THE RISE

THE
RISE

KOBE BRYANT AND THE PURSUIT OF IMMORTALITY

MIKE SIELSKI

ST. MARTIN'S PRESS
NEW YORK

For Kate, Evan, and Gabe

First published in the United States by St. Martin's Press, an imprint of St. Martin's Publishing Group

THE RISE. Copyright © 2021 by Mike Sielski. All rights reserved. Printed in the United States of America. For information, address St. Martin's Publishing Group, 120 Broadway, New York, NY 10271.

Designed by Jonathan Bennett

www.stmartins.com

Library of Congress Cataloging-in-Publication Data

Names: Sielski, Mike, 1975- author.
Title: The rise : Kobe Bryant and the pursuit of immortality / Mike Sielski.
Description: First edition. | New York : St. Martin's Press, 2022. | Includes bibliographical references and index. | Summary: "The inside look at one of the most captivating and consequential figures in our culture—with never-before-heard interviews."— Provided by publisher.
Identifiers: LCCN 2021037759 | ISBN 9781250275721 (hardcover) | ISBN 9781250275738 (ebook)
Subjects: LCSH: Bryant, Kobe, 1978-2020. | Basketball players—United States—Biography. | African American basketball players—Biography.
Classification: LCC GV884.B794 S54 2022 | DDC 796.323092 [B]—dc23
LC record available at https://lccn.loc.gov/2021037759

Our books may be purchased in bulk for promotional, educational, or business use. Please contact your local bookseller or the Macmillan Corporate and Premium Sales Department at 1-800-221-7945, extension 5442, or by email at MacmillanSpecialMarkets@macmillan.com.

First Edition: 2022

10 9 8 7 6 5 4 3 2

CONTENTS

PREFACE:
THE SIGNS OF
THINGS TO COME

ON THE DAY AFTER KOBE Bryant died, a high school classmate and friend sent me an email that carried the force of a fist that I couldn't see coming. "Thought you'd find this interesting," Ben Relles wrote.

Embedded in the message was a link to a thirty-six-second video. On the right side of the video's split-screen shot was Kobe, wearing a charcoal, scoop-neck sweater, sitting at an expansive cherry desk, riveted to flickering images on a laptop. He was in the executive offices of YouTube, where Ben was working to find new content for the channel. Kobe had come to the company's Southern California headquarters in January 2018 to pitch a show based on Wizenard, a series of children's books he had created that combined the themes of sports, fantasy, and magic. As it turned out, YouTube wasn't funding children's programming at the time and didn't buy the show, but "it was genuinely one of the most impressive pitches I've heard," Ben said later. "He was incredibly passionate about the idea and clearly hands-on in every aspect of it."

On the video's left side were the images that had grabbed Kobe's attention: footage of a basketball game between two suburban Philadelphia high schools—his alma mater, Lower Merion, and mine, Upper Dublin. Ben and I were seniors then. He was a backup forward on the team. I was an editor of the student newspaper and lacked the skills and athleticism to play organized ball beyond intramurals. Kobe Bryant was a freshman. It was the second game of his high school career.

On December 7, 1992, as part of its high school boys' basketball preview package, *The Philadelphia Inquirer* had published a pair of brief articles, one about each team. Both squads were green and were expected to struggle, but according to Jeremy Treatman, the correspondent who had written about the Lower Merion Aces, one player represented a glimmer of hope for them: "Remember this name: Kobe Bryant."

The following week, the teams squared off in the consolation game of a four-team tournament at Lower Merion. In that thirty-six seconds of footage from that game, the Upper Dublin player closest to the camera—a senior guard named Bobby McIlvaine, the number 24, also Kobe's number, huge on the back of his red jersey—whipped a cross-court pass to a teammate, Ari Greis. After Greis caught the ball on the right wing, he used a left-handed dribble to surge past Kobe and bank in a floater from the lane. A family friend of Ben's had filmed the game, and Ben, having kept the tape all these years and knowing he would be sitting down with Kobe, had converted the recording to a digital file. Then, once the YouTube meeting had ended, Ben had played the footage on the laptop, and one of his coworkers had taken care to capture Kobe's reaction to it. There it all was, in cosmic juxtaposition. You could watch Kobe as a thirty-nine-year-old watch himself as a fourteen-year-old in real time.

"That is hilarious," he said. "Great defense, Kobe. . . . That's horrible defense. . . . You can replay that all fucking day. . . . Oh. My. God. . . . Nawwwww! . . . That's funny. . . . We only won four games that year."

SO WHERE were you when that helicopter slammed into that Calabasas hillside in January 2020? Fixing yourself a midday snack in the kitchen? Relaxing in your recliner? Cleaning the garage? Me, I was in my car, my two sons in the backseat, hustling home so my eight-year-old could change and get to his 3:45 basketball game. And when we got there—I didn't notice it, but my son did, and he didn't tell me about it until after the game—there was a player on the opposing team, his arms peeking out like sapling branches from underneath a white T-shirt and a green tank top, the word "KOBE" written in black marker on his sleeve. You don't forget a day like that. You don't forget a death that causes the global compass to tremble.

That was Kobe Bryant's reach and power. We attach so much to our athletes. We see what they have done and can do. That's their gravitational pull, the attraction they have to us. They give us a standard to aspire to, a bar against which the rest of us can measure ourselves, and with Kobe, that pull was even stronger, because he was not limiting himself to basketball. He had been the executive producer of a short animated film, *Dear Basketball,* that had won an Academy Award and was based on a poem he wrote when he retired. In his post-Lakers life, he was, by all appearances, a loving husband to his wife, Vanessa, and a doting and demanding father to his four daughters. With time, with a media and fan base willing and eager to forgive, with the purchase of a gigantic diamond ring for Vanessa, he rendered the scandal that once stained his reputation—a rape accusation and his arrest in Colorado in 2003—an afterthought to most, though not all, of the public. He had put aside his petty wars with Phil Jackson and Shaquille O'Neal. There seemed great things ahead for him, things beyond the five championships and the fifteen All-Star Games and the 33,643 points and the 2008 NBA Most Valuable Player Award and the self-certainty—a belief in himself so absolute and obvious that it practically glowed and radiated from him—required to take the final shot when everyone in the arena knows you're going to take it. And now all that excellence and redemption and promise had been extinguished, and there was no sense of it to be made. It was barely worth trying. You sat there and it sank in and you gaped and shook your head.

Those great things had begun in and around Philadelphia. It might not *feel* that way any longer, because Kobe was so much a part of Los Angeles for so long—had gone from boyhood to manhood there, always under the spotlight's glare—that it seemed as if he had sprouted as a fully formed seventeen-year-old, complete with exquisite jump-shooting form, out of one of Hollywood's hills. But no. The great things had begun at Lower Merion, located on the Main Line, the posh suburb that hugged Philadelphia's western border. They had begun on the courts of those neighborhoods and playgrounds and parks, in the stuffy gymnasiums of local high schools, and in the tournaments of the country's AAU circuit. Sure, many Philadelphia natives still note that Kobe technically wasn't from the city, wasn't one of them, but ask yourself: Was there ever a player who better embodied what being a Philadelphia basketball player meant, what it looked like—the edginess, the kill-or-die-yourself competitiveness? "It taught me how to be tough, how to have thick skin," he said in late 2015, before his final game in Philadelphia against the 76ers. "There's not one playground around here where people just play basketball and don't talk trash."

Those great things had begun with his high school coach, Gregg Downer, who formed and was formed by Kobe, who won a championship with him, too, and would love and be loyal to him forevermore, who collapsed to his kitchen floor, disbelief accelerating into despair, when the news of Kobe's death broke. Those great things had begun with Treatman, who went from covering Kobe to befriending him, from a freelance sportswriter to one of Kobe's most trusted confidants and to a mover-and-shaker in the world of Philly hoops. His 1992 *Inquirer* story would be the first mention of Kobe in any major mainstream news outlet. *Remember this name?* Treatman did his best to make sure that no one would forget it. He became an assistant boys' basketball coach at Lower Merion at Downer's request, charged with handling the never-ending interview requests, keeping the media close but not so close that they became a burden and distraction, tracking the tail of Kobe's comet. He told anyone who happened to ask an offhand, casual question about Joe Bryant's son that Kobe was the next big thing, that we were all going to end up saying we knew him when, which we did. He grew so close to Kobe that the two of them collaborated on a series of interviews for a book that Treatman never got the chance to write, though he made sure to preserve the microcassette tapes and transcripts of several of those interviews—the fresh thoughts and memories of a Kobe who was not yet twenty years old—and has given me access to them for this book. And then on January 26, Treatman answered his cellphone from Jefferson University, in the East Falls section of Philadelphia, where he was overseeing a girls' basketball tournament, and he could barely get the words out. "I can't believe it," he said.

Those great things had begun at a school whose boys' basketball program had faded into irrelevance years earlier but became a traveling circus—and the best team in the state—because of Kobe. They had begun within a community that touted its racial and economic diversity and harmony but whose members were in reality hungry for a common point of pride to unite them. They had begun in summer-league and pickup games that instantaneously became the stuff of apocrypha and myth and remained so for decades thereafter, stories that didn't need to be embellished because the reality was flabbergasting enough: that a kid who was just turning seventeen already was the equal of or had surpassed the best players on those courts, which meant that he already was the equal of or had surpassed some of the better players in the NBA. They had begun at practices and workouts that the Sixers would hold at St. Joseph's University in the mid-1990s, when a teenaged Kobe would walk into the gym and upstage many of those NBA veterans and coach John Lucas could only wish that the team would have the good sense to draft the kid. As an undergrad at La Salle then, as an editor and sports columnist for the student newspaper, I had read and heard rumors about those workouts. Like everyone else on campus who wanted to see La Salle men's basketball return to the success—the twenty-win seasons, the conference championships, the NCAA tournament berths—that had been common, and perhaps taken for granted, just a few years earlier, I hoped Kobe would choose to go to college and to play in the same program where his father had such strong ties. *Joe Bryant is a La Salle alum and a La Salle coach! He and Kobe are so close! It's meant to be, right?* But how realistic was that scenario once Kobe saw that he stacked up pretty well against pros, that they could try their sly tricks and throw their elbows and he could not only take it but give it right back to them? The great things had begun with that realization. They had to have begun then.

They had begun at a moment in our cultural history when a traditional path to athletic stardom was seen as the only appropriate path to athletic stardom—a presumption that Kobe managed to follow and eschew at the very same time. They had begun with a youth who was in some ways completely typical and in others unlike anything a teenager could possibly experience, a youth that seems so far away now. They had begun in December 1992, when Kobe was just fourteen. And look where it all had led.

THE BRIEF snippet of film that Ben Relles preserved for nearly thirty years didn't tell the game's full story. Lower Merion beat Upper Dublin, 74–57, and Kobe's moment of embarrassment, captured forever, as if in amber, by that camcorder, was hardly representative of his overall performance. He scored nineteen points, and in a five-minute excerpt of the game that Ben later discovered, Kobe is the most arresting figure in the action. He drives into the lane and scores. He pulls up for two. He frees himself on an inbounds play and rattles in an open jumper from the left baseline. For a while, the longer video seems a highlight reel of Kobe and Kobe alone, and to watch him is to wonder how the Aces would ever lose as long as he remained in the lineup. But lose they did. Kobe was right: The team won just three more times while he was a freshman, finishing 4–20.

More illuminating than his perfect recall of that season, though, was the look on his face as he watched the game: smiling, snickering, and cursing at himself for his lazy defense, chomping on a piece of gum, his eyes on the computer screen but his mind searching, groping backward for that moment and that time in his life, for the prodigy he used to be. The footage clearly had surprised him, had sent him hurtling deep into his past, and if he went back far enough, he could make out the shape and contours of the mold for the man he became. The template was already in place. So many traits that shaped and characterized him were already present at that point in his life—the cockiness, the competitiveness, the warmth and the coldness that would emerge depending on the circumstances and his own desires and aims, the boyish insecurities, the comfort with fame, the beyond-his-years commitment to basketball brilliance and the preternatural understanding of what it took to achieve it, the traits he had retained over time, the traits he had shed. Memory is a gift often hidden away within a box locked tight, and that game film was the gliding, turning key, allowing Kobe access to sights, sounds, places, and people made tactile and intimate again. He was seeing himself anew. What follows is an attempt to see him that way once again.

PART I

I'm sure it seems to you like I have the perfect life right now.

—KOBE BRYANT

1

AFTER
THE FIRE

ATOP THE GRAY CONCRETE WALKWAY outside the entrance to Kobe
Bryant Gymnasium, a makeshift memorial garden was blooming
with colors and remembrances: candles and wreaths and sneakers and
jerseys, maroon and white for the Lower Merion High School Aces, purple and gold for the Los Angeles Lakers, orange and brown from the basketballs, yellow and red from the roses. It had been forty-eight hours since
a Sikorsky S-76B helicopter, its body white and striped in royal blue and
periwinkle, had lifted off from John Wayne–Orange County Airport
in Southern California, hovered in circles above a golf course, tried to
slice through a fog bank as thick and blinding as gauze, and crashed into
a hilly ravine, killing the nine people aboard: Kobe; his thirteen-year-
old daughter, Gianna; the pilot; and six people involved in Kobe's AAU
basketball program, including two of Gianna's teammates—all of them
bound for a tournament at his Mamba Sports Academy, forty-five miles
northwest of Los Angeles. That was Sunday, January 26, 2020. Now it
was Tuesday, a crystalline afternoon in the suburbs west of Philadelphia,
the middle of the school day, breezy and chilly. Students, heading from
one class to another, stopped to gaze at the items and whisper among
themselves. Middle-aged men and women parked their cars blocks away,

then walked to the site, as quietly as if they were entering a church. A sixty-four-year-old Lakers fan from central New Jersey, Mark Kerr, drove ninety minutes that day with his wife and nephew, just to visit the memorial, just to feel a connection to Kobe. Three members of the school's 2006 boys' basketball team, which had won a state championship ten years after Kobe had led the school to one, set a framed photo there; in the photo was Kobe, sitting on a bench with them. A WNBA player had written a letter to him in lavender ink, in curlicued Palmer method, on lined notepad paper: "I feel selfish for just missing out on what else you would have done with your time with us . . ."

For those two days, Gregg Downer had not watched TV, had avoided listening to any radio reports, and had not stopped once at the site. How many times had he kept his head down and kept striding past it and into the gym? How many times would he have to contemplate what he had lost, what the world had lost, in the foothills of the Santa Monica Mountains? He couldn't say, but he knew he couldn't bear to spend any time there yet. There was so much of him blanketing that ground, too. He was fifty-seven now, his face finely wrinkled and more weathered than it had been when he and Kobe were together, when he was in his early thirties and so boyish that the two of them could have been mistaken for college roommates. They were so close, knew each other so well, respected each other so much, that they might as well have been.

In his kitchen on the morning and early afternoon of that Sunday, Downer had been overseeing a playdate between his daughter Brynn, who was seven, and one of her friends. Whenever Kobe saw Brynn, towheaded and pigtailed, he scooped her up, nuzzled her face, and squeezed her tight as if she were his own, as if she were his fifth daughter. Downer had not become a father until he was fifty, until after Kobe and Vanessa had already had two girls, Natalia and Gianna. There was always a gleam in Brynn's eyes, Downer noticed, whenever she saw Kobe and the gleam in his when he saw her. But now Brynn and her friend were padding past Downer and his wife, Colleen, and Downer's phone was buzzing. A reporter. Downer guessed why he'd be getting such a call: The night before, in Philadelphia against the Sixers, LeBron James had moved into third place on the NBA's career scoring list, leapfrogging Kobe. The sportswriter must be looking for a quote from Downer on the nugget of news. That's what he told Colleen. He didn't bother to pick up his phone. But then, for the next ninety seconds his phone didn't stop, buzzing and jumping so much it seemed possessed by a poltergeist, and finally he went online and read a TMZ post on Twitter, the first report that Kobe was dead, and after Downer prayed for five minutes that the gossip site had gotten it wrong and that some sick internet troll was guilty of a cruel hoax, Brynn's playdate was over and the Downers' kitchen was a vale of tears.

He walked upstairs, walked back down again, walked through his front door, and walked around the suburban development where he and Colleen had moved fifteen years earlier, past lawns gone brown and swimming pools shuttered for the winter, past the houses of friends, past all the people who had known for a long time that Kobe's coach lived in their neighborhood. He could gain no mental and emotional traction. Had this really happened? Who else had been aboard the helicopter? Who already had heard? Would he have to tell people? The other men who had coached Kobe at Lower Merion—the long-ago players and teammates who had been Kobe's closest friends when they were teens and now didn't often hear from him once he became a star and Los Angeles became his home and they remained Guys Who Had Been Teammates And Friends With Kobe Bryant—Jeanne Mastriano, who had taught English at the school for thirty years, who had no formal connection to the basketball program but remained a mentor to Kobe nonetheless, who had coaxed and fanned the intellectual curiosity within him into a fire—who would tell them? Tears leaked from him in small, sporadic bursts. On a table in his house, his cell phone continued to hum with calls and texts, each one a thread in a web of horror and grief. He walked home, not knowing who he should reach out to first, or if he could pick up the phone at all.

THEIR FOUR children, all under age eleven, were bored, with pent-up energy to burn off, with nothing to do at home on a winter Sunday afternoon. So Phil and Allison Mellet took advantage of who they were and where they lived. The couple were Lower Merion alumni, members of the class of 1998—they had started dating as seniors and been together ever since—and Allison, who taught Spanish at the school and directed its world-languages department, could get access to the building even on a weekend. A quick bit of packing, a short ride to Bryant Gymnasium, and there they were—Allison on a treadmill in a room down the hall from the gym, Phil shooting a basketball or throwing a football with the kids. Mellet propped his phone against a wall in a corner of the gym, next to the lumpy mound of jackets and long-sleeved shirts that the children had stripped off once they felt the gym's sticky warmth, granola bars and applesauce pouches stuffed in the pockets and piled nearby.

The gym—named for Kobe in 2010, after he donated $411,000 to the school district—was far bigger than the old one that he and Mellet had played in back when they were teammates in 1995–96, when Kobe was a senior supernova and Mellet, now a corporate attorney who hadn't spoken to him in years, was a scrawny sophomore guard happy just to ride the bench. With the bleachers pushed in against the wall, as they were now, the place seemed even bigger. The kids' voices echoed as if they were at the bottom of a canyon. The only other person in the school was a janitor. Still, Mellet managed to notice that his phone was droning and lighting up with text messages. They were from old friends bearing horrible news.

As he read them, he was filled with an odd emptiness. Though he had not maintained a relationship with Kobe—how many of those guys, even with those old friendships and a state championship binding them to him, really had?—Mellet had always considered himself lucky to have played with him, to have gotten to know him a bit. Whenever he met someone through his work, investors or stockholders or other attorneys, he had always found a way to loop his connection to Kobe into the conversation. It was a marvelous icebreaker, better than asking about kids or golf or the same-old, same-old. *You were on the same team as Kobe? Well, tell me about THAT!* They lit up, and to Mellet, there was a thrill, a tiny electric charge, in retelling and reliving the stories. Now that wire had been severed. Now a piece of his life, one that had significance, was gone.

Within twenty minutes, the janitor came by to tell him that he and Allison and the children would have to leave. The building was going to be locked down.

IN THE frozen-food aisle of an Acme in Narberth, Pennsylvania, a mile and a half from the high school, Amy Buckman perused the options behind the glass, bags of vegetables crackling and crunching in her hands as she took care of the grocery shopping for her and her husband, Terry. Before the Lower Merion School District had hired her, a 1982 alumna of the high school herself, in March 2018 to be its spokesperson, Buckman had worked for a quarter century as a producer and on-air reporter for Channel 6 Action News, Philadelphia's ABC affiliate. Terry, home watching TV, texted her. They had been married thirty-two years. He knew what she needed to know.

They're reporting that Kobe's helicopter crashed.

He continued to funnel her updates, confirmations, and details as she rushed through the checkout line. She drove home, unpacked the groceries, sent texts to the school district's superintendent, Robert Copeland; to the high school's principal, Sean Hughes; and to the district's facilities director, Jim Lill. *I'm going to my office. We're going to be the news.* She called Downer, then Doug Young, who was one of Downer's assistant coaches, one of Kobe's former teammates, and her predecessor as the district's spokesperson. From the somber, halting whisper that was Downer's voice over the phone, she could tell that he wasn't up to speaking publicly yet. He gave her one six-word sentence, which Buckman included in the 189-word statement that she wrote there at her desk. It was not merely that her job required her to write the statement. It was that she, unlike Downer or Young or any number of people still tethered to Kobe, possessed the distance and perspective to do it. She had never met him. In her television career, she had covered the O. J. Simpson trial, had interviewed Oprah Winfrey, had produced a morning talk show and spoken with dozens of Philadelphia newsmakers—that was the evergreen term in the business for any chef or senior citizen or nonprofit director who might fill six and a half minutes on an hour-long local TV program, "newsmaker"—and Kobe had become Polaris in the region's constellation of celebrities, the newsmaker of newsmakers. Yet they'd never crossed paths. This was not a hindrance to her at this moment. This was an asset. Someone had to be clear-minded enough to speak for the community. Someone had to be the face of Kobe Bryant's alma mater on the day of Kobe Bryant's death.

Already the impromptu shrine was spreading, like holy kudzu, from the sidewalk in front of the school's gymnasium entrance to the doors themselves, and reporters and camera crews were lingering there, interviewing those who had come to the site, waiting to see if they would be allowed inside the school to shoot footage for that night's newscasts—the trophy case, the memorabilia therein, Kobe's name on the gym's walls, the obvious images. At 4:30 P.M., Buckman rooted herself just outside the doors and read the statement.

The Lower Merion School District community is deeply saddened to learn of the sudden passing of one of our most illustrious alumni, Kobe Bryant. Mr. Bryant's connection to Lower Merion High School, where he played basketball prior to joining the NBA, has raised the profile of the high school and our district throughout the world. . . .

Gregg Downer coached Mr. Bryant from 1992 to 1996. Mr. Bryant led the team to the 1996 state championship. Downer said that he is completely shocked and devastated by this news, adding, "Aces Nation has lost its heartbeat." The entire Lower Merion School District community sends its deepest condolences to Mr. Bryant's family.

She told the media that they could enter the building and get their footage. They could get it then and only then. No one would let them back in for more on Monday. Monday was a school day. The reporters filed in and gathered their B-roll, pointing their cameras to the sparkling hardwood court and the championship banners hanging inside the gymnasium, to the kaleidoscopic mosaics of Kobe on the walls outside the gym, to the glass trophy case where the school displayed five of Kobe's sneakers and four framed photographs of him and the 1996 state-championship trophy, the lustrous golden basketball that he held above his head that night in Hershey.

The reporters filed out. The mourners continued to arrive. The carpet of letters and flowers and basketballs—officials eventually collected more than four hundred basketballs, donating many to local boys' and girls' clubs, keeping some in boxes and black trash bags that would remain stacked on storage shelves until they could be displayed at the school— snaked all the way to the lip of the entrance, blocking the doors, creating a fire-code violation. Buckman, Hughes, and Lill roped off a nearby section of lawn and began picking up the sheets of paper and the lilies and the roses, carrying them with caution and care, as if they were handling fresh-blown glass, and setting them next to the doors, near withered bushes and a plot of mulch and dirt. It took them until the darkness of early Monday morning to move all the items and clear a path to enter and exit the school, Amy Buckman still in the tan corduroy leggings and black down coat she had worn to the Acme.

AT AROUND the same time that his old friend's helicopter had lifted off that morning, Doug Young had folded himself into a coach seat for a short flight from Alabama to North Carolina. A communication strategist, he had spent the week in Mobile for the Senior Bowl, which was both a chance for NFL executives and coaches to scout college players and a networking opportunity for several of Young's clients: trainers and up-and-coming coaches and aspiring quarterback gurus looking to build their brands and businesses. Six foot four and lean, Young had a stylish appearance and re-fined deportment that belied his earnest loyalty to and affection for his high school. No one knew more about the history of Lower Merion, and of its boys' basketball program in particular, than he did, and with the exception of Downer, no one had done more to maintain the connection between Kobe and the school. When the team traveled to Los Angeles in 2018 to visit Kobe, for instance, Young handled the itinerary and accommodations, arranged a ninety-minute roundtable chat between Kobe and the players at Kobe's office, and made sure every player got a signed copy of his book *The Mamba Mentality*. Whenever Downer wanted to inspire his players, Young went to the trouble of fitting a conference call / pep talk snugly into Kobe's schedule. His junior and senior years had coincided with Kobe's freshman and sophomore years. He had been there for the dawn.

For the hour and forty-five minutes that the plane was airborne, Young had kept his cell phone and laptop off. But once the plane landed, he looked around and noticed some of the passengers crying, all of them looking at their phones and freezing in place, person by person, row by row, a domino array of shock and sadness. He turned on his phone, then went numb.

Until he wandered toward the terminal for his flight to Philadelphia, the coincidence of his location didn't occur to him: Charlotte Douglas International Airport. Charlotte, home of the Hornets. The team that had drafted Kobe.

OVER THE two days after the crash, Downer responded to just a few of the calls that he had received Sunday. He remained in the same half daze that he had lapsed into that afternoon, and Hughes had told him not to come in to try to teach. *Stay home. Take what time you need.* Downer had exchanged text messages with John Cox, Kobe's cousin, but he had not heard from Kobe's parents, Joe and Pam. No one had. They had said nothing publicly. Downer hoped he might reconnect with them soon, but until then, there were more immediate matters to which he had to attend. Hughes and Jason Stroup, the school's athletic director, would be gathering Downer's players before the team's regularly scheduled practice to speak to them, and Lower Merion still had a game on Tuesday night. Several of the players had met Kobe during the team's recent visit to Los Angeles, and Downer didn't want to leave the task of calming and reassuring them, of speaking with authority about who Kobe was and what he might want them to do now, to Hughes and Stroup. He drove to school for the meeting.

He talked to his players about Kobe's death in a manner that, he hoped, would resonate with teenage boys. *There are a lot of circulating emotions here, guys,* Downer told them. *We have to get those ten or fifteen emotions down to three or four. When I try to think what Kobe would want to have happen in a situation like this, I think he would want to get back to the bouncing ball as soon as possible. We have an important game Tuesday. We should want to bounce the ball. We should want to squeak our sneakers. We should want to compete like crazy, and we will. Let's respect that we have our health. Let's respect that we have the ability to do this, to play basketball, and let's try to have a heck of a lot of fun while we're doing it.*

He had said nothing publicly since Buckman had released the statement, but now he would have to. A wave of interview requests for Downer had flooded the school district's offices. In response, Buckman arranged a midafternoon press conference at the administration building with Downer and Young. It was a strategy straight from the textbook of modern media relations, and given the power of Kobe's fame, it was understandable. Buckman would give the local TV stations and newspapers and websites, and maybe a national outlet or two that might travel a couple of hours to suburban Philadelphia—*The New York Times, The Washington Post*—one fair and open opportunity to talk to Kobe's coach in person. Then—and Buckman gathered the thirty reporters on hand and insisted upon this condition—the district wouldn't allow reporters to ask Downer or anyone else at Lower Merion about Kobe for a good long while. Downer still had a basketball team to coach. He needed time to mourn. Everyone did. So here was your chance, journalists. Take it.

ONE BY one, twenty to twenty-five in all, the media members marched into a conference room to stake out their positions for Downer's appearance. The room held a large, horseshoe-shaped table with thick wooden chairs, and the phalanx of tripods closed off the open end of the shoe. A maroon banner hung behind the table's head. Set on an easel was a poster-size photo of Kobe that had been snapped during one of his high school games. He was clad in a white jersey and cradled a basketball in his right hand, his mouth open and his eyes turned upward toward a net as he prepared to flip the ball over his head for a reverse layup—a flawless, frozen coup d'oeil of his athleticism and grace on the court.

With Young behind him, Downer stepped into the conference room from a door behind the banner, his thinning, straw-gray buzz cut perfect for the archetype of his profession: He had been a physical-education teacher at the school for more than twenty years. Minutes before, he had dug through a closet in a storage room next to the gym and removed from it a precious artifact: Kobe's white warm-up jacket from his junior and senior seasons, the number 33 on the sleeves. It had stayed in that closet for twenty-four years since Kobe last wore it—*24,* Kobe's first jersey number at Lower Merion, his second jersey number with the Lakers. Was the coincidence odd? Fitting? Maybe both. Downer, as he prepared to meet with the press, had donned the warm-up himself, as if it were a protective cloak. He felt that he had to wear it, that he would be somehow safer and stronger if he did.

"He's giving me strength in a moment like this," he said later that afternoon. "Wasn't sure I could get through yesterday. Wasn't sure I could keep my emotions together. And I found . . . the ability to do that. It's coming from him. It means the world to be in a jacket like this. If there's some sort of small connection between him and me with his warm-up he wore . . ."

He sat at the table's head; Young sat in the chair to the left, his body bowed toward Downer's in deference to him. "I appreciate your patience," Downer said to the assembled media. "The past few days have been poor sleep, poor nutrition, and lots of tears," and the evidence was obvious— his face puffy, his eyes rimmed red. To his right, in a corner of the room, mingled a loose group of men with connections to the program: former players and coaches, alumni, friends of Downer's. Jeremy Treatman stood there among them, his arms crossed against his chest, his head dangling below his shoulders as if he were hanging by his nape from a hook.

The gathering was a testament to Kobe, of course, but to Downer, as well. Kobe's freshman season with the Aces had been Downer's third as the school's varsity head coach. The first time he had seen Kobe play, when Kobe was an eighth grader, Downer had joked, *Well, I'm definitely going to be here for four years.* Four years had stretched to thirty years. Lower Merion had won fifteen league championships over that time. It won the state title in 1996 with Kobe, then won two more thereafter. Downer had never experienced again a year like Kobe's senior season—the autograph and ticket demands, the crowds, the media attention, games becoming rock concerts—but without that year, he believed, none of the success that followed would have been possible. "The pathway of our program would be very different had we not met him," he was saying at the table. "He taught us how to win. He taught us how to work hard. He taught us how to not take shortcuts. The bar got very high. . . . I don't think the momentum for any of this would have been there if we hadn't been blessed enough to meet this amazing player and this amazing person."

He was searching for his words, and the hunt became harder when someone asked him, "Have you talked to anyone from Kobe's family?" The question cut him. Joe and Pam Bryant had practically been members of Downer's family, too. Joe, in fact, even served as Downer's junior-varsity coach during Kobe's career there. But Kobe's relationship with his parents had fractured during his years with the Lakers, both because of his decision to marry Vanessa when they were so young—he was twenty-one, and she was eighteen—and because of a dispute with Pam over the handling and sale of some of his personal items and memora-bilia. *You're not ready to be married. . . . Yes, I am. . . . I'm going to sell some of your things. . . . No, you can't.* There had been fights and cold wars and temporary reconciliations and the tearing apart again and maybe, still, the faint but lingering possibility that there might yet be full healing . . . all of that conflict, in the end, over *stuff*—high school jerseys and Lakers jerseys and rings, just stuff, and what did that stuff matter now? The wounds had been deep, so deep, Downer knew, that they had to be the reason Joe and Pam had yet to issue any public comment about their son's death. Downer had never met Vanessa, but he had maintained his relationship with Kobe. He had seen him three times in the previous eighteen months, had flown his team to L.A., had met up with him in Philadelphia at a book signing. Kobe had published a series of novels for elementary school students in March 2019, and he was giving the books away—not selling them at the signing, giving them away. That was the last time Downer had talked to him in person. He couldn't remember the last time he had talked to Joe and Pam in person, or at all, and now here was this question, here were these cameras . . .

"I had a wonderful relationship with Pam and Joe. . . . I learned about coaching from Joe, and I think of him in the highest of regards. . . . If they're out there, I badly want to be supportive of Vanessa and the other three girls. I badly want to be there for them in any small way that I can be. And I definitely . . . uh . . . want to get in touch with Joe and Pam."

Now he was crying. Now the words stopped.

"Joe and Pam, we lost a great one. I love Kobe, and I love Joe and Pam also."

He reached for a bottle of lemon-lime Gatorade that he had set on the table in front of him. He held it to his lips for a few heartbeats. He wiped his eyes with his right hand, then with his left. There was no sound in the room.

ONE MONTH later, at 8:00 A.M. on Tuesday, February 25, the day after the memorial ceremony for Kobe and Gianna Bryant at the Staples Center in downtown Los Angeles, Downer sat aboard a cross-country flight back to Philadelphia, racing home to coach in a district-playoff game at 7:30 P.M. that night. He had missed his team's last four practices and not watched one second of film on the Aces' opponent, Pennridge High School. His assistant coaches had been in contact with him, and he had no doubts that his players would be ready for the game. But in truth, his mind was elsewhere, dwelling on the day before.

Downer, Treatman, and Young had followed through on a tentative plan they had laid out not long after Kobe's death. No matter when the Lakers might host a memorial for Kobe, the three of them would travel to the West Coast for it. Now Downer's mind reached back. Obtaining tickets for the ceremony had been a chore, because so few were available and because the ceremony would be so NBA- and Los Angeles–centric, to align with Vanessa's wishes. But Tim Harris, the Lakers' senior vice president for business operations, had interceded on their behalf. Harris had done more than intercede, in fact; he had procured a couple of extra tickets, allowing Jeanne Mastriano and Downer's younger brother, Brad, to attend, as well.

The group left their hotel early on the morning of the ceremony, Brad driving them to the Staples Center. To Gregg, ten minutes early was always ten minutes late anyway, and they had anticipated, correctly, delays beyond the normal Los Angeles rush-hour mess. Some streets were blocked off. Traffic choked the rest. Outside the arena, giant murals of

Kobe painted on brick building walls in the days since his death, phantasmagorical in their colors, towered over the passersby, most of whom wore Lakers jerseys, some of whom wore Lower Merion jerseys. Lower Merion jerseys in California, in China . . . the reach . . . Kobe's reach . . . even in this setting . . . Young marveled to himself at the community created by this one human being. Vendors sold Kobe T-shirts. *People are buying them?* Downer thought. He had trouble stomaching it . . . the inappropriateness. Kobe's ghost was everywhere, and it could be yours, screen-printed on rayon, for fifteen bucks.

They shuffled past the security guards and X-ray screeners into Staples. At another time, in another context, the scene around Downer inside the arena would have been a dream: Gregg Downer, blue-collar kid from Media, Pennsylvania, surrounded by Michael Jordan, Bill Russell, Kareem Abdul-Jabbar, Elgin Baylor, Jerry West, Shaquille O'Neal, Magic Johnson, Tim Duncan. He had always assumed that he would be sitting among these immortals during Kobe's induction into the Naismith Memorial Basketball Hall of Fame, except the purpose of this gathering was his worst nightmare. He was still struggling to process his new reality.

For two decades, he had kept West Coast time, learning to get by on five hours of sleep so he could track Kobe's struggles and triumphs every night. He saw Kobe's air balls in Utah during that humiliating playoff-series loss his rookie year, his eighty-one-point game, the five championship rings. Before he died, in the fall of 2018, Downer's father, Robert, would record all of the Lakers' late games and watch them the following morning, then begin every phone conversation with his son the same way— *Did you see what Kobe did last night?*—unless Kobe happened to have an off night, in which case Robert simply erased the game from the DVR. For Gregg, though, there were too many memories to erase. He shot free throws with Kobe at the old Forum before Lakers practices. He swam and ate meals with him at Kobe's house overlooking the Pacific. He traveled to games all over the country, just to see him play. He worked Kobe's basketball camps. They exchanged emails about strategy. In a private moment, in the halls of Lower Merion, Downer shared the news that he was going to be a father, and Kobe wrapped him in an embrace.

ANOTHER MEMORY, this one fresh: He had shared the same tight embrace with Joe and Pam Bryant, with Kobe's sisters, Sharia and Shaya, seconds after the ceremony, Treatman and Young there, too, all of them crying, all of them together. The ceremony had been lovely but, from a Lower Merion perspective, perhaps incomplete. There was no mention of Kobe's high school years, or even of Joe and Pam. Vanessa had handled the program's agenda and themes, and of course she sought to honor and acknowledge her daughter as much as she did her husband, but the iciness between her and Kobe's parents was still apparent. From what Treatman saw, they never interacted with or so much as glanced at each other before, during, or after the ceremony.

Rob Pelinka, Kobe's former agent and the Lakers' general manager, spoke. Connecticut women's basketball coach Geno Auriemma and one of his greatest players, Diana Taurasi, spoke. Vanessa herself spoke. Shaq spoke. Magic spoke. Michael spoke. That last speech, Jordan's, had moved Downer so much, had reminded him of the conversations he'd had with Kobe during their years together, when Kobe was fifteen, sixteen, seventeen years old, so obviously mimicking Jordan's moves and mannerisms on the court. The speech had moved Downer because Jordan, ever so stoic and prideful, had finally called Kobe his "little brother," an amazing player, and imagine how Kobe, at any age, at any stage of his too-short life, would have reacted to hearing that! And once the ceremony ended, he and Treatman rushed down to Joe and Pam's seats, near the stage, and when she saw Treatman, Pam had shouted, "It's Jeremy! It's Jeremy!" And when a security guard stopped the two of them, Downer said something he had never said before, played a card that he had never played before. He looked at the guard and said, "I'm Kobe Bryant's high school coach. I have to see his parents now. That's why I'm here." And the guard let him pass, and Joe, who had been hugging Shaq, let go, grabbed Downer instead, pulled him close and smiled wide and began massaging Downer's shoulders, as if to relieve the tension and the strain and the men's shared misery, and repeated the same phrase again and again.

"We made a kid for the world," Joe Bryant said. "We made a kid for the world."

And now that the speeches had ended . . . now what? Downer had always viewed himself through four prisms: teacher, coach, father, and husband. Now what? He wasn't sure. Memories and flashbacks were everywhere at Lower Merion. Ten months each year, six days each week, he coached in the gym that Kobe had funded, that Kobe had built, that bore Kobe's name. Kobe might pop into his head at any moment for any reason. One morning weeks earlier, for no reason that he could explain, Downer spontaneously dropped to the floor of the school, flattened his chest against the tiles, and cranked out twenty-four push-ups.

He began to scribble down thoughts, random ideas and aphorisms. *Kobe needs me to be strong. My current players need it. My students need it. I need to continue to affect players and students in a positive way, as I've been trying to do for thirty years. Kobe needs me to stand tall and sharpen my resolve.*

He thought of Brynn, of the hashtag that had spread brushfire-like over social media in the days after the plane crash, after a clip of Kobe on a late-night talk show, referring to himself as a "girl dad," had gone viral. The movement felt tangible to him now. Maybe this was the connection to Kobe he needed. Brynn always came to her dad's basketball games. Brought her own clipboard. Sat in on all the film-study sessions and pregame pep talks. Soaked her dad with water during postgame victory parties in the locker room. Swam with her dad. Had sleepovers by the fireplace with her dad. Played soccer and baseball with her dad. Made her first basket on a ten-foot hoop not long ago. He kept writing.

She can be whatever she wants to be, and I want more than anything else to guide her through the good and bad. Kobe's love for his girls, his legacy as a father, strengthens me. The bond we shared in raising our daughters is the greatest gift of our relationship. It's what inspires me most. I am going to focus on three words for my own motivation and peace of mind: courage, resilience, and love.

Every coach, he believed, needed a game plan at all times. For the first time since January 26, nearly thirty years after he first met Kobe Bryant, he believed he had one. The plane cruised through the clouds, shepherding Gregg Downer home, back to where the journey had begun.

I know that the players who competed before me and who are still performing are the people who made the NBA what it is today. How could I not understand that after watching my dad play and knowing what he went through?

—KOBE BRYANT

2

A SAFE
HAVEN

THE DETAILS AND ANNOUNCEMENTS, PRIVATE and public, of Kobe
Bean Bryant's birth on August 23, 1978, at Lankenau Hospital were
rife with ambiguity and errata. If Philadelphia never fully embraced
him, if many of its sports fans maintained a resentful, tribal posture
toward him for most of his life—*He is not one of us*—they could always
cite a delicious truth that spiced their attitude: He was not, in fact, a
native of the city. Lankenau was located within Philadelphia's borders for
its first ninety-three years before it was relocated in 1953 to Lower Merion Township in Montgomery County, to ninety-three acres of sprawling suburban land. So no: technically, Kobe was not from Philadelphia.
But the occasional misidentification of his birthplace was a less egregious
mistake than those made by the two newspapers that first heralded his
arrival. The day after Kobe was born, *The Philadelphia Inquirer* and the
Philadelphia Daily News—the former an austere broadsheet, the latter a
gritty tabloid—announced his birth in the same erroneous manner: by
spelling his first name "Cobie."

No matter the explanation, one could understand the blunder. It was
an unusual name with an unusual genesis. As August 1978 was nearing
its end and the start of Sixers training camp was approaching, Joe Bryant

was about to begin his fourth season with the team, and over those years he had developed a fondness for a particular restaurant: Kobe Japanese Steak House in King of Prussia, Pennsylvania. The restaurant—attached to a Hilton hotel and a stone's throw from the suburb's primary attraction, the King of Prussia Mall—had opened in the early 1970s, and its owner, Christ Dhimitri, touted it as an exotic alternative to the tried, true, and staid American steakhouse, though not too exotic. It served teppanyaki-style food—broiled, grilled, pan-fried—which meant that there was no sushi or sashimi on the menu, and ironically, there was no Kobe, either: An outbreak of hoof-and-mouth disease in Japan had made it illegal for anyone in the United States to import the succulent beef.

During Joe's years with them, the Sixers held their annual September training camp first at Ursinus College and later at Franklin & Marshall College, each of which was a lengthy drive west from Philadelphia or Wynnewood that could include, if someone so desired, a stop along the way at the Kobe Japanese Steak House. The restaurant became a hangout of sorts for Sixers players—several of whom Dhimitri befriended, Julius "Dr. J" Erving and Maurice Cheeks among them—as they commuted to and from camp. The Bryants patronized it frequently.

"At that time," Dhimitri said later, "Japanese food was really unique. That's why they came. All the food was fresh. It was kind of fun."

When he told *Sports Illustrated* in 1998 why he and Pam had given Kobe his name, Joe admitted, "I don't know if I should say [why], because they might want the rights." But Joe had no cause to worry. Dhimitri never bothered trying to collect any royalties from the Bryants. The chance to tell the tale, to link his Kobe to *the* Kobe, satisfied him, even if it might make someone wonder about the kind of man who would enjoy a restaurant so much that he would insist on naming his only son after it.

TODAY, THE street on which Joe Bryant lived for most of his childhood, the 5800 block of Willows Avenue in West Philadelphia, is 530 feet of zigzag sidewalk with starburst patches of weeds bursting forth from splits in the concrete, of seven decayed row houses with jury-rigged plywood doors and rust-tinged screen doors that swing and creak in the breeze, of curbside cars parked front to back as closely as a jigsaw puzzle's edge pieces. Step out of one of those row houses, turn the corner, cross the Cobbs Creek Parkway, and head north, and there is an oasis: a gleaming verdant park, with the full basketball court that Joe himself played on as a boy, the two hoops outfitted now with fresh white nylon netting. But the block itself retains little of the aspirational gleam, the promise of a purer form of freedom, that drew Joe Bryant Sr.—Kobe's grandfather—there from Dooly County, Georgia, one of hundreds of thousands of Black people who trekked from the South to Philadelphia during the Great Migration. They settled primarily in Philadelphia's northern, southern, and western neighborhoods, seizing on the city's industrialization during the twentieth century's first two decades, abutting and sometimes mingling with the ethnic enclaves already carved out nearby—Russian Jews in the west, Italians in the south, colonies of row homes amid ironworks shops, carpet and clothing manufacturers, apartments stacked atop convenience stores, windowless tan-brick warehouses with trolley cars trundling past. At one point, more Black people owned houses in Philadelphia than in any other city north of the Mason-Dixon Line, and the men who owned them were construction workers and steelmen and truck drivers, their hard work earning them the license and satisfaction to sit on the porches and stoops of their own homes on cool evenings, to look around at their children playing on the capillary streets of their sliver of the city, to know that they had gotten out of hell and forged something good and solid for themselves. They were not rich, and they did not have to be rich, because the money they made was *theirs,* which made it priceless. By the time Joe Sr. had turned twenty-five, he had become one of those men: a husband, a father, well over six feet tall, a body like a gigantic barrel, a deep and guttural voice, a *presence.* He had made that same journey and bought two of those houses—the first at 42nd and Leidy in West Philadelphia, the second at 58th and Willows, three miles south—and secured one of those jobs, spending sixteen years with a uniform-rental company as a plant manager. He built a family—a wife, two sons and a daughter, his oldest child his namesake, his eye's apple.

PICTURE THE sight, the strange, strange sight: a sixteen-year-old kid, six feet nine inches tall, a gap between his front teeth that made his smile appear wider and brighter, skinny as string, running, running, running. Joe Bryant would do that, just take off and go whenever he and his father were butting heads, whenever Joe Sr. let him know in no uncertain terms that there would be no excuses for violating the rules of the Bryant home. One of those rules: *Never bring daylight to this house.* It meant that under no circumstances was Joe to come home too late, and if he did, the cost for him, the reckoning at his father's iron fist, would be steep.

Big Joe was a natural disciplinarian, as fathers of that era tended to be. But there was cause for him to be concerned whenever Joe wasn't home. Philadelphia throughout the 1960s was a haven for street gangs, their numbers growing over the decade until, in 1969, the Philadelphia Crime Commission estimated there were three thousand members of seventy-five gangs responsible for forty-five murders and 267 injuries that year. As a ten- and eleven-year-old, Joe was involved in his share of skirmishes: the schoolyard, near the public pool in Fairmount Park. Once, he and several friends went at it with a gang called 39th and Poplar, named for the corner its members guarded as if the intersection were their castle. Joe was the youngest in his group, and when the fighting began, he felt a sensation in his left hip like a pin pricking him. He looked down and saw blood penciling down his leg and pooling near his foot. He'd been sliced by a knife, the wound leaving a scar that remained visible for years.

Basketball was his safe haven. The sport had hooked him long ago. Standing six foot six by the end of ninth grade, as a basketball star and track athlete at Bartram High School, he could play ball just about any-time, anywhere he wanted in the city. He had a backboard and hoop that had been bolted to a utility pole right there at 58th and Willows. He had Cobbs Creek Park. After his family attended Sunday services at New

Bethlehem Baptist Church, around the corner from his grandmother's house, Joe could get a game at the court next door. There was Bartram, where Joe played for coach Jack Farrell, muttonchopped and cheery-faced but tough on his team, and there were the summer leagues in Philadelphia and its suburbs. Joe started out at the Narberth League—in Lower Merion Township—then moved up to the premier summer basketball institution in the city: the Sonny Hill League. It was the place for players and prospects to see and be seen by high school coaches and college recruiters, from Philadelphia and around the country, and it was where Joe, regarded as the best player in the Philadelphia Public League, met and befriended Mo Howard, who as a senior point guard at St. Joseph's Prep was regarded as the best player in the Philadelphia Catholic League.

So Joe ran to those games, wherever they might be, or he ran to Howard's house in North Philadelphia, winding through some six miles of city blocks, seeking out Howard for support in the streets and on the court, tempting fate to a degree that only a young athlete of his stature could. The culture of the gangs came with a code, a single saving grace: If you were a good athlete, you were more likely to get a pass. Sonny Hill, a former union organizer with the magnetism and salesmanship of a carnival barker, used his negotiating skills to broker truces between gangs, to earn dispensation for the kids who played in his league and peace of mind for their parents, and word trickled through the neighborhoods: If you were involved with the Sonny Hill League like Joe was, if you excelled for your high school team like Joe did, people recognized that you were trying to achieve, and were capable of achieving, something bigger, better, more. People admired you. People shielded you from the violence. It would have been a valuable lesson for Joe Bryant, one that he could appreciate fully only after he himself became a father of a son: that he could make himself untouchable through basketball, that he could survive the unpleasant and uncomfortable aspects of inner-city existence and use them to his advantage. Understand where your opponents come from and how they will size you up, the tactics they will use to gain a mental and physical edge on you. You didn't have to live in the city to learn those things, but you did have to play in the city to learn them.

THE BEAUTY of Joe as a ballplayer and an athlete was that his speed wasn't his only elite trait. He could do whatever his coaches asked him to do, be whatever his teams needed him to be. His playground model was Earl Monroe, a Bartram alumnus who went on to a Hall of Fame NBA career with the Baltimore Bullets and New York Knicks, and though he grew to be six inches taller than the six-foot-three Monroe, Joe strived to match the Pearl's style and skill set. As his skinny body grew corded with muscle, he retained the showy hand-eye coordination he'd always possessed, dribbling the basketball between his legs, swirling it behind his back, spinning to the hoop as if he were smaller, as if he were a guard.

Which, at times, he was. Joe had gifts that other kids his height didn't or, if they did, weren't permitted to utilize then. A coach who happened to have a player six foot nine or taller stuck that player in the post, in the center of the team's offense and defense. Stay close to the basket, son. Shoot layups, maybe a hook shot. Protect the rim. But Joe . . . mercy. Joe averaged 27.4 points, seventeen rebounds, six assists, and six blocked shots during his senior season. Joe scored fifty-seven points in a game against one Public League team, Bok, and had forty points and twenty-one rebounds against another Public League team, Overbrook, in his final home game for Bartram. Joe ran the mile in four minutes, forty-five seconds and the 880 meters in two minutes, one second, long-jumped nineteen feet, and triple-jumped thirty-nine feet, nine inches for Bartram's track team. Joe was so damned athletic and looked so good being so damned athletic—liquid, no jagged edges to his game, always playing at his own pace, a zoot-suit dance slowed down until it was ballet—that the other guys at the playgrounds gave him a nickname born of the old Glenn Miller tune, a big-band song title shortened to slang. *Gotta be jelly 'cause jam don't shake!* Joe's game didn't shake. Joe's game swished and flowed. Now Joe wasn't just Joe. Joe was Jellybean. Perfect. "I eat about four pounds of jellybeans a day," he said in high school, and even if he was exaggerating, it was a righteous exaggeration, because it reaffirmed what everyone already knew: Even for a kid, Joe was a kid.

Jack Farrell told a reporter that Joe was "the best in the city," the top player in a basketball-mad town, and Joe didn't let a sense of humility or graciousness stop him from letting all his friends and peers know that, deep down, he thought the same thing, too—that he was the best. When Bartram won a game, he called them all for some good-natured gloating, to remind them who the true prince of the city was. But when Bartram lost? Well . . . somehow Joe was never home after a Bartram loss. Funny how it worked out that way every time.

I was lucky to grow up in a loving, nourishing family. . . . Some people don't have families like mine.

—KOBE BRYANT

3

GOD AND THE
DEVIL IN THEM

T HE CHURCH WAS THE CENTER of the Cox family's lives. Founded
in 1893, its walls castle-gray brick, St. Ignatius of Loyola remains,
according to the city archdiocese, "the oldest Black parish in Philadelphia." One of its earliest congregants was John A. Cox, Kobe Bryant's
great-grandfather, who lived a half mile from the church, who joined the
Knights of Columbus and for more than forty years managed St. Ignatius's thrift shop, and whose only son, John Cox Jr. . . . well, you could
find worse antecedents for the man Kobe Bryant would become than his
maternal grandfather.

Both sides of Kobe's extended family fed basketball into his blood,
and John Cox Jr. was a primary source—a standout who, when he was
sixteen, set a single-season scoring record in his local boys'-club league,
then set the sport aside so he could sprint into adulthood. He enlisted
in the Army in February 1953 and married Mildred Williams when he
was twenty and she just seventeen. The couple had two children, Pam
and John III, and John Jr. joined the Philadelphia Fire Department,
which had begun to integrate its companies only in 1949. He finished
his career as a lieutenant, his rank an indication of how hard he had
worked, how well he had performed, and how resilient he had to be

to rise so high. His personality, tough and stern, had an edge to it, a necessary edge.

John III, whose family took to calling him "Chubby" because he was such a pudgy toddler, inherited his father's tenacity and his love of basketball. Within Pam, John Jr.'s toughness and Mildred's sweetness commingled, and though she played her share of pickup basketball—"I hear she has a mean jump shot," Kobe once said—she had other, stronger interests than sports. At Overbrook High School, she was one of two female students selected to serve on the John Wanamaker Teen Board, arranging youth events at the famous department store in the center of Philadelphia. A panel of Wanamaker's employees had based its choice of Pam, according to one news report, "on scholarship, personality, poise, and physical attributes." Five foot ten, possessing high cheekbones and a shock of lustrous dark hair, Pam resembled, as she aged and matured, the singer Diana Ross, and indeed one of the spoils of her selection to the board was the opportunity to model in several fashion shows at the store.

That she would cross paths with Joe Bryant seems, in retrospect, only a matter of time and course. Her grandparents lived on the same street as his. One day, Joe was sitting on row house steps with friends when Pam walked by. The whispers and whistles and catcalls commenced. *Look at Pam! She looks good!* Joe was the only one on the steps who said, "I'm going to marry her one day."

YOU WOULDN'T have known that the campus, without a suitable arena—or any arena at all—for its men's basketball team, its academic buildings hidden within a dense urban trapezoid of duplexes, storefronts, and small-rise apartment buildings in the Olney section of North Philadelphia, was the home of one of the better programs in college basketball. La Salle College was a commuter school, mostly, affordable for the city's blue-collar Catholic families, accessible by bus or car or train or trolley, and its students had to use those modes of transportation to attend one of the school's home basketball games. They couldn't just walk. The Explorers played their home games at either the Palestra or the Philadelphia Civic Center, each in West Philadelphia, each a fifteen-minute drive from campus.

The city was so flush with basketball talent, though, that La Salle and the four other Division I programs that made up the Big Five—Villanova, Temple, St. Joseph's, and Penn—had an always-available pool to replenish themselves. La Salle had won the National Invitational Championship in 1952 and the NCAA tournament championship in 1954, featuring the biggest star in the sport at the time, Tom Gola, a six-foot-six guard/forward and a local hero for being born and raised in Olney. After a scandal in the mid-1960s landed La Salle on probation for two years—its coach had paid certain players and withdrawn scholarships from others—the school hired Gola as head coach in an attempt to restore its respectability and esteem. In Gola's first season, the 1968–69 Explorers, though banned from postseason play, went 23–1 and were ranked as the No. 2 in the nation, behind coach John Wooden, star center Lew Alcindor (as Kareem Abdul-Jabbar was known at the time), and the UCLA Bruins. The team is still, more than a half century later, regarded as the finest in Big Five history.

The afterglow of that 1968–69 season shone warm and bright three years later, as the best high school basketball player in Philadelphia weighed his college choices. Joe Bryant had spent much of the spring of 1972 showcasing himself at various all-star games and tournaments to more Division I coaches. He had particularly grabbed their attention when he was named the most valuable player at the Dapper Dan Roundball Classic in Pittsburgh, which pitted the state's top players against high school stars from the rest of the country and was organized and put on by a businessman and promoter from western Pennsylvania: Sonny Vaccaro.

AS HE winnowed his list to La Salle, Temple, Oregon, and Cincinnati, Joe and his parents grew confused over the recruiting process. They were overloaded with information and weren't certain whom to trust. To simplify things, to maintain a sense of comfort, Joe made staying close to his mother and father one of his highest priorities. "I might get homesick," he once said. "All I have to do is put forty cents in the toll box and come home or walk down the hill to my grandmother's." And La Salle offered him a dimension that the other programs did not: Gola had stepped down after two seasons, and his successor, Paul Westhead, coached a free-flowing, offense-oriented style of play that appeared a match for Joe's array of skills. Westhead's pitch to Joe was direct and without artifice: *Stay home and play in front of your friends and family. You were so successful at Bartram, and you can continue that success at La Salle. It's a natural segue.* Joe agreed.

"This was before the national recruiting kind of set in," Westhead said. "Local players wanted to stay local. For a player in Joe Bryant's era to say, 'I could go to Arizona' or 'I could go to Cal Berkeley,' it wouldn't really be a possibility."

Westhead's analysis of Philadelphia's recruiting scene was generally true over time, but there were exceptions to it. Wilt Chamberlain had been so dominant at Overbrook High School, averaging more than thirty-seven points a game and setting the city career scoring record, that he could have gone to any school in the country. In 1955, he picked Kansas. Gene Banks of West Philadelphia High headed to Duke in 1977. Rasheed Wallace left Simon Gratz in 1993 for the Southern environs of Chapel Hill, the genius of Dean Smith, and the University of North Carolina. Contrary to Westhead's assertion, not everyone wanted to stay local. Every now and then, a transcendent player from Philadelphia or from its penumbra of suburbs decided that the Big Five was not for him, and yearned for something else somewhere else, and went for it.

JOE HAD not qualified academically to play as a freshman, so he sat on the bench for every game of that 1972–73 season, the delay only increasing the anticipation surrounding his debut. In his first game for La Salle, with his mother and father on hand, he lived up to the billing: nineteen points, fifteen rebounds, one blocked shot, and three behind-the-back passes in a fifty-point win over Lehigh. But his performance on the court was hardly the highlight of the evening for him.

La Salle–Lehigh was the first game of a doubleheader at the Palestra; the second was Villanova–Richmond. The Wildcats would have four freshmen contribute to their 71–58 victory, among them point guard John "Chubby" Cox. Pam, an undergraduate at Clarion State in Pittsburgh, was home from college and attending her brother's game with John Jr. and Mildred. Across the packed Palestra, Joe saw Pam's parents, and Pam saw Joe's parents. He walked around the gym to say hello to Mr. and Mrs. Cox. She was already on her way to say hello to Mr. and Mrs. Bryant.

"It was kind of a Miss Piggy and Froggy thing," Joe once said. "'Hey, how you doing?' That type of thing. That night, we went on our first date."

They were married before the following summer, neither of them old enough to drink legally, both of them entering their junior year of college. Pam transferred to Villanova so that she and Joe didn't have three hundred miles of Pennsylvania land separating them, so she could be at his side while he was at La Salle, pointing himself toward a career in pro basketball.

For Joe and those who knew him well, his shift personally and socially was seismic. Playboyish? A partier? You might have said that. Joe was charming. Joe had had a girlfriend, Linda Salter, throughout high school, but Joe couldn't help who he was. If you were a young man, he could make you feel like you'd been friends forever, even though you'd just looked each other in the eye and pumped each other's hand for the first time. If you were a young woman, he could make you feel like you were the center of his world, even though he'd just noticed and smiled at you seconds earlier. One writer pegged Joe best: He had two minutes for everyone and two hours for no one.

Pam was the exception. Pam expanded his vision for what his life could and should be. "I'll say this to my dying day: Pam was really good for Joe," Mo Howard said. "All of us wanted to have equal to or better than the kind of family we grew up in. Pam put Joe in a place that made him a little more focused and responsible. He was a free spirit. Because of his relationship with Pam and her upbringing, it solidified who he would become as a father. He was finally settling in."

THAT STARTLING first game, against Lehigh, soon became the norm for Joe at La Salle. It had everything that would define his playing career in college: the gaudy statistics, the showmanship, the breathtaking fullness of his game. As a sophomore, he averaged 18.7 points and 10.8 rebounds a game, and the Explorers went 18–10, won the Middle Atlantic Conference Eastern Division, and advanced to the conference's championship game. The following fall, letters from agents wanting to represent Joe started flooding into Westhead's office, even though Joe still had two years of eligibility left. To enter the NBA draft after finishing his junior season, Joe would have to apply for hardship status—ostensibly an official acknowledgment from the league that the player was turning professional out of financial necessity, in reality a rubber stamp.

Initially, Joe wasn't certain that he wanted to leave; he and Pam were receiving financial help from his father while they were in school. But then, in the winter, Joe Sr. fell, broke a bone in his back, and couldn't work, and Joe began to reconsider his future. "He wants to maintain a certain lifestyle, and it's a scuffle now," Joe Sr. said then. "He does not like being dependent on anybody. I guess everything depends on what they're going to offer him."

Westhead viewed Joe's situation with the usual divided loyalties and conflict of interest that any college coach would. Of course, it was Joe's decision to make, and he had to do what was best for himself and his family, and Westhead, who would go on to coach six years in the NBA but hadn't worked in the league yet, pleaded ignorance when asked if Joe was ready for it: "I don't know the pro game." He felt on much firmer ground, though, when it came to evaluating Joe against other collegiate players: "I'll say this: If he gets another year of experience, he could be the best basketball player in the country."

Except, more and more, Joe believed he didn't have to wait. He was itching to go, and given the season he was having, it would have been hard to persuade him otherwise. He was leading the Big Five in scoring, at more than twenty-one points a game, and his hunger to test himself against the best players on the planet, to find out whether the tricks and flash that made him so distinctive would translate to the NBA, was growing more apparent by the game. Westhead had allowed Joe to play with the same style that Joe had wowed everyone with at Bartram. The coach was an agnostic about it, neither encouraging it nor discouraging it. He regarded it simply as part of the package with Joe—that sometimes Joe would bring the ball up court like a point guard, that sometimes he would shoot a twenty-footer from the wing like a two-guard, that he would rebound like a center, that he would put the ball between his legs, shake, bake, shimmy, double-pump, and take a contested shot just because the spirit had so moved him. Late in his sophomore season, for instance, he torched Rider for thirty-seven points, the most he scored in any college game, hitting seventeen of his twenty-seven shots, dropping all the theatrics and just dominating the game with layups and strong drives to the basket. His performance was a case study in how he ought to have played all the time, yet he seemed to have done it on a whim. After the game, he told a reporter, casually, "I should do a little more rebounding tomorrow." *Oh, OK, Joe.* There was no keeping his head out of the clouds. The exception to all that freedom from structure was a single set play that Westhead relied on whenever the Explorers had to have a basket: He'd have Joe post up six to ten feet from the basket, tell La Salle's guards to get him the ball, and have Joe shoot a feathery little turnaround jumper. Otherwise, there was no point, and little benefit to the team, in trying to limit Joe's options on offense. "He did not comply with the way big men were supposed to play," Westhead said later. "Back then, everyone had a slot. Every coach had a scheme, and everybody respected everybody's scheme. It was a ritual, and Joe was breaking the ritual, for sure."

La Salle was 21–6 entering the 1975 East Coast Conference Tournament championship game, against Lafayette at the Kirby Center in Easton, Pennsylvania, with a berth in the NCAA tournament on the line. And that night, Joe broke something else, too. At the time—and the concept sounds so antiquated today that it's humorous—dunking was prohibited in college basketball. The NCAA had banned the dunk in 1967. (The ostensible reason was that the association wanted to limit the influence of big men, particularly Alcindor. The actual reason likely had more to do with players' race than their height: that the NCAA was trying to squelch the quintessential expression of Black dominance of the sport.)

Whatever the intention of the transparently absurd rule, it was still a rule. If a player dunked during a game, the referees were to assess him a technical foul and give the opposing team two free throws and possession of the ball.

Everyone, including Joe, knew the rule. He would finish with twenty-eight points in a 92–85 La Salle victory, one that both won the Explorers the conference title and catapulted them into the NCAA tournament. But with seven seconds left and La Salle ahead by eight points, Joe stole the ball at half-court, sized up the Lafayette basket as he dribbled toward it, and couldn't resist. You could almost see the thought bubble floating above his head: *We have this game wrapped up. I've been compliant the entire season. I haven't dunked a ball once. I have to do it at least once!*

Two seasons' worth of pent-up dunking desire exploded forth, as if Joe were a just-jiggled bottle of seltzer. He threw down, without apology, a thunderous slam.

The Kirby Center stopped. Westhead couldn't believe it. Joe walked toward him and the La Salle sideline, a smile stretched across his face.

"Coach," Joe said, "I had to. I had to. I've been waiting all year to do this."

That's Joe, Westhead thought. All instinct, no calculation. It would surprise Westhead years later to see the stark difference between Joe and Kobe in their approaches on the court. Whatever happened to flit through Joe's brain, that's what he would do in a game. No-look pass? Why not? Off-balance leaner? Hell, yes. Kobe was the opposite. Kobe was all calculation. *I'm going to go three steps to the left. Then, I'm going to spin back to the right.* Everything for Kobe, from what Westhead saw, was precise and planned. Joe was all flow. Joe could just let go. Joe could treat the most important game of his college career, La Salle's East Regional semifinal game of the 1975 NCAA tournament, against Syracuse at the Palestra, as another afternoon on the courts at Cobbs Creek Park.

And he could make even that game look like an ordinary summertime playground pickup run—twenty-five points through the first thirty-nine minutes, Syracuse with no answer for him. Of course he could. This was the Palestra. This was the gym he knew best, where his best personal moments and basketball moments had taken place: meeting Pam, all those spectacular scoring nights. This was going to be one more. Now the score was tied at seventy-one with sixty seconds left in regulation, and Westhead had the Explorers bleed the clock down to the final ten seconds before going to their most reliable play: Joe in the post. They got the ball to him six feet from the basket, just like they were supposed to, and with his back to his man, with no chance of the shot being blocked, Joe turned and took that soft fadeaway . . .

. . . and the ball hit the front of the rim . . .

. . . and rolled around the rim . . .

. . . and the buzzer sounded . . .

. . . and the ball fell off the rim.

The game went to overtime, and overtime was awful for Joe. He fouled out with one minute, forty-two seconds left. Syracuse scored on a back-door layup to take a late lead. The Orangemen won 87–83. La Salle's season was over.

So was Joe's career. One by one, he withdrew from his roster of classes, or just stopped showing up to them. He didn't quit school outright. No, that would have required Joe to look someone in the eye—his professors, the college's registrar, Westhead—and declare his intentions and actions and open himself up to confrontation, to direct disapproval. Joe preferred to avoid that awkwardness if he could. "I backed down some," he said. "Everybody cuts classes. It's natural." In early April, with the NBA draft a month and a half away, he filed for hardship status, and the league approved his request. Was he ready? The numbers said he was: 21.8 points and 11.8 rebounds a game, a shooting percentage of 51.7, the consensus best player in the consensus best college basketball city in America.

Pam still had her doubts. She and Joe were a newly married couple, both still college-aged. What if no team drafted him? What if the team that drafted him cut him? What if he ended up playing in Philadelphia for his hometown team, the Sixers? Being the wife of a Philadelphia college basketball star was difficult enough. She was defensive about the manner in which the city's newspapers covered Joe. "When he's playing good, which is most of the time," she said, "nobody hardly mentions him except to say, 'Well, he made *this* mistake.' And when he's playing really good, people say, 'Well, he ought to play *better.*'" Surely the criticism would be harsher and sharper if he were a full-fledged professional, and what if it didn't work out for him in the NBA one way or another? It didn't even have to be his fault. Suppose he ended up with the wrong team—too many veterans, not enough talent. Suppose he ended up with the wrong coach, one who couldn't make the most of his skills, who wouldn't tolerate a six-nine player who didn't have a fixed position on the floor and didn't particularly want to have one, who thought that Joe was still too skinny compared to the average NBA player and would get pushed around in the post. Suppose Joe became just another local hero who didn't live up to expectations; a kid who *wasn't* ready, who wasn't mature enough to thrive at basketball's highest level; a ballyhooed prodigy who turned out to be a bust.

Joe was courting that naysaying by bolting early for the NBA. He didn't care. "I know where I'm at," he said. "I know where I'm going. Everything's cool." Come the night of the draft, everything was. The Golden State Warriors, who had won their first NBA championship just four days earlier, selected Joe in the first round, with the fourteenth overall pick. The only thing preventing Joe from starting his career with the Warriors was an obscure league edict: Once a team drafted a player, it had to tender him a contract by September 1 to retain his rights. Otherwise, the player would become a free agent. But the rule was a formality, met by a simple form letter from Golden State management to Joe's agent, Richie Phillips. Easy enough, one would think. Then Joe and Pam would be on their way to the West Coast.

AS FAR as Pat Williams, the Sixers' general manager, was concerned, September 1 passed without anything of note transpiring in the NBA. He assumed that the team he had assembled was complete and ready for training camp, and he assumed it right up to the moment, a few days after the contract-tender deadline, that Richie Phillips, Joe Bryant's agent and attorney, called him.

"We haven't gotten a contract from the Warriors," Phillips told Williams. "Does that mean Joe is free to sign anywhere?"

"Richie," Williams said, "that is my understanding."

"Well," Phillips said, "they still haven't given him a contract. If he's a free agent, would you be interested in signing him?"

Williams advised Phillips to wait another day or two to see if the contract arrived. It never did. The Warriors had simply neglected to mail it. Because of that clerical error, they had lost Joe's rights. He could sign with any team he wished, and he wished to stay in Philadelphia, and Williams was sold. He signed Joe to a long-term contract. Williams once wrote that the deal was for five years and worth $140,000 per year. Some media reports at the time said it was far more exorbitant: as much as six years and $1.4 million. The newspapers never did nail down the details. Regardless of the specifics, it was a magical sum of money for Joe, who used it to buy himself a sports car: a white Datsun 280Z. "It's unbelievable," Joe Sr. said. "How many people can see a son play in junior high, high school, college, and the NBA all in the same city?"

And what they saw for a while . . . wasn't very good. Joe missed thirty of his first thirty-six shots as a pro. When he finally scored ten points in a game for the first time, in an early-December victory over the Kansas City Kings, he savored the attention of the writers so much that some of his teammates started laughing at him. "Just talking jive," Joe said. "I can't talk jive like I used to."

The Sixers made the playoffs for the first time in five years, then were eliminated in the first round by the Buffalo Braves. Joe had settled into a bench role, playing sixteen minutes a night, scoring seven or eight points a game, instant offense when he was fully engaged and his shot was true, inconsistent otherwise. Now it was mid-April. He and Pam had become parents just a month earlier, when Sharia was born. He had the summer ahead of him to settle into the home that he and Pam had purchased for $82,000 on Christmas Eve, a five-bedroom colonial at 1224 Remington Road in Wynnewood. Joe was a husband. Joe was a father. Joe had security and wealth and, if he wanted, better days ahead as a promising professional basketball player. Joe Sr. had said it: Joe wanted a certain lifestyle. Now he had it. But Joe was still young, twenty-one years old, and Joe couldn't yet help who he was.

AT 11:37 P.M. on Wednesday, May 5, 1976, two officers of the Philadelphia Police Department's Eighteenth District, responsible for patrolling the Fairmount Park West area of Philadelphia, noticed a white Datsun 280Z ease past their van, then park at an intersection. One of its taillights was out. Inside were Joe Bryant and a twenty-one-year-old woman, Linda Salter, his former girlfriend.

The officers approached the Datsun and asked Joe for his license and registration. Joe stepped out and handed over the registration, then turned around to reenter the car, presumably to retrieve his license. He did not retrieve anything. He slipped behind the wheel, turned the key, and, without bothering to turn his headlights on, sped off, heading south.

One of the officers, John Pierce, radioed in a call for backup before following Joe in the van, commencing a high-speed chase that Officer Robert Lombardi, in an unmarked police car, joined. The chase lasted three miles, and it culminated on the 900 block of South Farragut Street in a sequence fit for a Steve McQueen film. The Datsun hit a stop sign, careened across the street and slammed into a no-parking sign, swerved back and plowed over another street sign, bounced off the left front end of one parked car to the rear of another to the front end of a third. Finally, it jumped a curb and crashed into a wall.

Joe leaped out and tried to run, but he got only about five feet away from the Datsun. "I grabbed him," Lombardi said later, under oath in a courtroom. "He raised his fist, and I struck him. I subdued and handcuffed him." "Struck" and "subdued" likely were euphemisms for actions that were far more specific and violent: Joe received six stitches later that night at Philadelphia General Hospital.

He told police that he had no driver's license, only an expired learner's permit. When they searched the Datsun, police found, on the front seat, two plastic bags, each of which contained a vial of cocaine.

Joe was charged with drug possession, reckless driving, and two counts of resisting arrest. At Joe's trial, Richie Phillips paraded twenty character witnesses into City Hall's courtroom 285 to testify on Joe's behalf. Pam, Sharia, and Joe Sr. appeared alongside Joe, completing the united front of family and team and community in support of him, and a photograph in the next day's *Philadelphia Daily News,* taken and distributed by United Press International, captured the couple as they entered the courtroom: Joe in a dark suit, his tie knotted in a long and bulky triangle, his mouth half open; Pam to his right, in a light-toned dress, a scarf around her forehead, her right finger touching her chin, a look that hinted she had just heard something that had at once surprised and disconcerted her.

The witnesses' pleas for leniency persuaded the presiding judge, J. Earl Simmons. He wiped Joe's slate clean—legally, anyway—ruling the search that uncovered the cocaine vials to be illegal, calling it "a bad reaction to what essentially was nothing more than a traffic violation." He found Joe not guilty of the remaining charges.

Joe returned to Phillips's law office, where the two of them granted an interview to Phil Jasner, a sportswriter for the *Daily News.* Joe would play harder, concentrate more, he told Jasner. Already, he had learned more about how he should carry himself. People would keep bringing up the incident for the rest of his life, and he would have to overlook that criticism and hope that it made him a better man. It was the classic media-relations move, the establishing of a narrative of redemption for public consumption: Young athlete does wrong, heeds difficult lesson, changes ways, and thrives. But what about the days and nights away from the court and the cameras, the moments when it was just Joe and Pam and his betrayal and carelessness likely hung heavy in the air between them?

That was the aspect of their relationship that only those closest to Joe and Pam could understand then and now. Pam would always put Joe and her family first—preserve them, support them, even coddle them. To her, *Till death do us part* wasn't a throwaway line. Why did she stay? No one who knew her well had to ask such a question. She was a strong, Black, Catholic woman, and a married couple stayed together. End of explanation. No matter what, a wife was supposed to stand by her husband; a mother was supposed to stand by her children. There would always be hard times in any marriage, and it just so happened that the

Bryants' hard times had played out in a manner for the world to see, just as their son's would.

KOBE BRYANT'S immersion in basketball began in the earliest days of his life, as one would expect. The Bryants attended so many Sixers home games that the Spectrum itself might as well have been an extension of their living room. Joe's parents sat in Section H, and the Bryants became such fixtures that Pat Williams grew accustomed at each game to saying hello to Joe Sr., now walking with a cane in the wake of his back injury, and to Pam as she pushed Kobe in a stroller. "He grew up at the Spectrum," Williams said.

The baby was happier to be there than his father was. On the surface, he was Good Time Joe—audacious silk shirts, platform shoes, a beret capping his head, that quick and easy grin—and since his arrest, he had caused no off-the-court problems, had handled his business. But he regarded his place on the team's hierarchy, as a backup forward, as an eighth or ninth man, as a slap in his face. What had the Sixers done in the aftermath of Joe's incident, instead of trusting that he could and would continue to improve? They had spent $6 million to acquire and sign Julius Erving from the ABA's New York Nets, burying Joe deeper on the bench. One night in September 1979, outside a motel bar in Lancaster, Pennsylvania, where the Sixers were holding training camp, Joe was chatting with two beat reporters when the name of another player came up in their conversation. The player was a rookie on the Lakers: Earvin "Magic" Johnson. The bitterness in Joe's words was still palpable four decades after he uttered them.

"He comes into the league with all that stuff, and they call it magic," Joe said. "I've been doing it all these years, and they call it 'schoolyard.'"

One month after Joe bemoaned his station in the NBA, fourteen months after Kobe was born, the Sixers traded Joe to the San Diego Clippers for a first-round draft pick. He welcomed the change of scenery, vowing that "the Sixers will look bad in the deal. I mean, I can play defense, I can play offense, and there are not too many players who go both ways, and I have the ability and capability of doing that. . . . That's the confidence I have in myself. Remember this: I'm gone, but I will not be forgotten."

While keeping the house in Wynnewood, he, Pam, and the children relocated to Southern California, the first clean break they had made from Philadelphia and their family. Without Joe on the Sixers anymore, there were now, for the first time in years, a couple of empty seats in Section H of the Spectrum, just six seats to the left from a boy whose dad and brothers had season tickets themselves. Just six seats to the left from a kid named Gregg Downer.

By growing up in Italy, I learned how to play basketball the right way through a teaching of fundamentals first. I'll always be grateful for the teaching I received from my coaches there. . . .

I knew it was going to be different, that the culture was different. I actually do remember the first time we went in our house and turned on the TV. There was an Italian cartoon, and me and my sisters were rolling. We were dying. "Oh, my God. This cartoon." It was on in Italian, but they had the same cartoon in America. It was the same exact cartoon, but it just had Italian words. It was weird, man. We were tripping, man.

—KOBE BRYANT

4

CHILD OF THE WORLD

LOOK AT THE CHILD, THREE years old, the precocious little child, standing in a hallway of his family's temporary home in San Diego. Look at him pick up his mini basketball with his mini-mini hands. The ball is the moon in them, too large for him to grip with just one. This would seem an impediment to his developing into a wondrous basketball player. In fact, the opposite will turn out to be true. Because, throughout his adolescence, he will be unable to palm a basketball, and because even once he develops into the most wondrous basketball player in the world, each of his hands will grow to just nine inches long—neither big nor small by NBA standards, forcing him to cup the ball against his wrist whenever he rises to dunk—he will labor to make his fundamentals absolutely flawless, to knead any glitch or imperfection out of his footwork, his shooting technique, any of his technical skills. But those often-solitary praxes are still years away. For now, he merely holds the mini basketball in his hands, and he can see, at the other end of the hallway, a tiny trampoline in front of a miniature basketball hoop, and he does something that brings him joy and that always will. He runs down the hallway and hops onto the trampoline, and the trampoline catapults him into the air, and he slams the ball down through the hoop. His mother warns him, *Don't dunk, sweetheart. You'll break the basket.* He picks up the ball again. He dunks again. He is three.

BEFORE THE Sixers traded Joe Bryant to the Clippers, his teammates in Philadelphia already had coined a couple of nicknames for Kobe. Those late-1970s Sixers teams featured an unusual number of players who had sons who went on to become elite basketball players themselves. Henry Bibby had Mike, who was the No. 2 pick in the 1998 NBA draft and spent fourteen years in the league. Mike Dunleavy had Mike Jr., who was the No. 3 pick in the 2002 NBA draft and spent fifteen years in the league, and Baker, who played college ball at Villanova. But Joe had Kobe, and Kobe was the only one whom the players and their families— and his own parents—called "the Chosen One" and "the Golden Child."

Now the Golden Child would spend some time growing up in the Golden State, and Joe, at first, hated that idea. He had wanted to be traded, right up to the instant he was traded. Then the realization that his hometown team really did regard him as expendable, and treated him as such, wounded him. The Sixers, Joe said, had "hurt me right in the heart." He was two weeks away from his twenty-fifth birthday when the trade went down, entering his physical prime, and the Clippers did afford him some obvious advantages and benefits: more playing time, a clean and fresh start.

Joe played twice as much as he had for the Sixers, but the results were no different. He had no green light to shoot, to display his wizardry with the ball, to be himself, and the Clippers were such a mess that he didn't even experience the same meager satisfaction that he had in Philadelphia: that at least he was, in some small way, helping his team win more games than it lost. The Clippers improved only marginally from Joe's first year with them to his second, from a 35–47 record to 36–46. In 1981, he had surgery on each of his big toes, and if any doubt remained about how much Joe missed the Philadelphia area, he erased it every summer, when he and the family returned to Wynnewood so he could play in the Baker League. Plus, he phoned his dad after every game, and Big Joe in turn fed the local papers, *The Bulletin* and *The Tribune* in particular, a steady stream of newsy tidbits from their conversations.

The upshot of San Diego, perhaps the only one, was the city itself—the weather, the people, everything sunny and charming and relaxing. Joe and Pam took the children to Disneyland and SeaWorld and the San Diego Zoo, and he was so approachable, just another dad wearing an orca T-shirt or a hat with mouse ears, that fans felt at ease waving hello to him or shaking his hand. Sharia, Shaya, and Kobe were enrolled in school, and Kobe grew fond of giving his teacher updates on Joe, as if the toddler were a sportscaster narrating highlights on the 11:00 P.M. news. *My daddy's team won last night, and my daddy slam-dunked.* At night, when he watched his daddy's games on TV, he'd sling a towel over his shoulder, like the grown-up players did. *Mom, I'm sweating.*

THE CLIPPERS nose-dived in '81–'82, winning seventeen games, finishing dead last in the Pacific Division, and Joe all but dared them to trade him at the end of that season, when he took exception to a cost-cutting move by the franchise's notoriously parsimonious owner, Donald Sterling. To save on expenses, Sterling demanded that the Clippers' coaches and players fly coach instead of first class. "The younger guys would have flown with the cargo," Joe said, "but as a veteran, I stood up for the players' rights." Given that, in 2015, NBA commissioner Adam Silver banned Sterling for life after the revelation of racist comments to his mistress, Joe's objection probably should have been regarded as an early warning of what the league would be in for with Sterling for the next thirty-three years. When the Clippers arranged a trade with the Houston Rockets in June 1982, Joe considered it a favor.

He was also considering something else: becoming a college basketball coach. Not only did he play in the Baker League during his summers in Philadelphia, he coached in the college division of the Sonny Hill League. He enjoyed the experience and thought he could serve a Big Five team well as an assistant and especially as a recruiter, putting that gregarious personality of his to good use. "I believe I could persuade the best players to stay home," he said. "Then I would work very hard to help those players reach their full potential."

LOOK AT the child, four years old, the precocious little child, wearing a white karate gi, standing in a dojo in southeastern Texas. He is, as his age suggests, a neophyte in the martial arts, but the sensei sees something within him. He decides to test him. There is an older, physically stronger, more experienced boy in the dojo, a brown belt, and the sensei tells the child to fight the bigger opponent. Tears pour down the child's face.

He's so much better than I am, he says.

The plaintive words anger the sensei. *You fight him!*

A head guard covering his skull, sheened red combat gloves on his hands, the child shuffles onto the fighting mat. The other children in the class encircle him and the bigger boy, all the better to bear witness to the beating. The child is overmatched. The child is scared. The bigger boy hammers him with a punch, a kick, another punch, but the child stops crying, stays in the ring, takes the punches, punches back. Lo and behold, he lands a few good shots. He loses the bout, but he has stood up for himself, and when the fight is finished, he comes to a liberating conclusion. He had envisioned the worst possible outcome, but the outcome and the consequences of the battle were not as bad as he thought they would be. It is a kind of instinctual recognition, an awakening that shapes him forever. He is four.

IN HOUSTON, with another bad team bound for nowhere, Joe provided a clearer answer to the question that had defined his spotty NBA career: Was it that circumstances had never been favorable to him, or was he the cause of his own exasperation and resentment? In Kansas City, he was two minutes late for the team bus to a morning shootaround, and when the bus left without him, he couldn't get a cab to the practice because he had been cleaned out of cash during a poker game the previous night. So he went back to his hotel room and went to sleep. Pam joked within the family that she would slide a five-dollar bill into one of Joe's socks before he left on the team's next road trip. It never seemed to occur to Joe that if he were more diligent in his habits, more professional, he might have earned the benefit of the doubt from his coaches, and his teams and his career might have been better for it. It didn't seem to occur to him at that time, anyway.

As bad as Joe's final season in San Diego had been, his only season in Houston was somehow worse. Under coach Del Harris, the Rockets went 14–68, the worst record in the league. The franchise was rebuilding. It had no need for Joe anymore, not on the court. His contract expired, and neither Houston nor any other NBA team bothered to sign him. But Charlie Thomas, the Rockets' managing partner, liked Joe enough to offer him another job, one that Joe accepted. Thomas had an ownership interest in some fifty car franchises, many of them Ford dealerships. Joe was twenty-eight. Joe was no longer an NBA player. Joe was married with three kids to provide for, and Joe was now a car salesman.

Forget that night full of bad decisions in Fairmount Park years earlier. At least Joe was still a basketball star then. At least the Sixers stuck with him, gave him a second chance. This was his nadir now. No one saw any value in him anymore, not on the court, not in the locker room, all that reputation and reality melding into the perception of him as a giant goofball, a perception he wasn't going to shed, and the worst part was he wasn't some aging has-been whose skills had deteriorated. He wasn't yet thirty. Jellybean could still shoot. Jellybean could still shake. But who was going to give him his second chance now?

Sonny Hill gave him an idea for who might. *Try Europe,* Sonny told him. *They will appreciate you there.* Of course. Go abroad. It made sense. There was good money to be made in the professional leagues overseas, and such a drastic lifestyle change wouldn't be unprecedented in the Bryant-Cox family. Joe's brother-in-law Chubby Cox already had made the jump, failing to make the Chicago Bulls' roster after they drafted him in 1978, treading water in the Continental Basketball Association for a while, abandoning the CBA for a team in Caracas, Venezuela. There, he had thrived. There, he and his wife, Victoria, had their son—John IV, Kobe's cousin—before returning to Philadelphia. If Chubby could do it, Joe could, too. He and Pam sold everything they had in Houston. He drove his Mercedes to her parents' house, parked it in the garage, and off he and Pam and the children went, across the Atlantic. They could be strangers in a strange land, if they had to be.

LOOK AT the child, nine years old, the precocious child, bounding down the aisle of the bus as it rolls through Italy's cities and countryside, speeding on the autostrada and rumbling along roads clouded in dust. The child isn't so little anymore. His torso is short and high because his legs are so long, and it is obvious that he will zoom beyond six feet in height once he enters his teenage years. He bops around the bus, which is filled with Italian basketball players and coaches on their way to a game, until he reaches the two *americani* in the last row. One of them is his father. The other is his father's friend.

The child loves these trips. He accompanies his father on them frequently. Depending on where the game will be played, the ride might last two or three hours, or it might last five to six. Depending on the route, the vehicle fills with the aromas indigenous to the regions and towns that it passes through—the pungency of the cheeses sold at the street markets of Bologna, the briny odor of fish in Venice, basil flavoring the breeze wafting along Italy's southeastern coast. His father and his friend, the only American-born players on the team, chat throughout the trips, often about their families, and the child joins the conversations.

Someday I'm going to show you old guys how to play, the child tells them. *I'm going to show you how it's done.*

Son, the men say, doubled over in laughter, *get your skinny butt outta here!*

One day, the child's father confesses something to his friend. The father's grandmother had once prophesied that someone would come along who would change the entire structure and direction of the family, who would accomplish great things and allow the family's members to live new lives.

And the father looks at his friend and says, *I know it's not me. I'm getting close to the end of my run.* And the two Americans look at the child bounding around the bus, and the father says, *It might be him.* And neither of the men is laughing.

★ ★ ★

HIS FAMILY'S move to Italy, when he was six years old, was a formative change at a formative stage of Kobe Bryant's life. Had Joe remained committed to pursuing a career in the NBA, and had another team offered him an opportunity to extend his career, the family's peripatetic existence would have continued. But it would have continued within the confines of the United States' borders, and for all the diversity and variety of people and life within those borders, the experience wouldn't have provided the full immersion in a foreign and exotic culture that Italy did. Nor would it likely have fostered the dynamic that the family carried forward for years thereafter. Italy's professional basketball clubs, including the one with which Joe signed, Sebastiani Rieti, operated with more relaxed and less demanding schedules than those of NBA teams. There were just thirty games in a regular season, and the team played only once a week, on Sundays. In Rieti, a hilltop town of more than forty thousand people an hour northeast of Rome, nestled within the Apennine Mountains, the club found the Bryants a cottage with a wooden gate and a garden and a basketball hoop mounted on an outside wall, gave Joe a new BMW, and made all the necessary arrangements for the children's education. The kids attended school six days a week, enrolling first in an American school in northern Rome—the team provided a chauffeur for them, as well—before transferring to an elementary school in Rieti. Immersed in Italian during their four-hour-long school days, which lasted from 8:30 A.M. to 12:30 P.M., and often convening at home to practice their new dialect among themselves, Sharia, Shaya, and Kobe learned the language faster than their parents did, and Kobe still had time to accompany Joe to practice each afternoon and be back for bedtime at 10:00 P.M. sharp. Already close, now living as a Black family in Europe, the Bryants developed even stronger, tighter bonds, becoming a self-contained unit in a land where they were both curiosities and celebrities. When they strolled through town, strangers offered to buy them coffee, cover their check at a restaurant, or let Kobe and the girls have a taste of pasta or chocolate.

"People treat others as equals there," Kobe once said while in high school. "They don't mistrust each other. They say hello when they see you on the street. And family—family is big there."

Those open hours that Joe used to fill having a blast on the road? Now he and Pam jogged five to six miles a day. Now he shot baskets in the driveway with Kobe and neighborhood kids, as if the Bryants' home were in Hamelin and Joe wielded a wind instrument. Now he brushed up on his Italian, expanding his vocabulary until he went from knowing just a few phrases—*Attento,* or "Watch out!" was a good one for him, as a father of young children, to learn early on—to mastering much of the language. Now he opened up packages from Joe Sr., videotapes of NBA games for Kobe to watch. Certain games captivated Kobe. They usually involved the Los Angeles Lakers. Those bold gold-and-purple jerseys, the manner in which Magic Johnson controlled a game, the funky goggles that Kareem Abdul-Jabbar wore, the combination of imagination and self-control within each man's game: Kobe couldn't stop watching them. How was it that Magic never made the wrong play? And the joy in his eyes—it was the same joy that Kobe saw in his father's. And how had Kareem taught himself that sky hook? No one else shot it! "He would watch those games like they were a movie," Shaya would say later, "and he knew what the actors were going to say next." And there was Joe, sitting next to him, watching the tapes with him, delivering analysis and commentary, explaining to Kobe what was about to happen, what this player or that player was about to do and why, and Kobe couldn't get enough. *See where Olajuwon sets up in the post. It gives him enough leverage and room to spin to the baseline if he wants.* He replayed the games so frequently and watched them so intently that he absorbed every nuance, as if Joe had permitted him entrance into a secret, thrilling world that Kobe would never want to leave. He started rolling up his dad's tube socks into a ball and flicking them into a garbage can, and he wasn't a six-year-old boy when he did it. No, he was a Laker, too, playing before a shrieking sellout crowd at the Great Western Forum, Jack Nicholson and Dyan Cannon and all the other glitterati in the front row. He was emulating, on his hoop near the garden, what he saw on the videos. He was waiting until his mother turned her back, and he was rappelling from the cottage's second-floor balcony to the backyard, scurrying across a dangerous highway, and sprinting across a field to a playground near a Catholic church, a snowcapped Terminillo

Mountain twenty kilometers in the distance providing a breathtaking backdrop, as he honed his basketball moves more. He was recruited by Claudio di Fazi, the son of Sebastiani Rieti's general manager, to play in a basketball league with boys two, three years older than he was, and he dribbled and shot and shot and dribbled and scored so many points— scored the first ten points in his first game—that the other nine players started crying and their parents started screaming to get this spoiled little *scuro* off the court. And when di Fazi complied and sent Kobe to the bench, it was Kobe's turn to burst into tears, running into the stands to Pam's side so she could comfort him. And Joe wasn't off in some hotel, thousands of miles away, in Atlanta or Portland or Salt Lake City. He was there, every day, to see his son score and sulk and dream.

"I've become a family man," Joe told *The New York Times* in 1985. "In the United States, I was more of a traveling man."

It was Pam, though, who was the household's true leader. She kept everything in order, insisted on the children being well-rounded as people, that they treat others as they would like to be treated, that they open themselves up to their new surroundings, disciplining and indulging them at the very same time. They would embrace the new and exotic aspects of Europe. "The travel helped them see different people, different religions," Joe once said. "I think they look at people as human beings, not as a color or religion, so they don't feel trapped in any kind of stereotypical situation." Kobe would immerse himself in basketball, sure, but he would love soccer, too. Sharia and Shaya would discover volleyball. They would carry themselves with respectfulness for adults and their peers . . . until those adults or peers transgressed them in some way, and then it was time for a show of strength or assertiveness or ice-cold defiance, and the three children had to look only at their mother for such demonstrations. Sometimes, when Pam was out on her morning jog, a male motorist would roll down his window and shout a catcall at her, and before he could say something really inappropriate, she would casually turn her head, without breaking the rhythm of her run, and respond: *Fuck you.* They would build on those self-guided Italian lessons, speaking the language so well that they would become popular interview subjects on Italian TV, which in turn would make them better students. She would expose them to American popular culture when possible; when Pam dressed Kobe in a bow tie and accompanied him to a friend's birthday party, he impressed the other kids and the adults with a spontaneous display of breakdancing. She would keep Catholicism at the forefront of their lives and thoughts: Eventually, while the family was living in Tuscany, Kobe would don a dark blue blazer, crisp white slacks, and a white shirt, and, just as he would have done had he been an ordinary American second grader in an ordinary parochial school, fall in among his classmates and make his first Holy Communion, just as Pam, as a young girl, had made hers. During Kobe's early years with the Lakers, when he would isolate himself on a team plane, slap headphones on his ears, and curl up in his seat to watch the film *The Ten Commandments* over and over again, there was a reason.

JOE ENCOUNTERED faces from his past, and those faces influenced Kobe's future. One of Joe's old Sixers teammates, Harvey Catchings, had come to Italy, too, with his daughters, Tauja and Tamika, the latter of whom was a year younger than Kobe. The children befriended each other, sometimes sharing slices of pizza, and remained in touch as Kobe progressed through his career with the Lakers and as Tamika won four Olympic gold medals with the United States Women's National Basketball Team, a WNBA championship, and a WNBA Most Valuable Player Award. "We had a vision of a different life," Kobe once said of him and Tamika. "It's crazy. We grew up thinking anything was possible." The two of them were inducted into the Naismith Memorial Basketball Hall of Fame on the same night: May 15, 2021. "This," she said, "was going to be the storybook ending."

Leon Douglas had met Joe when they were seventeen, at the Dapper Dan Classic in Pittsburgh, before they went their separate ways: Joe to La Salle, Douglas to Alabama. Douglas was the starting center for Fortitudo Bologna, one of Rieti's rivals, and the fresh connection, away from the pressure of pro basketball in the United States, rekindled his friendship with Joe, helping the Bryants to ease into their new surroundings. In Italy, the games had an atmosphere comparable to that of a college football game or a European soccer match, banners flying, a pure and merry energy pulsating throughout the arena. When Joe would start scoring, when he'd begin dominating a game, catching the ball on the wing, sizing up his man, Pam and the girls and Kobe would start shouting from the stands, *Bust him up! Bust him up!* No one was yelling at Joe to play team ball, to set a pick at the top of the key. He could be the player he'd always wanted to be, and was never permitted to be, in the NBA—a six-foot-nine small forward, launching deep jumpers over zone defenses, driving past anyone who tried to guard him man-to-man. His nickname was "The Show," for obvious reasons. Through the first twenty-five games of his second season with Rieti, Joe averaged 34.8 points, leading the league in scoring and assists, the latter statistic mostly a function of his having the ball in his hands so much. Finding an open teammate? Only if the pass was preceded by a 360-degree spin move that buckled a defender's knees. Only if Joe threw it without looking. Only if the play had some pizzazz. His scoring sixty points or more in a game wasn't uncommon, and he played without tactics or tact. He might as well have been alone on the court, trying trick shots just to amuse himself. A few years later, the Italian-league franchise in Pistoia recruited both Joe and Douglas to play there, purchasing Joe's contract for $115,000 American. Their families lived a half-hour drive from each other—the Douglases in a condominium, the Bryants in a mountainside villa—and often socialized. Their children celebrated their birthdays together, went to the same school. Sharia, Shaya, and Kobe would babysit the Douglases' daughter, Lenae. Joe and Leon would have lunch together each day, but if Joe was happy to split the bill after each meal, his sharing mood didn't extend to the court.

"It was good for me in one sense because I played with a very good friend," Douglas said, "but Joe didn't pass the ball too often. That's where Kobe got that from."

It was a weekly demonstration of education by osmosis. After plopping down on the floor, watching the first half from a safe spot that allowed him to pick up on the subtleties of the players' movements, Kobe would grab a mop or broom to sweep the court at halftime. (Once, in exchange for working an all-star game while wearing a sweatshirt advertising the business of Pistoia's owner, Kobe made the owner a deal: *Sure, I'll wear your sweatshirt while I mop, but you have to buy me a red bicycle.* The owner did.) Then, he would put on a basketball show of his own. There he was, mimicking what he had just watched, dribbling between his legs, practicing his jumper, heaving shots from too far out, a miniature version of Joe. The arena crowd would stay put and stare, and it never bothered the boy, and the game officials would have to kick him off the court so they could restart the real game. He befriended Luca Rusconi, the son of Joe's coach, a perfect workout partner. At home, they cut the bottom off a plastic vase, hung it from the top of a garage, and used it as a makeshift basket. They shot around before one of Joe's games, and Kobe challenged Luca, two years older, to a three-point shooting contest, and Kobe made all ten, leaving his friend speechless and dazed: Luca let the ball slip from his grasp, extended his hand to Kobe, shook hands with him, and walked away. On those bus rides, Kobe had told his father and Douglas of his plans, and they had chuckled at his braggadocio. But all this—the crowd and the setting and he himself, alone on the court before them—was just the necessary first step.

"He wasn't afraid," Douglas said. "That's what people don't realize. The great players are able to play where their confidence doesn't vary. What distinguishes a great player sometimes is his level of confidence. You can be put in a negative situation that will damage your psyche, and you'd shy away from the things you'd normally do. Kobe never had that problem. His dad was the same way: never shot a bad shot. If he missed ten, he might make the next ten. I'm sure being around pros reinforced that for Kobe."

But it was a particular kind of pro who made an impression on him. From his father, Kobe could appreciate basketball's individualist nature, the spectacular selfishness of a single-minded player. His gratitude for the coaches he had while in Italy? It was a polite sentiment, a nice bit of lip service, because when it came down to it, from whom was he going to learn more: the coaches who wanted to corral him, or the father who wanted to free him? It wasn't just that Joe could walk him through how to pull off the acrobatic moves that had been his, Joe's, signature. It was that Kobe could hear his father's what-ifs and might-have-beens from an NBA career that Joe still believed could have been so much more than it was, and Kobe was entirely sympathetic to those lamentations. Dad had been so respectful of his teammates, his coaches, the fans. Hadn't he played eight years in the league when there were fewer teams, when it was harder to make a roster? Hadn't he kept himself in shape all those years? Dad took nothing for granted. He was himself, played the way *he* wanted to play, maintained the integrity of his game, and look at the scoring numbers he'd put up in Italy, the acclaim with which the people had showered him, the warm hug that the country had given to the whole family. It hadn't been Dad's fault that no one in the NBA gave him the break he deserved. Someday Kobe would fix that. Someday, he vowed, he would right those wrongs.

From the men his father played against, though, Kobe could see how he could extract the best of Joe and the best of the systems and discipline to which his father hadn't paid enough mind. He could appreciate the basics of basketball, the importance of its fundamentals. Put your foot there to cause the defender to rock backward just enough that you can shoot over him. Lower your body at this angle to curl, tight as a stripe on a candy cane, around the man guarding you and knife toward the rim. The power forward should be here, exactly six and a half feet from the point guard there; otherwise, the offensive set you're supposed to run with so much timing and synchronicity will devolve into a crowded mess.

In 1986 and 1987, while Joe was with another club, Standa Reggio Calabria, Kobe played organized youth basketball, blending in with the other children, polite to everyone at first. His coach in the league, Rocco Romeo, described him as having "a splendid smile stamped on his face." But once the scrimmages or games began, Kobe would scream at Romeo, "Rocco! The ball! The ball!" And Romeo, to quiet Kobe and avoid the embarrassment of having a child yell at him, would encourage the other players, *Come on, kids. Pass the ball around. . . .* Predictably, once Kobe took control of the ball, he never relinquished it. He did not pass it back, and he did not smile, and he didn't care for playing defense. He carried himself on the court with his father's style and his mother's intensity, with the same tidy, elegant movements and actions that Romeo would come, over Kobe's career in the NBA, to find familiar—"He moved like a panther," Romeo said—and with the unspoken understanding that he was special. It was usually unspoken, that is, and his parents did little, if anything, to disabuse him of it. Joe brought Kobe with him to practice one day, and Santi Puglisi, Reggio Calabria's head coach, gathered the players at midcourt to explain a strategic concept that he wanted to develop and implement. Wearing one of his father's team T-shirts, the hem drooping below his knees, Kobe grabbed a basketball and started dribbling at a far end of the court. Distracted, Puglisi said with a laugh, "Kobe, stay seated." Kobe looked at him.

"Fuck you," he said. "Fuck you."

How do you handle a child who dares to speak like that to adults? How do you mark the line between encouraging him to believe and trust in himself and giving him carte blanche to behave as if the word of someone older and more experienced wasn't worth his bother, as if he could spit at a reasonable request from an authority figure? If you're Joe and Pam Bryant, you send him to private schools with the strictest of discipline codes, that challenge him intellectually, but you coddle him when it comes to basketball and his conduct relative to it. When he was eleven and twelve years old and his Italian was perfect and his father was playing for Reggio Emilia in northern Italy, Kobe played for Cantine Riunite, a junior team sponsored by the commercial winery of the same name. The team's uniforms were white with red and blue trim, resembling the jerseys that Bryant and the other members of the U.S. Olympic men's basketball team wore at the 2008 Summer Games, in Beijing. There is one photo from that time that is particularly revealing. It shows Riunite's two coaches and thirteen players posing for a typical team picture, the front row sitting, the back row standing. Several of the players smile. A few appear bored. Kobe, standing on the far left, has raised his chin and is scowling, as if the photographer has captured him in the midst of a self-assured nod. It is a look that says, *I'm the man,* and if you don't like or accept that truth, you already know what Pam Bryant and her son would say to you.

In the summer, once Joe's playing season would end each May, the Bryants would return to the Philadelphia area, and they'd volley between their home on Remington Road and Pam's parents' house in the Green

Hill Farms section of Philadelphia. Kobe, at age eight, now had a couple of playmates in his cousins: Sharif Butler, who was eleven and was Chubby Cox's older son, and John Cox IV, who was five. The trio were as close as brothers, but even then, at those tender stages of their lives, John was less a playmate to Kobe than he was a sparring partner, a tool that a budding basketball star could use to improve his game. The boys would broker agreements with each other. If Kobe wanted John to play basketball with him for an hour, then Kobe and John had to play with John's toy action figures for the next hour. If Kobe wanted to play more basketball, fine. But afterward, he and John had to spend the same amount of time swimming in their grandparents' pool, or pretending to be Batman and Robin, or wrestling with each other. Then, and only then, would John consent to be a part of the highlight of Kobe's daily routine: watching game films of Magic Johnson and the Lakers, maybe some Larry Bird, too, before practicing in the driveway what he had just seen on TV.

As Kobe and John got older, basketball occupied more and more of their time together. It occupied so much of it, in fact, that Pam referred to their basketballs as their "girlfriends" and teased the pair whenever she noticed that neither of them had a ball tucked under his arm. *Where are your girlfriends?* she'd say. *Where'd you leave your girlfriends?* For Kobe, his routines with his younger cousin were a respite from his routines with his older one. He and Sharif went at each other one-on-one each day in the driveway at Remington Road, at Tustin Playground in West Philadelphia, at courts throughout Ardmore, and the games were more one-sided than Kobe's first foray into the karate ring. By his thirteenth birthday, Sharif was six foot three, physically mature for his age, and Kobe could not beat him. How many times did they play each other? They played each other a thousand times, John said, and Kobe lost a thousand times. Worse, Sharif tortured him with a torrent of trash talk that sometimes escalated to cruelty. The eff-yous flew at Kobe now, not from him. "Sharif was an asshole," John said, "but he was always trying to make Kobe tougher."

He had help. In 1991, Joe signed Kobe up for the Sonny Hill League, presenting him with his first exposure to the rougher kind of basketball on which Sharif and every Philadelphia player had been weaned. The league promised to challenge Kobe physically and mentally. His circumstances, his genetics, his upbringing in the game had shaped his notion of what a basketball player looked like, how a basketball player was supposed to play, and mercy, was he a soft target. His twig-thin legs were covered, armor-like, with thick knee pads, in part because he suffered from Osgood-Schlatter disease—an affliction that developed because he played so much basketball and that caused inflammation, pain, and fragility to his knees' bones and tendons—and in part because he had seen other athletes wear them: NBA players, his sisters while playing volleyball. Though his sight wasn't impaired and he hadn't sustained any injuries to his eyes, he wore goggles. Kareem Abdul-Jabbar—six-time NBA MVP, six-time NBA champion, one of his heroes on the Lakers—wore goggles. So did James Worthy, another Lakers great. Why couldn't he? He knew little to no American slang; his fluency in Italian might have wowed the adults he encountered, but it earned him no quarter at Temple's McGonigle Hall, where the league held its games and the city kids chewed him up.

Near the end of his career with the Lakers, before his final game in Philadelphia against the Sixers, Kobe would tell a conference room full of media members at the Wells Fargo Center that some of his fondest memories came from playing in the Sonny Hill League, and he noted that the summer of '92 was one that he treasured. He couldn't possibly have felt that way at the time. In twenty-five games, playing up a level, against players who were a year or two older than he was, he did not score a point—not a meaningless layup in a blowout, not a wing-and-a-prayer jumper, nothing. He had shamed his father and his uncle, and he briefly considered giving up on basketball and focusing on soccer, a natural and facile transition, given that he was living in Europe. But instead he rededicated himself, learning of the half-true story of Michael Jordan's getting cut from his high school team—in reality, Jordan was merely assigned to the junior-varsity squad—and using this common ground with the sport's greatest player to inspire him. More watching game films with an eagle eye. More studying basketball's history and evolution and timeless basics. Humiliation became motivation, and motivation became obsession. "It was a turning point for me," he said. "It really was. Zero points the whole summer, and that became a big motivating thing for me, to make sure when I came back to the Sonny Hill League, I was ready to play. I was ready to compete."

Joe no longer was. One more season, for Mulhouse, a team in France, and that was all. He retired, officially. He felt like he could have played another two years, but he was whipsawed now by guilt and hope. His wife and children had sacrificed for him and his career, and it was time now for him to sacrifice for them. The time had come to go home. When Magic Johnson was diagnosed with HIV in November 1991, for instance, Pam's parents called her and Joe at 2:00 A.M. to tell them, and upon hearing the news, Kobe was so distraught that he skipped most of his meals for the better part of a week, his sadness dismaying Sharia, she once said, because she "never imagined feeling that way about somebody I'd never met. It hurt him as if it was a family member." As much as Joe hurt for his son's pain, he didn't want Kobe to lose that connection to his home country and to basketball's significance there. The Bryants were back in Wynnewood later that fall, with Kobe enrolled at Bala Cynwyd Middle School for his eighth-grade year. He was now six foot one, and he recognized that, for him to become the basketball player he believed he was born to be, he couldn't stay in Italy, though into adulthood he said he still missed the carefree nature of his years there, still wished he could go back in time to meet up with young friends in the piazza to share a gelato. To Joe, the family's return to Lower Merion Township was just in the nick of time. He was always quick to say that those years abroad were the source of what he considered Kobe's early maturity—"Italy was the key," Joe once said—but he also kidded that he wanted his son to live in America permanently, before Kobe forgot how to speak English.

LOOK AT the child, eleven years old, the precocious little child named Ashley Howard. He loves basketball, loves it so much that he accompanies his father to gymnasiums and playgrounds all over Philadelphia just so he can watch his father play or sometimes play alongside him. And on a Sunday morning, Ashley has accompanied his father, Mo, to the Gershman Y, at the corner of Broad and Pine in Center City Philadelphia, for the mother of all father-son pickup games. All of the men played Division I ball, in the NBA, or both. There's Mo with Ashley. There's Lynn Greer Sr., drafted by the Phoenix Suns in 1973, with Lynn Greer Jr., who will go on to star at Temple for John Chaney. There's Mike Morrow, who played at St. Joseph's University, with Mike Jr. There's Chubby Cox with John. And there's Joe Bryant. With Kobe.

This is a regular Sunday game, and the sons usually stay on a side court, shooting at a basket that's not quite ten feet high, while the fathers go full-court five-on-five. This Sunday is different. One father couldn't make it. They have only nine. One of the sons gets to play. Kobe is thirteen. Kobe gets to play.

Oh, wow, Ashley thinks. *Let's see how this goes.*

On the first possession, Kobe brings the ball down court. Mo Howard is guarding him. Mo Howard, Joe Bryant's buddy since they were teenagers, the former Philadelphia Catholic League Player of the Year. Mo Howard, who teamed with John Lucas at Maryland in the mid-1970s to form one of college basketball's best backcourts. Who played thirty-two games in the NBA. Who isn't yet forty years old.

Chubby Cox shouts at his nephew: "Yeah, go at him. Go at him." Oh, yes, the child wants to see how this goes. Kobe dribbles at Mo, shakes, pulls up, knocks down a jumper. The child is stunned. *Didn't Dad always take pride in his defense?* Ashley thinks. *He must be taking it easy on Kobe. He doesn't want to abuse the kid.*

The next time Kobe comes down the court, Mo presses up on him. Kobe slips around him, drives past him, banks in a layup. A puzzled look drops over Mo's face: *Shit, I've really gotta guard this young fella a little closer.* On the side court, still watching, Ashley Howard files away this memory. He had seen Kobe Bryant play, really play, for the first time, and Kobe wasn't intimidated. Kobe wasn't going through the motions, running up and down the court with no hope of having someone pass him the ball. Kobe was holding his own against men. Kobe was doing what he had been trained and groomed to do. The retribution to all the assholes—cousin, competitor, friend, foe—would be fierce.

PART II

I didn't want any special treatment in school because I was a good basketball player, and my school, which was and is known for high academic standards, wouldn't have pushed me through anyway.

—KOBE BRYANT

5

ANGELS
AT SUNRISE

ABOVE KOBE BRYANT'S QUEEN-SIZE BED at his family's home at 1224 Remington Road, on the wall behind the headboard and the pillows where he laid his head, his mother had hung a picture. Rimmed with a gold frame, shaped as a lengthwise rectangle, the picture depicted two guardian angels, a male on the left side, a female on the right, both of them Black in race. The male angel, shadowed in amber, posed in a tall church window as if he were standing guard, eagle-like wings protruding from his back and poised as if he had just descended and landed from flight. He held in his left hand, like a walking staff, a white sword, its point stabbing the window's landing. The female angel was cloaked in white, bestrode a snowy mountaintop, and had lifted her arms above her head. Hovering in her hands was a halo that threw off rays of blue light. Between the two images were these words:

> *God has given each of us*
> *an Angel in our life*

The house was middling by the standards of the opulent, old-money areas of the Main Line: thirty-four hundred square feet not in a secluded cul-de-sac but on a busy artery, gray stone and tan siding and white fencing and lush beds of red roses and a semicircle driveway. Inside, it seemed that everything was black or white or green, and the decor was warm, nurturing. A gorgeous table of African wood was the centerpiece of a room where teenagers might read or play board games, and Black-culture-themed artwork adorned the walls of the first and second floors. Sliding glass doors in the den—the home's gathering place, with a couch and a gigantic television—led outside to a small backyard. In the house's crawl space, someone, in permanent black marker and capital letters, had scribbled "2ND FLOOR KOBE'S ROOM" on a heating pipe, and when Joe and Pam sold the house in 2008, the couple who purchased it from them, Richard and Kate Bayer, thought that detail so endearing that, when they had a few repairs and upgrades done to the house, they asked the workers to cut out a piece of insulation large enough that the words would remain exposed. In Joe and Pam's bedroom, two black cushioned chairs rested in front of the bed, angled toward another large TV. Stacks of books and Italian magazines filled the shelves of the wall unit in Joe's study. It had not taken Kobe long, upon returning to the United States, to begin subscribing to *Sports Illustrated,* and he saved some of the back issues and stored them in the study, sometimes piling them on Joe's desk. One—the June 22, 1992, issue, published two months before Kobe turned fourteen and a week after the Chicago Bulls had beaten the Portland Trail Blazers in the NBA Finals—featured on the cover a single player, smoking a victory cigar: Michael Jordan.

Out in the driveway, of course, was the basketball hoop: a black pole, a rusting orange rim, and a canvas-white backboard set between the doors of the house's two-car garage. Because the hoop was centered against the garage, and because the driveway wrapped around the house, anyone who played at the Bryants' had enough room to simulate anything that he or she would do during a customary full-court game of basketball. Over time, the front of the rim bent and curved downward an inch or so, an inviting imperfection that made it easier to send a leather ball through the metal hoop, a testament to all the mornings and afternoons and evenings that Joe and Kobe played one-on-one against each other there—dunks thrown down, elbows crashing to the upper chest and jabbing into the solar plexus, every bump and pump fake a tutorial. The games weaved themselves into the scenery and the ambient noise of the neighborhood, as did the unceasing hours that Kobe spent alone in the driveway, practicing, each scene so common that motorists cruising through Wynnewood stood a good chance of glancing out their driver's-side windows and glimpsing a moment in Kobe's apprenticeship. In time, the house would become a kind of tourist attraction, Lower Merion Township's own Liberty Bell, an object of historical meaning and curiosity for passersby, many of whom parked their cars around the corner or paused their three-mile jogs to knock on the front door and ask the Bayers, *Is this where Kobe lived? Yes,* the Bayers would say. *Yes, it is. Come in. Have a look around.* This is where the Bryants became part of the community. This is where their son and brother, from the instant he returned there and for the rest of his life, was at once of that community yet separate from it.

IT IS IMPOSSIBLE to tell the story of Kobe Bryant without telling the story of Lower Merion: the township and the school district, the history and the diversity, the facile stereotypes and the complex reality, the high school broadly and the boys' basketball program specifically. As much as his environment there shaped him, he shaped it even more. He arrived as if he were a spaceman, aware of his new habitat, eager to explore it but unfamiliar with its history and customs and language. He defied pigeonholing; only so many of the trends and developments and presumptions that had been baked into the region's evolution and collective thinking, and into American society's, applied to him. He fit into some of those trends and developments seamlessly. He blew apart most of those presumptions.

The Bryants' home—its location, the path they took to settle there—was itself a relative anomaly. That the Bryants resided in Wynnewood was a break from the sociological patterns that had long defined Lower Merion, and those patterns had long been defined by one thing: the Pennsylvania Railroad. "More than any other person or entity," according to a history of the region, "it was the Pennsylvania Railroad that built the Main Line." To expand, the railroad's executives purchased, from the state, the Philadelphia & Columbia Railroad in 1857, then bought farms and land to develop that prime property—close enough to access Philadelphia but far enough away to feel removed from it—into a rural sanctuary for the rich and the beautiful. One hamlet, Bryn Mawr, emerged as a residential neighborhood, but the rest of the area became a summer refuge and resort for the upper class. Why stay in the city during an oppressive July heat wave, the dirt and smog and airborne sediment of industrialized Philadelphia filling your lungs and choking you into a phlegmy cough, when you could breathe deeply the clean air and the musk of azaleas, when you could wake up to sycamores and red maples and hackberry? To this day, Gladwyne, in Lower Merion, ranks as one of the wealthiest communities in America—the second-richest in the entire Northeast, as of 2018. The driveways are winding and private. There are few sidewalks. Along the twenty-five miles of the Schuylkill Expressway, only one exit empties commuters into Gladwyne, and once drivers zip past that exit as they head west on the highway, away from Philadelphia, there isn't another one for five miles. Gladwyne remains exclusive in every regard.

As the Pennsylvania Railroad added more stations and trains, more men and women of means and privilege saw the Main Line as a desirable place—no, *the* desirable place—to live in the Philadelphia region. For a half century, from the late 1800s through the Jazz Age, mansions sprouted around the Main Line as if money had been their water and sunlight, which it was. The railroad tycoons, their friends, and other developers and magnates built and bought them. "Life in the golden era was just about perfect, if one had a lot of money," the author James Michener, born in nearby Bucks County, Pennsylvania, once wrote. "The winter was spent in Florida. In summer, a few families moved to Newport, but most preferred the most sedate and rural life of Bar Harbor. Most families kept a city dwelling in Philadelphia's famed Rittenhouse Square. And the rest of the time they lived in their palaces along the Main Line. These massive and sprawling homes were fabulous."

The train depots alone were characterized by their Victorian-style architecture, and Isaac Clothier, the co-founder of the Strawbridge & Clothier department-store chain, owned perhaps the most ostentatious edifice on the entire Main Line: Ballytore, his home in Wynnewood. Built in 1885, it was a turreted, crenellated castle with four sentry gatehouses; a porte cochere to allow for convenient entry for a horse and carriage or, later, an automobile; and a covered porch that snaked halfway around the estate as if to protect it. A moat apparently would have been a touch too extravagant.

In the early twentieth century, the makeup of the township's population was predominantly Protestant, and the typecasting of the region during that era, as an exclusionary haven for WASPs, continues to this day. As they unfolded over the subsequent years, the demographic changes to the area only reinforced that image, the elite and the working poor living in tight juxtaposition, the difference between having and having not rarely so stark. The railroad meant jobs. The railroad meant residents hiring laborers to build their mansions and servants to wait on them. It meant Italian stonemasons settling in Narberth, and it meant Black men and women finding work as laborers or domestics—butlers, maids, chauffeurs, laundresses, gardeners—and nestling into the row houses and twin homes in the town of Ardmore. In turn, many Protestants began relocating to suburbs even farther to the west—Radnor, Conestoga—opening the Main Line to Jewish and Black families from southwest Philadelphia eager to leave the city. The student bodies of Lower Merion High School, which opened in 1894, and the district's other high school, Harriton, which opened in 1958 to accommodate this population surge and shift, grew more diverse, though the elementary and middle schools that fed them were themselves mostly homogenous pockets of Black, Italian, Irish, and Jewish people. Deed restrictions and covenants against Jewish and Black people were ugly facts of life then, and though areas of the Main Line were opening up, the residue of that racism wasn't washed away immediately. "A lot of people don't even realize the homes out there, the deeds on them say these homes are not to be sold to Negroes," said Dayna Tolbert, whose family moved from Cincinnati to Bala Cynwyd, who grew up near the Bryants, and who was friends with all three Bryant children. "They literally say in print, 'This house is not to be sold to a Negro.' My house was built in 1926. The only way that we could move in was that we were from out of state, and, on paper, they couldn't tell my parents were Black. They didn't realize until we showed up at the signing."

Those tendrils of the past would reach up and tether themselves to Kobe Bryant in myriad ways.

THE NEIGHBORHOOD where Arn Tellem was born and spent the first six years of his life was one of Russian-Jewish immigrants. His parents attended Temple University, and his father introduced him to Big Five basketball, which became his sports obsession. His extended family were all around him. "You knew everyone in a ten-block radius," Tellem said. "I had my grandparents, my great-grandparents, all my aunts and uncles and cousins. You could walk to synagogue and pass your family's homes." His was a mirror image of the childhoods of Joe and Pam Bryant, the same sense of inclusiveness, a shared experience of a clannish existence.

Just after President Kennedy's inauguration, in 1961, Tellem's parents bought a house in the Penn Valley section of the township, going from one Jewish neighborhood to another. It wasn't a move to Italy, but it was a disruption to his family nonetheless.

"I remember being in the car with my father and grandfather," he said, "driving down the Schuylkill Expressway to Penn Valley, and my grandfather didn't understand why we were moving to the suburbs. What was so great about the suburbs? What was the point? That was a huge generational shift, the move from the city. It changed the way of life. The togetherness you all felt through good times and bad times, sharing it together, became more remote. It was more about your smaller family."

Tellem retained his love of the Big Five and Philadelphia high school basketball, though. A senior at Harriton in the spring of 1972, he bought a ticket to the Palestra to watch the city championship game, to watch St. Thomas More beat Bartram and a player, wearing a puffy Afro and black low-top Keds, who fascinated him: Joe Bryant. "Packed house," he said. "It was just so exciting. The thing that struck me was that Joe could play anywhere, his unbelievable skill level." Tellem continued his education at Haverford College—just three miles from 1224 Remington Road—earned his law degree at the University of Michigan, and embarked on his career as a sports agent, and he couldn't have known at the time, as a teenager, how often he would come to think of that day at the Palestra and everything that followed it.

WENDELL HOLLAND did not grow up in Gladwyne or Wynnewood. His ancestors streamed to Ardmore from southern Delaware, and his mother, who was a domestic, and his father, who was a doorman at a ritzy apartment building, were what he called "classic Main Line Blacks." Ardmore had its benefits. There were other clusters of Black families on the Main Line, but of all its communities, Ardmore, particularly a five-block area on its southwestern side, was the "safest" for Blacks—that is, it was where they didn't have to question or doubt that their neighbors had their best interests at heart. If Holland and his friends, on a Saturday afternoon, walked or rode their bikes over to Suburban Square in north Ardmore, to see a movie or wander around the sporting-goods department of Strawbridge & Clothier, police might stop them, or store owners might eyeball them. They didn't have to worry about such anxious situations within their slice of the world. There were just two white families in Holland's neighborhood. "The joy of Black Ardmore was that you were literally around people who were like you," he said. "It was the Nairobi of the Main Line." Best of all, parents there could send their children to Lower Merion's public schools, regarded even then as among the finest in the nation.

Fine, but far from flawless. When Holland entered Ardmore Elementary School in 1958, the school was a model of de facto segregation. Just 9 percent of students throughout the district were Black, but at Ardmore Elementary, 85 to 90 percent of the students were. The school building by then was already fifty-eight years old. Textbooks were dog-eared and outdated. The teachers were the least qualified in the district, many of them marking time until their retirements. A grass field, the size of three average front yards in Gladwyne, was adjacent to the school, but no student was permitted to play on it at recess. Instead, the students jumped rope and played all their games—hopscotch, softball, kickball, rough-touch and tackle football—in the school's parking lot. Holland took part in all those games, and on Friday nights, he went to Downs Gym to see Mitch McDaniels, the Aces' basketball standout, the first thousand-point scorer in school history. McDaniels and Lower Merion basketball gave Holland a hero, and they gave him hope.

"As students, we had an overwhelming sense of apathy and belligerence," Holland said. "It was a lot like going to a parochial school, where a nun would whack you on the hand. That kind of corporal punishment was readily available. As many educators talk about the importance of educating kids from age three to sixth grade, that period of time was virtually lost to us for quite some time. How did I get through it? I had a tremendous drive to succeed. Why? Because I was part of a community and family that had a rich athletic legacy."

Under pressure from the Main Line chapter of the NAACP, Lower Merion's school board voted to shut down Ardmore Elementary on August 26, 1963, a relatively minor development in a year of upheaval: The vote took place two days before the March on Washington, seven months after Alabama governor George Wallace's speech demanding "segregation now, segregation forever," less than three weeks before the 16th Street Baptist Church bombing in Birmingham, and less than three months before President Kennedy's assassination. Holland and his classmates transferred to Penn Wynne Elementary. To him and his peers from Ardmore, wearing someone else's clothes and shoes, clothes and shoes with holes in them, and eating nothing but cheese sandwiches for lunch was normal. Yet on the morning and afternoon bus, with schoolmates of much greater means, Holland for the first time in his life *felt* poor. All the girls wore dresses that fit and had no stains on them at all, and all the boys wore brand-new sneakers. Come December, some of them looked forward to taking trips to Florida for the holidays. Florida? Florida, to Holland, might as well have been Mars, and Penn Wynne might as well have been a stately Ivy League campus. "Lunchtime came," he said, "and we went out there, and we saw this grass that we could play on for the first time. I'll tell you, it seemed like Franklin Field."

Holland went on to earn a basketball scholarship to Fordham University and graduate from Rutgers Law School. He became a judge and the chairman of the Pennsylvania Utility Commission, coordinated trade missions for the City of Philadelphia with China and South Africa, was on hand for Nelson Mandela's inauguration in 1994 and still keeps a ballot from that election as a souvenir. He and his wife live in Bryn Mawr, and he joined the Merion Cricket Club, and he still relishes that the club is across the street from a home where his father served meals and answered the phone, and the topic that will move him to tears is the one that differentiates him from Kobe Bryant. When, in March 1969, Billy Holland—Wendell's cousin and the senior captain of Lower Merion's basketball team—was suspended from school after an altercation with a white teacher, Wendell and fifty-four other Black students staged a sit-in to protest the punishment, arguing that the teacher's harsh and inappropriate treatment of Billy had provoked him. The demonstration lasted five hours before Billy was reinstated.

These were experiences that Kobe Bryant did not, and probably could not, have, and this was no meaningless stand for Wendell Holland to make. He was the team's best basketball player, a lithe shooting guard who averaged more than twenty points a game. He wore No. 33 before Kobe wore No. 33. "I don't think Kobe or anybody, ten years before or later, went through what we went through," he said. "Athletes are gray. They're not Black. They're not white. Because of their status, they enjoy the luxury of being the exception. Kobe really epitomized that. It can be a blessing and a curse."

When it came to his athletic life at his alma mater, however, Holland's lasting perspective had been formed by one place, the Ardmore Avenue playground, and one man, Vernon Young, a longtime high school track coach, the supervisor of the township's parks and recreation programs, and, in Holland's words, "the pooh-bah of the playground." Lower Merion won three consecutive state boys' basketball titles, from 1941 through

1943, and Young, a junior guard on the '43 team, had sunk the decisive free throw in that championship game. He told the community's kids the story of that game often, instilling in them a sense of pride about hailing from Ardmore and playing for Lower Merion. "There was somebody there—not my father, not my neighbor's father, but Vernon—who told us to be excellent," Holland said. "On hot summer days, when we were at the playground, talking trash and all that stuff, I'd say something like, 'In your face.' And he'd say, 'Yeah, but you ain't won a state championship.' That was my goal ever since I was about eight years old: to win a state championship." The Aces won forty-one of their forty-eight league games during his career, but Wendell Holland never did win that state championship. He swore that he would be honored to support and celebrate the kid who did.

THAT KID didn't show up for more than two decades. The Aces won a pair of district championships, in 1976 and 1978, but couldn't sustain those spikes of excellence. The regression was steep. From 1979 through 1990, they had six seasons in which they won no more than seven games. The uniforms were ratty hand-me-downs, often mismatched; a player might wear shorts with the number 43 on them and a tank top with the number 21 on the back. Soccer, lacrosse, and wrestling emerged as the most popular and respected boys' sports at the school, which was hardly surprising, given the area's history and demographics. "One of the beauties of living in Lower Merion, which I know to many folks in the area is seen as everyone driving a Mercedes in Beverly Hills and we're the most stuck-up of the stuck-up, is that it has all kinds of people," Evan Monsky, one of Kobe's friends and teammates, said. "There are nice people. There are dickheads. There are intellectuals. There are boneheads. There are creeps. I found that pretty much wherever I go." But in the aggregate, the area's affluence was undeniable. By 2004, the household income within the school district averaged more than $86,000, the median home cost $334,500, and the district spent more than $19,000 per student every year. Volvos, BMWs, and sports cars didn't just serpentine through the streets of the community; they filled the high school's parking lot. The school district's motto—ENTER TO LEARN, GO FORTH TO SERVE—was carved in serif font into a large stone placard just outside the entrance to the tan-brick high school building, and the desirability of life and the quality of education were reflected in the high school's increasing enrollment, which eventually topped fourteen hundred. Basketball was an afterthought. There was no image, no feel, no aesthetic to the program, nothing that defined Lower Merion other than that it was a school with a diverse collection of students—two-thirds of whom were white, 8 to 12 percent of whom were Black, the ratios shifting slightly depending on the year—that featured many academic achievers, kids who were smart and had scored well on their SATs and were headed off to prestigious colleges and didn't need scholarships or Pell Grants to go. It wasn't a bad reputation to have. *U.S. News & World Report* and the other institutions and publications that judged such matters perennially ranked the school among the best high schools in Pennsylvania, and a press release from the district, heralding the ten to twelve students who were National Merit Scholarship semifinalists, became a springtime tradition. But its academic reputation didn't strike any fear in anyone within Philadelphia basketball circles. In that world, Lower Merion's was just another boys' basketball program in the 'burbs, until the Bryants crossed an ocean to come back.

*To achieve a goal, you have to set
a goal. Mine was to play in the NBA
directly out of high school. . . . It took a
lot of hard work. And I was fortunate, at
age thirteen and fourteen, to know that
it would.*

—*KOBE BRYANT*

6

BATS AND MICE AND
THE RIDE OF A LIFETIME

KOBE BRYANT'S FIRST COACH IN the Lower Merion school system was a trim, forty-three-year-old man who earned his Ph.D. in health education from Temple University, ran at a five-minute-mile pace every day during his lunch period, and believed a middle school basketball team should pass the ball at least three times before someone took a shot. Dr. George Smith went nearly a quarter century without speaking to anyone from the media, perhaps because his everyman's name made him difficult to track down, perhaps because Kobe attended Bala Cynwyd Middle School for less than a year, in eighth grade, and no journalist considered finding Smith to be worth the trouble. In 1996, a reporter asked him one or two questions about Kobe. There was nothing thereafter. No matter. Smith was comfortable with his anonymity.

"Once Kobe left for the Lakers, I didn't keep in contact with him," Smith said. "But I kept reading articles about him."

To know even the most elemental details of Kobe Bryant's life and career is to understand why he and Smith didn't become longtime pen pals. For his twenty-seven years as a health and physical-education teacher at Bala, Smith was respected and admired, an Ardmore native and Lower

Merion alumnus who coached football, track, and basketball. Just before each basketball game began, he changed out of his sweatsuit and into clothes that exuded a greater air of formality and professionalism—button shirt, nice slacks, dress shoes—and he accented team play at all times, to give his young players a good foundation with the sport's fundamentals. On defense, they always played a basic 1–3–1 zone, and because most of their opponents played zone, too, Smith insisted, in a gentle but firm manner, that his players pass the ball until an opening in the defense's shell presented itself. "If you take a shot after one pass, you're not forcing them to play defense," Smith said, and anyone who took a shot before a third pass took a seat on the bench next to him. The instruction and the strategy, the nature of the program itself, seemed unchanged from what they had been forty, fifty years earlier. Dr. George Smith really had no idea what he was getting into in December 1991, when a fellow Bala teacher knocked on his office door and said, *I have a new student here who has just come from Italy.*

"Yeah," Kobe Bryant said. "I want to play basketball. My father played. I just want to get started."

"That's going to be a little difficult," Smith said. "We've already completed tryouts, and we have a scrimmage tomorrow. I can't really let you play until you get your physical completed."

The next morning, Kobe was back in Smith's office, paperwork in hand. "OK," he said, "I'm ready to play."

Smith gave Kobe a uniform—white, No. 24—and added him to Bala's roster in time for that afternoon's scrimmage, though he took care to warn him that he might not play in the game. "You don't know the offense," Smith told him. "You don't know what we're doing."

Kobe nodded. "No problem," he said.

He sat next to his new teammates. The team played well through the scrimmage's first several minutes, sticking to Smith's timeless and rigid game plan. Smith thought it was a good time to see what Kobe could do. He put him in the game. Immediately, Kobe blended into the offense, and subtly he began to assert himself, shooting more, dribbling around defenders. The kids on the bench looked at Smith, who shrugged his shoulders. *How was I supposed to know?*

"This was something I hadn't expected," Smith said. "From that point on through the rest of the season, it was just amazing, what he was able to do. I'm just sorry I didn't realize he was going to turn into such a player. I could have utilized him more, but I didn't want to give the ball to just one player. I probably held him back too much. Looking back, it was just unbelievable, what he could do."

WHEN KOBE became a student at Bala, there was no announcement, of course. No one got a heads-up that a future Hall of Famer had entered eighth grade. A pencil-skinny Black kid with a lilting, sibilant accent to his speech simply began showing up to class, and the rumor mill began churning, mixing fact and speculation into a mysterious milkshake. *Dude, that new kid in math class, he lived in Italy for, like, eight years. . . . I hear his dad played for the Sixers. Has two older sisters who are already at LM. I hear he takes a limo to school every day. . . . Have you seen him play? He's freaking good. . . . One kid challenged him to play one-on-one on the first day of school, and Kobe shut him out.* Word was that God or genetics or a combination of those two powerful forces had bestowed a precious gift upon Joe Bryant's only son, and that son was like nothing Dr. Smith or anyone else at Bala had encountered before. Gregg Downer, in just his second season as Lower Merion's head coach, heard the rumors, too, and he wanted an unfiltered view of the phenom for himself. In early 1992, he stopped by a game one afternoon to see Kobe Bryant play basketball for the first time.

It did not go well.

Dr. George Smith's rules had long become, in Kobe's mind, too burdensome for him. As talented as Kobe was, Smith's highest priority wasn't developing his skills. It was coaching the entire team. This, Kobe could not abide. He shot quickly once. Smith benched him. He shot quickly again. Smith benched him again. He pouted and grimaced each time he left the court, putting on such a petulant display that his father, to calm him down, whispered something in his ear in Italian.

Downer approached him after the game. The kid's talent was obvious. "Maybe you should come up and practice with our varsity," he told Kobe. "Maybe that would give me a better look at you."

There was no three-pass mandate at Downer's practices, and there were no tantrums from Kobe when he scrimmaged with the varsity team days later. The players had heard the rumors, too. How could they not? Matt Snider, a sophomore center on the team and an emerging star on Lower Merion's football team, had a little brother, Stevie, who was at Bala, and every day during basketball season, Stevie would come home and breathlessly tell Matt, *There's this kid named Kobe from Italy. No one can stop him. He's tearing it up.* Matt's response: *OK, we'll see about that.* Sophomore guard Sultan Shabazz had been Kobe at Bala before Kobe was Kobe at Bala: the dominant middle school player, the subject of tall tales and expectancy. How much better could this Bryant kid be than he was? "I was like, 'Bring him,'" Shabazz said. "'Let him come.'"

He came. With Joe Bryant standing impassively in a corner of the gymnasium, thirteen-year-old Kobe had his way with those bigger, stronger, older players. They couldn't slow him down, and it didn't matter if two of them guarded him at the same time. They couldn't handle his handle, his long arms whipping the ball behind his back and around his rail-thin waist to split those double-teams, and they damn sure couldn't meet him near the rim. Five minutes into the practice, Downer turned to his assistant coaches. "This kid is a pro," he told them. He had no idea at the time how understated his assessment would be, but he recognized immediately what was ahead for him.

"I was in," Gregg Downer said later, "for the ride of a lifetime."

THE DRIVEWAY of the Downer family's house in Media, a bourgeois suburb twelve miles west of Philadelphia in Delaware County, was a picture of basketball privilege in the early 1970s. There wasn't just one hoop. There were two: one the regulation ten feet, the other lower, maybe seven or eight feet high, so that Gregg and his two brothers—he was sandwiched between Drew, two years older, and Brad, seven years younger—could dunk. In the winter, Gregg would set three or four basketballs against the radiator in the house, to make sure that they were warm once he had shoveled the driveway clean of snow and was ready to play. A warmer basketball bounces better and truer in the cold. Out there he stayed in that driveway, playing all day and, because of a spotlight he had set up nearby, well after sunset—left-handed, little guy, soft blond hair flopping like a patch of lamb's wool as he hoisted jump shot after jump shot—until the neighbors started to complain about the damn noise and the bats that lived in the trees overhead started to get braver in the darkness. He always knew it was time to go inside once the bloodsuckers swooped in.

The court was where he went to get away when the shouting started. His mother, Marjorie, taught for years at an elementary and middle school for children with learning disabilities. His father was a salesman, natural-born, in a few jobs. He was an executive with Scott Paper. He sold Hoover vacuum cleaners door to door, and Robert Downer wasn't above a rascally trick to move product. *You use your vacuum, ma'am,* he'd say, *and I'll use my Hoover.* And when the credulous housewife wasn't looking, he'd toss a pinch of the dirt that he carried in his pocket onto the floor and ruefully shake his head. *Look at that. Yours missed a spot.* He and Marjorie divorced when Gregg was ten.

At Penncrest High School—one of Lower Merion's rivals in the Central League—Gregg made the varsity basketball team as a junior, working his way into the starting lineup, at two-guard, as a senior, for a team that finished 27–6 and carried a four-point lead into the final six and a half minutes of the 1980 Pennsylvania Interscholastic Athletic Association District One Class AAA championship game. Norristown High came back to win by six, though, and all the loss did was whet Downer's desire to keep playing competitive sports. Off he went to Worcester Academy in Massachusetts, one of the nation's elite boarding prep schools, for a year as a postgraduate. He was still just seventeen, and, eager to challenge himself, he was leaving home. But when his father eased his big blue Continental into that sweeping, pastoral campus and Gregg hopped out, the sight of the car pulling away tempered his excitement: *I'm all alone here, and I don't know a soul.* The experience, that feeling, would prove a helpful connection later, with one of his Lower Merion players.

AFTER FINISHING up at Worcester, playing four years of Division III ball at Lynchburg College in Virginia, and graduating with a phys-ed degree, Downer had learned pretty much just one thing: He wasn't a shirt-and-tie guy. He didn't want to be a banker or accountant or lawyer or salesman. Actually, he had no idea what he wanted to do until, while working at a sporting goods store in Media, he got his first coaching job: the freshman team at Penncrest. The Shipley School, a private day school in Bryn Mawr, then hired him as a gym teacher and its boys' basketball coach. At a Villanova camp and through a couple of summer basketball leagues on the Main Line—the Narberth League was the granddaddy of them—he got to know John Dzik, the head men's coach at a local Division III school, Cabrini College. Dzik brought him on as a volunteer assistant, no pay, just an apprenticeship. Downer was never going back to selling sporting goods. He was just twenty-seven, but he was gaining some name recognition in Main Line basketball. Young coach. Sharp. Passionate. Worked his ass off. When Mike Manning retired in 1990 as Lower Merion's coach, Downer applied for the vacancy. In his sit-down with Downer, Tom McGovern, the school's athletic director, told him that he was looking for a coach who could jolt the program back to life, and Downer explained how much potential there was at Lower Merion, how good the program could be, given the wide and varied area from which the team could draw its athletes. "We struck gold," McGovern said.

Downer would have been forgiven if he didn't quite feel the same way. Under Manning, the Aces had won just thirteen games over the previous two years. The perception of the program—and there was no small amount of truth to this perception—was that Lower Merion was a school for rich-kid scholars, not basketball studs. The Central League's other teams, most of them from the gritty, predominantly white working-class towns south and west of Philadelphia, could push the Aces around; never mind what teams from Philadelphia, where the caliber of competition and talent was far higher, could do to them. In one particularly telling game, Lower Merion lost, 54–13, to Ridley High School, traditionally one of the top teams in the Central League. Because so many players on the roster had already been deemed academically ineligible and a few more fouled out during the game, the Aces finished with just four players on the court. In the school's locker room, fat drops of condensed water parachuted from an air-conditioner to the floor, puddling in a far corner and rusting the lockers. The gym smelled of dried sweat—"Of basketball," Downer said, with optimism—and the backboards and bleachers were old wood. Downer learned quickly that, generally speaking, he would be provided little to no background about which incoming freshmen might be talented basketball players. There was no youth pipeline, no arrangement or agreement in which the eighth-grade coach understood that he was preparing his players to move up to the junior-varsity or varsity level, to play for a coach who expected certain things to be taught a certain way. There was no synchronicity between Bala's program and Lower Merion's, between what Smith was doing and what Downer might want done. The program was rudderless.

So what did Downer do at his first meeting with the players? He laced up his sneakers and told them: *Hope you brought yours, 'cause we're gonna go play.* He had to earn their respect and attention, and showing them that their coach could school them on the court, showing them that he wasn't going to put up with their thinking they were hot shit, was the fastest way to do it. "He's so brutally honest, and I think a lot of kids, especially in our community, are used to having things sugarcoated and being told how great they are," said Doug Young, who was a freshman when Downer became coach. "He did not mind giving us hard truths."

The Aces improved immediately, winning nine games in Downer's first season and twenty in his second, but he hadn't started to contemplate what heights they could reach until he followed those rumors wafting from the middle school and saw Kobe Bryant play basketball for the first time. Not long after he did, he ran into Lynne Freeland, who taught in the gifted program at the high school and was so enthusiastic and popular that she was known as "Mrs. Lower Merion."

She had already heard about Kobe; her daughter, Susan, was an eighth grader with him at Bala.

"Get ready," Downer told her. "You're in for a long ride."

FOR A student who showed up nearly two months into the school year, Kobe made an impression at Bala. "He was around all the time for everybody," Susan Freeland said, including on a class trip to Hershey Park, where the two of them rode a roller coaster together and Kobe, at a pop-a-shot basketball game, won stuffed animals for Susan and several of his female classmates. Per Pam's insistence that he couldn't play ball if he didn't keep his grades up, he polished off dinner each night and either scaled the staircase to his room or headed off to the library to finish his schoolwork. He even played first base on the school's baseball team, finding it relaxing, a diversion at an age when he still believed he could have diversions.

He was selected as one of the four outstanding athletes in his class, and to page through the 1991–92 Bala Cynwyd yearbook is to presume that he had been a fixture in the school's social and athletic culture. There he is, sitting on a rock wall, cradling a basketball in his lap, his hair buzzed into a high-top fade, with two boys gripping footballs and a brown-haired girl with a field-hockey stick. There he is, standing ramrod straight in the back line of the basketball team's photo, hands clasped behind his back, natural as can be. The photo of the baseball team is different, though. There are eighteen people in it: the coach, who was a frumpy science teacher named Robert Smith, and seventeen players. The players kneel and stand in two rows. All of them, save one, are wearing their Bala baseball uniforms: the jerseys, the sliding pants, the sneakers or spikes, their gloves on their hands. Kobe stands to the far right, a happy grin on his face. He is the only Black student on the team, and he is the only player not in uniform, wearing, instead, a warm coat and a multicolored sweater over a white dress shirt buttoned to the top. In the photo, he's the one who jumps out. He's the one who doesn't quite belong there. He was still a kid, more than merely a basketball player, but it was easy to see what direction his life was likely to take.

"He loved baseball, and he was actually pretty good at it," his friend Dayna Tolbert said. "When people started comparing him to Michael Jordan, I'm like, OK, people didn't realize he had other things in common with him. He just made his focus basketball, and we really watched that progress. We watched him go from playing like a kid to learning how to play like a man. It was unreal."

He had Wynnewood Valley Park, just three blocks from his house on Remington Road, where he could go with his friend Matt Matkov, hang out and goof off (as much goofing off as Kobe did when it came to basketball). It was Matkov whom Kobe trusted enough to let in on the secret that would drive him for the next four years: Even in eighth grade, he had his sights set on the NBA. It wasn't a dream. It was a plan, and he shared it with only so many people. At Bala, for instance, he considered Matkov his best friend, and he waited a year, until they were in ninth grade, before telling him, "I'm going to have the option of going to the NBA straight out of high school." Matkov was dumbstruck by the idea, just because it was so foreign to him, not because he didn't believe in Kobe . . . because he did. Even before Kobe confessed his future to him, Matkov would tell all their eighth-grade classmates, *He's gonna be a pro one day.*

"They'd say, 'Well, he's not that good now,'" Kobe once said. "That's because the coach wouldn't let me shoot."

So, as if to show up Dr. Smith and those doubters, Kobe offered the kids a dare. Each year, the high school held Hoop It Up, a three-on-three basketball tournament for students. Kobe would enter it, with Matkov and their friend Dave Lasman, and they would win. *Yeah, right. Wanna bet? You're going against high school kids. You're not gonna win.* And after he and Matkov and Lasman won, Kobe predicted that he would start for the varsity team the following season.

"Everybody started laughing," Kobe once recalled, "like, 'Yeahhh, right.' My classmates! . . . It was funny, man. There was a lot of doubt then. Matt said, 'He's going to be a Division I college player.' 'Yeah, right. He can't do this. Can't do that.' There was a lot of doubt right there. Then, he said, 'He's going to be a pro and could probably go out of high school if he wanted to.'"

But even though Matkov's loyalty to Kobe seemed unshakable, even though he wanted to practice with him all the time, even though Matkov believed in Kobe and hoped to accompany him on that journey—not that Matkov could conceive of playing pro ball himself, but he could be there, alongside Kobe, Alfred to his Batman—their gap in talent made it unproductive for Kobe to spend too much time there with him. Playing at a suburban park so close to home wasn't going to get him better. It was great for building a friendship. It was a waste of time for growing his game. Matkov would remain a close friend throughout high school, but Kobe didn't have many others. His sisters already were at Lower Merion; he had no one to lean on at Bala, no one to help him muffle his culture shock. Lock up his valuables during the school day? He and Sharia and Shaya had never had lockers at their schools in Italy. Why was it necessary in America? He was stunned when someone stole his stuff. He didn't know slang, the trendy terms of a typical American teenager, so he had no easy point of connection with anyone. If a friend or classmate or peer said something to him that he didn't quite understand, couldn't quite pick up on, he'd just nod his head and stay silent. He was around for everyone, as Susan Freeland said, but he maintained distance between himself and most of his peers. Which was fine, as far as he was concerned. It left him more time to devote to basketball.

In truth, both on the court and off it, he was a thirteen-year-old version of the twenty-three-year-old version of Michael Jordan, believing that he could do it all alone, that he was his team's only hope and salvation, that passing was inherently unproductive, every shot he took acting as a salve for his own ego. Jordan did not win his first NBA championship until his seventh year in the league, until June 1991, before Kobe had entered eighth grade. The Jordan who would go on to win six NBA titles, who learned to trust John Paxson in the final minute of one championship-clinching victory and Steve Kerr in another, who gave in to Phil Jackson and Tex Winter and the selfless cohesion inherent in the triangle offense and saw his game flourish for it, had just emerged, just broken through his chrysalis. So why not allow Kobe to see, up close, this fuller iteration of Jordan? Joe, as a former NBA player, could make that meeting happen. Joe could get Kobe into the Spectrum when the Chicago Bulls came to Philadelphia to play the Sixers.

And he did. Before the teams' game on March 8, 1992, father led son into the arena's locker room, and Kobe said hello to Michael Jordan. Jordan said hello back and gave him a wristband. There is no lasting indication that Kobe was nervous or stuttering or in any regard intimidated by Jordan. That was merely the entirety of their conversation; Jordan had nothing else to say. Neither did Kobe, who introduced himself to Bulls forward Horace Grant.

"Do you play basketball?" Grant asked him.

"Yes," Kobe said, "but I'm only in eighth grade."

"Are you going to be a superstar one day?"

"Yes," Kobe said, "I might be."

TWENTY DAYS after Kobe first came in contact with his archetype there, the Spectrum was the site of what has since come to be regarded as the greatest of all college basketball games: Duke vs. Kentucky in the East Regional final of the NCAA tournament. The Blue Devils were the defending national champions, with a superstar coach, Mike Krzyzewski, and a roster of superstar players: center Christian Laettner, point guard Bobby Hurley, forward Grant Hill. Rick Pitino, flashy, fast-talking, innovative, was running the show for Kentucky, and he had revitalized the program, embracing the three-point shot to a degree rarely seen in college basketball at the time. Duke was 31–2 and the No. 1 seed. Kentucky was 29–5 and the No. 2 seed. And the game ended, in overtime, after a marvelous court-length pass by Hill, on Laettner's catch/dribble/turnaround jumper at the buzzer. Duke 104, Kentucky 103.

The following week, the Blue Devils beat Indiana and Michigan in the Final Four to become the first team to win back-to-back national championships since John Wooden's UCLA Bruins in the mid-1970s. Laettner was graduating later that spring, but Hurley had one year of eligibility left, and Hill had two. There was no reason to think, yet, that Duke wouldn't remain atop college basketball's mountain. Mike Krzyzewski had lifted the program so high, and he now possessed such prestige within the sport and around the country, that he had his choice of virtually any elite prospect who sought out or could handle the rigors of an Ivy League–quality education.

THAT NCAA tournament was the fourth that La Salle University's men's basketball program had reached in Bill "Speedy" Morris's six years as its head coach. Sure, Seton Hall had knocked the Explorers out in the first round, by two points, but expectations for a team from the Metro Atlantic Athletic Conference could be only so high, and Morris and La Salle kept meeting them. He kept doing more with less than just about any college basketball coach in America.

How much less did he have? Before Morris became La Salle's men's coach, in 1986—he had been the women's coach for two seasons before that—the university had done the minimum to modernize its basketball program. In 1989–90, La Salle went 30–2 and nearly reached the round of sixteen in the NCAA tournament. In response, Tom Gola, arguably the university's most esteemed alumnus, presented plans to its board of trustees for an eight-thousand-seat on-campus arena. It would cost $5 million to build. Gola offered to raise the money. The trustees and administration said no. Too expensive. Unnecessary. In the MAAC, La Salle could compete for a conference title and a tournament bid every season against Manhattan and Siena and St. Peter's while pulling its purse strings tight. Morris's recruiting budget never surpassed $24,000. Each season, he would help fund the program by scheduling three games, usually on the road, that would come with a healthy payout from each opponent. His starting salary as the men's coach was $37,000. Adjusted for inflation, it was the equivalent of less than $88,000 in 2020 dollars.

He always claimed, publicly anyway, that he didn't need much more. He was born in the city, got his first full-time coaching job at his alma mater, Roman Catholic High School, when he was twenty-four, and still lived in the city, in a row home in Manayunk. He got his nickname when he was twelve, when a youth basketball coach ragged him for dogging it while the team was running laps—*Come on, Speedy!*—and nobody who met him called him anything else. A former bar owner, a part-time stand-up comic, he had a round, Santa-style belly, and when a player's error or an official's bad call angered him during a game, he might crack the player in the head with the thick, laminated game program he had rolled up into a baton, or he might allow his temper to erupt in a lava flow of expletives. There was one Division I basketball coach in the country who didn't have a college degree, and it was Speedy Morris, and that fact was irrelevant to the people devoted to him, and as long as La Salle kept winning, it was irrelevant to everyone else. He was as Philadelphia as Philadelphia could be. He was, one writer put it, "rowhouse and neighborhood, soft pretzels seasoned with bus exhaust, and cheesesteaks dripping *agita,* a lifelong gym rat."

The basketball camp that Morris directed every summer fit that motif. Three hundred kids would crowd into La Salle's practice gym, on the third floor of Hayman Hall, the university's athletic headquarters, from eight in the morning until eight in the evening for three days and three nights in July. The gym had no air-conditioning and was as hot as a convection oven. Morris would have several off-duty police officers, buddies of his from Manayunk and Roxborough, hang around to make sure everything was in order. The counselors were other coaches with Philadelphia ties. All the coaches and players slept in La Salle's concrete-walled dorms, if they didn't allow the distractions that came with the setting—an all-night discussion of the best guards in Philly history, the scratching sound of mice feet scurrying across the top of the ceiling panels, the 2:00 A.M. jingle from an ice-cream truck whose driver was selling something stronger than a chocolate cone—to keep them awake.

"It was Philadelphia basketball in its truest sense," said Villanova head coach Jay Wright, who, as a twenty-three-year-old assistant coach at the University of Rochester, worked at Morris's camp. "When you came in, Speedy would give you a case of beer to take to your room, and at night, you'd stay up and talk basketball. It was all Philadelphia basketball guys: high school guys, street guys, Sonny Hill guys, college guys. You'd sit around, eat peanuts and pretzels, drink beer, and tell basketball stories."

It was that way for years, unchanging, but there was upheaval ahead. The next season, La Salle was leaving the MAAC for the Midwestern

Collegiate Conference, the move the brainchild of athletic director Bob Mullen. Though La Salle had little in common with the conference's other programs, which included Wisconsin–Green Bay, Detroit Mercy, and Illinois Chicago, Mullen approved the change on the expectation/promise that three other schools—Xavier, Dayton, and Duquesne—were joining, too, and that their inclusion in a stronger league would lead to more revenue for La Salle. The Explorers were moving up in weight class, and there would be pressure on Morris to recruit better players as his program prepared to push west.

AS SPRING warmed into summer, the nature of Kobe's basketball education shifted. Gone were the restrictions imposed by Dr. George Smith. Summertime meant the developmental level of the Sonny Hill League and assorted camps where he could either play or volunteer as a counselor. La Salle's was only one. The summer of 1992 was the beginning of a balancing act that he would carry out until he entered the NBA: the long-term, team-oriented goals of the Lower Merion program versus his long-term, individual goals; his polite, respectful demeanor away from basketball versus his cutthroat disposition on the court. Tracing the arc of those months, one can see with clarity who he was, who he was becoming, and where he was going.

The summer began with a phone call from Gregg Downer to his mentor John Dzik to ask for a favor. Downer had mistakenly scheduled two basketball camps for the same week, and there was no way he could supervise both at the same time. One of them was a day camp, 9:00 A.M. to 3:00 P.M., for thirty to forty-five kids at the Agnes Irwin School in Bryn Mawr. Was Dzik willing to oversee one for him? "I'd be happy to do it," Dzik told him. Even better, Dzik's son Mike, a sophomore guard at The Haverford School, could work as one of John's counselors.

Great, Downer said, *and I'll give you this kid Kobe Bryant.*

John, Mike, and Kobe ran the camp's drills for the week. "Glorified babysitting," Mike said. The real fun was lunch. Every day, Kobe would play Mike one-on-one and in H-O-R-S-E, four or five games. Every day, Mike, a deadeye jump shooter who himself had played for years in the Sonny Hill League, beat him. And every day, Kobe reacted with the same shrug of indifference: *Doesn't matter. I'm gonna be a pro someday.*

"I knew he was going to be good, but I would never have guessed he was going to be what he was," Mike Dzik, who went on to play at Penn, said later. "At the time, Philly was stacked with talent: Cuttino Mobley. Rasheed Wallace, Alvin Williams. The list goes on. He was younger, of course, but you'd look around and think, 'I don't know. These guys are all major players. Is he going to be as good as those guys, let alone better than them?'"

Mike Dzik wasn't alone. For all Kobe's confidence, it didn't take long for the Sonny Hill League to expose further his limitations as a player, such as they were for someone approaching his fourteenth birthday, and the speed with which he learned first to compensate for them and then to erase them entirely. Donnie Carr, a promising eighth grader from the Point Breeze neighborhood of Philadelphia, in the southern part of the city, had heard chatter about Kobe before the two met and faced each other for the first time. The Philadelphia basketball community, from its instructional leagues all the way up to the Sixers, was close-knit, and once the Bryants were a full-time part of it again, Carr felt like he heard nothing but *Kobe Bryant this, Kobe Bryant that.* Now he was in a gym with Kobe, sizing him up, this kid who looked like an Erector-set robot—tall and thin, knee and elbow pads hanging off him, goggles on his face— and now he was on the court with him, bodying him, Carr pushing his squat, sturdier frame against Kobe, and he wasn't impressed.

"I didn't think he was that good," Carr said later. "He was slow. He was skinny. And he couldn't bend down because he was so straight up and down. Everybody in basketball knows the low man wins, so I was able to get underneath him and push him off his spot. He wasn't athletic. He was just tall. He could dribble, but you get underneath him and dictate his movements. He wasn't anything special at that age, to be honest with you."

Still, Dzik and Carr were among the few who thought that way. When he looked at Kobe in that padded, goggled getup, Ashley Howard didn't see an easy mark. From those Sunday-morning pickup games in Center

City until now, everything about Kobe seemed beyond the realm of someone so inexperienced in the sport. In one Sonny Hill game against Kobe, Howard—a point guard, just like his dad—stole the ball and took off on a breakaway, and he could sense something behind him: Kobe, chasing him down. As he closed in on the hoop, Howard, younger and smaller than Kobe, stopped suddenly. Kobe didn't. He jumped, flying over Howard, who ducked, then banked in a layup. As they jogged back down the court, Kobe whispered to him, "I let you have that one." In another game, Howard was the youngest player on the floor, and he hung back, passing the ball immediately after it was passed to him, getting out of the way, soaking in the sight of Kobe controlling the game in every way a game can be controlled. "He's the tallest guy on the team, but he's handling the ball like a guard," Howard said. "He's making all the right passes. He's posting up. He's shooting threes. He's getting dunks in transition. And this is a fourteen-and-under game. I'm thinking, 'Yo, I was just with this dude on Sunday mornings at the YMCA!'"

The topper, though, was when Kobe showed up at Gustine Recreation Center in East Falls, one of the many spots in the city where pickup games raged every summer morning and afternoon. After each game he played, he wrapped his knees in bags of ice. The pros in Italy had done it to maintain their strength and ward off soreness, to take care of their joints and muscles and tendons. His father had done it. Why couldn't he? Why wouldn't he? It puzzled Howard at first. *What's wrong with this dude?* Only later did the precociousness and meaning of it dawn on him. "He was being taught, groomed, at an early age to be the player he eventually became," Howard said. "His dad was one of the greatest players in the city of Philadelphia. His uncle was one of the greatest players in the city of Philadelphia. You look at his pedigree and his genes on both sides, and a lot of who Kobe was, was genetic. But the mindset he had to watch and learn and perfect certain things was off the charts, unbelievable."

Howard wasn't the only one who noticed. Allen Rubin, a scout for the recruiting service Hoop Scoop, happened to be at Gustine, too. Who was this kid? Rubin knew all the good high school players in the Philadelphia area. He didn't recognize this one. He asked someone. *Oh, that's*

Joe Bryant's son. Name's Kobe. He'll be a freshman at Lower Merion next fall. Rubin often recommended players to the prestigious ABCD Camp, held each July in central or northern New Jersey. Eighth grade? He filed away the name. *Give it a year,* Rubin told himself. Then he would call the man who organized and operated the ABCD Camp, the man who had been Nike's director of grassroots basketball since the late 1970s, the man who had handed out hundreds of thousands of dollars in endorsement deals to the best and most celebrated coaches in college basketball, the man who signed Michael Jordan to his first sneaker contract and turned him into a global icon. Yes. Give it a year. Then Rubin would call Sonny Vaccaro and tell him about Kobe Bryant.

Growing up in Italy . . . it took a while for me to relearn "American" English and the way of life of a Lower Merion student. When I started to become accepted by my fellow students, they started to ask me to parties, movies, and social functions. Believe it or not, most of the time, I passed.

—KOBE BRYANT

7

LOSING

THEY STRODE THROUGH THE HIGH school every weekday for nine months, towering over many of their fellow students, sometimes wearing dashikis as an homage to their Black heritage, sometimes wearing Italian shirts or skirts or robes, big logos and bold colors, because they were accustomed to wearing them, sometimes trading greetings and questions and raillery, like verbal high fives, as they passed each other in the halls. Those little exchanges were usually in Italian, too, a reassuring crackling among three siblings that reminded them, no matter the angst and stresses endemic to their still-new milieu—the daily existence of suburban American teenagers—that they had each other. It would be lovely to think that Kobe Bryant and his sisters, Sharia and Shaya, eased into their lives at Lower Merion without trouble, and in a short time, most of their hiccups had settled. But those hiccups did shake them, just a bit, Kobe in particular.

"When they moved back, it was a little tough for them," said Guy Stewart, who was a year ahead of Kobe and one of his basketball teammates. "They were in Italy, so they didn't have that experience of being around so many minorities. I can still see in my head the clothes they used to wear. People would just . . . not necessarily make fun of them to their faces, but that was the talk. Getting through that was probably a little rough."

Rough, of course, is relative. Lower Merion had resources and norms, within its school district and its community, that other high schools in and around Philadelphia did not, and no matter how bad his day might have been, Kobe could come home to be mothered by Pam and dared by Joe to a game-to-eleven in the driveway, and all would be right again. It has become something of an urban legend that Kobe had an especially privileged upbringing, that Joe's fame and career earnings from basket-ball afforded the Bryants a life without want. But if anything, the Bryants were in an economic sweet spot. They led a fairly typical upper-middle-class existence, and many of Kobe's friends and classmates were better off materially than he was. "I grew up in a bigger house," one of those friends said. To suggest, though, that Kobe wasn't still adjusting to his surroundings and that those surroundings didn't present some challenges would be incorrect.

He was still learning American slang, for instance, and the catchphrases of the era puzzled him. Buggin' out? Eat my shorts? He had no sense of popular culture in the early 1990s, of the zeitgeist, of the novelty and freshness of Bill Clinton playing the saxophone on Arsenio Hall's late-night talk show—who had time to watch TV when there were Magic and Michael videos to study?—and sometimes that innocence and ig-norance are all it takes for a high school kid to start out as an outcast. Black students in the district had long gotten used to adjusting how they carried themselves and spoke, depending on where they were and with whom they were interacting. When they were in the presence of some of their teachers or the parents of some of their white friends? That was one thing. When they were in a more homogenous setting—among themselves in Ardmore, for instance? That was another thing. "You act differently," Stewart said. "You were definitely aware of that, and you were aware of that in elementary and middle school to the point where, in high school, it was just second nature. At that time, you knew what people were friendly to you and what people weren't." But Kobe didn't yet possess the cultural vocabulary to toggle between those two worlds. He set out to learn it.

He also was immediately a potential target for ridicule and practical joking for another reason, though he wasn't alone in this regard. He was a ninth grader. The school had a long-standing tradition that each year, on Friday the 13th, the sophomores and upperclassmen would haze the freshmen. The tradition was known, in a peak of creativity, as "Freshman Day." The older students might spray the younger ones with water from Super Soakers, or punch them in the arms, or drop eggs on their heads, or smear shaving cream in their faces, or dump perfume or urine on them. One student even had bong water poured on him. Tall enough, at six foot three, to be somewhat intimidating, Kobe managed to avoid the worst of it, though he likely never knew how close he came to suffering at least one indignity that day. A sophomore acquaintance of his, Sterling Carroll, saw him jogging up a stairwell as Carroll was coming down and thought, *You know, if you weren't so tall, I'd get you right now.* "But he was just one of those guys who commanded respect," Carroll said, "and even though it was all fun and games, I wouldn't give him a punch in the leg or the arm or anything."

That Kobe was no ordinary freshman was obvious from his arrival, and the respect that he commanded from an older student like Carroll was the same that Lower Merion's Black students and their parents had for years been clamoring for, despite all the progress that Wendell Holland and his peers had spurred. To the 90 percent of its students who weren't Black, the school was, in the main, a place free from racial tension, where students of all colors and backgrounds mingled in social harmony and received superior public-school educations. To many of the 10 percent who were, there was a sense that the deck was stacked against them. Throughout the 1980s and into the 1990s, Black students showed up at school-board meetings to complain about their treatment, that they were not encouraged and supported academically in the way their white peers were. In 2007, more than a decade after Kobe had graduated, seven Black families filed a civil lawsuit alleging that the school district "intentionally and systematically segregated African-American students by placing them in below-grade classes." A federal appeals court rejected the suit in 2014, ruling that the segregation had not been intentional, but the figures had been stark: Only twenty-seven of the district's five hundred Black students, or 5 percent, had been identified as gifted, compared to 13 percent (790 of 6,000) of its white students. One-fourth of all Black students were enrolled in special ed.

The Bryant siblings transcended that power misalignment to a certain degree, and it's no wonder why. "It was like," Doug Young said, "a royal family had arrived at Lower Merion. They were a huge force of nature in our lives there." Sharia, a senior, was five foot ten and a standout on the girls' volleyball team. Shaya was six foot two and played volleyball and basketball. (Neither of the girls had been on an organized basketball team while the family lived in Italy, and Shaya's inexperience frustrated the school's girls' coach, Dennis Dool. "She is weak on fundamentals," he said. "She is not very aggressive and sure of herself on the court.") The Bryants and their extended family—including the Coxes, including Big Joe, now in a wheelchair because of diabetes, now needing to cart around an oxygen tank that pumped air into his lungs to help him breathe—attended every sporting event that involved one or more of the kids, all of them sitting together and taking up a section of the bleachers. The siblings were smart and disciplined and cooperative and unfailingly polite to teachers and coaches and any authority figures. Both of the girls served on the student council, and their friends became Kobe's friends, a group of ten to fifteen who would ensconce him in a cocoon of support and keep an eye on him to make sure he stayed out of trouble and that trouble stayed away from him. The Soul Shack, Ardmore's community center, was their primary hangout: basketball games, holiday parties, a place to go after school. "It was almost like a protective thing," Dayna Tolbert said. "Kobe never went anywhere without Shaya. He was very smart and knew where to be, when to be there, and what not to do. We knew all he wanted to do was have fun and play basketball. To do that, you definitely have to have people around you who you trust and who you love and who you know have your best interests at heart. He had that a hundred percent."

Within the high school's walls, the uniting institution for those students was Student Voice, which had been founded by Katrina Christmas, a longtime librarian, and was Lower Merion's equivalent of a Black student union. The organization put on plays for local schoolchildren, arranged guest-speaking engagements and assemblies, performed concerts, and advocated on behalf of students of color to the faculty and administration. Though its membership wasn't limited to Black students—it comprised Asian-American and Hispanic students, as well—most of its members were Black. "We encompassed all the underdogs of Lower Merion," Christmas said, and as a ninth grader, still feeling his way around high school, Kobe was, in that context, an underdog. "I met him as a freshman, and I didn't deal too much with freshmen," Christmas said. "They were so silly, and I didn't have the time. But he showed more maturity." One of the group's leaders, Corella Berry, had encouraged him to join. As the school year went on, Kobe would have to duck out of some Student Voice meetings to get to basketball practice on time. But on days he didn't have practice, he would deliberately not get on his bus, then walk slowly outside the school until he saw Berry about to drive herself home.

Corella, he'd say, *can you take me home?*

Kobe, she'd reply, *your bus is right there!*

Students on the bus would yell at him: *Kobe, come on! You're going to miss the bus!* "But I was a sucker," Berry said. "I would take him home." Their conversations were never about basketball and never betrayed that Kobe had any kind of crush on Berry. They would talk about music—rap, gospel, Berry's love of singing and her role as a featured voice in the Student Voice choir—and Kobe would ask question after question, as if he were interviewing her, trying to learn more about how and why music had become such a big part of her life. "I could see him figuring it out, what was cool, who to hang with, just being curious," she said. "He would say, 'Corella, I like when you sing. When you sing, I get chills.' I would tease him and say, 'That's the Spirit in you.' He'd say, 'What do you mean?' 'It's the Spirit that's giving you the chill bumps.'"

Kobe's and the Bryants' zone of social comfort expanded further to include the Jewish Community Center in Wynnewood, where Joe worked part-time as a trainer in the fitness center and coached players to prepare them for the Maccabi Games in Israel. Kobe joined him on evenings and weekends—they had a key to the place—playing pickup against teenagers and twenty-somethings on Saturday mornings and afternoons and against men of middle age on Sunday mornings, and father and son became friendly fixtures there. "His dad was the same as him," said Audrey Price, one of Kobe's classmates, "ear-to-ear smile, so sweet and warm, would talk to anybody and everybody who wanted to talk to him." But the training sessions did only so much to scratch Joe's itch to coach, so he accepted an offer from Akiba Hebrew Academy, in Merion Station on the Main Line, to become its girls' basketball coach. From grades six through twelve, the school had an enrollment of 320, required students to learn Hebrew and another foreign language, and gave them the opportunity to spend their junior years studying in Israel. The position was Joe's first official coaching job, the perfect one to ease him into the profession that he had contemplated pursuing since leaving the Sixers. "My objective," he said, "is to have fun and compete."

Yes, Joe still had that engaging personality. But he was a different kind of good-time guy now, with his family and not his playing time or his nightlife as his top priority. He and Gregg Downer had hit it off immediately, meeting on the day that Kobe, while in eighth grade, worked out with the varsity team and ended up dominating the practice. All it had taken was for Downer to usher Joe on a walk down memory lane . . . *I used to sit in Section H of the Spectrum, near your mom and dad, and watch you play* . . . and the two had established a measure of trust between them. Downer had played basketball against Kobe the previous summer, while Downer was coaching in the Narberth summer league and Kobe was hunting for any game he could get, part of the getting-to-know-you process for a coach and the player who, he knew, would define his next four years. Kobe, at thirteen, had beaten Downer often enough to reconfirm in the coach's mind that the kid was more than special, that Downer had to be daring, had to be unorthodox in his decision making, to maximize Kobe's potential and the team's potential with him. Now

Downer had an opening on his staff: he needed someone to coach the junior-varsity team. He had an idea that he brought up to Joe one day.

"You want to help us out?"

"Yeah," Joe said, "I'll do it."

There was a long-range strategy behind Downer's proposal. Here he was, a young coach, far from a finished product, who knew he didn't know everything. Here was a way for him to get to know Joe better. Having Joe coach the junior-varsity team would show him that he, Gregg Downer, was secure in himself and had no ego, and above all, having a good relationship with Joe and Pam would be crucial to coaching Kobe. In the best-case scenario, Joe would bring two vital elements to the team—his wealth of basketball knowledge, and his ability to control and reassure Kobe, who, as any freshman playing at the varsity level would be, was still maturing and still mercurial—and he would stay out of Downer's way, let him coach the team as he saw fit. Day to day, Downer and Joe wouldn't even have to coach together, wouldn't have to have their voices compete. The varsity would practice in one gym at the school, the JV in another. Downer liked separating the teams; it allowed for more hands-on teaching and coaching. Nevertheless, it was a proposal with a fair amount of peril for Downer himself. What if Joe wanted Kobe coached more aggressively, or less aggressively, than Downer did? What if they didn't see eye to eye on anything? When push came to shove at a practice or during a game, who would Kobe listen to—his head coach or his father? Downer had now imbued Joe with enough power, with a formal role on the coaching staff, to complicate that question. Based on his interactions with Joe, Downer believed it a risk worth taking. Fittingly, a December 1992 article in *The Merionite*, Lower Merion's student newspaper, about Joe's hiring ended with this quote from him: "It should be fun!"

The next stage of Downer's strategy was a sit-down with Kobe. He might as well have written out a speech, then committed it to memory.

Kobe, you're a freshman. You want to be a McDonald's All-American your senior year. That's the ultimate honor for a high school player, right? OK. To make that team, you have to be one of the top fifteen seniors in the nation. I have a four-year plan to get you there.

Right now, there are one hundred freshmen in the country who have your ability to play basketball. Fifty percent of them, each year, are going to be eliminated by drugs, bad grades, bad attitudes, poor work ethic. Next year, there will be fifty sophomores with your ability who still have a shot. Your junior year, there will be twenty-five. Your senior year . . .

You've got to have a work ethic. You've got to be coachable. You've got to have good grades. You've got to steer clear of drugs. You keep to that same progression, and we'll reduce that number from one hundred to ten or twelve.

Following that plan meant narrowing the tunnel, shedding hindrances and making sacrifices that Kobe would have been liable to shed and make himself anyway. Perhaps to make the transition to high school easier, perhaps to hold on to a piece of his time in Italy, Kobe decided early in his freshman year to try out for the varsity soccer team, which at the time was more popular, prestigious, and successful at Lower Merion than boys' basketball was. Only during the 1991–92 school year, when the Aces reached the district playoffs in Downer's second season as head coach, did basketball begin to reemerge as an interesting and respected sport within the school's culture. Soccer had more cachet, but Kobe's affiliation with the team lasted only a week or so, before Downer and Joe found out. Downer went directly to athletic director Tom McGovern and told him, *You can't do this. You have to pull him off the team.* Like baseball had been in middle school, soccer was a hobby for Kobe, not the focus of his future. He could stand giving it up. He admitted as much to his guidance counselor, Frank Hartwell, during their first one-on-one meeting of the school year. The tête-à-tête was procedural for Hartwell, who had taught and counseled students at Lower Merion since 1970; he met with all his freshmen, on the presumption that any or all of them might be feeling overwhelmed or uncertain about the transition to high school or their futures in general. Kobe was not overwhelmed or uncertain, not when Hartwell asked him about his interests and long-term goals. Kobe already had received his first basketball recruiting letter—from the United States

Military Academy at West Point—and he told Hartwell that he was going to play in the NBA.

Bespectacled and bookish in his manner, Hartwell might have appeared a pure intellectual to his core. In fact, he had founded the school's ice hockey club in the early 1970s and had played the sport himself as a youth in New England. He appreciated the pull that athletics could have on a teenager. Nevertheless, he had never seen Kobe play basketball, and even if he had, would he have recognized what he was seeing, what was buried within that bony body? He wasn't inclined to advise Kobe, or any high school athlete, to pour himself or herself into the pursuit of a professional playing career.

This is my dream, Kobe said.

I understand, Hartwell said, *but remember: Only so many people attain this dream.*

In his farewell feting during his last season with the Lakers, 2015–16, as he reflected on his NBA career in interview after interview, Kobe mentioned "a guidance counselor" who had told him to put aside his dream. "I thought, 'If this is so hard to accomplish, how in the world am I going to accomplish it if I don't put all my eggs in one basket?'" he said. "'If I don't focus a hundred percent on this, I'm never going to get there.'" No, he did not take Hartwell's response, this recommendation for prudence, as wise advice. He took it as a dare, almost an insult, and he would never forget it.

JEREMY TREATMAN wanted everything fast. He wanted everything *now.* A million thoughts and ideas and proposals and plans flitted through his mind and shot into people's ears like little arrows from his mouth. They always had. His had been one of the first and few Jewish families to move to Gladwyne, on the Main Line, in the early 1970s. He went from kindergarten straight to second grade, skipping first grade entirely—a low hurdle to clear academically but a social nightmare for a small kid who loved sports. When you're in a fourth-grade-level math class when you're seven, when you're in ninth grade and still just thirteen, when your classmates are at least a year older and a head taller than you and are finishing puberty just when you're starting it, when you're a Jewish kid without many other Jewish kids around, life isn't likely to be pleasant. His older brother got beat up in school. His father, after becoming a Cub Scout leader, heard the whispers from the other parents: *Why is this guy leading our kids?* Oh, yes, Jeremy Treatman knew what it meant to be a little different from everyone else around him.

His favorite idea? The thing he wanted most? To work in sports media. He went to Phillies games with his dad, sitting in the faraway bleachers of Veterans Stadium. He memorized NBA and NHL box scores in the morning newspaper. He went to Temple University, won a competition to become the radio voice of the women's basketball team, started covering Philadelphia sports for the student radio station. Nineteen years old, and he was lifting a mic to the faces of Julius Erving, Ron Jaworski, Larry Bird. Once he had finished up at Temple, he hopped right to *The Philadelphia Inquirer* to cover high school sports . . . on the Main Line, while freelancing for another local paper, *The Jewish Exponent.*

And so he covered Lower Merion during Gregg Downer's first season there, and the two of them ran into each other at a local pub, and they spent the night throwing back beers and talking into the morning and becoming friends. And so Treatman went to Akiba one day to write a story about one of their boys' basketball players, and he befriended the team's head coach, Tom Riley, who encouraged him to get involved in the Narberth League, as did Downer. And so he did, and he gained enough coaching experience that when Riley told him Akiba's JV boys' coach had resigned, he put his hand up for the job, and got it. And so now he was covering Main Line high school basketball and he was coaching at one school and hanging out with the head coach at another, and this crazy gumbo of connections and coverage and coaching finally finished cooking for Jeremy Treatman in the fall of 1992, when, in Akiba's gymnasium, he watched a fourteen-year-old boy not dunk a basketball.

Treatman was just twenty-six himself then, but knew his local hoops history, and he often remained in the gym after the boys' JV team's practices so he could chat with Joe Bryant. Among the teenage girls he was coaching and despite their remedial skills, Joe was cultivating the same frolicsome approach to the sport that had flavored his game, mixing ball fakes and showy footwork into their dribbling and shooting fundamentals. He wasn't just cashing in his $1,500 stipend and letting these basketball neophytes fend for themselves. He taught them how to fight through picks, had them weaving around cones to improve their ball handling, walked them through set plays step by step. He was, Treatman thought, as enthusiastic as hell, and the girls loved playing for him, and Treatman loved talking basketball with Joe—the coaching tips, the stories from his time with the Sixers and the Clippers and the Rockets and his career in Europe, his carefree view of his mostly charmed life, always upbeat, always peppering a conversation with his favorite expression of agreement: "You right, you right!"

Then, for the first time of many times, Kobe tagged along with Joe to practice. He isolated himself at a side basket in the gym, far from his father and the players and their drills. There was no one slowing him down or double-teaming him. There was just Kobe, leaping into the air with the basketball in his hands over and over again, high enough to dunk it but not dunking it, no, just dropping the ball through the hoop, as if he were tossing wads of paper into a waste can as he walked by.

"What's he going to be like?" Treatman asked Joe. "You're not expecting him to be another Joe Bryant, are you?"

"He's so much better than me at this age," Joe said, "it's not even funny."

"So," Treatman replied, "are you saying he's going to be better than you? You played for the Sixers, Clippers, and Rockets and were an MVP in Italy. And you're six ten."

"He's going to be so much better than me," Joe said, "it's not even funny."

As the two men talked, the boy continued his lonely workout. He emitted the occasional throaty grunt, noise born of effort, but nothing more. It seemed impossible that a kid that skinny could jump that high. And yet . . .

Up. And drop.

Up. And drop.

Up. And drop.

It was easy for him. It was so easy. From then on, whenever someone asked him when he first thought Kobe would be as good as he turned out to be, Treatman always would point to this moment, inside a gymnasium at a Jewish day school in the autumn of 1992, as the true beginning of the unveiling. Up. And drop. He couldn't look away. Better than Joe? *You right, you right!* Jeremy Treatman had been granted a rare privilege, a peek at what the world, soon enough, would see in full, and he meant to savor it.

TO UNDERSTAND Kobe Bryant's influence on his high school's basketball program, think of him as a dose of slow-acting medicine. The benefits of his presence did not manifest themselves instantaneously. Garry Kelly, one of the top players on the Aces' twenty-win 1991–92 team, had graduated and gone to junior college in Maryland, and that single excellent season wasn't enough yet to establish a full-fledged renaissance for the program, even with Kobe joining the team. The next season began with a road trip to Connecticut, for a scrimmage against Fairfield Prep. It was the first time Kobe wore a Lower Merion jersey, but it was the players' warm-ups that made a lasting impression: T-shirts that read GET HIGH ON HOOPS, NOT ON DRUGS and that had outlines of tank tops screen-printed onto the shirts. Downer put Kobe in the starting lineup, and already jealousy and frustration were apparent among several of the older players: *Why is this kid playing all the minutes? It's our time.* At the motel where the team stayed that night, rabble was roused, and a window was smashed, but in a decision that would become standard operating procedure for most of the basketball-related overnight trips Kobe took in high school, he never left his room. "He had no interest in participating in any of the bullshit," Doug Young said. "There was a level of seriousness right out of the gate with him: 'Who are these jokers?' Off the court, it didn't really matter; he was cool with you. But he was very quick to determine who he respected and who he didn't as a basketball player."

Two years older than Kobe, Matt Snider had moved to the township from Iowa, and he observed in Kobe what he himself had experienced.

"You're very shy," he said. "You take your time to get to know people. Who's going to become your friend? Who are you going to trust? I could tell he was doing that, which was totally fine in my book. He wasn't very talkative to some of his teammates, and he sort of sensed that he and I were going to be the top two guys on the team." Their relationship was friendly but competitive. As players, they were opposites: Snider was a six-foot-two rock, a tight end and defensive end who would head to Richmond to play Division I football and would eventually play two-plus years in the National Football League, as a fullback, for the Green Bay Packers and Minnesota Vikings. Kobe was six foot three and 140 pounds. After every game, the two of them would scan the scorebook, to see who had scored more points that night. Over a season in which the team lost five out of every six of its games, its two future professional athletes had to extract their little pleasures when and where they could. Otherwise, they would have extracted none at all. "We were godawful," Young said. "That year was a complete and utter train wreck." After beating Upper Dublin in their second game—the game that Kobe watched again on that laptop in YouTube's offices years later—the Aces lost their next eight. They lost in routs: In a Christmas/holiday tournament sponsored by the Ardmore Rotary Club, Bartram embarrassed them, 113–76, even though Kobe scored twenty-five points against his father's alma mater. The next day, Malvern Prep beat them, 74–47; Kobe scored twenty-four of those forty-seven points. They lost by two in double overtime to Conestoga and by two in regulation to Marple Newtown. Resentment within the team festered not just because Kobe was playing so much, but because of how he was playing: his gunner's mentality, the exaggerated nature of every move he made on the court, the explicitness that he was trying to show everyone who the best player out there was. "He had a herky-jerky game, almost a corniness to him," Evan Monsky said. "He had a lot of shake-and-bake that you didn't need." Junior Joe Dixon, the team's starting point guard, considered transferring to Harriton once the season ended, in part because of all the losing, in part because he didn't like that Kobe was commanding so much attention. "There was a lot of jealousy," he said. Still, one had to be inside the Aces' locker room after each of those losses, when Kobe would grind his teeth and try to compose himself before answering any questions from any reporter, to appreciate why those closest to him trusted that he would push himself to reach his full potential. Following a December game against a local rival, Upper Darby, a nineteen-point home loss in which Kobe scored seventeen points and was the only Lower Merion player to have more than eight, Treatman said to him as Kobe stood in front of his locker, "You don't look happy."

"We lost," Kobe replied, his face a scowl, his voice a knife's edge.

Few of Kobe's teammates were inclined to invoke the same tone. For that team's upperclassmen, basketball wasn't necessarily part of their central experience at the school. Some of them thought they were better players than they actually were. Some of them were placed on academic probation or suspension. Some of them were suspended. Sultan Shabazz, counted on to be one of the team's playmakers and leading scorers, tore ligaments in his ankle and missed the season's first seven games, and his availability became uncertain over time anyway. After every practice, either Joe or Downer would stay with Kobe, rebounding for him and chest-passing him the ball as he fired hundreds of shots from near and beyond the three-point arc, and Kobe would ask Shabazz, *Hey, man, how come you don't stay?* Kobe—and Downer, and most of the players—had no idea that, once practice ended, Shabazz would catch the 105 SEPTA bus from Wynnewood to a neighborhood in West Philadelphia. There, he would spend the night selling crack and cocaine, smoking his share of marijuana himself, before hightailing it back for classes and practice the next day. The contrast between his habits and Kobe's was stark even at lunch, where Kobe would eschew junk food but hoard his teammates' milk, lining up five or six of the little cartons on his cafeteria tray. *You're not gonna drink that? Let me get it.* "This kid was actually getting his body ready to play in the NBA, eating right at a young age," Shabazz recalled. "I look back on that, and people ask me, 'What do you think?' I say, 'What I saw, y'all didn't see.'" On weekends, knowing that Kobe was hungry to prove himself anywhere in the city to anyone, Shabazz would bring him to a gym at 57th and Haverford, in the teeth of Shabazz's drug territory, to play pickup. Kobe got what he needed from those excursions, the chance to sharpen his game, the chance to impress others, but after a while, he began to figure out why Shabazz spent so much time there, and the excursions stopped. "Me protecting him, I would not bring him around," Shabazz said, "because I knew he had a career." It was the career, Shabazz acknowledged years later, that he himself might have had . . . and had thrown away. By the start of his senior year, he was making $6,000 to $7,000 a night on his West Philly corner, and once he was ruled academically ineligible for basketball, he dropped out of Lower Merion and didn't bother going back. (Shabazz eventually earned his high school degree and graduated from Cheyney University.)

With Shabazz's reliability in question, Downer moved Kobe to point guard late in the season, all the while maintaining that the losing was having no effect on the prodigy's development. "He's right on schedule," Downer said in January. He was on schedule . . . until February, when he bumped into an opposing player during a game. Kobe's knee already fragile because of his Osgood-Schlatter disease and his spindly frame, the collision fractured his kneecap. He sat out the team's final two games, finishing with an average of 17.1 points per game as a freshman, leading the team in three-pointers and free-throw percentage.

So no, the Aces didn't have Superman for all of that mostly awful season, but they did have Superfly. No one can say if Joe Bryant was the coolest junior-varsity basketball coach in the Central League in 1992–93, but this much is certain: He chased the title whole hog. He'd roll into practice wearing a red leather suit, as if Lower Merion weren't a high school but a disco joint. "Just couldn't have seemed more comfortable," said Monsky, a point guard on that JV team, "strutting in, probably sweating his ass off. He wasn't a twenty-eight-year-old NBA pro. He was in his late thirties, father of three teenagers, still trying to wear red leather. But to us, what a god. It was great to have a former Sixer who knew so much about the little nuances of the game that came so easily to him—and probably to Kobe—but that JV players would never think of." What other coach would stop practice because his players weren't play-ing with enough flair? Joe would. Mid-set, he'd halt play, incredulous.

Don't you see this pass? It's so obvious! And he'd take the ball and thread a behind-the-back pass through three guys, and the players would look at each other: *Well, no, Jellybean. That pass might be obvious to you, Mr. Six-Foot-Nine Point Guard, but not to a bunch of five-foot-nine sophomores.* When practice grew stagnant, Joe had the boys play soccer. At halftime of one JV game, the players waited for him to enter the locker room . . . and waited . . . and waited. They sat there for several minutes, wondering where he was, why he apparently had abandoned them, before a couple of them spoke up about a strategy for the second half. *We should probably guard that one guy better.* When they exited the locker room, there was Joe, chatting with someone. "Nobody does that in tenth grade," Monsky said, but Joe had been through a thousand halftimes. Sometimes a coach just needed to shut up and let the players figure things out themselves. These were insights he already had shared with Kobe, and these underclassmen would be juniors and seniors when Kobe was peaking as a high school player, and maybe it wasn't the worst idea to present a more relaxed approach to coaching to contrast with Downer's intensity, to get them figuring out answers on their own once in a while, to understand that, if they were going to become the players and the team that they wanted to be, they had to learn to keep up with Kobe—his work ethic, his intelligence—as best they could.

In June and July, Downer stenciled a stark line of demarcation between Kobe and the other players, an indication of his true standing on the team and, increasingly, among all the high school players in the Philadelphia area. Suddenly, even in the more relaxed atmosphere of suburban summer-league basketball, Lower Merion was beating schools that it had never beaten before: St. Joseph's Prep, Archbishop Carroll, Monsignor Bonner, strong teams in the Philadelphia Catholic League. But the victories themselves weren't as much a telltale sign of Kobe's status as one moment was.

This was the moment: His team down by one, Downer—still coaching summer ball at the time—called a time-out. Snider was the co-MVP. Snider was the senior. Snider had to be getting the ball, right? No. Downer drew up a play that put the ball in Kobe's hands.

Monsky couldn't believe what he was hearing. He asked himself, *Is Downer an idiot?* Matt Snider was an ox. Matt Snider was a beast. But with his team down a point, with the clock melting to 0:00, Matt Snider was not getting the ball.

Kobe was. Kobe missed a pull-up jumper. Lower Merion lost. And Downer gathered his players in a corner of the court.

We couldn't have asked for anything more, guys. We got our best player the ball at the last second with a chance to win. He didn't make the shot, but that's all right.

Evan Monsky acknowledged the truth years later, and he was self-deprecating about it. There was only one idiot in that huddle who thought Kobe Bryant shouldn't take the last shot, and it wasn't Gregg Downer.

LA SALLE had gone 14–13 in 1992–93, what would be Speedy Morris's last winning season as the Explorers' head coach. When the season ended, one of Morris's assistants, Randy Monroe, said goodbye. He was off to Nashville for another assistant coaching job, at Vanderbilt. Morris had always been tight with Sonny Hill. Who in Philadelphia basketball wasn't? And Hill recommended one name to Morris to fill Monroe's spot on the staff: Joe Bryant. Morris liked the idea. A La Salle alumnus? A former pro who, in the Sonny Hill League, had coached several of Philly's top high school players? A guy with that affable personality? Joe could help recruiting. That alone made it worth it to hire him. Oh, and there was one more thing.

"Of course, he had Kobe," Morris said years later. "That was part of it."

THE YEAR had been tumultuous for Sonny Vaccaro. Nike had fired him in 1991, and neither he nor the company had offered or, in the years that followed, would offer an explanation for his dismissal. But Vaccaro had held on to the rights to the ABCD Camp and the Dapper Dan game, and he remained as plugged in to grassroots basketball as he ever was. Seizing on a chance to challenge Nike in the athletic shoe market, Adidas had hired him. Nike was still Goliath, with a marketing budget that dwarfed its competitors', but in this battle, Adidas considered Vaccaro a potential equalizer, the world's best slingshot.

So Allen Rubin did as he had sworn to himself, a year earlier, that he would. He called Vaccaro, telling him there was a kid in suburban Philadelphia, Kobe Bryant, who was good enough to be at the ABCD Camp later that summer. *Well, we really don't want freshmen,* Vaccaro told him. *That puts too much pressure on them. We're just concentrating on upperclassmen.* Rubin did not mention who Kobe's father was, and Vaccaro, even after hearing the name *Bryant,* did not think to make the connection.

THE GROUP of professional and collegiate players, all of them with Philadelphia ties, would rotate to gyms around the city then, during the late spring and summer of 1993. It was how they stayed sharp, stayed in shape: pickup games at Community College of Philadelphia, Hayman Hall at La Salle, the Philadelphia Sporting Club at the Bellevue Hotel, McGonigle Hall at Temple. Trainers from the Sixers' medical staff would show up to tape players' ankles, no matter who they were, what team they played for. Tim Legler, who had been a sharpshooting guard at La Salle and had just finished his third season in the NBA, his first with the Dallas Mavericks, was on the training table one morning, casually watching the game going on in front of him, when he noticed "this young dude," long and gangly, who was holding his own against the NBA veterans. Legler didn't recognize him. He figured the youngster played at one of the schools in the Big Five.

"Who is that guy?" Legler asked the trainer.

"Oh," the trainer said, "that's Kobe Bryant, Joe Bryant's kid. He's, like, a freshman at Lower Merion."

Legler, who went on to play ten years in the NBA and analyze the league for ESPN, was floored. "Number one," he recalled, "just think about what it would take from a physical standpoint to go onto a court at fifteen years old with NBA players or high-level Division I players and fit in. But on top of it, what really stood out was that his confidence level made absolutely no sense for any fifteen-year-old person doing anything.

He wanted to go at guys. He wasn't just surviving, like someone did him a favor by letting him in the game because they knew Joe Bryant."

From his brief time in the NBA, Legler already had learned that the primary attribute that a player needed to possess to fashion a long career in the league wasn't skill or determination. It was physical strength. "You have to play through a level of contact that you don't play through at any other level," he said. If a player couldn't maintain his balance off the dribble, if he couldn't get to a spot on the floor where he could pull up for a jump shot without being off-balance, if he couldn't finish plays at the rim through contact, he couldn't play in the league. And Kobe was trying to make every play happen every time he caught the ball, no matter where he was on the court, no matter how many men were blocking his path to the basket. Once or twice, he drove the baseline with just one dribble and two giant strides and threw down a dunk. But there were lots of guys who could do that and who had no prayer of sticking in the NBA. "You have to learn how to play at multiple speeds," Legler said. "You've got to learn to be patient. You've got to learn how to be more efficient as a player. All of those things were going to be ahead of him, but it was impossible to know that at that age. All I know is, I've never seen a person in my life that young, that confident at anything."

The contrast between Kobe's physical capacities and mental/emotional approach, at that stage of his life, was as much an impediment to him as it was a gift. He completed the most trying year of his early basketball life by playing for a local AAU team, the Sam Rines All-Stars. Sam Rines was not just one man. Sam Rines was two men, and Sam Rines was a brand. Sam Rines Sr. was an elementary-school teacher in Abington, just north of Philadelphia, who had been a part-time assistant coach at La Salle from 1980 until the early 1990s. Sam Rines Jr. had himself played at La Salle under Morris before becoming Abington's director of parks and recreation and founding, with his dad, a basketball program that was known just by their shared nomenclature: Sam Rines AAU. Joe had worked and coached with Sam Jr. in the Sonny Hill League, and Sam Sr. was as well known and well regarded around Philly as Hill. So when it was time for Kobe to fill his non–Lower Merion basketball schedule, Sam Rines AAU was a natural fit . . . for a while.

Kobe's game was a complete Jordan derivation. "You could tell he was imitating and mimicking players, but he looked natural doing it," Sam Jr. said. "His whole swag was TV-like. Joe would tell me that. He'd say, 'When you see him play, you're going to like his game. But he's going to remind you of someone.' I was like, 'Damn, you didn't tell me he was this good.'" Once the games began, however, Sam Jr. wasn't so sanguine about coaching Kobe. In Kobe's first game, yes, he drained six consecutive jump shots from the top of the key and got open for a good dunk—all that while playing up an age group, playing for an under-seventeen team when he was just fourteen—but it didn't take long for him and Sam Jr. to clash over Kobe's greed for personal glory, his refusal to play a team game. One player quit because Kobe wouldn't pass the ball, and you know what? Sam Jr. couldn't blame the kid. As an adult, Kobe would explain away his behavior by saying that, once he turned thirteen, he started "playing the longer game, because my game wasn't about being better than you at thirteen. It was about being better than you when the chips were really on the line. Playing at thirteen, I would size you up and see what your strengths and weaknesses are. How do you approach the game? Are you silly about it? Are you goofy about it? Are you good at it just because you're bigger and stronger than everybody else, or is there actually thought and skill that you put into it?" But Sam Jr. couldn't cater to Kobe and his farsightedness. He had other players to coach, and these players weren't Kobe's Lower Merion teammates. These weren't kids for whom basketball was just a thing to do in wintertime. These kids, all of them, were chasing Division I scholarships. The team played roughly eight tournaments a year in Delaware, in Maryland, in upstate New York, and a player needed to kick in fifty dollars a tournament to cover travel and food and lodging. An investment of four hundred dollars wasn't much for the Bryants, but what about the other kids on the team and their families? They were trying to get exposure, too. They were trying to get some love from the recruiters and the scouts. They were trying to show what they could do, yet if a player passed the ball to Kobe, that player damn well knew he wasn't getting it back. Sam Sr. would signal to Sam Jr. during games whenever Kobe got into one of those chuck-it-from-half-court-'cause-I-can modes, raising and lowering his hand as if to say, *Get off his back.* "But he was a jack," Sam Jr. said. "He was cocky. These other kids were trying to get scholarships, and I tried to explain to him, 'Kobe, you can't shoot every time you touch it.'"

How was he going to put Kobe in his place? How was he going to make him understand? One day, Sam Jr. played one-on-one against him. Sam Jr. wasn't even six feet tall, and he had averaged exactly 0.9 points over his thirty-four games at La Salle. But he'd widened some since then, and he was still a former Division I player, which meant that he had enough game to chasten any mouthy fourteen-year-old. So in he went on Kobe, body-bumping him, driving him down into the post, pushing him around and shooting over him, Kobe's anger and frustration rising. Once . . . twice . . . OK . . . that was enough.

"He couldn't finish the game," Rines said. "He was so competitive, there were damn near tears in his eyes. I was pushing him to be what I thought he could be, and he didn't like it."

What Rines was trying to do, really, was break him. Kobe took everything personally, and if he came to realize that a middle-aged coach who had let his body go puffy could whup him one-on-one, maybe he'd come to understand that passing the ball to an open teammate was not an admission of his own failure to create, take, and make a more difficult shot. It was merely the smarter play, the right play. His team would be better for it, and he would be a better player, and be regarded as a better player, for it. There would be occasions throughout his career, in high school and beyond, when it appeared that he had never learned that lesson at all. There would be occasions, too, when it appeared that he had learned it so well that everything he ever wanted out of the sport would be his for the taking.

I never took my studies lightly. . . . I'm interested in writing, especially poetry, and am active in music, as you may have heard.

—KOBE BRYANT

8

SWAGGER

FOR KOBE BRYANT, ANOTHER NECESSARY humbling was always and only just a few steps away from his front door. At Lower Merion, his arrival had caused, and his selfishness had cultivated, tension throughout his first varsity season. In AAU ball, he had been in conflict with his coach, who in turn had pushed Kobe to the brink of humiliation by bullying him just as his cousin Sharif Butler had, on the one place where Kobe believed himself to be bullyproof: the basketball court. But Kobe did not love Sam Rines Jr., and in their first summer together, he didn't listen to him much, either. Kobe loved his father. Kobe listened to Joe. Kobe liked Gregg Downer. Kobe respected Gregg Downer. But when Kobe got worked up during a game, when his temper flared, Joe could calm him every time, usually by speaking to him, whether a whisper mouth to ear or a sharp shout from the stands, in Italian. When they went to Sixers games together, players and officials and fans would stop Kobe and tell him what a great player Joe was, and Kobe basked in that rose-colored recasting of his father's career. "Whenever I step on the court, I think of that," he said, "that my dad went through this, and now I'm going through it." In the pantheon of people who could advise him on and teach him about basketball, about life, Kobe put his father first.

Their driveway on Remington Road was their private laboratory. Through the summer, Kobe had added two inches and was now six foot five. He had put on muscle, some of it born of natural pubescent testosterone, some of it from intermittent weight training at Lower Merion and at the Jewish Community Center. There was only one true way, in his mind, to test his physical improvement: Play Dad one-on-one.

One of their games from that summer stood out to him. Kobe took the ball out, dribbled past Joe, scored. Kobe was feeling good. Kobe got a bucket on his old man. Why couldn't he do this every time? Ah, Joe's ball. Joe went all out this time. Joe decided to give his son a taste. Joe drove right past him and dunked on him. Kobe was shocked. Kobe had no idea that an NBA player, even one that hadn't suited up in the league for ten years, could be that quick. It was his dad. There were no tears. There was no pouting. There was only the realization of the journey ahead and the lessons yet to learn, in all kinds of classrooms.

JEANNE MASTRIANO approached teaching writing, in her honors-level survey course for tenth graders, in the same manner, she believed, that an athlete would approach his or her preparation for a game or meet or contest. "You do different things to train and strengthen your body," she said, and her goal was to have her students do different things to train their minds, to develop flexibility and confidence by having them cycle through writing styles and forms—poetry, playwriting, personal essays, narratives—then having them critique each other's work without pulling punches. They didn't keep journals or diaries. They kept writers' notebooks, and at her say-so, like a starter's pistol in a sprint, they would write like runaway trains for three minutes, five minutes, letting ideas tumble out of their brains and hearts until something beautiful landed on the page. Whenever they discussed each other's work, they should bare their teeth. From the moment she joined Lower Merion's English department as a full-time faculty member, in 1987, she cultivated an environment in which it was safe for her students to speak freely, but not mushy-safe. *Does the piece work? Does it not work? Why? Let's dig into it. You're entering the unknown here, and you need to take risks. Everyone does. If you don't, you're not going to have an exhilarating experience. You need to scare yourself.* On one of her classroom walls, she had tacked a full-body photograph of Michelangelo's *David;* when a parent objected to the display of nudity, Mastriano cut hot-pink Post-it notes into the shape of bathing suits and stuck them to the photo to cover the statue's crotch. She was charismatic and witty, had studied English literature for a year at the University of London, and oversaw her classroom with a simple set of rules and standards. She didn't want, in one of her favorite phrases, "sunshine blown up my skirt." If you showed up unprepared, if you hadn't read the assignment, shut up. Sit there, save your snappy patter and your CliffsNotes-level insight, soak up what you can during the class period, and make a vow that you'll catch up on your reading and come back tomorrow ready to contribute. It was no wonder she connected with Kobe Bryant.

When it came to academics, Kobe lived at home under rules similar to the ones that Mastriano established at school. Pam had an edict: In her house, academics took precedence over athletics or even a robust social life. Yes, Kobe and Sharia and Shaya could play basketball or volleyball or chat on the phone with their friends or, in Kobe's case, sequester himself in his room to pore over his Magic and Michael videos. But only after they'd finished their homework and taken care of their few chores around the house. Pam, for instance, often harped on the condition of Kobe's bedroom after a weekend of AAU basketball: His sweaty and smelly clothes were strewn all over. Once, Mastriano arranged for each of her students to tell a short story to a kindergarten class. In his story, Kobe turned those dirty clothes into monstrous apparitions that dragged kids from their beds. She had unlocked in him a side of his personality that he didn't know existed, and that would define his post–NBA career.

"She was so good and so passionate about what she was teaching," he once said. "She firmly believed that storytelling could change the world."

If most of Kobe's courses were obligations to him, Mastriano's was an escape—as it turned out, an essential one. She centered much of her course material around the concept of "the hero's journey," showing *Star Wars* in class to give her students, in Luke Skywalker, an easily accessible case study before drawing on Greek mythology and the writings of

Joseph Campbell, particularly his seminal work, *The Hero with a Thousand Faces*.

It was obvious to Mastriano that Kobe, even at fifteen, saw himself on that trajectory. The course material was a drug in his veins, feeding the grand vision he had of himself and his future. He read the *Iliad* and asked himself: *Do I identify with the rage-driven Achilles or the honor-bound Hector?* The "call to adventure," Campbell wrote, "signifies that destiny has summoned the hero and transferred his spiritual center of gravity from within the pale of his society to a zone unknown." To Mastriano, Kobe was mulling that call, grappling with its perils. What else was his style of play but a zone unknown to and apart from the other nine players on the floor? Her class had read book 9 of the *Odyssey,* in which Odysseus pulls off an inspired, brilliant escape from the Cyclops, only to fall into arrogance and taunt the monster, who in turn rips off the top of a mountain and hurls it at Odysseus' ship, nearly killing him and his men. What else were those whispers and complaints from Kobe's teammates—their anger over his refusal to share the basketball, their assertion that his egotism threatened to hurt the team more than help it—if not a parallel to that parable? "That swagger that alienated the Greek gods," Mastriano said, "also caused some of Kobe's peers to dislike and reject him." At its basest, the metaphor of the "hero's journey" was a self-serving rationalization for Kobe's me-first behavior on the basketball court. At its best, it was a coat of emotional, intellectual, and inspirational armor. This was his destiny. Nothing could or would stop him.

Mastriano, at the time, wasn't entirely certain of the wisdom, the ramifications, and the costs of Kobe's perspective. She required each student to submit a one-act play to the Young Playwrights festival in Philadelphia. Kobe's was titled "For My Homey," and it was, of course, about basketball: The protagonist, Trajar, is a high school basketball star, ticketed for the NBA, whose best friend, Dom, is shot and killed by a drug dealer. Everything he wrote for Mastriano's class was about basketball, which annoyed her no end. Didn't he realize there was more to life than the bouncing ball? She despaired that he would be consumed by the sport, that his authentic self would be devoured or swept away. "I really didn't get the big picture," she said. "I had more than one conversation with him about how ludicrous it was, to think about going pro. I kept saying to him, 'Do you know what a long shot it is? Try thinking about other things.' I didn't see where he was headed at all."

Still, she became and remained an adviser to him. Most of her students called her "Mastriano." Kobe called her "Mrs. Mastriano," maintaining the formality that Pam had insisted on but always rolling the *r*, flavoring his favorite teacher's name with Italian flair when he lingered in her room after the bell rang or stopped by before study hall. In class, among his peers, he did not talk much, though in Mastriano's memory, he was the type of student who would not have hesitated to say, and not in a terribly antagonistic tone, *Why are we learning this? I don't see where this is going. It's not doing anything for me. Could you please justify it?* She would have welcomed such feedback. She loved an edgy student who asked impertinent questions, who challenged her. It was so much better than the alternative, than the smarmy brown-noser just out to tell her what she wanted to hear for the sake of an A. She wished that Kobe had spoken up more. She had an inkling why he didn't.

"He seemed to be part of the larger group but not settling into a niche," she said. "He told me he was very lonely much of the time, and that he dribbled himself to sleep."

JERMAINE GRIFFIN was what Kobe Bryant needed, and in some ways he was what Kobe Bryant wasn't. He'd had the tough childhood in urban America that Kobe hadn't, in a housing project in Far Rockaway, Queens. Drugs were ubiquitous. A friend of his had been shot and killed before the two of them had graduated eighth grade. A serious student and fond of basketball, Griffin was finishing his ninth-grade year at Benjamin Cardozo High School when a teacher suggested that he enroll in a national program called A Better Chance, or ABC, which would allow him, with all room and board and school expenses paid, to transfer to and live in a school district with a more favorable educational setting. Griffin would have to leave behind his mother, Vanetta, and his twin brother, Jermell. He jumped at the chance anyway, banking that a fresh, clean start would be the best thing for him. After taking the program's admission tests, he found out where he was headed: to a house in Ardmore with eight other students in the program, and to Lower Merion High School.

Six foot three with shoulders like a picture-window curtain rod, Griffin kept his head down and his mouth closed as he walked the halls for his first few weeks there. In Queens, most of his friends and classmates were Black, as he was, and from working-class or impoverished backgrounds. Now most of his classmates were white, and many were wealthy. On his tour of the school, he met Downer, who helped him get over his culture shock by explaining to Griffin how valuable he could be to the basketball team. And once Griffin met Kobe, the two formed a fast friendship from their shared and complementary traits: their intensity about basketball; their love of music, rap in particular; their early outsiders' view of the school. "Jermaine was the savior," Kobe once said, "because for him to come to Lower Merion at the right time, it was like, 'Where did this guy come from?' He was someone I could relate to on the basketball team, someone I'm comfortable with." In the cafeteria, Kobe, Griffin, and Matt Matkov would engage in rap battles that in time continued in apartments and clubs around Philadelphia and included Kevin Sanchez, regarded as the school's best rapper, and Anthony Bannister, a teenager who worked at the Jewish Community Center in Wynnewood. Their interest and involvement in the city's rap scene kept Kobe, Griffin, and Matkov close even as their roles in the Aces' basketball program diverged. Kobe was . . . well, Kobe. Matkov was never going to be much more than a bench rider. Griffin bisected them. He wasn't in Kobe's league as a player—who was?—but his length, his leaping ability, and his tenacity as a rebounder were elements that the team had been missing throughout Kobe's freshman season. It wasn't just that Downer needed to surround Kobe with more-talented players if the Aces were to improve. They needed more kids who played with a toughness and an edginess that approximated Kobe's. After coaching Kobe for a year, Downer understood how the expectations on Kobe and the team—and the pressure on him as head coach—would mount over the subsequent three years. Lower Merion was a member of the Pennsylvania Interscholastic Athletic Association's District One, which comprised more than sixty schools in the towns and suburbs around Philadelphia. Winning a district championship, amid that level of competition, would be an achievement in and of itself, and winning a state championship had been too far-fetched to contemplate. Downer knew that it wasn't anymore, not with Kobe. For a long time, there was no chance that the Aces could compete with such teams. Their players could never be as tough as those teams. They could never have as much passion and heart. They could never get over . . . what other way to put this was there? . . . their *fear.* Maybe, with Kobe, that fear would disappear.

"We always had this label on us as the silver-spoon kids," Evan Monsky said. "That was definitely a chip on our shoulder that we carried with us in any gym we played in or summer-league tournament. Or at least, from a personal aspect, I felt that way. I'm sure Kobe felt that way, as well. You heard it all the time: We were soft Main Liners. No. Fuck, that's ridiculous. I'll elbow in the face for a loose ball, and we want to shove it down your throats. We grew up watching Charles Barkley! Charles Barkley will shove you through a plate-glass window and then joke about it. We loved that as well, and even though we are in this cushy little suburb outside West Philly, we feel like we're part of Philly."

Feeling like they were part of Philly and its basketball culture was one thing. Proving it was another. Most of the returning players used the summer to grow closer as friends, bonding over afternoons at the Shack in Ardmore and nights at the movies: *Jurassic Park, The Fugitive, In the Line of Fire.* "But Kobe would be working out at the JCC or in his driveway," Guy Stewart said. "So he was constantly, constantly working. You would get these glimpses of him. 'Oh, he's different now.' Narberth Summer League, Ardmore Summer League. Then you would see him play pickup somewhere, where you could see how hard he had worked to change his game. He's just doing it with ease now, whether it was his jump shot, whether it was his handle, his vertical. He made such a leap from his freshman to his sophomore year that it was just insane."

It took Lower Merion just four games, all victories, to match its win total from Kobe's entire freshman season. The last of those four, a 75–58 victory over Strath Haven, featured a performance by Kobe that, in a more modern era of media, would have made him a sensation. Showing no ill effects from the fractured kneecap and a summertime schedule loaded with AAU games, he scored thirty-four points—a Pennsylvania high school basketball game had just thirty-two minutes of actual playing time—and hit five three-point shots. Of course, there was no social media, no Twitter, no Instagram, no Facebook video to spread the legend, but even *The Philadelphia Inquirer* and the *Philadelphia Daily News*, the region's two most widely circulated and read newspapers, didn't catch on right away to the nature and magnitude of what was developing in Wynnewood. The son of a former Philadelphia high school and collegiate star and a former Sixers player was now putting up eye-popping point totals and leading a renaissance season for a once-lowly program in the city's suburbs? It would seem an obvious and alluring story line. Yet *The Inquirer*'s coverage of the Strath Haven win, in the paper's suburbs-centric Neighbors section, focused not on Kobe, but on his teammate and rival Joe Dixon, who had eight points and seven assists. Kobe went unmentioned until the midpoint of the 416-word game story, and only in the final paragraph did the story note that, after Strath Haven had cut Lower Merion's lead to six with less than five and a half minutes left in regulation, "Bryant, the son of former 76er Joe Bryant, answered with two of his five three-pointers to give the Aces some breathing room." Still coaching at Akiba, still stringing for *The Inquirer,* still hanging out with Downer and talking regularly with Joe Bryant and stopping by practices when he could, Jeremy Treatman begged his editors to increase the paper's coverage of Kobe. Treatman wasn't chatting with Joe just because they were friends, either. Treatman was in his first season as the radio play-by-play voice of La Salle's men's basketball team, on hand every night as Speedy Morris and Joe and the Explorers labored through their second season in the Midwestern Collegiate Conference, going 11–16, the university's geographic distance from its intraconference competitors already doing damage to Morris's and Joe's recruiting efforts. Why the hell would a Philly kid with his pick of big-time college programs want to spend four years playing against Wisconsin–Green Bay, Detroit Mercy, and Illinois-Chicago? It would take a transcendent player to reverse La Salle's fortunes. It would take Kobe, and here was Treatman, with an inside track to what, he was certain, would soon be one of the biggest stories in Philadelphia sports. But the editors kept saying no to his story pitches, insisting that the programs in the Philadelphia Public League and the Philadelphia Catholic League, for their more prestigious histories and better quality of play, mattered more. Treatman was dumbfounded. Why didn't they believe him? They might have understood better had they been in Lower Merion's gym with him one afternoon, when he was standing next to Downer, both of them watching Kobe dominate another practice, when Downer turned to him and asked a question.

"Do people realize that Michael Jordan is in this gym with us right now?"

No, people did not. The editors weren't alone in their blindness. Two or three times a week, Kobe hitched a ride home from practice with his friend Audrey Price, who was in Jeanne Mastriano's honors English class, too, and who was a point guard on the JV girls' basketball team. Occasionally, they would have playful games of one-on-one when the girls' and boys' teams were in the gym at the same time, and the two were a sight together: Kobe closing in on six foot six, Price just five foot one with a nickname that Kobe gave her that belied her size: Diesel. "I was one of the lucky ones; my mom would come and pick me up," Price said. "Often, Kobe would peek in the window and say, 'Oh, Mrs. Price, do you mind, could I have a ride?' And my mom would say, 'Of course, Kobe! Hop in.' It was just Kobe. It wasn't a potential superstar in my backseat—and in the backseat! You would give him the front seat if anything, but he was in the backseat with his long legs in our little Chevy."

One Saturday at the JCC, Kobe ran into Price, who confided in him that she was considering quitting basketball. She showed up at every practice on time and ready, put her heart and soul into the team, but once she entered a game, she froze, her anxiety overtaking her, and the coach would take her out. She felt stupid, sitting on the bench, a fifteen-year-old girl self-conscious about how people viewed and judged her. *Diesel,* he told her, *you don't quit. You don't give up. You play, even if you sit on the bench. You learn by sitting on the bench.* "I played that year, and I played because Kobe made me play," she recalled. "He didn't want me to give up. I loved the game too much to give up, and he knew that. That was the kind of guy he was. He saw potential in everything and everyone." To Audrey Price and most other people in and around Lower Merion, though, he was still just Kobe.

MAYBE YOU had to be in the hurricane's eye to see clearly its path. Williamsport, in northeastern Pennsylvania, watched three games' worth of film on Kobe before devising a game plan—take the charge when he drives, double him in the post—that led to the worst game of his high school career. He had just seven points, and the Aces lost for the first time that season, 63–43. But then they ripped off a seven-game winning streak, a stretch over which Kobe averaged 26.3 points a game and—in a win over Haverford three days before Christmas, just before an ice storm in the Philadelphia region wiped out two weeks of the high school basketball season—posted his first triple double: 26 points, 17 rebounds, 10 assists. The Aces staggered down the stretch, going 5–4 over their final nine regular-season games, and two losses to Ridley, the first when a Ridley player hit three free throws in the final thirteen seconds, the second on a buzzer-beater, prevented them from winning their first league championship in more than a decade. Nevertheless, the team entered the district playoffs with a 15–5 record, with as well-rounded and deep a roster as the program had had in years. Three starters—Matt Snider, Joe Dixon, and Doug Young—were seniors, but Griffin, Monsky, and Stewart would all be back the following season. That was great. That was nice. That wasn't the real reason for the turnaround. Kobe was.

It was Kobe who, during a drill that season, leaped with both of his hands up and didn't block one of Young's shots as much as he smothered it at the apex of Young's release. It was Kobe who, as the two of them wrestled for possession, said to Young, "Doug, get your hands off the ball because this is starting to look bad." It was Kobe who was slowly drawing students and teachers and Main Line residents to the high school on Tuesday and Friday nights. "I don't think Kobe was responsible for some mass awakening," Young said. "That would be overstating it. But he was a person everyone could be proud of. You had community members bringing their kids to games. That hadn't happened in generations."

It was Kobe who scored thirty-five points in a 76–64 first-round-playoff victory over Pennsbury. It was Kobe about whom Brad Sharp, Pennsbury's coach, said, "He is the best sophomore I've seen in twenty-one years of coaching. He did whatever he wanted out there." And it was Kobe who had twenty-four points in the Aces' final game that season, their 86–77 loss in the district tournament's second round to a more talented, more experienced team, Plymouth Whitemarsh. Who scored fourteen of his points in the fourth quarter. Who drilled three three-pointers in the game's last eighty-five seconds just to keep Lower Merion close. Who gritted his teeth and scrunched up his face and broke the stone silence of a losing locker room by saying, *Never again. This is not going to happen again. This is not how we're going out. Next year, we're going to win the state championship.*

"It was his team from the time he arrived," Young said. "The success of the program and our teams would not have happened without him setting a bar for us of unsurpassed work ethic and an absolute hatred of losing. You could see, even as a sixteen-year-old, that the passion, the drive, was something we, as multiple-sport athletes, as kids just walking the halls of a high school, had never experienced before. I had no doubt that the team was going to come back next year and be even better, and whatever this kid wanted to accomplish as a high school basketball player, even at that young age, he would. I had a sense that something was about to happen."

Young was right, in more ways than he could possibly have known.

I don't believe I have ever consciously tried to imitate him. I just try to be Kobe. But I'd be lying if I said that Michael Jordan didn't make a big impression on me.

—KOBE BRYANT

9

SE DIO
VUOLE

N THE RETELLING, SONNY VACCARO described the moment that he met Kobe Bryant with a kind of wonder reserved for those who have experienced the transcendental, as if he could not explain or account for the encounter in rational terms, as if it could only be the hand of God at work. "History was rewritten in New Jersey," he said, "because of a quirk of circumstances, a freak of time." Of course he described it that way. This was Sonny Vaccaro, seller of shoes, maker of sneaker kings, the man who brought Michael Jordan and Nike together, the man who found Kobe when no one else was looking for him. It couldn't be that Kobe had come to him through the groundwork that Vaccaro had already laid and the grunt work he had already done, through the system of sources and contacts that Vaccaro had constructed years earlier, through Allen Rubin of Hoop Scoop picking up the phone and saying, *This kid should be at your camp.* No, if Kobe saw himself as the hero of his own myth, then Sonny Vaccaro could attach some mysticism to his role in Kobe's rise.

Vaccaro had his own remarkable story—a former teacher and professional gambler from Trafford, Pennsylvania, just outside Pittsburgh, with expressive, serving-dish eyes and the affectionate manner of an Italian grandfather and a salty tongue and an ability to connect with high school kids, who parlayed a part-time job as a recruiter for Youngstown State's men's basketball program into the Dapper Dan Classic, into a job with Nike, into a meeting with Jordan at the 1984 Summer Olympics, in Los Angeles. He had seen Jordan play one game, one, but it was enough for him to give him $500,000, Nike's entire signing budget for the '84 class of incoming pros. He could have given it to Charles Barkley, or split it between Sam Bowie and Sam Perkins. Why didn't he? How did he know to go all in on Michael, that the 1985 release of the Nike Air Jordan sneaker would revolutionize the whole freaking industry and turn Jordan into the most popular and powerful athlete on the planet? It was just Sonny being Sonny, doing what Sonny does.

"As I've gone through my life, when I made my bet on a guy, I can't explain it," he said. "I wasn't a scout. I didn't have training and all that bullshit. It was just this instinct. But I knew it. I quite obviously knew it, because the quest was the quest. We got him."

But now he was starting anew with Adidas, with forty small-college coaches as clients but no superstar players, with the ABCD Camp still attracting coaches and recruits, with his connections and friendships with AAU and high school coaches still unbroken and strong. The NCAA still hated him, still hated that he had such influence with its bottomless well of unpaid basketball talent. And he hated the association right back, believing that it was exploiting those players—most of them poor, Black kids—by building a multimillion-dollar machine on their backs and, through the veneer of amateurism, denying them any of the spoils. If there was any opportunity to pull a high school player away from college basketball, to help that kid make good money for himself and his family (and, in fairness, for Vaccaro, too), and to stick it to the NCAA, Vaccaro was going to take it. He didn't have the budget and the resources yet at Adidas to sign such a player, but he knew he would. And he had a mandate there to find the next Michael Jordan, and he knew he would.

In 1994, he moved his camp to the Rothman Center on the campus of Fairleigh Dickinson University in Hackensack, New Jersey, less than two hours from Wynnewood. Then, on the day before the camp opened in early July, "out of the clear blue sky," he said, "the world changes."

The camp was free but invitation-only, and Joe Bryant had taken a chance. He had reached out to Gary Charles, the coach of the Long Island Panthers AAU team and a go-between for Vaccaro. It was the easier, less risky route than going straight to Sonny. Joe had his array of contacts, too, through his time coaching in the Sonny Hill League and his job at La Salle, and besides, what if Sonny didn't remember him from the '72 Dapper Dan, from all those years ago? What if Sonny didn't remember that Chubby Cox played in the Dapper Dan, too? That would be embarrassing. Better to contact Charles first for what Joe had to ask: Could Kobe, entering his junior year, get into ABCD? Could he go against the country's best? Could Sonny grant Joe this favor? And in Sonny Vaccaro's retelling of his place and emergence in Kobe Bryant's origin story, Allen Rubin's phone calls and tips about Kobe never came up, because where is the drama in that? Where is the magic?

"So Joe walks in," Vaccaro said, "and I remember him immediately. Gary says, 'Sonny, Joe Bryant is here. He wants to talk to you about his son, who's been in Italy and who no one knows about.' Joe comes over. Now we're reunited. It was the thing called sports, the thing called opportunity and happenstance. That's the pattern of a life. What if Joe wasn't picked? I meet Pam, and she tells me, 'My brother played in the game, too.' All these things add up."

And the sum . . . the fulfillment of what to Sonny Vaccaro could only be destiny . . . didn't reveal itself until Joe and Pam Bryant walked into Fairleigh Dickinson with their son. "Until the Child comes in," Vaccaro said. *The Child.* "That's who Kobe Bryant is."

WHO WAS Kobe Bryant during the spring and summer of 1994? He was a kid who had no free time because he wanted no free time, a kid who played in at least six basketball leagues and at least two basketball camps and traveled the East Coast for AAU tournaments and who carted his school-books with him on those trips so he could complete his homework and whose typical July day began with a game at 9:00 A.M. and ended with a game at 9:30 P.M. He was a kid obsessed. The blare of the final buzzer of that district-playoff loss to Plymouth Whitemarsh had barely begun to fade when Kobe embarked on a schedule that would have left a less committed player exhausted and sick of basketball by its conclusion. Each league, each trip, each camp, each game refined a particular aspect of his evolution, both individually and collectively at Lower Merion. By playing so much, by playing with and against such varied opponents and teammates, he took himself from being an excellent high school player as a sophomore to being a great high school player as a junior. He worried not at all that the volume of this work, the pure physical exertion and demands, would lead to his injuring himself again. The broken kneecap was too deep in the past, he believed, to be a cause for ongoing concern. He had gotten taller, put on muscle. "The way I think about it," he said that summer, "if I get hurt and can't play anymore, God didn't want me to be a basketball player. If that happens, then I'll just move on and do something else with my life." But he wasn't hurt, and he wasn't about to move on anytime soon.

First was a drive down to Newark and the University of Delaware, with the Sam Rines All-Stars, for the Delaware Shootout AAU tournament, at the time one of the hottest college basketball recruiting events on the calendar. And among the hundreds of coaches at the Bob Carpenter Center for that early-April event was Mike Krzyzewski, less than a week removed from Duke's excruciating four-point loss in the national-championship game to Arkansas. It was the third time that the Blue Devils had reached the championship game in Grant Hill's four years with them, but now Hill was graduating, moving on to the NBA, and Krzyzewski would be more than happy to sign a similar player—a small forward / shooting guard with intelligence and a feathery jump shot and compression springs in the soles of his shoes—if he could find one. In Kobe, he thought he had.

The irony of the discovery was that Kobe was shell-shocked on the first day in Newark, for, after his high school season, he wasn't accustomed to competing against so many players who were older, taller, and stronger but also every bit as skilled as he was. Time and again, he drove the lane for a dunk or layup, only to have his shot blocked. By the tournament's end, he had tweaked his approach, shooting with an earlier, quicker release. There were splashier performances from better-known names. Stephon Marbury, a guard entering his senior year at Brooklyn Lincoln High School, was named the tournament's most valuable player, scoring eighteen points in the championship game, and Paterson (New Jersey) Catholic's Tim Thomas, a rising junior like Kobe, was terrific, displaying point-guard skills rarely found in a player his height, six foot nine, a Joe Bryant for the 1990s. But Krzyzewski was impressed enough with Kobe that he tracked down both Bryants and told Joe, *I'm going to give your son a scholarship to be the next Grant Hill.* It was a hell of an offer to back-pocket.

AT THE Sonny Hill League, Philadelphia's best players—Donnie Carr and Arthur "Yah" Davis at Roman Catholic, Rashid Bey at St. John Neumann—laughed at Kobe when he strutted onto the court. They remembered, from the previous summer, his physical weakness compared to them, and they had an air, a look. *All these people say that you're the best this and the best that. We don't care.* "We didn't have to say a word," Carr said. "He'd just see it in our eyes, and he felt it." But he was growing out of that scrawniness, and his skills were more developed, more refined, and even the crowds surrounding the court, thirty to forty people deep around the perimeter, some of them jeering him and all of them loud one way or another, had no effect on him. Players and spectators would stalk the sideline, smack-talk him, and it would only heighten his focus, make him pick up his level of play. "You could see what was inside of him," Carr said. "He was fearless." After games, Kobe would join Carr and those city kids, moseying down Broad Street to Roy Rogers or KFC for something to eat. No, he was never going to understand fully what they had experienced. He hadn't lived it. But he wasn't oblivious to the differences between them, and because he wanted their respect and acceptance, he didn't flaunt those differences, either. He didn't walk into a fast-food joint, slap a fifty-dollar bill on the counter, and declare, *Get whatever you want.* He did what the crowd did, pooling the money in his pocket with theirs. *Well, I want to get a No. 2. How much do we have?* Then they could grab a booth and rank their favorite rap groups and albums—*Enter the Wu-Tang (36 Chambers),* by Wu-Tang Clan, was at or near the top of Kobe's list—and he could ask them about their neighborhoods, their upbringing, the ways they were alike, the ways they weren't.

"We grew up in poverty, man," Carr said, "so we're seeing everything under the sun. He would always be interested in those stories: 'What happened here? What happened there?' I tell people all the time, man: He might have grown up in the suburbs, but he had an inner-city mind and heart, always."

He saved much of his vitriol and immaturity, it seemed, for his complex and stormy relationship with Sam Rines Jr., who kept trying to break Kobe of his egotism and kept succeeding only in pissing him off. One game, Rines put Kobe at point guard, and Kobe proceeded to lose the ball on seven straight possessions. He had it stolen. He threw it away. He kicked it out of bounds. Rines had worked to assemble more Division I recruits on the team, and Kobe was taking the plan to turn Sam Rines AAU into a bigger, better-regarded program, crumpling it into a ball, and firing it into a trash can. Who would want to play with a ball hog like this? Who would want to play for this program? "While everyone else was trying to get scholarships," Rines said, "Kobe was working on a crossover." He was still treating AAU ball like every court was his own driveway—deaf to Rines's instructions, blind to the other players, focused solely on *his* skills, *his* development and improvement, himself, himself, himself. Sam Jr. would bark at Kobe, and Sam Sr., sitting next to his son, would tell him to settle down, and Kobe would remain at point guard. And so, in another game, when the same thing happened, when Kobe turned the ball over again and again and his team was down 14–2 and could barely get off a freaking shot, Sam Jr. had finally had it. He told Kobe to let another player bring the ball up. Kobe waved him off and brought the ball up anyway. "That's like a fuck-you," Sam Jr. said. "So I subbed him out. I said, 'Listen, you can't flag me during the game. I'm trying to help you out. You're hurting the team. Just get the shit together, and let us get into a flow, and we're going to get you the ball.' He wasn't crying, but he was visibly upset. Joe pulled him over, talked to him in Italian. I put him back in. Everything was fine. But I swear, he hated me after that." He was evolving fitfully, the only way a personality as extreme as his could evolve, the heat of his vanity flaring up and cooling, flaring up and cooling, his father there to soothe him, his mother reminding him to be polite.

SPEEDY MORRIS, as usual, held his annual overnight basketball camp at La Salle's Hayman Hall, but this time, something was different. A future celebrity and star, just a teenager then, was in attendance. The young man had persuaded his mother to pay the camp's entrance fee, and he still couldn't believe that she had come up with the money. He was a nobody then, just another kid from a tough background with big dreams. You couldn't tell him that he wasn't going to play in the NBA someday; it was only a matter of what route he would take to get there. Duke? Playing for Coach K would be awesome. North Carolina? He didn't care for sky blue, the Tar Heels' signature color, but that dislike wasn't necessarily a deal-breaker for him. Maybe he'd stay in Philly and play for John Chaney at Temple, make his mom happy. He felt he was the best defensive player, at his age, in the city, perhaps the country, and he gave himself a nickname: The Bug. Step on the court with him, and he'd warn you: *You don't wanna make The Bug mad.*

But then Kevin Hart met with some hard realities once the drills and games began.

He noticed, immediately, that Kobe Bryant was at the camp, too, with Joe, working alongside Morris. Excellent. Hart had heard about Kobe, what a terrific player he was. He roomed with Kobe at the camp, sneaked around La Salle's dorms with him late at night to play pranks on other campers, followed him everywhere, just wanted to be in his vicinity, whether it was a layup line or a communal restroom. There had to be something that Hart could glean from him, could show him. Day one . . . day two . . . Hart hustled. He defended like a Doberman even when he, who would never grow to be taller than five foot four, had to guard Kobe. He Greco-Roman-wrestled for rebounds with the giants down low. One night, he worked up the gumption: *Hey, Kobe, where do you think I'll end up? You know, D-I-wise?*

Kobe laughed and walked away.

After he had become a famous stand-up comic and actor, Hart would describe that camp as an awakening: Basketball was Kobe's calling, but it wasn't Hart's, and he had better find another vocation. He has insisted, even during an appearance on *The Tonight Show Starring Jimmy Fallon,* that Kobe played left-handed during the entire camp, toying with everyone. "The opportunity that I thought was going to be the biggest of my life," Hart said, "turned out to be a goddamned practice pad for Kobe Bryant." Whether Hart's tale was true or tall, it didn't escape Morris's attention at the time that his assistant coach's only son had proven himself—one hand, two hands, no hands—to be far and away the best player there.

THE NARBERTH and Ardmore summer leagues weren't quite the respite, the relaxing opportunity to hone his craft on his own terms, that the La Salle camp was for Kobe, but compared to Hackensack and Delaware, they were warm blankets. His Lower Merion friends and teammates surrounded him, and these games allowed them to measure themselves against the players and teams who would stand in their way in the district and state playoffs in the spring of 1995. In the Narberth League, he averaged 33.5 points over one three-game stretch, including a forty-point performance in which he scored thirteen of his team's fifteen third-quarter points. All the while, Joe shouted advice at him from the bleachers. The strange part was that Kobe didn't shout back; on the court, he could always hear Joe's voice. In an earlier game, with his team holding an eight-point lead in the fourth quarter, Kobe barked to Joe, *I'm gonna pull up for a three.* Joe started yelling at Kobe, who smiled and kept dribbling to let him know that he was kidding all along, that he just liked seeing his old man get worked up.

These local summer leagues, really, even with Downer coaching in Narberth, were extensions of the pickup games that sprung up organically among the Aces and those who aspired to be Aces—imagine such a thing in the recent years before Kobe's arrival—at Remington Park or the Shack or the other courts on the Main Line. Kobe had established himself, locally at least, as a bona fide star, and word had been out for a while about who he was and where the program might be headed with him. One example: Dave Rosenberg, a year younger than Kobe, graduated from Bala Cynwyd Middle School but considered attending a high school other than Lower Merion. His primary sport was football; maybe there was a better option, with a better football program, elsewhere. But he loved basketball, too, and he was shooting hoops by himself one day at Remington Park when Kobe and his cousin Sharif Butler showed up.

"I could not have been more thrilled," Rosenberg said. "For a fourteen-year-old kid, second to Magic Johnson, the next superstars in my life were anyone on the high school varsity team, let alone Kobe."

The three of them played a couple of games of roughhouse, a play-ground game of one-on-one-on-one, before Kobe pointed to a spot near the lane's left elbow. "Hey," he told Rosenberg, "play some defense on me. I want to work on some things." Butler, still beating Kobe every time they went head-to-head, though the gap between them had closed some, eventually left, but Kobe and Rosenberg stayed for another hour. "I hung around like a happy dog on defense," Rosenberg said, "as Kobe practiced a mix of fadeaways and quick moves to the basket." When he told his parents that he had decided to go to Lower Merion, Rosenberg, an excellent student, cited its strong academics . . . and something else. "I told them I thought I could make the varsity basketball team in a couple of years and play with this guy named 'Kobe,'" he said. "I told them he was going to be great, and I remember their eyes rolling at both ambitions." True to his prediction, Rosenberg had made the freshman team, putting him on track to play varsity as a senior, and now he was part of a group of players who could both complement Kobe and ride his coattails.

"But Kobe would be working out at the JCC or in his driveway," Guy Stewart said. "So he was constantly, constantly working. You would get these glimpses of him. 'Oh, he's different now.' Narberth Summer League, Ardmore Summer League. Then you would see him play pickup some-where, where you could see how hard he had worked to change his game. He's just doing it with ease now, whether it was his jump shot, whether it was his handle, his vertical. He made such a leap from his freshman to his sophomore year that it was just insane." It was the total trust that Kobe was bound for greatness that stayed with his friends and coaches. It was his entire mien that they could never forget. One game, with the clock run-ning down at the end of a quarter, he threw the basketball like a baseball from the opposite foul line to his team's basket, seventy-five feet, maybe eighty. In it went. The crowd around the court caught its breath and re-leased it in a long *Woooo*. Kobe just walked right back into the huddle and took his place there next to Downer, as if he expected the shot to go in. "I guarantee he did," Downer said. *I'm special. Special people make shots like this.* Already, the most important event of his summer had shown him so.

★   ★   ★

THERE WERE 157 players at the 1994 Adidas ABCD Camp, and among them were four of the best juniors-to-be in the nation: Lester Earl from Baton Rouge, Louisiana; Shaheen Holloway of St. Patrick High School in Elizabeth, New Jersey; Tim Thomas; and Kobe. They became friends, the four of them, each of them a regular on the AAU circuit, each of them his own player, none of them a facsimile of the other: Earl a six-foot-nine low-post presence, Holloway a five-ten point guard, smart, tough, a future coach; Thomas able to play anywhere, the game coming so naturally and easily to him, maybe too easily; Kobe the scorer and closer, driven. They would have fit together nicely on the same team. They thought so themselves.

The country's top senior prospect, Kevin Garnett of Mauldin (South Carolina) High School, was there, too, and he was a sight: six foot ten, intense, ribbed with muscles, possessing a body that no one doubted would withstand the rigors and attrition of an eighty-two-game NBA season. Dick Vitale, the most famous and influential college basketball voice in America, took a seat in the FDU bleachers, ready to take in some dipsy-doo-dunkaroos and see some diaper dandies and wonder if these kids were SERIOUS—WERE THEY SERIOUS? with their moves and their skills and their savvy. Kentucky's Rick Pitino, Villanova's Steve Lappas, Wisconsin's Stu Jackson, and dozens of other coaches looked on.

Marbury, who would accept a scholarship to Georgia Tech and play one year there before entering the NBA draft in 1996, was named MVP of the camp, just as he had been in Delaware. In the wake of his proximity to a racially motivated fight between Black and white teenagers, Garnett later that summer transferred to Farragut Career Academy in Chicago. But neither the incident nor his performance at the ABCD Camp did anything to hurt his standing as the one player in the class of 1995 who was seriously contemplating, and could seriously contemplate, bypassing college and entering the draft directly from high school. No player had done that since Darryl Dawkins and Bill Willoughby in 1975.

That 1994 ABCD Camp, though, might have been a more powerful statement for Kobe and his future, more influential to his rise, than it was to either of those more publicized players. There was no shell shock or timidity from him at FDU, just thoughtful questions during the critical-thinking and sports-psychology classes that the players took during the camp, just excellent play from beginning to end that earned him a place, on the final day, in the junior all-star game. Sonny Vaccaro himself couldn't stop shaking his head over it. This kid didn't play for a nationally renowned AAU team. The Sam Rines All-Stars were hot stuff in and around Philly, a good team, but they weren't Gary Charles's Long Island Panthers or Jimmy Salmon's Playaz—teams in New York and New Jersey that had reputations and esteem everywhere. And this kid, from a suburban high school that no one had heard of, had lived in Italy for eight years . . . he was practically a foreigner. Look at what he had done . . . and what he might do.

As the junior all-star game ended, and the mixture of players' families and New York, New Jersey, and Philadelphia residents who had flooded FDU to see the game filed out of the Rothman Center, the Bryant family—all of them: Joe and Pam and Sharia and Shaya and Kobe—stopped Sonny Vaccaro right there on the court. Joe gave him a hug, and Pam gave him a smile, but Kobe . . . Kobe grabbed him in a big, tight embrace, Vaccaro's face pressing against Kobe's left shoulder.

"Thank you very much, Mr. Vaccaro," Kobe said, "for allowing me to come to camp. And I apologize."

Vaccaro pushed him back gently. "Kobe," he said, "why are you apologizing?"

"Because I'm coming back next year, and I'm going to win the MVP for the whole camp."

"Kobe, God willing. I'll see you next year."

"*Se Dio vuole,*" Kobe said.

Vaccaro was taken aback. His heart warmed. The gears in his brain began to grind. "*Se Dio vuole*" means "God willing" in Italian, and it was a phrase that had been part of Vaccaro's vocabulary since his childhood. Whenever he left the house to play, to cause the mischief that little boys cause, he would say, *Mama, see you later,* before ducking out the door, and his mother would reply, *Se Dio vuole.* The interpretation and implication were obvious and unspoken: *You'll be back. You'll be here. You'll be alive. You'll be well. And I will be here, waiting for you.*

My teammates needed to see me as someone who never slouched in a drill, who never got complacent, and who never got too cocky. My sisters wouldn't have allowed that, anyway.

—KOBE BRYANT

10

OK,

LET'S PLAY

THE PEERS OF KOBE BRYANT'S past don't remember him as a Los Angeles Laker, as a five-time NBA champion, as a nonpareil of competitive nature who bestowed upon himself an audacious nickname—Mamba—that he built into an eponymous lifestyle brand. This was what Evan Monsky was insisting, the point he was driving home, one night over the phone. That Kobe was not their Kobe. That Kobe? Monsky couldn't be sure what that Kobe had in common with their Kobe. "People kissed this dude's ass from the time he was eighteen until his dying day," he said, "and it's a type of ass-kissing that's bonkers. It's not a normal life and not one that would be cherished by many. It seems absolutely horrible." And what did that life do to Kobe? How did it change him? Those who knew him when he was young remembered him a certain way. Was he still that person?

There is a part of Monsky, and perhaps of everyone who encountered Kobe at Lower Merion, that doesn't want the answers to those questions. The person whom Monsky remembered was a kid, a sixteen-year-old kid, who loved to talk hoops, who wasn't the funniest guy in the room but could crack a decent joke now and again, who got nervous whenever the vehicle he was traveling in, whether his car or his parents' car or a school bus full of basketball players, had to cross a bridge. Those memories aren't precious to Monsky because they're rare. They're precious to him because they aren't, because they're memories of a sixteen-year-old kid and not of the most famous athlete in the world. They're memories of a kid who shared a seat with him on afternoon rides to games and nighttime rides from games, who would glance out the window and whose lungs would expand and contract out of terror at the silvery water below. There was no explanation for Kobe's fear in those few seconds, none that he would admit to his teammates, anyway. But they would tease him about it as if he were just one of them, which in their minds he was and always would be, and he would white-knuckle it until the bus had safely reached the other side.

COME THE beginning of Kobe's junior year, it had become clear to Gregg Downer, even as he allowed himself to envision winning a district or even a state championship, that if the Aces were to reach such heights, he needed to make some changes, and his best player needed reinforcements. Some of those changes would occur and reinforcements would arrive naturally, just from the maturation of Kobe and several key players who would be returning for the 1994–95 school year and basketball season. Lower Merion's 16–6 record and even its district-playoff loss to Plymouth Whitemarsh, a strong team that qualified for the state-championship tournament, had reaffirmed to Downer and the upperclassmen that the Aces could be, and probably should be, among the best teams in the Philadelphia area and all of Pennsylvania. Downer spoke to his players often about aspiring to reach the semifinals of the District One tournament, because those two games were held annually at the Palestra, and to play at the Palestra was to experience and achieve something special. But he also recognized that the team was missing some important components, tangible and intangible, that it had to have not only to advance that far in the postseason but to win once it got there.

One such component showed up in the fall of 1994, when Dan Pangrazio transferred in for his freshman year after his family relocated to the Main Line. Pangrazio had been an athletic phenom as a preteen in his hometown of Fairfield, Connecticut. Already an elite soccer goalkeeper for his age, he was nine when he won the Connecticut and New England titles in the Elks Hoop Shoot, a free-throw-shooting contest sponsored nationally by the Benevolent and Protective Order of Elks—an accomplishment that *The New York Times* deemed worthy of a 671-word story in its April 9, 1989, edition. Pangrazio would step right into the starting lineup as the Aces' shooting guard, balancing the alignment of the offense and forcing opponents to honor his ability to make a long jumper, or several. As much of a blessing as Kobe's presence was, Downer and the Aces couldn't rely on him too much. What if he got in foul trouble? What if he suffered an injury? Downer liked to joke to people: *I'm one Kobe Bryant sprained ankle away from being a total schmuck.*

The boost of offense that Pangrazio was likely to provide would be welcome, but Downer's more urgent task was to improve the Aces' defense. Over their final eight games of the '93–'94 season, they had given up an average of seventy points, a figure that placed too much pressure on Kobe and his teammates to go basket for basket against teams that had more overall skill. Through the Narberth League, Downer had met Mike Egan, an Ardmore native who had just completed his second season as an assistant coach at Wilmington College, an NAIA program in New Castle, Delaware. Living in the Overbrook section of Philadelphia, working as an insurance underwriter in southern New Jersey, and coaching in northern Delaware made for an exhausting schedule, even for a guy like Egan, who was twenty-nine, single, and with few attachments and obligations. Coaching at Lower Merion would cut down the time he spent in his car, and it would allow him to work with Kobe; Egan had seen him play in Narberth summer ball and had played pickup against him at the Jewish Community Center. "I was like, 'This kid is worth going back to the high school ranks to coach,'" he said, and Downer made him an enticing offer: *Be my defensive coordinator. No basketball team that didn't play great half-court defense has ever won a championship. I'll give you twenty minutes every night to run practice, to coach your system your way.* Egan couldn't say no.

The third and final component on Downer's list was perhaps the most vital and profound. If the Aces were to contend with, let alone beat, the best competition in the region and the state, they had to become accustomed to playing such teams before the postseason rolled around. So Downer set to strengthening their nonconference schedule. They would have their sixteen annual games within the Central League, but Downer filled in any open date he could with a higher caliber of opponent: St. Anthony in Jersey City, led by Bob Hurley, Bobby Hurley's father and one of just three high school coaches to have been inducted into the Naismith Memorial Basketball Hall of Fame; Glen Mills, a youth detention center in Delaware County whose high school basketball team competed against public and private high schools throughout Pennsylvania; and Coatesville, with a blade-thin junior who was sharpening himself into one of the area's best guards: Richard "Rip" Hamilton. Downer had spent several days in Harrisburg the previous summer coaching a Philadelphia-area all-star team at the Keystone Games, which were akin to the Olympics of Pennsylvania. The kids he had coached there came from the city's perennial blue-chip boys' basketball programs and from one program located not within Philadelphia but just outside it: the Chester High School Clippers, the class of District One, the defending state champions. Those teams were similar to those Downer had added to Lower Merion's souped-up schedule. Those kids had an edge, a toughness, to which he wanted to expose his players. Kobe had it, but the rest of them needed to experience it, touch it. Chester, in particular, embodied that edge, that toughness, that excellence; its state championship, in 1994, was its third in twelve years. Already, Downer and Kobe were keeping their eyes on the Clippers, for the two of them regarded Chester as the standard they sought to reach, as the greatest threat to their achieving their goals.

ANTHONY GILBERT'S friendship with Kobe Bryant was born of Anthony Gilbert's gentle flirting with Sharia Bryant. There she was, a standout on Temple University's women's volleyball team, an outside hitter with that Bryant family leaping ability, thwacking one kill after another until she finished her career fifth on the Owls' all-time list, five foot ten with striking features but so approachable and down-to-earth off the court. There he was, a part-time freshman at Temple who was working in the university's athletic department to pay his way through school, who didn't know the first thing about volleyball when he started handling statistics and research for the team. He was five foot eight, which meant he not only looked up to Sharia, he looked up *at* Sharia. He was impressed with her, and he wanted to impress her.

"Look," he told her one day, "I'm from Philly. I play *ball*."

"Dude," she replied, "you couldn't even beat my little brother."

Gilbert had never heard of Kobe. He would soon. As with Kobe's basketball games, every available member of the Bryant and Cox families attended Sharia's volleyball matches. (The crowds at the matches were sparse, so the family's presence stood out even more than at Kobe's games.) Kobe sometimes didn't accompany them; basketball was too great a demand on his time. But after Gilbert and Sharia's tête-à-tête, Kobe showed up at his sister's next match at McGonigle Hall, picked up a volleyball, dribbled it like a basketball, and introduced himself to Gilbert in his own inimitable way.

"We can do this right now," he said.

What? Gilbert thought. *You're the younger brother? Who are you?*

From those awkward introductions to Sharia and Kobe in the fall of 1994, Gilbert became a contributor to *SLAM* magazine and a friend to Kobe and the entire Bryant family, admiring them for their unity among and loyalty to one another, giving himself a window into the family's dynamics and the disparate sides of Kobe's personality that only so many people shared. There was Kobe within basketball: cutthroat and cunning and bulletproof. And there was Kobe away from basketball: courteous and naive and sheltered. The split couldn't have been cleaner.

"A lot of people don't realize he was a big geek," Kobe's friend Dayna Tolbert said. "We never saw him as this big star. He was Kobe. We didn't act differently around him, and he didn't act any differently around us. The home videos that you can find him geeking around with his family, that was the real him. The Black Mamba that everyone sees on the court, that was competition. Those were two different things."

That dichotomy was at its starkest in Kobe's dating life, in that he didn't really have one. There was a girl, Jocelyn Ebron, whom he met at a family barbecue, who found him quiet and mild-mannered and became the closest thing Kobe had to a girlfriend through most of his high school years. At that barbecue, he didn't seem to have much *game,* didn't appear to be prowling for the latest pretty thing to put on his arm, and Ebron, a student at an all-girls Catholic high school, liked that. They spent most of their time together at the Bryants' house, where Ebron, who when she met him had hoped that Kobe wasn't the typical American guy, learned just how atypical he was. Their "dates," such as they were, consisted largely of Ebron doing exactly what Kobe's Lower Merion friends and teammates—Guy Stewart, Matt Matkov, Jermaine Griffin, Evan Monsky, others—would do when they were hanging out with him. She would take a seat on the couch next to Kobe as he watched videos of Magic and Michael and Kobe himself, from his games and workouts in Italy. Whatever moves he had, romantic or otherwise, were confined mostly to the court. Pam, Ebron noticed, did all of Kobe's laundry, made him his breakfast every morning, and made him the *same* breakfast every morning: bacon, eggs, and Cream of Wheat. "Everything sort of focused on him and around him," Ebron said in a 2003 interview with *Newsweek.* "His two sisters just seemed to accept that. He was the only son and the king of it all." Sharia and Shaya were protective of Kobe, sizing up and fending off any teenage girls who wished to get to know their brother more intimately. There were many with that wish. One could understand why, especially when Kobe, as was his habit whenever he was uncertain of himself or searching for words, flicked his tongue out of his mouth to lick his lips, adding a touch of vulnerability and soulfulness to his rich brown eyes and disarming smile. But even Ebron, a beautiful girl with an interest in Kobe, was regarded by the Bryants as an outsider, even though she was permitted, at times, within their circle. Sharia told Gilbert once that she didn't consider Ebron to be Kobe's official girlfriend, which suggests that Kobe didn't, either. Because she lived on Temple's campus, Sharia also took it upon herself to counsel him on how to negotiate the world outside leafy Wynnewood and the nearest basketball court. "She has this maternal instinct," Gilbert said, "and she learned a lot about the city and how it moved, how we talked and spoke and dressed. She passed it on and translated it to Kobe, who was still kind of green on a lot of things, just in terms of being a young Black kid around the city. You say certain things, and he's just kind of quiet. But on the basketball court, OK, this guy does talk."

As their friendship deepened, Gilbert, by Kobe's design, would talk *at* him nearly as much as he talked *to* him. *Hey,* Gilbert might ask, *wanna go hang out on South Street? Let's go meet some girls.* He knew the answer already: No chance. Gilbert was from West Philadelphia, so he was familiar with Kobe's real haunts, the places where Kobe enjoyed himself most: Remington Park, Ardmore Park, Tustin Playground. Drive to South Philly? Why do that when Kobe had the keys to the Jewish Community Center? For Kobe, experiencing the city didn't mean taking in the tattoo parlors and the record stores and the social scene along the main drags in town. It meant having Gilbert join him at the JCC or those playgrounds. It meant having Gilbert rebound each of Kobe's shots and snap chest passes to him. And it meant having Gilbert, while Kobe was shooting and driving and refining his footwork, mimic the insults that Kobe heard either to his face or behind his back.

You're good, but you don't play in the Public League.
Dribble . . . dribble . . .
You live in the suburbs.
Spin . . .
You go to a white school.
Swish.
There's no competition there.
Hard dribble . . . hard dribble . . .
You're not one of us.
Dunk.

This was Kobe's emotional chain mail, his defense against the criticism he heard that he wasn't hard enough, wasn't Black enough, wasn't worthy of respect from the players who shared his skin color but assumed they had little else in common with him. "His family was loved wherever they went," Gilbert said. "They didn't have an air about them. They were loved and respected because they embraced everybody. Kobe never really had that 'Black experience' like my friends and I had, but the disrespect that he got from the city had more to do with his zip code than his basketball skill set. Kids his age in the city playing in the Public League, playing in the summer leagues, they were like, 'Listen, Kobe, you're good. People write about you. But you don't play in the Public League. You go to a white high school. You live in the suburbs. I don't care what anybody says, you're not one of us.' Basketball was his way of getting vindication: 'You know what? Y'all are right. I'm none of those things. But once this ball goes up in the air, I'm going to show y'all who's Black and who's not.' He knew he wasn't like anybody else, but he used that to his advantage. If somebody was mouthing off, he was quiet, and it was like, 'OK, are you done? Because we're about to play now.' And that would throw anybody off. Most guys would be ready to fight, but Kobe was like, 'Is that it? OK. Let's play.'"

More, it was his way of honoring and defending the reputation of the person who had introduced him to basketball and fostered his obsession with the sport: his father. Joe had bounced from team to team because those teams didn't believe they could trust him. Joe had never established any staying power in the NBA. Joe had to go to Europe, go into exile, to reach his highest heights. Kobe was determined to equip himself with the right skills and attitude and ethic to avoid the same fate. *They're not going to have a question about who I am, what they should do with me, and where I belong. I'm going to work so hard that they never forget the Bryant name.* "He wanted to be like his dad and to redeem his dad," Gilbert said. "It was an homage to Joe." And there was no time to waste in following this road map to a father's redemption and a son's greatness. Once, Kobe told Gilbert that he had certain benchmarks that he wanted to reach, things he wanted to do in his life, and he wanted to do them all while he was young. He wanted to get to the NBA while he was young. He wanted to marry while he was young. He wanted to have children while he was young. He didn't want to wait to be a man, on his terms alone. "That was his mantra," Gilbert said, "and that's how he attacked things. He was on a different page from everybody else." He wanted to do everything early, but first, he had to do something else, for his high school and its burgeoning basketball program: win a championship.

ENTERING KOBE'S junior season, the coaching staff signaled his standing within and importance to the Aces by naming him team captain. Not a team captain. *The* team captain. Not all of his teammates greeted the decision with understanding and aplomb. Monsky had presumed that, as seniors, he and Guy Stewart—the former outspoken, the latter a lead-by-example type—would share the duties of captaincy, and he was hurt that the coaches had bypassed them for Kobe. It was the first of a few occasions of tension and haughtiness in the season's early going. Kobe had gotten ahead of himself in an interview with Stacy Moscotti, a reporter for *The Merionite,* when he boasted that the Aces had a very good chance of winning a state championship. "I look around at those other teams," he said, "and they're not close to as good as we are." Through his first few practices with the team, Egan scribbled his impressions of each player in black felt-tip pen on loose-leaf paper, and his evaluations of Kobe revealed the new assistant coach to be an unforgiving grader: "offensive, foul prone; lateral movement; work on rebounding, shot selection . . . lackluster play, <u>must</u> rebound more, dominate from 15 ft + in + then 3 will come. You are only as good as your intensity. Don't be sloppy." Then, in some karmic retribution for Kobe's comments to *The Merionite,* the Aces opened their season of greater expectations with a 62–60 loss to Sun Valley, a game in which they squandered a fourth-quarter lead and Kobe, with thirty-one points, and Dan Pangrazio, with sixteen, combined for 78 percent of the offense. That distribution suggested that the team was still too top-heavy, that the same question that for two years had hovered over Downer's head like an anvil—when is there too much Kobe, and when is there too little?—still hung there, unanswered. Before the team's second game, its first Central League game of the season, against Upper Darby, Downer and Egan pulled Kobe aside and urged him to be more vocal with his teammates, to involve them more. Kobe told them that he would show his leadership through his play.

What he showed them, over the next two months, was stunning. He averaged more than thirty points a game over the Aces' next three games, each a victory with a margin of at least fourteen points. He entered his next game, against Marple Newtown, five days before Christmas, knowing that he had 994 career points, six away from one thousand, and after he hit his first two shots, he tightened up, missing his next three and committing a turnover, his anxiousness over reaching the milestone causing him to press. Finally, he flushed a jump shot from near the foul line with three and a half minutes left in the first quarter. Lower Merion won, 63–58. He had thirty-eight points, a career high, which he then eclipsed two nights later, scoring forty in a thirteen-point win at Penncrest that was more noteworthy for something else, something darker: The game featured what can be reliably called the first documented and sustained public criticism of and backlash toward Kobe Bryant in his life, and to call what happened "criticism" is to be kind.

In 1986, the NCAA had enacted Proposition 48, a rule that a high school student who wished to play Division I sports in college had to meet certain standards, in his or her grades and SAT score, to qualify academically. The minimum SAT requirement, for instance, was 700 points when a perfect score was 1600. Quickly, "a Prop 48 kid" became racist, stereotypical shorthand to insult a basketball player, almost always a Black basketball player, by labeling him or her as too stupid to be admitted to college. So it didn't take long, once the referee tossed the ball up for the opening tip-off, for a group of Penncrest fans, white Penncrest fans, to start flinging racial epithets and chanting at Kobe: "PROP 48! PROP 48!"

As usual, the entire Bryant clan was there, clustered together. But it wasn't the sensitive Joe or the fiery Pam who betrayed any obvious anger or dismay or who leaped to Kobe's defense. It was Shaya, the high school senior, the reticent middle sister, stretching her six-foot-two frame into a flagpole to stand up in the Lower Merion section of the bleachers and shout back . . .

"Sure, but my brother's an honor student. What do you have to say about that?"

Lakers fans write messages on a Los Angeles mural honoring
Kobe in February 2020.

Three members of the '95–96 Lower Merion Aces, from left to right: Oral Williams, Jermaine Griffin, Kobe Bryant COURTESY OF MIKE AND CONNIE EGAN

From left to right: Gregg Downer, Kobe, Jermaine Griffin, Mike Egan COURTESY OF MIKE AND CONNIE EGAN

Kobe fell in love with soccer during his childhood years in Italy.

Mike Egan, shown here between Kobe and Jermaine Griffin, joined Gregg Downer's staff as an assistant coach in 1994.

The 1995–96 Lower Merion Aces

The Aces got off to a slow start in Kobe's senior season, losing three of their first eight games.

Several of Kobe's teammates had never been on a plane before the Aces' trip to Myrtle Beach in December 1995.

Kobe throws down a left-handed dunk during the Beach Ball Classic slam dunk contest.

A rare stint on the bench

By the time he was a senior, Kobe had become the most recognizable and popular figure at Lower Merion.

Kobe particularly enjoyed his English and public-speaking classes with his mentor, Jeanne Mastriano.

Gregg Downer instructs his players with assistant coaches Mike Egan and Jeremy Treatman (far right) looking on. Kobe and the Aces wore warm-up shirts with No. 53 on them, a reminder that Lower Merion had last won a state championship 53 years earlier, in 1943.

Kobe led a big second-half comeback for the Aces in the '96 district-championship game, avenging their loss to Chester a year earlier.

ABOVE: At first, Gregg Downer had Kobe bring the ball up against Chester's press in the 1996 District One championship game. Because the Aces were losing at halftime, Downer changed that strategy.

OPPOSITE: Kobe rises for a dunk over a Chester defender.

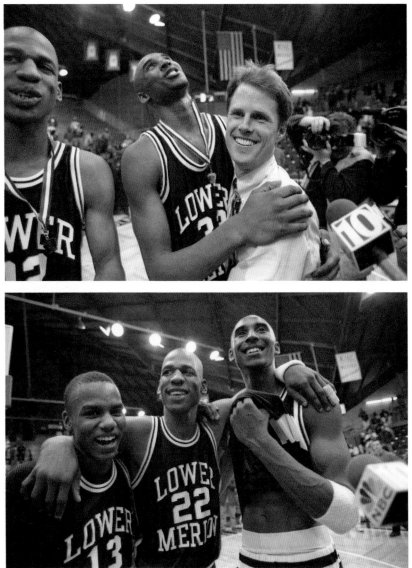

COURTESY OF AL TIELEMANS

OPPOSITE: Kobe scored 34 points and had 11 rebounds against Chester in the 1996 district-championship game.

AT TOP: Kobe celebrates the 1996 district championship with Gregg Downer and Jermaine Griffin (left).

ABOVE: With Emory Dabney (left) and Jermaine Griffin (center)

Kobe, hanging out at school, his muse by his side   COURTESY OF AL TIELEMANS

Kobe splits two Erie Cathedral Prep defenders in the 1996 state-championship game. He scored just 17 points, which matched his second-lowest point total for any game his senior season.   COURTESY OF MIKE AND CONNIE EGAN

Kobe sank two clutch free throws to tie the state-championship game.

Kobe, Gregg Downer, Mike Egan, and Jermaine Griffin celebrate at the Aces'
state-championship parade.

Kobe poses at the 1996 McDonald's All-American banquet.

Kobe, just moments after the Charlotte Hornets
selected him with the 13th pick in the 1996
NBA Draft

TOP: Kobe returned to Lower Merion once a year or so, to catch up with his old coach.

BOTTOM: When Gregg Downer learned that he was going to be a "girl-dad," Kobe was one of the first people he told.

LOWER MERION HIGH SCHOOL

Kobe returned to his alma mater when Lower Merion retired his jersey.

LOWER 33 MERION

ACES

Lower Merion retired Kobe's No. 33 jersey in 2002.

Nothing, as it turned out. The chant stopped.

It was only the beginning, though. Kobe's profile was getting higher, as were the stakes for everyone involved, the Bryants included. Kobe's games had become such a priority for the family that Shaya—the starting center on the girls' basketball team, averaging more than thirteen points a game herself—skipped a couple of her own games to go to Kobe's. "And, of course, we would lose," said Tolbert, who was one of Shaya's teammates, "because she was who everyone feared, and I was only five ten. The machine around him was extremely tight-knit." Tales of Kobe's talent now spilled out across Philadelphia and its suburbs from locker-room gossip and coaches' meetings and college scouts' insight swaps, so much of the chatter organic. Jeremy Treatman, still stringing for *The Inquirer,* still talking with Joe regularly and checking in with Kobe once a week, still visiting Lower Merion's practices and games, couldn't persuade his editors that Kobe warranted a major profile piece or even increased attention, but he soon had an alternative medium available to him: He had begun working as a producer and on-air reporter for *The Inquirer High School Sports Show,* a weekly TV program that the paper sponsored and that highlighted local athletes. Once the district playoffs rolled around and interest started to increase, he could tell Kobe's story there. Until then, to be in the know about Kobe, you had to be on the ground, going to the games or reading the local dailies and weeklies on the Main Line and in Delaware County. Nevertheless, mouths were spreading the word.

In the championship game of the Ardmore Rotary Tournament, just before the new year, Lower Merion trailed Malvern Prep by six points at halftime and four points after the third quarter. Early on, with Kobe off to an ice-cold start—he missed twelve of his first fifteen shots—a gaggle of Malvern students and fans tried to rattle him with another chant, one less demeaning than Penncrest's: "OVERRATED! OVERRATED!" Silence would have been the more prudent course of action. The Aces dominated Malvern in the fourth quarter, pulling away to win, 71–64, and though Stewart had nineteen points and Pangrazio kicked in ten, one player was the difference in the game, and it wasn't either of them. Kobe scored twenty points in the final quarter and finished with thirty-six. He wasn't just racking up gaudy offensive numbers or pulling off breathtaking plays and moves for his own amusement. He was making his team better than it had been in a generation or more, and short of having Kobe scrimmage with his eyes closed and paperweights taped to his legs, Downer found himself struggling to create scenarios and obstacles that would provide Kobe a genuine test. Because Monsky and Stewart complemented each other so well in the backcourt, Kobe frequently played down low on offense, posting up shorter opponents, which led Downer to have Brendan Pettit, a hulking six-foot-five sophomore who played mostly for the JV team, not only practice with the varsity squad but also guard Kobe. Pettit considered himself a tough player who wouldn't back down from anyone, and he was not above throwing an elbow or two if it meant grabbing a rebound or intimidating an opponent. He did the same to Kobe, and several times, the jostling between the two nearly led to a fistfight. But other than Pettit and his size and tenacity, none of Kobe's other teammates could offer him much resistance, and instead of a head coach having to inspire his team's most gifted player, Downer felt he had to prove his own competitiveness and work ethic to Kobe. So he egged him into three-point and trick-shot contests after each practice, then begged Egan and Pangrazio to join them: two-on-two, coaches versus players. *Can you make a half-court shot? Can you bank one in from the baseline?* These weren't goof-off, time-wasting sessions. Kobe thrived on them, and Downer believed that he had to show him that he could coach him with the same discipline and authority that he coached the rest of the team, and beating Kobe in a game of H-O-R-S-E, humbling him once in a while just as Joe used to in the Bryants' driveway, was one of the best ways to remind him who was boss. "I needed to challenge him," Downer said. "I couldn't baby him. 'If you want all these things, if you want the NBA and the greatness we've talked about, you've got to let me coach you tough. I'm going to be hard on you. There are standards here, and you need to follow them.' All the shooting after practice, that helped." The contests carried on so long that Downer, Egan, and the other assistants started arguing, just as practice was ending, over who had time to stay and shoot with Kobe for a couple of hours—*Hey, man, I've got work to do. . . . Yeah, but I'm supposed to meet my girlfriend at seven*—and Pam started calling Downer and the school's new principal, Jack Maher, to complain that they were keeping her son late at school, when it was the other way around.

"That's why he'll be different from his father," Joe Bryant Sr. told a reporter at the time. "I remember Joe was a great player in high school and college, but Kobe, he's doing things now that Joe started doing in his first year in college."

The Aces' winning streak had stretched to eight games ahead of the first of their two games of the season against Ridley, whose coach, John DiGregorio, had provided Kobe with another injection of motivation. *If you hold Kobe to fifteen points,* DiGregorio had told a local newspaper, *you'll win by thirty.* Kobe considered the theory a demeaning slight against his teammates, and after Monsky picked up four early fouls, including a technical, consigning himself to the bench from the second quarter until the fourth, Kobe took over for him at point guard and took pleasure in the role as the offense's facilitator. "Dan told me he was feeling it," Kobe said after the game, "so I started looking for him." Double-teamed all night, he would drive into the lane and kick the ball out to Pangrazio, alone in the corner, for a three-pointer or slip a pass down low to Griffin. Rob Knox, the correspondent covering the game for *The Philadelphia Inquirer,* had seen Kobe play before, but he had not seen *this* Kobe play before. "He didn't have to score," Knox recalled. "I'm sure he could have scored if he wanted to, but that was a game where he really trusted his teammates." This time in a Lower Merion–Ridley matchup, there was no embarrassing finish with just four players on the court. There was no heartbreak, no buzzer-beater, no clutch foul shot to crush the Aces' spirits. This time, there was Pangrazio with a career-high twenty-three points, and there was Griffin with ten, and there was Kobe, scoring just fifteen points but, miracle of miracles, collecting seventeen assists in a 59–37 rout, finding open shooters just for the sake of shoving DiGregorio's own words back in his face. Then, later that week, in a 90–61 blasting of Strath Haven, he returned to his customary style of play, with a box-score line for the ages:

fourteen made field goals in eighteen attempts, ten made free throws in eleven attempts, forty points, eight rebounds, four blocked shots . . . all without playing a second in the fourth quarter because Lower Merion entered the frame with a thirty-four-point lead. Downer sat him for mercy's sake, not knowing how many points Kobe had. "Someday," he said after the game, "he'll get fifty." The part of the performance that pleased Kobe most, though, was the two three-pointers he hit. He hadn't made one in six games, and he was relieved to rediscover his shooting stroke. "I needed that," he said.

Still, those victories in the Central League, as satisfying as they were, were never going to be the truest measure of Kobe's and the Aces' standing in the state. Those non-league games that Downer had scheduled would be, and they had been on the collective mind of the coaching staff since the preseason, so much so that they influenced Egan's defensive strategy and stretched Kobe's patience and stubbornness to their limits. Egan's system called for the guards and forwards to pressure the ball and lure the dribbler into a double-team or trap, and it called for Kobe, playing in the post, to front his man at all times. At first, Kobe didn't understand Egan's thinking, arguing that he should play behind his opponent. "I'll block every shot," he said, and at one preseason practice that Joe happened to attend, Joe raised the same objection. Egan explained his reasoning to both of them: First, the main purpose of the defense was to speed up the opposing team's offense, to harass it into bad decisions, to force turnovers and rushed shots. To do that, Kobe had to be able to sprint out to the wing or the baseline to create a double-team, and he couldn't do that if he was playing behind his man in the post. Second, having Kobe try to snuff out every shot would be fine against the land-bound centers and power forwards of the Central League. But a superior team, with bigger, more athletic, and more refined post players, would go right at him, which risked putting Kobe in foul trouble. Egan's discussion with the Bryants lasted ten minutes. "That sounds great," Joe said. "I like that." It was the last time he questioned Downer or Egan about anything, and Kobe never played behind his man in the post again.

Now, here was the first opportunity for the 11–1 Aces to put that preparation to the test: on the road on a late Saturday afternoon against Rip Hamilton and a 12–3 Coatesville team. Nothing about the setting was comfortable or comforting for them. The gym felt like the Louisiana Superdome compared to their cozier venue. It included a scoreboard that flashed the numbers of the players who were on the court and that kept track of their points and fouls, a mind-blowing sight for the Aces. The teams had no recent history against each other. They were supposed to have played the season before, but the game had been canceled because of an ice storm, which meant that Hamilton remained as mythical and mysterious a figure to most of Kobe's coaches and teammates as Kobe remained to Hamilton's. Downer told the Aces that the Coatesville star—crafty, with a quicksilver game, penetrating and setting up teammates one minute, shredding a defense with drives and midrange jumpers the next—would be the best player they would face all season. Likewise, when someone had first told Hamilton that there was a guard at Lower Merion who was his age, who was his size, who had better shooting range and more jazz to his game, who could do everything Hamilton could do and a few things he couldn't, it had seemed incomprehensible to him. Hamilton had rarely played a game of basketball outside of Coatesville. He hadn't been tutored and cosseted as Kobe had—he had shown up to his first high school basketball tryout wearing platform shoes without heels—and he had struggled to process the possibility that, compared to anyone, he was the lesser player. *Lower Merion? There are no kids there from the kind of neighborhood where I grew up,* Hamilton thought. *It's like a private school. He's still not as good as me. He still can't outplay me.*

"You hear so much about a kid who's good," said Rick Hicks, a Coatesville assistant coach, "and you think you've got one of the best players in the area. Skill-wise, you're thinking, 'Somebody's better than him? Gotta see him.' It was Kobe's whole swag, and I ain't talking about an arrogant swag. It was, 'I'm telling you I'm going to steal the ball, and I steal it. I'm telling you I'm going to do this, and I do it.'"

Kobe's performance that afternoon embodied that ethos. The Red Raiders played a box-and-one against him, and during one time-out,

Downer told the rest of the team, *You guys are going to have to make open shots for us to win*. Stewart, Pangrazio, and Jermaine Griffin did; the trio combined for forty-three points, each scoring in double figures, and Lower Merion led by two with less than ten seconds left in regulation. But Hamilton, from the right wing, made a balletic spin move, ducked under Kobe, and dropped in a layup with five seconds to go, sending the game to overtime. He fouled out with seventy-five seconds left in the extra period, finishing with twenty-one points, but Coatesville still forged a four-point lead after his departure. In the NBA, even in college basketball, a four-point deficit in a game's final minute is far from insurmountable. In high school basketball, a four-point deficit in a game's final minute meant the Aces were pretty much dead meat. Pretty much.

Twenty-five years later, Jim "Scoogie" Smith could see it all clearly in his mind's eye, and it still brought him a pang of pain and admiration. Like Hicks, Smith was an assistant coach for Coatesville that day—he took over as head coach the following year—and he was on his feet as a Lower Merion player pulled down a defensive rebound and hit Kobe in stride with an outlet pass. Kobe darted to his right toward the sideline and, after four dribbles, crossed half-court. "The thing that was so awesome," Smith said, "was that once he got over half-court, he didn't do what most players do. He didn't launch a shot with one hand. He took another one and a half, two dribbles at most, and he shot a jump shot."

Kobe was right in front of Smith and Hicks and the Coatesville bench, twenty-five feet from the basket, when he rose to shoot. Hicks thought, *There's no way in hell that shot's going in.*

The shot went in.

It was now a one-point game. The Aces committed a foul to stop the clock. A Red Raiders player missed the front end of a one-and-one. Kobe gathered in the rebound and, again, pushed the ball up court along the right sideline. This time, he cut back to his left, dodging a defender near the free-throw line, and slipped into the lane, pulling up for a six-foot jumper. The ball fell like a feather through the basket's netting with two seconds left on the clock. Lower Merion 78, Coatesville 77. Back at home later that night, Hamilton replayed the game in his head, comparing himself to Kobe and finding himself wanting. *Bro, you ain't what you thought you were.*

"That might have been," Egan said, "the best basketball game we played in all of Kobe's years."

The Aces took their showers, changed, and carried their duffel bags out to the court to greet their family members mingling there. Monsky had played the entire game without scoring, and Shaya Bryant looked up at Coatesville's giant scoreboard, still glowing with the players' final statistics. There, next to the No. 31, Monsky's jersey number, was a 0. Next to Kobe's No. 33 was a 32. Shaya seized the opportunity to tease her younger brother's teammate.

"Zero points, Ev?" she said. "You've got to be kidding me."

"Shaya," Monsky said. "They don't keep assists there."

Despite Monsky's deadpan retort, the jab pricked his pride a bit. First Kobe was named a captain ahead of him. Now Shaya was busting his stones? How many times did Monsky have to be reminded that he wasn't on equal footing with Kobe? The sting didn't linger much longer, though. Before another game later that month, as the teams' captains conferred with the referees at half-court, Kobe ducked out, scurried back to the huddle, and grabbed Monsky and Stewart. "Come on," he told them. "We're going to the circle." From then until the season's end, Monsky and Stewart joined him there before every game.

"That always stuck with me," Monsky said later. "Being a captain of a high school team—who gives a shit? You shake hands with the other captains. It's nothing. But to a seventeen-year-old kid, it matters, and for him to go out of his way to bring us in was really something I appreciated. I never got to mention that to him."

A RIP-ROARING start—victories in their first five games—hinted that the La Salle Explorers might be returning to a place of prominence in Philadelphia basketball and, relatively speaking, in the country. Instead, the team would stagger to a .500 record, 13–13, ahead of the 1995 Midwestern Collegiate Conference tournament. The mediocre season was a microcosm of the circumstances and poor decision making plaguing the program, students and alumni apathetic about seeing the team face opponents from Illinois and Wisconsin, opponents that had no rivalries with or emotional connection to La Salle and East Coast basketball fans. The Civic Center held ten thousand people; the Explorers were fortunate if they drew two thousand for a game. One night, a Philadelphia sportswriter perused the cavernous arena from the press row and quipped, "You know, if you put everybody in this place on the court, no one would get called for three seconds."

Speedy Morris's decision to hire Joe Bryant as an assistant coach wasn't yielding any material benefits, either. The players liked him—who didn't like Joe on a surface, personal level?—but his coaching duties and diligence about his job often appeared less important to him than Kobe's next game was. At one practice, while the Explorers were honing a set play on offense, Joe stepped into the middle of the drill and delivered a hard pick on senior Paul Burke, the team's starting point guard, that sent Burke tumbling to the floor.

"Joe," Morris said, "what the hell are you doing?"

THE NOTION that basketball didn't rate more than a passing interest from Lower Merion's student body or surrounding community was fading with every victory, every spectacular Kobe moment. The school's tenor and culture were realigning, removing a stigma of arrogance and intimidation associated with athletics, and he was at the center of the shift. Dan Gross, a member of Kobe's class, who went on to become a gossip columnist for the *Philadelphia Daily News,* was a punk-music aficionado and had not followed any of the school's sports teams, preferring instead on weekends to join his friends for concerts at fire halls, in church basements, or at the Trocadero, a historic theater in the Chinatown section of Philadelphia. "But there was something about this," he recalled. "It was infectious knowing there was someone who was so good at your school. Watching Kobe play at that level, destroying every other person in high school, that was the thing that made us pay attention for the first time." One of Maher's first mandates as principal was to do away with Freshman Day and its attendant hazing, and it helped the cause that in the boys' basketball program, in what was emerging as the most popular sport on campus, the head coach had never allowed hazing in the first place and the best player, universally perceived as respectful of teachers and students alike, had never participated in it. "Sports had gotten run down some at Lower Merion, for whatever reason," Maher said, "and I think that made it OK again. It was OK to try out for sports. You didn't have to go to a private school and play. You could stay at Lower Merion and play." With the annual three-on-three Hoop It Up competition approaching, with Kobe's teams having won it three years running, Maher bumped into him one morning outside the principal's office and asked if he'd be competing in the event. "I don't know," Kobe told him. Maher suggested that, rather than dominate the tournament again and leave the other students frustrated over the inevitable outcome, Kobe should referee instead. He agreed. "He understood who he was," Maher said.

When it came to basketball, there was little doubt of that. Sterling Carroll, the captain of the track team, who once had considered pranking Kobe on Freshman Day but thought better of it, tried to recruit Kobe to run track. "At least you could do the high jump," Carroll told him. But Kobe wouldn't bite. "He was one of the most focused people I've ever seen," Carroll said, "but he was strictly focused on basketball." One afternoon, Jimmy Black, an assistant coach at Notre Dame, came to a practice to scout Kobe. Afterward, he introduced himself to Kobe, who was cordial but hardly enthusiastic. When he gave Kobe a ride home that night, Egan asked him if he knew who Black was. "Yeah, assistant at Notre Dame," Kobe said, slumped in the front passenger seat. *There's more to him than that,* Egan pointed out. Black had been the starting point guard on North Carolina's 1982 national-championship team . . . with Michael Jordan. Suddenly, Kobe sat up, a surge of excitement running through him. "He played with Mike?" he said. "Oh, my God! Where is he now? Can we go talk to him?" The prospect of playing basketball for and getting a degree from the nation's most prestigious Catholic university had no purchase with him. Black's familiarity with and proximity to Jordan was what counted to Kobe. "He wasn't really that interested in Notre Dame," Egan said, "or Jimmy Black, for that matter."

When it came to everything else in his life—his identity, his intellect, his social life—Kobe was still learning, still probing. Only in certain circumstances and situations, with certain people, did he let his guard down and open up, a posture that his friends and family believed stemmed from his sense that he was different from other teenagers, from his recognition that he needed time to assimilate into American culture. "When he came from Italy," his classmate and friend Susan Freeland said, "we could be rude, talk fast, talk over each other. I mean, we're from Philly. That's not normal there in Italy. He was still learning English. He was quieter. He came to us as thoughtful." It would be facile to think that his future in basketball was the only thing on his mind, that his obsession with the sport occupied every aspect of his existence. It is better and more accurate to frame greatness in the sport as a destination toward which he kept himself steered, and to understand that, to assist him on the passage, he would marshal whatever resources and skills were available to him. Getting after-school tutoring for a geometry class wasn't a chore but a challenge. Egan asked him how it was going. "Good, really good," Kobe told him. "This shit is *fun*." Scoring 1080 on his SATs was to him not a benchmark that, combined with his athletic prowess, would gain him entrance to Duke or Notre Dame or another Ivy League–caliber university. It was a reflection, instead, of who he was and what he might yet do. He could go to any college he chose, and he would thrive there. But he didn't *have* to go.

"It's like the saying, too much of one thing can be bad, right?" his cousin John Cox said. "Not for him, because you knew that was his passion. He found his passion early, but he was still rounded enough. He read. He was a big reader. Read everything. It was more focused on people who were masters of their craft, to see what they did and how they were getting ahead, picking up little things. He was still doing it for basketball, but that wasn't all. He was reading to help himself be more articulate and educated. Since he wasn't sacrificing by going out and going to parties, he would still kick back and spend time with his family. That kept him real grounded to where we didn't think he was OD'ing on ball. It didn't seem like an overdose. He did work hard, but he still had balance."

He would show up to meetings of Student Voice when he could, stopping by the library to ask Katrina Christmas, the organization's moderator, what topics were on the next agenda. When he did attend, it wasn't as if he were taking over and running the meeting, but he would sit in a desk and unfurl those long legs of his into the aisle, raise his hand to contribute to the discussion and make suggestions, joke and laugh, and Christmas appreciated that, even with his devotion to basketball, he would make the effort to be there. Deirdre Bobb, a year younger than Kobe and a member of Student Voice, noticed that Kobe always seemed to have at least one girl following him into the meeting or from class to class. He liked the attention, but he seemed to be modest about it; Bobb liked that about him. Christmas noticed something else: Several Black male students, some West Philly–born, some Ardmore-raised, didn't like Kobe. They doubted and questioned his racial credibility. It was a charge that he couldn't escape either on the basketball court or in the halls of his high school.

"Jealousy—they were jealous," Christmas said. "They were saying, 'He don't know how to play no ball because he'd never been in the streets playing ball.' They distinguished him playing ball from them playing street ball. 'You're a different animal when you play ball in the street. You get pushed. You get knocked down. You get bloody.' They were saying he was the cutesy person. I understood what they were saying, but they didn't know his heart.

"That goes along with being Black and having to go into a different type of circle. You always feel like you have to prove yourself. I'm sure there are days when it made him sad. That stuff gets to you after a while. It really does. It really gets to you that people will judge you by what they see on the outside and not on the inside. Now, you have to do whatever you can do to show them, 'Hey, man, I'm human just like you.'"

He just happened to be a kid who defied categorization, who relished being an individual, who was content to connect with anyone through whatever interest or trait they might have in common, as long as he could funnel it back to his compulsion, to the thing he loved most. In February 1995, Student Voice's choir performed a concert to coincide with Black History Month, showcasing the music of Aretha Franklin, Lena Horne, and Cab Calloway. After hearing Bobb sing, Kobe approached her with a proposition: Would she perform the national anthem before a basketball game? Bobb was initially reluctant, but once she did it the first time, Kobe insisted that she sing the anthem before every Lower Merion game, that he would not take the floor without hearing her voice first. "It became so passionate," Bobb said, "that I made sure I was at every game, even away games. He would go up to the officials, 'Listen: I have a girl in that audience, and her voice is phenomenal. I want her to sing and open up this game before the team comes out.' I just felt really honored." Each time, Bobb would keep her eyes closed throughout the anthem until the final verses, when she would open them. Always, she would find the basketball team and look at Kobe, his head bowed, his eyes closed, too. Always, once she finished, "he would open his eyes," she said, "and give me the biggest smile and give me two thumbs up." *All right, Deirdre. I'm ready to go.*

THE COATESVILLE win was the Aces' twelfth consecutive victory, and the streak would continue for another nine games, stretching to twenty-one, lifting the program to a level with which its coaches and players and followers were not familiar. Chester still loomed over the entire district; the Clippers had lost five games, sure, but they played such a strong schedule that no one, Kobe and Downer least of all, was under any illusions about how good they really were. Nevertheless, the variety of and reasons for the string of wins only caused the team's confidence to swell. Griffin scored twenty-five and twenty-four points in back-to-back games, one an eleven-point victory over Glen Mills, the other a twelve-point victory over Haverford in which Kobe, stricken with the flu, spent much of the game spitting clumps of phlegm into a paper bag, shivering so much as he sat on the bench that Pam draped her red shawl over him. He still scored thirty-six points. Pangrazio hit eight straight fourth-quarter free throws to beat Marple Newtown. In the 76–70 victory over Ridley that clinched Lower Merion's first league championship in more than a decade, Kobe set his latest career high in points, with forty-two. "We felt like this was our year," he said. Dave Rosenberg, whose parents weren't originally from the area, had little knowledge of Philadelphia-area high school basketball and the region's rivalries. He was puzzled to see Downer and Egan and the other Aces coaches reacting to the Ridley victory as if they'd won the Super Bowl, and he wasn't the only player who was.

"Ridley was in the league," Rosenberg said, "and Kobe said, 'Ridley's not the one you want to beat.'"

Lower Merion's last regular-season game, against St. Anthony in Jersey City, was hardly a typical warm-up for the postseason. Perennially ranked among the top ten high school teams in the nation, the Friars were 19–2, and if Downer hoped that facing them on their turf, on their terms, would be a good gauge of his team's talent and toughness, the game ended up testing the Aces' resolve more than he could have imagined. Stewart didn't play—he had the flu—and in the second quarter, Monsky motored in on a partial breakaway and, as he jumped to bank in a layup, collided with a St. Anthony player. Bracing himself as he fell, he chipped a bone in his left wrist when he landed and missed the remainder of the game.

Hurley had never seen Kobe play in person before; despite having a cadre of friends and tipsters and hangers-on throughout basketball, he had just one scouting report on him. "We didn't have much information," Hurley said, "other than he was a great individual player." Hurley's teams played only man-to-man defense, and to motivate his players and try to make the task of containing Kobe appear more manageable, he exhorted them in the huddle, *Had a lot of players better than that guy come into this gym over the years.* Egan overheard what Hurley said and interpreted it as an insult to Kobe, but the Friars set to proving their coach correct. They held Kobe to twenty-two points and never trailed in their 83–67 win, and for Lower Merion, the cost beyond the final score had been substantial. Monsky would have to play with his left arm in a cast that, to protect his injured wrist, he kept wrapped in Styrofoam, and the district playoffs began just two nights later. The Aces were 21–3 and the No. 2 seed in the thirty-two-team tournament, behind only Chester. But they wouldn't be at full strength, and more pressure would be on Kobe than ever before, against the ones they wanted to beat.

I decided to spend most of my free time—nights, weekends—going to gyms and playing basketball. By myself.

—KOBE BRYANT

11
THE
PIT

THERE WAS NO SUCH THING as a short road trip for the 1994–95 Philadelphia 76ers, and when John Lucas, their coach and general manager, returned in late February from one—three games in five days, all on the West Coast—he greeted a surprising assertion from his wife, Debbie, with a mixture of exhaustion and bemusement. Those Sixers were terrible, the sort of terrible that seems amusing only in retrospect. They would go 24–58 and finish sixth out of the seven teams in the NBA's Atlantic Division; in many respects, they were embarrassingly retrograde in their thinking and culture. Nineteen players would appear in at least one game for them. Shawn Bradley, a center whom the team had selected with the No. 2 overall pick in the 1993 draft, struggled so much to build upper-body strength and gain weight that the training staff would bring cheesecakes to shootarounds and practices for him. He'd stuff his face, then throw up.

In temperament, in philosophy, in personal history, Lucas might have been the perfect coach for such a crew. A recovering drug and alcohol addict whose demons haunted and nearly destroyed his fourteen-year NBA playing career, he was upbeat to the point of Pollyanna, believing deeply that every human being was capable of redemption, no matter how severe or damaging his or her mistakes. *You learn humility,* he liked to say, *when you're passed out on the bathroom floor and your children have to step over you in the morning.* He was willing to see things in people, and in basketball players, that others might not—admirable qualities all, even if they didn't make him a particularly good coach. The Sixers had lost all three games on the trip, the last by thirty points in Denver to the Nuggets. The defeats were taking their toll on Lucas, but there were still silver linings to the situation. Moving to the Philadelphia area allowed him to strengthen his friendship with his backcourt partner at the University of Maryland, Mo Howard, and he and his family had settled in a lovely neighborhood, in an excellent school district, just west of the city.

He and Debbie had known each other since they were lovestruck teenagers in Durham, North Carolina, and she had always told him that he was the best high school basketball player she'd ever seen. But after Lucas walked through his front door, he found out that someone had pushed him down a rung on his wife's hoops hierarchy.

"I've finally seen a high school basketball player better than you," she said.

He had no idea who Debbie was talking about, despite a subtle, unspoken clue: Their daughter Tarvia was a junior at Lower Merion.

EVEN WITH their relative postseason inexperience and Monsky's broken wrist, the Aces coasted through the first two rounds of the district tournament, then got thirty-five points from Kobe—none in the first quarter, six in the second, eleven in the third, eighteen in the fourth—to beat Norristown, 75–70, in the quarterfinals. (Kobe also had twelve rebounds and eight blocked shots.) The victory assured them of a berth in the state playoffs . . . and of a matchup five days later against a familiar foe: Coatesville. Yet for all of Downer's goal setting, all of his speeches to the team about striving to play at the hallowed Palestra in the semifinals, most of the players didn't know what the district tournament was. Here's what they knew: *If we win, we have practice tomorrow. Someone bring doughnuts. . . . Oh, it's standing-room-only for this game? Cool. Where's the next one? The Palestra? Awesome.* It was all new and exhilarating. The Kobe experience was expanding everyone's conception of what Lower Merion basketball was, how the team could and should play, what it could accomplish. Downer felt it at a microlevel, in the plays he called in the huddle.

Take an alley-oop. Downer had hesitated to draw one up in the past— one, because he wasn't certain he had a player capable of catching a pass near the rim and, while still hanging in the air, dunking the ball; two, because the alley-oop requires such high degrees of timing and precision, especially between two high school players. "A bad alley-oop pass will devastate a play," he said. "That's the key connection." But with Kobe, all it took for an alley-oop to work was a decent back pick on his man and a pass that floated within two feet of the rim. Kobe would get free. He would catch it, even with one hand. He would hammer it home. "I remember driving in my car one day and thinking, 'There is no such thing as a bad alley-oop pass for this kid,'" Downer said. "One time, he caught one behind his head and threw it down. It dawned on me, 'There's no way this can be different from Grant Hill or Penny Hardaway. How can it be any different?'" And when you have Grant Hill or Penny Hardaway on your team . . . when you have Michael Jordan in your gym . . . what is impossible?

The flip side to that question, of course, was terrifying for Downer: What might happen if Kobe wasn't there? Against Coatesville, he got his answer.

THE NIGHT before the game, a *Philadelphia Inquirer* reporter placed a call to William Duffy, the assistant principal for academic affairs at Roman Catholic High School. There were rumors that Kobe Bryant would transfer to Roman for his senior year, and yes, Duffy had heard them, too. But any student's transfer paperwork would go through his office, and the Bryants had not contacted him. "My understanding of the situation," Duffy told the reporter, "is that it's not true." The Roman talk worried Downer a little. That Donnie Carr, Kobe's friend and competitor from the Sonny Hill League, went to Roman gave these rumors more credibility, and Downer had always been on guard for Kobe-is-transferring scuttlebutt, even going back to Kobe's time as an eighth grader. Not long after the Bryants moved back to Wynnewood from Italy, for instance, Joe Bryant had contacted Jim Fenerty, the coach at Germantown Academy, a well-regarded prep school in Montgomery County, to gauge his interest in having Kobe on the team. "I figured he would make me a good coach right away," Fenerty said. Kobe went so far as to take the school's entrance exam and qualify for acceptance, but because GA didn't give out athletic scholarships, because its students received only need-based financial aid, Joe elected to have him go to Lower Merion. Truth be told, Fenerty sensed that Kobe wasn't the one pushing to go to GA, that the kid would have been just as pleased to attend and play for his local public school, and Downer never picked up on any restlessness from Kobe, either. "It helped that his sisters were established at the high school," Downer recalled. "If it were today, Kobe would be on a plane to IMG." But what he didn't know at the time was that he had won over Kobe forever the first time they met. "I knew that Lower Merion was the right spot for me, even when I was in eighth grade," Kobe once said. "I really didn't know Coach Downer that well, but the simple fact that he accepted me when I was in eighth grade to come up to the school, practice with his team, allow me to stay after practice and work on my game, I knew there was no other place. There was never any truth to those rumors going around."

It was a conversation that night before tip-off, in fact, that proved to have far greater influence on Kobe's future. As he stepped from the late-winter chill outside the Palestra's doors into its cinder-block walkway, jostling through a crowd that would fill the old gym to its corners and rafters, Joe bumped into John Lucas, there with his family. Debbie had bought tickets to the game.

"What are you doing here?" Lucas asked Joe.

"My son plays for Lower Merion. What are you doing here?"

"My wife wants me to see some kid named Kobe."

"That's my son," Joe said.

A high school basketball game is thirty-two minutes long. Lucas saw Kobe for exactly twenty-seven minutes, twenty-two seconds against Coatesville. He saw Kobe score twenty-six points in that time. He saw him rip off ten in the third quarter to erase a ten-point Red Raiders lead. He saw Monsky throw a couple of nifty passes that Kobe turned into electrifying dunks. And, with four minutes, thirty-eight seconds left in regulation, with the Aces down by one, he saw Kobe foul out.

Alley-oops were no longer an option for Downer. "We have to play defense," a helpless Kobe said in the huddle as the two senior captains, Stewart and Monsky, exhorted their teammates to take advantage of the opportunity before them. Every morning in the newspaper, they read Kobe's name in the box score, Kobe's name all over the game story, quotes from Kobe, quotes about Kobe. So . . . were they a one-man team or not? "We have to win without him," Stewart said. "This is our moment to show we're more than him."

For the next two and a half minutes, they held Coatesville scoreless, forging a five-point lead, never allowing the Red Raiders to get any closer, Kobe raising his arms in a V after the 72–65 victory and Griffin, on a tender left ankle that he had sprained during the game, rushing to wrap his arms around him. Rip Hamilton, who had fifteen points at halftime, scored just seven in the second half; Egan's pressure defense worked even without Kobe there to front the post. Afterward, Downer praised the Aces' resilience—"A lot of teams would have been devastated if a player of that caliber fouled out," he said—and Joe put the Kobe-transfer speculation to rest. "It isn't true," he said. "He has a lot left to do at Lower Merion," starting, presumably, with winning a district championship in forty-eight hours. On a Friday night at Villanova's DuPont Pavilion. Against Chester.

John Lucas, meanwhile, was on his way home from the Palestra. He knew he wouldn't be able to watch the district-championship game in person. The Sixers were scheduled to play the New Jersey Nets that night in East Rutherford. Besides, he had already seen enough.

AT THE center of the William Penn projects in the city of Chester was a basketball court. Concrete and asphalt, the court sank into the ground like a pit. Boys, male teenagers, and men started playing there in the morning and didn't stop until the thick curtain of night had dropped over them. They chose up sides and picked each other up full-court, and the eldest among them shared stories steeped in the sport's history and heritage in their city. The youngest among them were scolded that settling for a jump shot was a pussy's way to play, that nobody earned the privilege of wearing the orange-and-black uniform of the Chester Clippers and representing that high school and this city by playing weak-ass basketball. In the pit, those kids learned that the sport could be as vital to their survival and flourishing as their beating hearts. In the pit, the sinister pops of gunfire and foreboding blares of police sirens, the awful sounds intrinsic to their lives, would fall, to their ears, silent for a while. In the pit, there was nothing to dread. In Chester, the pit was where you went to climb out.

From a thriving city hard on the Delaware River in the mid-1950s, from a diverse population of nearly seventy thousand residents and a vibrant main street and an economy fed by factories that built ships and trains and machines, Chester had deteriorated into an exemplar of postindustrial decline. Through local political corruption, through the suburbanization of the region and the resulting white flight, through redlining and race riots and blockbusting, the town had transformed into an urban cautionary tale. Chester's population plummeted to fewer than forty thousand people, 80 percent of whom were Black. It was the poorest city in Pennsylvania and the second-most-dangerous city in America. Its housing projects, author Christopher Mele wrote, were "open-air drug markets," and in the 1980s, the William Penn homes "became [a] one-stop hub for cocaine and heroin distribution, sales, and open consumption." Chester, put simply, was the inverse of Lower Merion.

What held its people together, what provided a measure of stability and social capital and pride, was basketball, specifically the high school's team. Club coaches were father figures to players, and those players who grew up to stay in the city handed down the tradition of the program's success. The 1994–95 team upheld that tradition; the Clippers' four victories in the district tournament suggested that Lower Merion might have a better shot of beating an NBA team: 90–44, 70–43, 74–38, 71–49. Chester came at its opponents in waves, playing eight, nine, ten players, pressing, trapping, forcing tentative passes and indecisive dribbles and generating layups and dunks. Its backup point guard, junior John Line-han, one of several Clippers who lived in the William Penn homes, was a five-foot-nine-inch ball of muscle, speed, and relentlessness, so fast that he could carry out a full-court press by himself, scurrying from one side of the floor to the other, hounding the opposing guards as they lofted passes to each other. Years later, Kobe would describe him as the best defensive player he'd ever faced, and Linehan, because he wasn't a senior, didn't even start for Chester. "The way we played," Linehan said, "we had probably two, two and a half starting fives. Anybody from our team could go anywhere else and start."

Linehan had been on those Sonny Hill League teams that Kobe had used as the furnace to forge his game, that had embarrassed and overwhelmed him and had done so much to inspire him to practice and improve. Given how far Kobe had come, he had earned Linehan's respect, but not so much that Linehan and the Clippers feared him. In anticipation of a matchup against Lower Merion, coach Alonzo Lewis had Zain Shaw, a Chester alumnus and six-foot-six swingman who was playing at West Virginia University, return to "be" Kobe at practice, to simulate his moves and style of play. *Yeah, Kobe's great, maybe the best player on the floor. So what? We're going to blow them out. We're Chester.* Shaw's participation in the practice was a testament to the depth of Chester's program over time and the loyalty it engendered in those who passed through it. More, the Clippers trusted that they had a psycho-logical advantage over anyone, let alone the money-softened kids who surrounded Kobe.

"We could go to places, and we would have the game won before we even started," Linehan said. "Our fans would come—I'm talking about the whole city traveling with us everywhere we went. If I'm going some-where and say I'm from Chester, people look at me like I'm crazy. We can get into the racial implications of it, but that's just the reality of it. The media put this image of 'Black kids from Chester' out there, and immediately, white suburban kids and people in general are going to be afraid. Now, if you add the basketball part of it, where we're rough and we play a different way, it just adds to it."

Not only had Kobe competed against several Chester players in varsity summer leagues, Downer's interactions with some of them at the Keystone Games were still fresh in his mind. As tip-off at a packed DuPont Pavilion approached, the former was as confident as ever; the latter's stomach was a bowline. Kobe was afraid of nothing, Downer knew, but neither was the average Chester kid. In the locker room, Kobe and the team could hear chants of "LET'S GO, ACES!" and the thumping and singing of Chester's step team and could feel the tremors of the sound, the slight quiver of the walls. Yes, Monsky's wrist was still broken, and yes, Griffin was on crutches, unable to play, and yes, this was Chester. But . . . maybe they could pull it off. Downer, calmer as his players charged out on the court, glanced around the arena. *Man,* he thought, *this is great stuff.* During the pregame introductions, one by one the Clippers' starting five dashed over to shake his hand, and each of them said the same thing to him: *Sorry for what we're 'bout to do, Coach.* They liked him, and they respected Kobe, but they damn sure weren't going to do anything but try to grind them into dust.

Which they did. The teams traded baskets throughout the first half, Kobe scoring fourteen points, the Aces straining to keep up with the Clippers' furious, full-ninety-four-feet pace. In the first quarter, Ray Carroll, a forward bound for Fordham on a full basketball scholarship, drove toward the basket, and Monsky stood firm in front of him in an attempt to take a charge and draw an offensive foul. Carroll lifted off to shoot and crashed into Monsky, knocking him over, and Carroll's foot landed, with all his weight, on Monsky's face. His arm in a cast, one of his eyes a swirl of black and purple, Monsky stayed in the game until the third quarter, when he and Stewart fouled out. A 12–2 Chester run caused Downer to stand up, rip off his sport coat, and heave it into the stands. It landed in his best friend's lap. The game was getting out of hand. With the Chester lead reaching eighteen points entering the fourth quarter, Downer pulled Kobe and the rest of his available starters and sent an all-sub lineup out on the floor, kids who played when a game's outcome was beyond all doubt. Then he turned to Egan on the bench.

"What do we do?" he asked.

"I don't know," Egan said.

The final score, 77–50, wasn't surprising; it reflected the gap between the two programs. Lower Merion committed a whopping twenty-nine turnovers. Linehan himself had six steals. "We were injured, and we weren't ready," Monsky said. "It was an environment we had never played in and Chester had probably played in a million times." Even Kobe could tip the scales only so much. He trudged out of the Pavilion exhausted, having scored twenty-three points, having come to a deeper understanding of what he and the Aces were up against if they were to win a district championship the following year. "They just wore us down," he said, and the lone consolation for him and his teammates, especially Monsky, Stewart, and the other seniors, was that the state playoffs began in little more than a week.

THE DAY after Lower Merion's loss, the La Salle University men's basketball season, and the team's tenure in the Midwestern Collegiate Conference, clanked to a close 550 miles to the west, in Dayton, Ohio, with a 54–46 loss to Wisconsin–Green Bay. With a 13–14 record. With another season in which the Explorers weren't among the sixty-four teams to qualify for the NCAA tournament. If there was to be a turnaround, the following season promised to be the inflection point. La Salle was leaving the MCC and entering a more appropriate conference, the Atlantic 10, joining Temple, St. Joseph's, and other schools that made more geographic sense as competitors. With that move, the program's problems seemed nothing that Kobe's presence couldn't solve . . . if he decided to go there . . . and there were already forces working, independent of each other, to try to make that happen.

WHERE ELSE would they want to be? The basketball was in the place that all the Aces, from Downer to Egan to every player on the roster to every player's parent, regarded as the safest place on earth: Kobe Bryant's hands. The game, in the second round of the Pennsylvania Class AAAA tournament, at Liberty High School in Bethlehem, was tied at fifty-nine. The opposing team—Hazleton, from the northeast part of the state—and its fans had commandeered most of the gym, comparable to Chester's contingent in size and enthusiasm, as disparate as could be in some other regards. "The crowd," Stewart said, "was not pro-minority." The setting was hostile, and the Aces' play in the closing minutes of the fourth quarter was sloppy. Ahead by one point, they spread out and ran a stall offense to try to bleed the clock, and one of their players, Tariq Wilson, was cradling the ball in one arm against his hip when he just . . . dropped it, and it rolled out of bounds. But Kobe had the ball in a tie game, and he had thirty-three points, even though Hazleton had been double-teaming and trapping him the entire night, just as the Cougars were now with the clock ticking down from :10 to :09 to :08, two players right up on him, waving their hands and arms to distract him or obstruct his view or maybe bat the ball out of his hands for a steal on the off chance that Kobe, in initiating his move to the basket for a game-winning shot at the buzzer, got a little careless. But such recklessness was inconceivable now, because the ball was in the safest place on earth . . .

. . . until it wasn't. Until one of those Hazleton players stripped the ball out of Kobe's hands. Until there was a scramble for it and Hazleton guard Ryan Leib grabbed it and dribbled in a mad dash to the basket, desperate to beat the buzzer with a game-winning layup . . . and getting there . . . and flicking the ball up toward the rim . . . and missing.

Overtime. There should have been a great exhale from the Lower Merion bench, a ripple of relief that the season had not ended, a relaxed team taking control of the game. There was none of that. Perhaps the sight of Kobe's mistake, his fallibility in such a crucial moment, had been too disquieting and disorienting. Hazleton continued double-teaming him. He couldn't get a clean look at the basket. No one else picked up the slack. The Aces didn't score a point in the five-minute extra period; on their final possession, Kobe pulled down a rebound and dribbled the length of the court . . . into three Hazleton players. He lost the ball, and Lower Merion lost the game, 64–59.

Afterward, Downer surveyed the locker room. Sniffles were the only sound. "Does anyone have anything to say?" he asked.

Guy Stewart and Evan Monsky did. Neither spoke very long, a minute at most. *We've all been playing together since we were little, and this experience was so cool, to think about the crappy team we were on, and here we were, playing in the state playoffs in a packed arena. I'll miss basketball, but I'll miss you guys more.*

At first, Kobe couldn't speak. At last, he started repeating the same two words:

"I'm sorry."

The rest of those minutes in the Liberty High School locker room are a blur in the memories of those who were there. Gregg Downer remembers wondering what Kobe would say next, whether he would maintain the sentimental tone of the moment, and hearing Kobe deliver a sermon without compassion. *Those are good stories, and we'll miss the seniors, and I'm sorry. But to every player in this room, let me make one thing clear: This is never happening again on my watch.* Stewart remembers Kobe's apology to the team and his promise to his older teammates, the ones who were graduating, that he would get payback for them. Brendan Pettit remembers his shock over the loss and his recognition of the pressure that would be on the team the following year, that he could be part of something special. Egan remembers nothing but Kobe crying. No purposeful, resolute speech. No defiance. just those two words, again and again. *I'm sorry.* Perhaps that's the reaction that would have made the most sense, that everyone should have expected from Kobe Bryant at that point in his life: still five months away from his seventeenth birthday, nothing else mattering as much to him as his own image of himself. He had averaged 31.1 points and 10.4 rebounds during a remarkable junior season. He had lifted his team to a level that it hadn't been near in years. But if he wasn't a district champion, if he wasn't a state champion, if he wasn't the best, who was he, and who did people believe him to be?

I'm sorry.

I'm sorry.

I'm sorry.

People made a point to tell me how shocked they were that I was this seventeen-year-old kid who was so sure of himself and confident in his abilities that I put myself in this unique position, to choose among the top colleges in the country or the NBA.

—KOBE BRYANT

12

MYTH
AND REALITY

JOHN KUNZIER, LA SALLE UNIVERSITY'S women's volleyball coach, found Joe Bryant to be an "awesome guy" during their time on campus together, amiable whenever they chatted in the athletic offices, the hallways, and the third-floor gymnasium of Hayman Hall. Volleyball was not a top-tier sport at La Salle. Kunzier's teams had staggered to a 17–78 record over his first three years as coach, and despite the impending move to the Atlantic 10, he did not anticipate that the university would begin splurging on his program. The NCAA permitted each of its member schools to have as many as twelve volleyball players on scholarship. La Salle, per its athletic budget, permitted Kunzier to have four. It *had* permitted him four, anyway, until the late spring of 1994, when athletic director Bob Mullen and senior women's administrator Kathy McNally delivered to him what they had to have regarded as good news.

You got another scholarship player, McNally told Kunzier. *She's a six-foot-two middle blocker, and her name is Shaya.*

Kunzier had never recruited Shaya Bryant to play volleyball at La Salle, and no one had ever discussed with him the possibility of her playing volleyball at La Salle. "There was no money" in the budget, he said. "There was nothing. But somehow, I get an extra player out of the blue who wasn't in any of the plans I had. I didn't even know who she was." She played one season, the fall of 1995, leading the team in blocks. But the Explorers' record didn't improve much—to 4–27, from 3–30 the season before—and Shaya stayed at La Salle for just one year. "Shaya was a lovely young lady," said Kunzier, who stepped down as coach after that 1995 season, "not the toughest player I ever had, but athletic and gifted and really, really sweet and nice." Don't misunderstand him: He was happy to have her, happy to coach her. Considering the team's struggles, he would have been happy to have anyone who possessed Shaya's qualities. It was the naked opportunism of the whole situation that bothered him.

"La Salle, at the time, was, I believe, willing to do whatever they needed to do to get Kobe," Kunzier said. "They were paying Joe's salary. They were willing to give Kobe a full ride, and they gave Shaya a full ride. It was a Bob Mullen move. It was a big mess when I was there. It was a real mess. I think Bob was looking at Kobe as his savior, and it was going to be his big turnaround."

For the one year that Shaya Bryant spent at La Salle, the value of her athletic scholarship—tuition, room, board, a meal plan, a twelve-credit course load—would have been roughly $20,000. But that sum wasn't the only price that Mullen was willing to pay if it meant coaxing Kobe to campus. Entering the summer of 1995, the salaries of Morris's two primary assistant coaches, Joe Mihalich and Joe Bryant, were $34,000 and $32,000, respectively. One day, Mullen told Morris that he had arranged a pay raise for Joe Bryant to $50,000.

That's great, Morris told Mullen. *But if Jellybean's getting $50K, Mihalich has to get $52K.*

Mullen exploded in anger and disbelief. *Are you crazy? Do you realize your neck's on the line if you don't get Kobe?* Morris didn't care. Mihalich had three children, and he had been on Morris's staff since 1986.

There's a loyalty thing there, Morris told Mullen. *Joe Mihalich is my top guy. If you don't give him the bump, Joe Bryant doesn't get one.*

Mullen stormed out of Morris's office. The next day, he told Morris that Joe Mihalich's new salary was $52,000.

There was reason, though, for Mullen to believe those bread crumbs would entice Kobe, for Kobe himself was considering La Salle . . . under a particular set of conditions and scenarios. That the university was entering the Atlantic 10 intrigued him—the conference already had natural rivalries in place for the Explorers with Temple and St. Joseph's—as did the prospect of playing with Lari Ketner, a six-foot-ten center from Roman Catholic High School. A grade ahead of Kobe, Ketner had verbally committed to La Salle in the spring, but he had signed no papers and made nothing official. Part of him still wanted to keep his options open, and one reason that he was holding off on committing fully to Morris and La Salle was that he was waiting to get a better sense of what Kobe's college decision would be. Teaming up for pickup games at Hayman, Kobe and Ketner dominated the players who were already on La Salle's roster—Kobe knifing into the lane at will, throwing alley-oop passes to Ketner for dunks, looking at the college kids' faces and recognizing that they were agog with the possibility of what the Explorers could be with him and Ketner. *If you tell me that you'll go to La Salle,* Ketner told him, *I'll sign tomorrow. Imagine turning the program around, together.*

Kobe could not and would not give Ketner any assurances, though, not merely because he didn't want to make a promise he couldn't keep, but because Joe had a pie-in-the-sky plan that, if the circumstances were right and if he could pull it off, would guarantee that Kobe would end up at La Salle. Neither Joe nor Kobe could be certain it would happen, but the plan was contingent on a sequence of events that, to Joe, seemed likelier by the day. The Explorers had gone through back-to-back losing seasons for the first time in the program's history, and their record had worsened each of the previous three years. Alumni and administrators were getting restless and impatient with Morris, as Mullen had so emphatically made clear to him. Another poor season, Joe reasoned, and Morris's firing would be a fait accompli, and the university would have no choice but to hire . . . Joe. The whispers were already on the wind, an open secret in some quarters, a complete secret to Morris. "They really talked about Joe getting the job at La Salle," Sam Rines Jr. said. "And obviously, if Joe had gotten the job, Kobe would go to La Salle."

Not just Kobe, either. From his contacts and Kobe's travels and friendships on the AAU circuit, Joe had assembled his own version of the "Fab Five," the famous 1991 Michigan recruiting class who had led the Wolverines to the 1992 and 1993 national-title games: Kobe; Rip Hamilton, who had developed a friendship with Kobe and had joined the Sam Rines All-Stars; Shaheen Holloway; Lester Earl; and, from Eau Claire, South Carolina, Jermaine O'Neal. Joe was certain that he could persuade most of them, if not all four of them, to join Kobe at La Salle. He was recruiting them anyway, talking them up to Morris and Mihalich. Hell, if he could tell them, *I'll be your head coach,* they'd commit on the spot—he had no doubt. Kobe didn't, either. He played with those four guys, played against them, batted around this very idea with them over the phone. Who wouldn't have wanted to play for his dad? Ketner eventually backed out of his oral commitment to La Salle and headed north to the University of Massachusetts. But those four guys would have been thrilled to play for Joe—Donnie Carr would have been thrilled, too, and what if they could add him to the party?—and it wouldn't have mattered that they'd be at La Salle, with its rinky-dink practice gym and with so much losing over the last couple of years. They wouldn't be as good as the Fab Five. They would be *better,* and they'd have to stay only a year before all of them bolted for the NBA, and Kobe wouldn't have to hunt for a college coach who would take care of him, a college coach who would nurture him. He would have one. He would have his dad. Speedy Morris . . . was Speedy Morris really going to be that kind of coach for Kobe? . . . Speedy Morris, who, when Joe recommended that La Salle recruit Sharif Butler out of junior college, told Joe, *No, we don't think he's good enough.* "It really hurt the family deep down inside," Joe said. "That means he didn't really understand the Bryant family at that time." . . . Speedy Morris, who didn't think Kobe was good enough to go to the NBA—not that Kobe shouldn't go, but that he *couldn't.* "If this guy doesn't think he's good enough," Joe said, "How am I going to trust him to raise my son?" . . . Speedy Morris, his anger on a hair trigger, so furious over a dumb play or a bad call that he often couldn't stop himself from stomping his feet like a toddler demanding a toy his parents refused to buy, his pants sometimes splitting, his voice reaching a higher pitch and ringing throughout the Civic Center . . . Kobe had been there to witness a few of those mushroom clouds. There was a time, early in Joe's coaching tenure at La Salle, when he would have been thrilled if Kobe decided to go there. But that was it: The decision was always Kobe's, and he thought that Speedy screamed at his players too much. He told Joe and Pam as much, and they didn't mind him saying so.

THE SPRING and summer of 1995 brought into full flourishing the blueprints and promises that Kobe Bryant and those close to him had been following and chasing since he was a baby. As dynamic and dominant as he was for Lower Merion, as much as winning a state championship drove him, that junior season was now the equivalent of those Remington Park pickup games with his middle school and high school friends. There would be no creative friction for him, no challenge, in pitting himself solely against teenagers who weren't in his league as ballplayers. "He was never in the moment," Sonny Vaccaro said. "He was always in the next moment." It is worth noting, too, that Kobe's accelerated self-training, his increased urgency and success in improving his game, coincided with a seismic event in professional sports. On March 19, 1995, just four days after the Aces' season-ending loss to Hazleton in the state playoffs, Michael Jordan, after his seventeen-month retirement/hiatus from basketball, scored nineteen points for the Chicago Bulls in a loss to the Indiana Pacers. MJ was back, and his return provided Kobe another goal in the distance, another marathon finish-line tape to break. Only so many outsiders could envision what his endgame was.

One day that spring, for example, Villanova assistant coach Paul Hewitt decided to drive to Lower Merion to watch him practice. Accompanying him was Jonathan Haynes, the Wildcats' starting point guard, who knew little about Kobe; he had never met him. Hewitt had been recruiting Kobe, hoping to add him to a boffo freshman class that would include Tim Thomas. The idea of joining forces with Thomas and tearing the Big East apart had some purchase with Kobe. Two of the Wildcats' top scorers—guards Kerry Kittles, a likely NBA lottery pick himself, and

Eric Eberz—would, in theory, graduate before Kobe arrived, opening up spots in the starting lineup right away for him and Thomas. *College basketball wouldn't be ready for two players like me and Timmy on the same team,* Kobe thought, and because his uncle Chubby Cox had played for the Wildcats, it was easy to envision Villanova as a potential destination.

After Kobe had what Hewitt later described as "an unbelievable practice" and chatted with him and Haynes, Hewitt left with his chest puffed, convinced that Kobe would stay on the Main Line for college. *Damn, that's a hell of a recruiting class. There's nobody we can't get.*

Except Haynes was laughing at him.

"What's so funny?" Hewitt asked.

"Coach," Haynes said, "you have no shot at getting this guy."

"What do you mean?"

"Coach, this dude ain't going to college. He's going straight to the NBA."

Haynes's insight into Kobe's thinking hit Hewitt like a bolt. "For a college kid to say that about a high school kid, that's when I started to realize this dude must be something different," Hewitt recalled. "Kobe and I would have frequent conversations. I didn't really appreciate it back then, but the thing he always asked about was the game. He always had questions about the game and loved talking about basketball, was always on a quest for information and knowledge. At the time, you're thinking that he's a seventeen-year-old kid, and it's great he's engaged in the conversation. Later in life, you realize that this kid was on a quest to be great."

One didn't necessarily have to be of Kobe's generation to understand Kobe's thinking, Kobe's trajectory. From that night at the Palestra, that playoff game against Coatesville, John Lucas could see Kobe in the same way that Kobe saw himself: not what he was at sixteen, but what he would be at twenty-one, twenty-two, beyond. To ensure his Sixers players would stay in shape, to maintain an NBA-quality competitive environment throughout the league's off-season, Lucas encouraged them to participate in the regular, informal pickup games, among pros and college players, at all the familiar locales throughout Philadelphia. The

Fieldhouse at St. Joseph's University was the Sixers' official practice facility, and Lucas assigned his old friend Mo Howard to oversee the practices: two a day, nine in the morning to seven at night. Lucas called the Bryants and invited Kobe to those workouts, and he gave Howard a mandate: *I don't care how you make up the teams, but Kobe has to play. If Kobe can play, if he wants to play, he plays. End of story.*

Even before his high school season ended, Kobe had contacted Phil Martelli, who was in his first year as St. Joseph's men's basketball coach, and asked if he could work out at the Fieldhouse. Martelli put Kobe's name on the guest list, where it stayed through the spring and until the following school year began in September. "If he played for Lower Merion on Tuesday and Friday," Martelli said, "he would come in Monday, Wednesday, and Thursday to our gym." So accepting Lucas's invitation didn't require Kobe to upset his meticulous, jam-packed schedule—pickup and practice, workouts and weight-training during the week; AAU tournaments and all-star camps on the weekends—and it gave him a chance, over his five-to-ten-minute drive to St. Joe's, to bond with his carpool mate, Emory Dabney. Sensitive and high-strung and two years younger than Kobe, Dabney had spent his freshman year at the Woodlynde School in West Philadelphia, a day school for students with learning differences and challenges. Having been the point guard on Woodlynde's basketball team, he had played summer-league ball with Kobe and the Aces, meeting Gregg Downer there, turning down several scholarship offers from private high schools, choosing instead to transfer to Lower Merion. He had caught Lucas's eye during those summer games, too, and Lucas took such a liking to Dabney that he offered him the chance to be the youngest player in a gym full of men. If it was strange to have Kobe, entering his senior year, work out with pros and experienced college athletes, having a kid still a few weeks shy of his fifteenth birthday do the same might seem ridiculous. But before meeting Lucas and Kobe, Dabney had found a basketball mentor who surpassed them both in his standing within the sport: Dabney's best friend at Woodlynde had been Cory Erving, Julius's son. Whenever Dabney visited the Ervings' home in Villanova, Julius would offer to play one-on-one against him. "We'd mess around," Dabney said. "Then he'd say, 'OK, you want to see what defense is like in the NBA Finals?' I was like, 'Yeah.' I couldn't even do anything. For years and years, I would get better, and he'd say, 'You're going to start playing in front of bigger crowds. This is what it's going to be like.' And I never thought twice about playing in front of a lot of people."

Cory Erving died in a car accident in 2000, when he was nineteen, and Dabney still lives with the losses, at such young ages, of two of his dearest friends. For their first workouts together, Kobe would pick up Dabney in the Bryants' old, white BMW and, later, in a new light green Toyota Land Cruiser; at St. Joe's, they would concentrate on cardiovascular exercises, mostly running on a track inside the Fieldhouse. "Kobe was always like a big brother," Dabney said. "He'd give me advice. I spent a lot of time with him off the court. He was at my house a lot. I was at his house. He just wanted to see you get better and succeed, even with schoolwork and grades. He was on you about that. He was just a great person to be around at that age. I get kind of emotional thinking about it. At that age, he gave you a foundation of what it takes to be successful in life, even with him being only seventeen or eighteen. You got that feeling just from being around him." Once the 1995 NBA draft took place in late June, though, the nature of those workouts morphed from the grind of daily sprints and drills to a still-surviving form of basketball mythology.

THE BELIEF that Jerry Stackhouse, either during his collegiate career at North Carolina or after the Sixers selected him with the No. 3 pick in the 1995 draft, would be *The Next Michael Jordan* was at once flattering and nonsensical to the young man who bore the burden of such heavy expectations. Of course, it was an ego stroke to be compared to the player who was arguably the greatest in the sport's history, but . . . the people making that comparison knew Jordan was a guard, right? Stackhouse wasn't. He was a power forward in high school, and he was a power forward at North Carolina. He had never played guard in his life, hadn't chased smaller players around and through screens, hadn't come off screens himself for jump shots or drives. He could handle the ball a little, but most of his game was predicated on posting up, on having the ball in his hands while his back was to the basket, and he had a long way to go to understand the nuances and develop the skills that would allow him to thrive as a guard . . . which is where the Sixers planned on playing him.

Based on his background, Stackhouse, once he joined the Sixers and the Philly pickup circuit, stepped into a situation for which he was not fully prepared, and that context is critical to sorting out and separating truth from fiction or embellishment in the stories of that summer. There's a natural inclination to grade Kobe on a curve, to elevate or exaggerate his feats in the Fieldhouse and at the Bellevue and at the other gyms that he and the Sixers and the other Philly pro and college players frequented, because he was so young and turned out to be so great, because the exaggeration amplifies his legend. Every person who shares an anecdote about Kobe's participation in those games filters those memories through his or her own interests and perspective. John Lucas thought he had unearthed a secret diamond. Assuming that he would still be the Sixers' coach and general manager in June 1996, he already had made up his mind that he would draft Kobe. He confessed this scheme to only those people in basketball whom he trusted most, and there is a powerful, prestigious legacy in being the coach who saw Kobe coming before anyone else did. Mo Howard was practically a brother to both Lucas and Joe Bryant. Jerry Stackhouse has had to listen to these stories for two decades, and every one of those stories is a needle pricking his ego, because implicit in every one of those stories is a slight on him and his career and his ability: *Kobe schooled you one-on-one. Kobe owned you. Kobe wasn't a high school senior yet, and he was demolishing the third pick in the draft, and the third pick in the draft was you.*

And so . . .

Willie Burton, a journeyman NBA guard, had played for the Sixers during the 1994–95 season. In December, he had scored fifty-three points in a victory over the Miami Heat at the Spectrum, setting the arena's single-game scoring record, and had explained his incredible one-off performance with two words: "Just hoopin'." He showed up at St. Joe's, got in a game, and had to guard Kobe. Burton scored the first time he touched the ball, then shot a word or two at Kobe. Over the rest of the game, Kobe scored ten of his team's eleven baskets. Burton scored just one. He immediately stomped out of the Fieldhouse, fuming. He didn't come back, to either the gym or, for a year, the NBA. He signed with a team in Italy and spent the 1995–96 season there.

And so . . .

After the Sixers practiced, Lucas would pair Kobe against individual players for games of one-on-one. Once, his partner/adversary was Vernon Maxwell, who had just completed his seventh NBA season and whose nickname was "Mad Max," for justifiable reasons. Just that February, the league had suspended him ten games for charging into the stands and punching a fan who had been berating and heckling him.

"They were playing to ten," Lucas said, "and it got to nine–nine. It was so rough, I thought they were going to fight with each other. I said to myself, 'I want somebody who's going to fight at nine–nine.'"

And so . . .

Bobby Johnson, who had played at Southern High School in Philadelphia and had been the sixth man on La Salle's three consecutive conference-championship teams in the 1980s, sometimes accompanied his former teammate Lionel "L-Train" Simmons to the runs at St. Joe's. Simmons, with the Sacramento Kings, and Johnson teamed up with Kobe, former Sixers center Rick Mahorn, and Philly native and former NBA guard Paul "Snoop" Graham for a game against five Sixers. First to ten won.

"The score is tied at nine; we have the ball," Johnson said. "Kobe brings the ball up, defended by Vernon Maxwell on the right wing. Here goes Kobe pounding the rock and directing NBA veterans to clear out. First Train posted up, and he cleared him out of the post, followed by Snoop. Waved off the screen from Mahorn. After seeing this, there was no need for me to take my butt anywhere near him."

Against Maxwell, Kobe dribbled between his legs, crossed Maxwell over, and took a sixteen-foot jump shot. "Dagger over Maxwell,"

Johnson said. "He called 'Ballgame' like he'd been there before. I was impressed beyond belief."

And so . . .

Kobe played a game of P-I-G against Sixers forward Sharone Wright, who had been the sixth overall pick in the 1994 draft. At stake: a chance to tool around in Wright's Land Cruiser. "I concentrated really hard, and I beat him," Kobe once said. "I was supposed to be gone for five or ten minutes, but I drove around for half an hour."

And so . . .

Howard was at every workout. During one game, Kobe took off from the foul line and tried to dunk over Shawn Bradley, the Sixers' seven-foot-six center. He missed. "But none of the pro guys were doing that," Howard said. "There was no fear. There was no indecision. There was alpha, alpha, alpha. You'd think, because these guys were older than he was, he would defer. But his thing always was, 'I'm going to be the best player on the court this session.'" On a morning the Fieldhouse was closed, the players and coaches, including Maurice Cheeks, one of Lucas's assistants, headed across City Avenue to the gym at Episcopal Academy. Stackhouse and Kobe guarded each other. "Jerry is a pretty good player," Howard recalled, "but Kobe is giving him the business. There was one play; I'll never forget it. Kobe is guarding Jerry, and he's defending Jerry pretty tough, and Jerry got a little frustrated and hip-tossed Kobe. Kobe gets up and gets the ball, and I swear to you, he hit a thirty-foot shot. He banked it, and he knew what he was doing. Maurice looks at me and says, 'If Jerry Stackhouse is No. 3, Kobe has to be 3A.'"

And so . . .

Kobe picked up Emory Dabney one August morning, and on the way to St. Joe's, he rolled up the windows and cranked the heat in the car.

"What are you doing?" Dabney asked. "I can't take this. It's ninety degrees outside."

"I'm about to play Stackhouse," Kobe said. "I've got to stay warm."

And so . . .

Jeremy Treatman got in to see a couple of scrimmages and workouts, and it was easier for Gregg Downer to attend, too, since he had just left his phys-ed teaching job at The Shipley School and accepted one at Episcopal. Kobe took Treatman's breath away on one play, driving into the lane, rising over Mahorn—six foot ten, 240 pounds, a former member of the "Bad Boy" Detroit Pistons, capable of flattening Kobe with a forearm and happy to do it—bending around Mahorn midair, his hand and the ball above the rim, for a layup. To Treatman, the most telling revelation of that July and August was that Bradley would sometimes bring Kobe home from the workouts, then call him each night to confirm that he would be there the next morning. That was something. That was significant. That meant Kobe *belonged,* that he fit in, and in the bigger picture, that belonging meant everything. The Minnesota Timberwolves had just selected Kevin Garnett with the fifth overall pick, making him the first player in twenty years to be drafted out of high school, and "that made Kobe want to do it even more," Treatman said. "College basketball wasn't as important to him, growing up in Italy, as it was to everyone else. During those workouts, the NBA thoughts became more serious."

And so . . .

Kobe continued practicing with the Sixers into September, and during a week when they held those practices at Episcopal's gym, Lucas asked a couple of Episcopal players to join the workouts as warm bodies: set picks, throw passes in drills, nothing that the average high school player couldn't handle. For Michael Weil, a sophomore on the JV team—six feet tall, 145 pounds, short blond hair, "pale as shit," he said—participating in the drills was a dream come true for a kid who had never been so close to a professional athlete before. It was Kobe, though, who drew most of Weil's attention and interest. A high school senior . . . playing full-bore against the Sixers . . . Weil marveled at it. Of all the players and big names there, Kobe's was the only autograph that Weil sought and got. He handed him a slip of notebook paper, and Kobe was happy to sign it, was talkative and friendly, and asked, "What sports do you play?" *This guy's only two years older than I am,* Weil thought, which made what Weil witnessed each day, once the scrimmages had ended, all the more memorable.

"Kobe and Stack were on one of the side hoops," Weil said, "and they were going at it. I don't know what number they played to or what the final score was or anything like that. But it didn't take being a basketball analyst to see that the two guys playing one-on-one on the side were of roughly equal capabilities at the time."

And so . . .

Stop. Just stop. Didn't everyone else in the gym those days see what Jerry Stackhouse saw? Doesn't everyone else who was there remember what he remembers? Didn't anyone else notice Lionel Simmons and former Temple stars Eddie Jones and Mark Macon and all the old heads from Philly basketball pulling Kobe to the side again and again: *You gotta pass the ball.*

So . . . stop. Yeah, Kobe had some good days scoring, because he could move and handle the ball so well, but his tunnel vision was total, all-encompassing. Nobody *really* wanted to play with Kobe. Sometimes, nobody would pick him for a pickup game. *Oh, he beat Stackhouse one-on-one.* Stackhouse was three and a half years older than Kobe. "Could you imagine a seventeen-year-old beating me consistently?" Stackhouse once said. "I'd have hurt him first. Real talk. I was just physically—that could never happen to me. Did we play one-on-one? Yes. Did he beat me? Did he maybe win a game? Yes. Did he consistently beat Jerry Stackhouse at twenty years old and he was seventeen? Hell. No. I'm putting an end to that story. Was he super talented and everybody saw great potential in him? Yes. But those scenarios that we hear in the lore of Kobe Bryant now, they have a little different story when you talk to people who were actually in the gym."

IN A later age of media, everyone at the 1995 Adidas ABCD Camp, at Fairleigh Dickinson University, would have already known that Kobe Bryant was the best high school basketball player in the country, because Kobe would have been the one telling everyone he was, posting on Twitter and Facebook, sharing video of himself on Instagram. But that July, the internet was still a curiosity to most of America, a new technology whose power and reach had yet to be revealed in full, and that allowed Sonny Vaccaro to keep hidden his strategy to regain control of the athletic-shoe market.

Entering that summer, without the financial resources and brand strength that Nike could wield and before Garnett had gone so high in the draft, Vaccaro had not intended to hitch Adidas' future to a high school phenom. His mission was to find the next Michael Jordan, but the presumed risk that would accompany signing a seventeen- or eighteen-year-old and putting him at the center of the company's hopes for a comeback would be too great. Perhaps Kerry Kittles—a long and supple shooting guard returning for his senior season at Villanova, his style of play similar to Jordan's—was the safer play. "He probably would have been the guy I recommended to Adidas," Vaccaro recalled. "Kerry was a big name, a legitimate player, and had a very good career. There was nothing negative about him. But Kevin opened the doors." And opened Vaccaro's mind. The '72 Dapper Dan Classic . . . the shared fluency in Italian . . . that hug and goodbye at the '94 ABCD Camp . . . he had this . . . sort of . . . *bond* . . . with Kobe Bryant and his family—with the father, Joe, a once-forgotten figure from the past, and with the son, loaded with so much precious possibility. They had found each other, after all these years, at this particular moment in time, and Sonny Vaccaro did not believe in coincidences.

IT HAD been easy, oh so easy, for Gregg Downer to goad Kobe in the years and months before this ABCD Camp, to refine the perfect method of motivation for a player who entered every gym believing, knowing in the marrow of his bones, that there wasn't another player in the place better than he was. All it took was a quick peek at a recruiting ranking, a list in a basketball magazine, and Downer had enough information for ammunition. Who was ahead of Kobe this week? Vince Carter, down at Mainland High School in Daytona Beach? Tim Thomas? The mere mention of a name or two set Kobe off. Even in the last few years of his life, Kobe would bring up that teasing from his old coach and its power to inspire him. *You used to tell me Vince Carter or Tim Thomas was better.* It wasn't exactly true—Downer always took care to point out that those two were rated higher as recruits than Kobe, not that they were better than he was—but it served its purpose, for both of them.

When Downer; his older brother, Drew; and Mike Egan headed north to Hackensack for the camp, they soon realized how ineffectual comparing Kobe to other outstanding high school players would be. Gregg had asked Drew to join his staff for the 1995–96 season, and Drew, working and living in Orlando as an executive for a flooring company, agreed, quitting his job and leaving the sunshine behind for the chance to coach Kobe. Anticipating that the pressure on him, Kobe, and the Aces to win a state championship could crush them if they weren't prepared for it, Gregg trusted no one more to be an emotional barometer for the team, to pick up on which players needed a pat on the back or an angry talking-to, than Drew. And Drew, in turn, noticed right away that Kobe would probably be the least of his concerns in that regard. None of the other campers were competing as hard as he was. "I kept waiting for Kobe to back off the throttle," Drew recalled, "and he never did." In fact, when the camp began, it was obvious that Kobe was overcompensating. "He played a game," Egan said, "and he was . . . not goofing around, but looking to do more than he should have been," trying too hard to be the best player on the court, to wow the college coaches and pro scouts in the stands. Egan pulled him aside afterward: *Hey, man, what are you doing? Just play your game. Just do what you do.* "The next game he played—I'm not saying it was because of me—he did a move where he did a stop, a spin, and a fifteen-foot bank shot, and I just saw every coach's jaw drop," Egan said. "It was an NBA-level, unstoppable move. No one ever at any level could stop a six-foot-six kid from making that shot. That's what the coaches want to see. He was really starting to separate from the pack there."

IN OCTOBER 1994, six months after Duke had lost by four points to Arkansas in the NCAA championship game, Mike Krzyzewski had undergone surgery for a slipped disk in his back, but he was still in so much pain for months following the operation that he doubted the disk was the problem. He was afraid that, just like his friend Jim Valvano, the former coach at North Carolina State, he had contracted cancer and was going to die. All he needed, as it turned out, was time and rest so that the disk could heal properly, but in his absence, the Blue Devils fell apart. Long-time assistant Pete Gaudet coached in Krzyzewski's absence, and Duke finished the '94–'95 season with a 13–18 record, the situation turning so fraught and tense that former NBA coach Doug Collins, who had been Joe Bryant's teammate with the Sixers and whose son Chris played for the Blue Devils, charged into the locker room after one loss, screaming at Gaudet for not utilizing Krzyzewski's players in the right way. It marked the only season in a thirty-six-year span that Duke failed to qualify for the NCAA tournament. Krzyzewski convalesced enough that he could resume coaching in the fall of 1995, and he returned to a program in dire need of a superstar to return to its previous glory.

Having targeted Kobe as that superstar, Krzyzewski had assigned his top assistant coach, Tommy Amaker, to act as the primary liaison between the Duke program and Kobe. And Amaker's primary contact at Lower Merion was Mike Egan. Amaker thought Kobe had all the qualities, basketball and otherwise, that Duke looked for in a player. There were layers to him—his intelligence, the depth of perspective and appreciation for different people and cultures that his years in Italy had fostered. But Amaker probably spent more time talking with Egan about Kobe's potential future at Duke than Egan did with Kobe. "Kobe was very private about this stuff," Egan said, "and we were very respectful of the fact that it was his decision and not really our business. 'Hey, if you ever want to talk about it, let us know.' But he had an amazing ability to compartmentalize things. We almost never talked to him about it."

Kobe, however, was talking to Krzyzewski, by phone, and he liked him immediately. When they spoke early on in the recruiting process, the two talked more about Kobe's experiences abroad and in his first few years back in the United States than they did about basketball. Kobe had admired the manner in which Krzyzewski had developed Grant Hill during Hill's four years at Duke, and Krzyzewski would tell Kobe stories and anecdotes about Hill: his taking over leadership of the team, his adapting to the media attention that the Blue Devils received. Hill had just finished his first season with the Detroit Pistons, who had selected him with the third overall pick in the 1994 draft, and he had averaged nearly twenty points a game for them, earning a berth on the Eastern Conference all-star team and winning the NBA's Rookie of the Year Award. Kobe could envision Krzyzewski having the same effect on him. Late in his senior year, he would admit to those close to him what he was starting to acknowledge to himself: If he decided to go to college, he would choose Duke, no question.

No one knew that at the ABCD Camp, though: not Krzyzewski; not Speedy Morris; not Rick Pitino; not Syracuse's Jim Boeheim, who had rolled off fourteen consecutive twenty-win seasons and whose leading scorer, guard Lawrence Moten, had just been selected in the second round of the NBA draft; not Connecticut's Jim Calhoun and his sharp New England accent, in which he touted to Kobe his career win-loss record and UConn's back-to-back Big East championships. Every coach at the camp had a chance to sell Kobe on him and his program, and every coach felt he had to, because no one knew yet what Kobe's plans were. So as Kobe, Gregg Downer, and Egan got on an elevator inside the Rothman Center, Krzyzewski slipped in, too, before the doors closed. It was the first time he and Kobe had met in person. Now the coach could make, quite literally, his elevator pitch.

At Duke, he told Kobe, *we polish diamonds. We know they're great, and we're going to make them better.*

Damn, Egan thought, *that's a great line.*

At a camp with Rip Hamilton, Lester Earl, Shaheen Holloway, and Jermaine O'Neal, with that "Fab Five" still chatting about joining forces at La Salle, Kobe fulfilled the promise that he had made to Sonny Vaccaro a year earlier. He was named the camp's most valuable player, claiming the de facto crown as the best high school player in the country. On hand for the coronation, Joe basked in the attention washing over his son. Phone calls from coaches had been flooding the Bryants' house, interrupting the family's meals; it wasn't like that for him when he was at Bartram, but he savored it on Kobe's behalf nonetheless. "You wouldn't believe how many people have commented to me about their enjoyment in watching him play," Joe said during the camp. The questions about Kobe's college choice? "I'm trying to steer talk away from college right now," Joe said. "There will be plenty of time for Kobe to pick a college. The important thing now is to soak this up, because this kind of thing is a once-in-a-lifetime experience." Besides, word was out now. Everyone knew, or would know, who would be atop those recruiting rankings from then on. Everyone knew, or would know, who the king was. Soon enough, Vaccaro had consigned poor Kerry Kittles to the recesses of his mind. Kobe, he decided, was the player commensurate with the scope of his ambition for Adidas. This would have to be done just right, with an agent and partner who was just right for Kobe. Who had a Philadelphia background similar to the Bryants'. Who believed, as Vaccaro did, that an aspiring professional athlete had the right to pursue his career as he saw fit, that college shouldn't be mandatory for a player to enter the NBA. Who would share Vaccaro's vision for turning Kobe into basketball's next god-child and who possessed the cachet to pull the strings and make it happen. Later that summer, Vaccaro called Arn Tellem.

TO GET another up-close look at Kobe, Krzyzewski arranged a trip to suburban Philadelphia to watch one of his games in the Plymouth Whitemarsh summer league. He chose a good one: against Donnie Carr and Roman Catholic. It wasn't often that a summer-league matchup inspired gamesmanship a full twenty-four hours before tip-off, but . . .

. . . the night before the game, Carr was talking on his home phone with his girlfriend when the call-waiting beeped. He clicked over.

"Hello."

"Yo, Don. What's up, man? What's going on?"

"Chillin'. Who's this?"

"Bean, man. How you doing?"

"Chillin', man. Talkin' to my girl."

"All right, man. Just had a quick question for you. Is Yah Davis going to be at the game tomorrow?"

There had been rumors that Davis, Carr's teammate at Roman and a

Division I prospect himself, was transferring to Frankford High School. Immediately, Carr's antennae poised. *This dude's fishin'.* This wasn't the same kind of question that Kobe used to ask him when they were younger, when he probed him about life in South Philly, about a childhood without the suburban comforts that Kobe enjoyed, about saving up money just to splurge once in a while at a fast-food joint. This wasn't born of genuine curiosity. This was a soft interrogation. This was a competitor searching for an edge over his equal.

"I don't know," Carr said. "Why?"

"Man," Kobe replied, "if Yah comes to the game, it's you and Yah against me, and we're gonna get it on. You and Yah against me—that would be a heck of a matchup. But if it's just you, man, I don't even know if it's worth me coming."

Carr lifted the phone over his head and slammed it down on the receiver, forgetting that his girlfriend was still on the other line. His sister and brother rushed into the room: *Yo, what's wrong? We heard this loud noise.* Carr couldn't get over the . . . *balls* on Kobe . . . to pick up that phone, dial that number, and engage in mind games with him. This was the skinny little joker Carr and his friends used to laugh at, used to push around the court.

"Man, this motherfucker just called me!" Carr shouted to his siblings. "Total disrespect!"

At Plymouth Whitemarsh the next day, among the twenty or so people sweltering in the gym's stagnant, heavy air sat John Lucas, Rick Pitino, and, in the ninth row of the bleachers, Krzyzewski. Dave Rosenberg, one of Kobe's teammates, glanced up at them. *Oh, shit,* he thought, *this season is going to be real.* That Krzyzewski had made it to the game at all was of profound relief to Mike Egan. Lower Merion's head coach in that league, Egan had given him directions to the gym and was worried that the legendary coach might end up in Allentown instead of Montgomery County.

Confronted with that array of coaches, Carr approached an assistant on Roman's staff. "I want to guard Kobe," Carr said. "I want to show Kobe and everybody else that I'm better." As they walked onto the court for tip-off, the two of them didn't shake hands or speak to each other, and when a Roman player batted the ball to Carr, Kobe dropped into "a big-time defensive stance," Carr recalled, "like when Jordan was guarding Magic in the Finals," arms and legs extended and wide, a giant spider. *Yeah, I remember what y'all used to do to me. But now it's a new thing.*

Carr came at Kobe at a nice swift clip and glided to the basket. Kobe caught up to him near the rim, lifted off from just behind him to try to swat away his shot, but no . . . Carr fooled him, passing the ball to a trailing teammate for a power dunk. The first half ended; he had twenty-five points, and Kobe had four. Carr laughed to himself. He knew he could score on Kobe anytime he wanted. "If I went side to side on him, going north and south with some shifty moves," Carr recalled, "he was going to have a hard time staying in front of me because his lateral quickness wasn't as good as it became." Nothing was different from those Sonny Hill League games, when Carr could manipulate Kobe like a chess piece, pushing him just about anywhere he wished through his advantage in pure size and strength.

Then the second half began, and for the first time between them, everything was different. On defense, Kobe began face-guarding Carr, denying him the ball, and on those rare occasions when Carr did have it, Kobe dropped his shoulders, refusing to let Carr get underneath him. On one possession, Roman's point guard tried to force a pass to Carr. Kobe stole it, tipped it ahead of himself, chased after it. A Roman player closed in on the ball, but Kobe grabbed it, whipped it around behind his back and in front of him again, kept going toward the basket. Two more Roman players came at Kobe, who this time threw the ball between his legs, from behind his butt to in front of his groin, an outlet pass to himself. The ball bouncing, he retrieved it one step inside the foul line, at full speed, and soared and dunked it with two hands—*BOOM*—and when he landed, he started screaming. "It was elation," Carr said. "He gave that look: 'I'm the best player on the floor, and don't you forget that.'"

Was Kobe finished? He was not finished. He later cruised down the right wing, sized up Carr, and crossed him over, just like Carr had done to him early in the game, shrugging him off with an in-and-out dribble, sticking a jumper and holding his arm and hand there like a tall bird standing in high grass, Jordan-like. Carr heard, from the stands, Joe Bryant shout out, "Awww, yeah, son. Just like I told you." He never forgot that, the father adding the exclamation point for the son.

From twenty-five points at halftime, Carr finished the game with twenty-nine points, nine rebounds, and nine assists. Kobe scored thirty-two in the second half, thirty-six in the game. When Carr missed a shot at the buzzer and the Aces won by a point, he fell to the court, and Kobe picked him up.

"Listen, man," Kobe said. "It's only a summer-league game. You bring out the best in me. I'll see you again."

Only a summer-league game. The line was laughable in light of the championship game a few days later. Lower Merion was matched up against a familiar opponent, Chester, whose coach and players continued to revel in their belief that the Aces, whether in their summer or winter iteration, couldn't beat them. That head coach was a new head coach: Fred Pickett, a longtime assistant at the school who reveled in the Clippers' status as the preeminent program in Pennsylvania basketball and their image as the most forbidding. Unlike his predecessor, Alonzo Lewis, who insisted his players speak only in anodyne clichés about themselves and their opponents and who spoke that way himself, Pickett wasn't above telling local reporters exactly what he thought or claimed to think. It was a tactic, a reaffirmation to his players of his confidence in them, and Pickett was willing to annoy other coaches in the name of keeping his team's psychological shield impenetrable.

Down by eight at halftime, Lower Merion scored the first basket of the second half, only to have the teenager who had volunteered to operate the scoreboard mistakenly give the two points to Chester. The Clippers actually led by six, but the scoreboard said they led by ten. Egan called the referee over. This was just summer league. No one kept an official scorebook. But this was the championship game, and this was Chester.

"Hold on," Egan said to the ref. "They got the score wrong."

Then, Egan motioned to Pickett.

"Fred," he said, "you know that it was eight points and we just scored."

Pickett just sat there, his arms crossed over his medicine-ball belly.

"I don't know that."

"Fred! Come on!"

The score was quickly corrected, but Lower Merion still lost. Another championship game against Chester, another loss. Downer, on hand to watch, and Egan ushered the team into a hallway outside the gym. The coaches didn't try to console the players. They didn't have to. From most of them, a loss in a summer-league championship game elicited the same reaction: *OK, now we can go to the pool or the beach.*

That was not Kobe's reaction. This was a championship game, and this was Chester. He started to speak, and as he did, he grabbed two handfuls of his damp T-shirt, wrinkling and wringing it until fat drops of his sweat beaded up on the fabric, fell from his shirt, and plopped against the floor.

"You motherfuckers had better be ready to play," he said. "I'm not fucking losing to this fucking team again. This is bullshit. You all had better be ready to get your asses in gear."

ON JULY 25, 1995, two weeks after the ABCD Camp, Mike Krzyzewski handwrote, in Duke-blue ink, a personal note to Mike Egan to express his fondness for Kobe.

> *Dear Mike,*
> *Nice win over Roman Catholic! You did a fine job with the kids.*
> *They play hard and well together. Mike, thanks for all of your help.*
> *I am very appreciative. Kobe is truly special and I want to coach him!*
> *My Best Always,*
> *Mike*

Egan was honored to receive the note, but as much as he wished he knew what Kobe's decision would be, he still had no idea. Today, he keeps the letter not in a desk drawer, not buried somewhere out of sight, but mounted in the center of a wall in his home office in Paoli, Pennsylvania, across from a bookshelf overflowing with autobiographies and fat historical narratives. Just fourteen miles away, on an early September day in 2020, a Duke basketball, striped blue and white with a Blue Devils head insignia, balanced atop a desk in Joe Bryant's old study at 1224 Remington Road. Richard and Kate Bayer, the couple who lived there, still didn't know exactly why Kobe had left it behind, but they, like everyone else, could guess.

IT DIDN'T take the Sixers' prospective savior long to see that the deck was stacked against him. On July 31, 1995, a month after the team had drafted Stackhouse, Joe Carbone, the team's strength and conditioning coach, watched a tall, lanky kid walk into the Fieldhouse and head straight to Lucas. The two talked privately for a moment before Lucas called Carbone over and introduced him to Kobe. Stocky and muscled and shaped like a fire hydrant, Carbone was a former competitive bodybuilder who had spent his entire life living and working in Rockland County, New York, before joining the Sixers that season. He knew nothing of Philadelphia's high school basketball scene and had no idea who Kobe was, and at five foot two, he gazed up at the six-foot-six teen.

You've got to get with Joe, Lucas told Kobe, *and get stronger.*

The reshaping of Kobe Bryant's body began immediately, with Carbone leading Kobe over to a loose pile of exercise equipment and machinery in the corner of the gym. The Fieldhouse didn't have a separate weight room, just a squat rack with two benches, a couple of selectorized and pin-loaded machines, some high-low pulleys and cables. "But if you know what you're doing," Carbone said, "you can get around that. You can do all the lifts." Since the Sixers and other players started their workouts at 9:00 A.M., Kobe began his with Carbone at 7:00 A.M., and they would continue in full view of all the other athletes. The arrangement was awkward, Carbone had to admit later, because it was clear who the real chosen one was.

Carbone created a spreadsheet to track Kobe's workouts and progress. He has kept it ever since, so he can show you, a quarter century later, that Kobe's first weight-training session with him comprised four rounds of exercises, from back-squatting 65 pounds for ten repetitions to three sets of twenty curl-ups to push-pressing 105 pounds for ten repetitions. By their third session, on Thursday, August 3, Kobe was closing with ten back-squat reps of 135 pounds. "He was built as an endurance guy," Carbone said. "His muscles were based on endurance. He wasn't a fast-twitch guy. Fast-twitch muscles help you sprint fast and get large, thick muscles. You see an NFL running back: very thick thighs, can bench four hundred pounds, squat six hundred pounds. That wasn't Kobe's style of body, so his gains came hard. They didn't come easy. But he did gain." Come summer's end, Kobe had gone from 185 pounds to 200, those fifteen additional pounds nothing but muscle and sinew. Phil Martelli, out of the corner of his eye, would catch him pedaling on an exercise bike or sprinting with a parachute attached to his torso, Carbone nearby monitoring him. *This is different,* Martelli thought, *from anything else I've seen from all these other great players coming through Philadelphia.* "He was there to prepare," Martelli said later, "not to play."

THE GENERAL manager of the Washington Bullets, John Nash, was, if such a characterization could be a title, a Philly Guy—an alumnus of St. Joseph's University, formerly a longtime executive with the Sixers, an insider who knew where all the bodies were buried, a man for whom a handshake was a bond. "If John says something," Frank Layden, the longtime president and coach of the Utah Jazz, once said, "you can put it in the bank." When Nash was the director of the Philadelphia Big Five in the mid-1970s, he and Joe Bryant had maintained a friendly relationship. They ran in the same circles, and Nash knew the Bryants, knew their reputation as a solid, grounded family.

One pick after the Sixers chose Stackhouse in the 1995 draft, Nash and the Bullets, already with two elite post players in Chris Webber and Juwan Howard, took the most talented player left on the board, even though he was another big man: Philadelphia native Rasheed Wallace, who had been Stackhouse's teammate at North Carolina. Nash, of course, as a consummate Philly Guy, knew that Stackhouse and two of Washington's guards, Doug Overton and Tim Legler, took part in those summer pickup games and workouts, and he knew that Lucas often sat in on them. So Nash would call Lucas once a week or so to get an update, just the friendly sharing of observations and information between colleagues and competitors.

One day, Nash asked, "How's Stackhouse doing?"

"Oh," Lucas replied, "he's the second-best guard in the gym."

Nash was taken aback. The Sixers thought Stackhouse to be a cornerstone piece to their franchise. Were Overton and Legler the only other NBA guards taking part in the workouts? Was Lucas talking about one of them? *Stack's probably better than they are,* Nash thought.

"Who's better than him?" Nash asked.

"Oh, Kobe," Lucas said. "Kobe is lighting up the gym."

Kobe, Nash thought. *If I get the chance to draft him, I'm not passing it up.*

SUMMERTIME WAS Sam Rines time for Kobe, and it was Sam Rines Jr.'s time with Kobe. Later in July, after the ABCD Camp, the Sam Rines All-Stars flew to Las Vegas for the Adidas Big Time Tournament. Entering the tournament was a break from the Rines family's approach to building its AAU basketball program, from keeping the program and its aims centered in and around Philadelphia. But Kobe had been pushing Sam Jr. to expand the team's reach, to take on more national competition, and on the flight out to Vegas, in a private conversation with him, Sam Jr. realized why. Kobe told him that he was planning to enter the NBA draft.

"The relationship became tight," Sam Jr. said. "Stuff got real."

It makes sense that Kobe would confess his plans to Sam Jr. first. Yes, the two had had their conflicts. Sam Jr. wondered when Kobe would learn to play a less self-centered game; Kobe bristled at Sam Jr.'s demands that he take his teammates into consideration. But as much as winning a state championship mattered to him, as close as he was to Gregg Downer and Mike Egan and Jeremy Treatman, Kobe kept separate those two worlds, high school ball and AAU ball, and in only one of them was he capable of proving that he was ready to turn pro. Scoring forty points against a Central League team in the middle of January was nice; excelling against the nation's best high school players, in front of hundreds of coaches and scouts, in front of the power people of America's basketball machine, at an event arranged by a sneaker mogul who was befriending him and his family, was cardinal. Rip Hamilton didn't make the trip with the Sam Rines All-Stars, and the team didn't win the tournament, but those matters were ancillary. Kobe's future was taking definitive form. In the closing seconds of one game in Vegas, he even passed the ball to a teammate for a wide-open layup. That the teammate missed the layup and the Sam Rines All-Stars lost the game was inconsequential. The pass, with all those eyes upon him and evaluating him and judging him, was an indication that Kobe was at last taking to heart Sam Jr.'s pleas for him to share the ball more, that he was allowing his full and multifaceted game, and not his ego and mouth, to speak for him. "He became my favorite player with that play," Sam Jr. said. "I even told him, 'That's the way you should play all the time. No matter what people say, you look like the best player, period, once you start making passes and don't play so selfishly.' I respected him after that play."

All those coaches and scouts surely did, too. But did they see what was happening, what Kobe had in mind for himself? Did they understand they were, to him and to Joe, a means to an end, that the Bryants, as much as they needed the validation and approval of those coaches and scouts, were looking past them, at the life and career to come for Kobe? They were tasting it already. At the Keystone Games in August, Joe, Sam Rines Sr., and Ron Luber—the father of one of Kobe's AAU teammates, Justin Luber—watched Kobe and Rip Hamilton romp to three victories over Pennsylvania all-star teams, then caught a quick flight from Harrisburg to Atlantic City for a night of craps and other gambling at Trump Plaza Hotel and Casino. Luber, a doctor, picked up the tab, a friendship forming among the three of them. And the basketball itself? Well, that was sweet for Kobe, because his team's opponent in the Keystone championship game featured several players from Chester and was coached by . . . Gregg Downer and Mike Egan. And when Kobe capped the tournament by scoring forty-seven points in that championship game, in a win over his coaches, the outcome and his performance became a witty and sharp retort to Downer's and Egan's instruction once Lower Merion's season began that fall.

Hey, Kobe, here's what we're gonna do on defense . . .

Yeah, will it work as well as it did that time I dropped forty-seven on you at the Keystone Games?

Looking back on what he called "that famous St. Joe's summer," Downer, now a father himself, could take on the perspective that Joe had then. Here's Kobe, going toe-to-toe with Jerry Stackhouse and Vernon Maxwell. Here's Kobe, trying to throw down dunks over his new chauffeur, Shawn Bradley. Here's Sonny Vaccaro, making moves. "Joe had to be thinking, 'It ain't happening,'" Downer said. "'It ain't happening for La Salle, Villanova, Duke, none of these people.'" Yes, Joe had to be thinking it . . . because *Kobe* was thinking it, especially when it came to the theory that the two of them would unite to revitalize the program at Joe's alma mater. The chatter among the "Fab Five" was already starting to dissipate. Sam Rines Jr. had encountered Lester Earl in Las Vegas, had stopped him for a quick question—*You gonna play with Kobe?*—and Earl had given a revealing answer: *Man, I don't know about that one, Coach. Kobe shoots a lot. I could play with Kobe, but at La Salle? I don't know.* Michigan coach Steve Fisher showed up at an open gym at Hayman Hall to scout Kobe, took in the surroundings, and said to someone, *Damn, this is where they play?* It wasn't, of course, but that didn't matter, because the truth was unveiling itself: It was too much to think that La Salle could attract Kobe and that Kobe could change La Salle once he got there. The place was too small for him. Above all, Kobe himself had no time for such treacle. He just wasn't ready to share his true thoughts yet. He had too far yet to go, and if people weren't paying attention, if they weren't completing the dot puzzle, that failure was on them.

There's no way I'm going to La Salle. If I were, I would have committed a long time ago, and I would have had those four other players come with me. Since I didn't announce during the early-signing period that I was going there, you would have thought everyone would have understood that. People can be so slow sometimes.

JOHN COX had issued warning after warning, admonition after admonition, to his older brother, Sharif Butler, before they joined Kobe in the back corner of the gym at St. Joe's one day that summer. Butler had been away from Philadelphia for a while now. A six-foot-five guard, he was playing for coach Billy Tubbs at Texas Christian University in Fort Worth, and he was back just to visit family, just to humiliate his little cousin Kobe one more time for kicks and giggles. *Yo,* Cox kept telling him, *you don't want to play him. It's done for you. It's over.* But Sharif Butler was a starting guard in the Big 12 Conference. Sharif Butler was a damn good ballplayer himself. And Sharif Butler had no clue of the monster that, with all that torment years earlier, he had helped to create. One more time, Cox told him, *Don't play him. He's going to destroy you.* Butler played him anyway, because he had been away for too long, because he hadn't been bearing witness to Kobe's transformation.

The game was to sixteen. Kobe won. No, that's not quite right, doesn't quite do it justice. Kobe beat him, 16–0. Kobe demolished him. Kobe dunked on him. Kobe unleashed a barrage of obscenities and manhood-questioning insults against a family member three years his senior, an expulsion of fury that had built up over hundreds of losses to Butler. "He annihilated him like he stole something from him," Cox said. When it was over, Kobe got a drink of water. Butler, chastened, trudged over to Cox.

"John," Butler said, "he's ready. He can play in the NBA right now. He's there."

PART III

*I love keeping secrets, in case
you haven't noticed that by now.*

—KOBE BRYANT

13

SECRETS
AND SHARKS

HE WAS A SENIOR NOW, and before his final season of Lower Merion basketball began, Kobe Bryant would wake to the darkness and stillness of predawn morning in late autumn, coil himself into the driver's seat of his Land Cruiser, and embark on a two-mile ride to his high school. Nothing would be open yet, not the supermarkets or the bagel shops. No one would be on the road or the sidewalks, not for a while. If he allowed himself a couple of more minutes' sleep, if he slipped out the front door a little later, he would, while driving, pass another car or catch in his peripheral vision a jogger or two, steady as metronomes, breath steaming the ten inches in front of their faces, the streetlights' soft glow glinting off their reflective vests. Otherwise, there wouldn't be much to distract him as he turned left out of the driveway, right onto Haverford Avenue, then right again onto Argyle Road. There, for all the tightly packed houses and the go-go-go lifestyles of the baby boomers living in those houses, all would be quiet, and only porch lights or a full moon's glare would puncture the canopy of night.

The speed limit wouldn't top 35 mph on any street on his route, so the drive would likely take him seven minutes or so. Perhaps it would take less than seven minutes, because he was a teenager and impatient and would want to get to school as quickly as possible, so his foot might give the gas pedal a heavier push, and the SUV might get up to 40 mph, maybe 45. Or perhaps it would take him more than seven minutes, because he was a Black teenager driving around the Main Line and would want to be cautious, because one never knew where a cop might be and what that cop might think upon seeing a Black kid driving around the Main Line in the predawn darkness.

His windows would be shut and his heat would be on, so sometimes the silence would be total. Would he picture and plan out the morning's workout in his mind, the foot drills and the three-pointers and the midrange shots? Would he think ahead to his team's next practice, its next game? Would he see himself in the NBA, the crowd throbbing, the winning shot his to take at the end? Sometimes, he wouldn't drive alone. Sometimes, he would swing by the house of Robby Schwartz to pick him up. A stumpy junior guard, Schwartz was one of the most personable kids on the team, a burbling fizz of one-liners and funny anecdotes. He had spent the two days of tryouts flinging himself around the gym, diving for every loose ball, taking every charge, winning every sprint. "I never practiced so hard in my life," he said later. "I *had* to make the team. I knew something special was going to happen, and I wanted to be part of it."

Kobe would park in the faculty lot, in a space close to an entrance to one of the school's three gymnasiums, an act of entitlement that, one could argue, he should not have been afforded. Construction at and around the school that fall had cut the number of student-allocated spots from seventy-nine to twenty-four, and since residents were so put out by the cars flooding their sweetgum-shaded neighborhoods, police were writing forty-dollar tickets to students who had the temerity to park on the streets near campus. *And Kobe gets to park his SUV anywhere he wants, like he's the principal?* But he could justify himself, weave the rationalization, so easily. He was arriving at school before 5:30 A.M., before any faculty members or students, and if he was spending more time in that building honing his craft than they were honing theirs, if he was bound for fame and immortality—and he was certain that he was—why were they more deserving of one of those parking spots than he was? So a janitor would let Kobe into the school, and he and Schwartz would enter either the main gym or its tertiary one, called "the Ardmore Gym." Either way, it would take five minutes for the lights to come on and a half hour for the gym to warm up to room temperature, and as Schwartz stood there, shivering in his shorts—"I have never been so cold as I was in that gym"—he asked himself why, when Kobe had asked several teammates if they'd join him for these shootarounds, he had been the one to say, *Sure*.

"I had all these thoughts that we're going to develop this great chemistry and somehow it would lead to me playing more, or playing at all," he said. "I just ended up rebounding for him for an hour. I never said anything. He's my teammate. He's a year older than me. I was a very small person in high school. I was not going to speak out of turn, and again, I just wanted to be part of whatever his journey was. 'I'll just rebound for him for a couple of minutes. We'll do some drills.' But it was just an hour of me rebounding for him.

"What's funny is, looking back on it, it was the most fun ever. It was amazing. People would have done anything just to be in my position, just to rebound for him. I didn't think about it like that at the time. Now I have such a high level of appreciation for every single second with him and with the team. That was the best year ever. Every moment, pregame, postgame, practices, I would kill to go back and do any of them."

A HIGH school senior possesses a confidence and a self-comfort that, to that point in his or her life, is unmatched. A high school senior has the run of the school for the first semester and can coast through the second semester, once the college applications have been submitted and the acceptance letters are filling his or her mailbox, once he or she has a better sense of what's ahead, once summer—his or her first as a high school graduate, as an eighteen-year-old, as an adult—and its new freedom are in sight. A high school senior is familiar with the landscape of his or her daily existence, what's cool, what isn't. A high school senior gets the bigger locker, the prime table in the cafeteria, the invites to the parties. A high school senior struts.

Kobe Bryant had cause to strut more than most high school seniors. All semblance of that shy, unsure freshman was gone, replaced by a seventeen-year-old who had proved to himself that his dream—playing in the NBA—was not merely attainable but at hand. That knowledge liberated him. He was aware at all times of his place and role and responsibilities in Lower Merion's ecosystem. But he was also ready and inclined to push boundaries—others' boundaries and his own, inside school, outside it, trying on moods and images and identities as if they were department-store clothes. When a vagrant approached him and Matt Matkov on a Philadelphia street and asked Matkov for money, Kobe picked the guy up and *threw* him away. Matkov got into a fight at the Shack in Ardmore, and after Kobe interceded on his friend's behalf and defused the situation, he told Matkov, "Matt, you can't be makin' n——s mad like that. You just can't." One night, a diner waitress served him a small piece of apple pie, and he told her, "Ma'am, I'm six-six. This ain't gonna fill me up." His desire to become the best basketball player in the world so consumed him that his friends didn't begin to understand its effect on him until after he was gone. "This is something I struggled with a lot after he died," Robby Schwartz recalled. "People say things a lot about him, and I think they're speaking out of turn. 'Oh, he was like this.' Nobody knows anybody. Everybody just wanted to have a story about what he was like, and nobody knew that. I've always thought that to be great at something, you have to be obsessed with it. For a seventeen-year-old, imagine that level of focus and intensity. He was just extremely focused on one goal. That is what people didn't understand. He had one goal in mind, and if you weren't a part of it, if you didn't contribute to that goal . . ."

That blinkered fanatic was not the Kobe whom Katrina Christmas encountered at Student Voice meetings and those mornings when he stopped by the library, sometimes to chat, sometimes to confide. That Kobe was respectful, inquisitive, eager for her advice, even about his interactions and relationships with the opposite sex, such as he had them. "He was like my son," Christmas said. "When we talked about girls, we talked about respect and looking for respect for them. I would tell him,

'You don't want those girls with the skirts real high.' I'm an old lady, and he was a young boy, so I'm coming from an old lady perspective. It was life in general and just how to get along with one another. That's what our relationship was: how to get along with other people and other people who may not look like you. He never had a cockiness to him. He was like everybody else, but he wasn't like everybody else."

It was one of the defining paradoxes of Kobe's entire life. He could relate, and he could not relate. He was in the same homeroom as Jordan Couzens, who was the star of the ice-hockey club, and Kobe often drove out to King of Prussia to watch the team's games and support him. "I think Kobe recognized he got all the attention," one of his classmates said, "but Jordan still owns every record at Lower Merion for ice hockey, and there was a kinship between the two of them." During an English class analysis of the Flannery O'Connor short story "Everything That Rises Must Converge," Matkov found a way to divert the discussion back to Kobe, arguing that the story's main character had fooled himself, had failed to be honest with himself, in a manner that Kobe never would. "A lot of people think he's living in a bubble, his own world," said Matkov, his ponytailed hair bobbing as he spoke and nodded toward Kobe, "but I know he's not. He's connected to me, and he's connected to himself. It doesn't get any truer than him." To be in the classroom at that moment was to be unsure whether to admire Matkov for his loyalty to his hero/ best bud or roll your eyes at his sycophancy. For a home-economics project, Kobe was paired with his friend Lauren Rodrick, whom he had met when as a junior she transferred to Lower Merion after attending Catholic school for six years. She had told him how out of place she felt as a new student, and he had told her that he understood. Now their home-ec teacher had handed them a Cabbage Patch doll for the time-honored exercise of high school students' learning what it's like to be parents, to care for a newborn. Fair-skinned, Rodrick burst into laughter when Kobe looked at the doll's darker complexion and asked her, "Are you sure this is your baby?" She thought him clever, a jokester who was more comfortable in one-on-one situations than he was in groups. The larger the crowd around Kobe, Rodrick noticed, the quieter he got.

When they were juniors, she had been surprised when he told her that, while of course he had hung out with two or three friends at a time, he had never been to a house party, never been among a couple of dozen high school kids without his or anyone else's parents supervising. "Kobe, you might be going off to college," Rodrick had told him. "You can't go without going to a house party!" So after trying to deflect Rodrick's insistence—*Naw, I'm gonna stay home, and you guys go have fun*—Kobe had accompanied her, her boyfriend, Shaya, and a few others to a house in Yeadon, a small city in Delaware County, and for one Saturday night he let the music and the attention from girls he had never met before take him away. "He was a hot commodity," Rodrick recalled. "He was so on guard about life, but he was enjoying the girls not knowing him for being Kobe Bryant. He was just a good-looking guy at a party. It was a pretty good night. He was very thankful that he went."

Such freedom and relative anonymity were no longer available to him at Lower Merion. On October 3, students turned their eyes to the televisions in the hallways and lobby for the conclusion of the O. J. Simpson murder trial, and the not-guilty verdict split the school, Black kids cheering, white kids disbelieving, the tension somehow never touching Kobe. "I don't know how much people saw him as Black or white as much as they saw him as Kobe, this looming figure," Schwartz said. "He was amongst us, but in a way, he was bigger than us."

He was growing more comfortable with his exalted place in its social strata, and with himself. He and Griffin went out more frequently on weekends, to clubs and other spots in and around the city. A rumor circulated through the school that he had begun dating actress Tatyana Ali, who starred in the sitcom *The Fresh Prince of Bel-Air,* a rumor that Kobe himself had started by joking with his friend Rennae Williams that he would take either Ali or the pop star/actress Brandy to the senior prom. (When Melanie Amato, a reporter for *The Merionite,* asked him if the rumor was true, he laughed. "No comment," he told her.) Because of his status, he left an impression in every interaction, with every person in the building. Early in the school year, his guidance counselor, Frank Hartwell, was meeting with some freshmen when Kobe came into Hartwell's office and interrupted. "Hi, Mr. Hartwell," he said. "How's your family?" The freshmen audibly gasped, then stared at him. *Here's Kobe Bryant! I'm up close to him!*

A later meeting with Hartwell had a different tone. In March 1995, the school board had adopted a revised policy on sexual harassment that required training seminars the following fall for the school's staff and students. As a counselor, Hartwell had to gather his students into small groups to review and teach them about the formal guidelines of the policy, which included learning "about the relationship between rules, laws, safety, and the protection of the rights of the individual" and "the differences between appropriate and inappropriate physical contact."

After Hartwell explained the purpose of the session, Kobe stood up and headed toward the door.

"Mr. Hartwell, I don't need this," he said. "I don't need this."

"Kobe," Hartwell said, "you need this."

Kobe sat back down, and Hartwell continued with the seminar.

THE PRESSURE of coaching Kobe and chasing a state championship had been weighing on Gregg Downer well before tryouts and practices began in the late autumn of 1995. He anticipated that the upcoming season would be his last at Lower Merion. He had accepted his new job as a phys-ed teacher at Episcopal Academy with two understandings: first, that he would have the opportunity to coach the Aces for Kobe's entire senior season; second, that once the season had ended, he would devote himself fully to teaching and coaching at Episcopal, that even if he never became the school's head basketball coach, he would make his career there. But what if there was no district title or state title? What if the season was somehow a failure? The daily challenge of Kobe, of pushing him and being pushed by him, was invigorating, but Downer couldn't quell those questions. Before Kobe came to Lower Merion, Downer would lie awake at night sometimes, worried not that the Aces wouldn't win their next game, but that they wouldn't *score*. It was silly, but it was real. Now the stress could cripple him if he wasn't careful, and other people were feeling it, too. At a pep rally for the football team, Kobe jumped into a seniors-vs.-juniors tug-of-war, five students on one side, five on the other, upperclassmen supremacy on the line. Students had tossed their book bags all over the place, creating a minefield on the gymnasium floor, and when Lynne Freeland, the teacher who had organized the pep rally and the mother of Kobe's friend Susan Freeland, saw how close Kobe was to stepping on the bags, she scrambled to kick and heave them out of harm's way. *Oh, God,* she thought, *Gregg will kill me if Kobe sprains his ankle.* The phone in the athletic office—a broom closet–size room barely big enough to fit the director, Tom McGovern, and the secretary, Mary Murray—never stopped ringing: coaches, scouts, media, parents, community members. McGovern bought an answering machine that could hold as many as a hundred messages. After two days of flicking on the lights in the office and finding the machine full because the calls had kept coming overnight, he unplugged it. There would be so many requests for tickets throughout the regular season, and the lines to purchase them would be so long, that McGovern had to move ticket sales out of the athletic office because the office was in an academic area, and the lines were disrupting hallway traffic during school hours. On game nights, hundreds of people who had assumed they could buy tickets just before tip-off would be turned away at the door, their retreating cars creating snarls along Montgomery Avenue and headaches for the township police. "By his junior and senior years," McGovern said, "Kobe occupied almost every minute of my day." And Murray's, too, though she wasn't as sanguine about it. Of everyone at Lower Merion, she seemed the person who most disliked or disapproved of The Kobe Experience, as if the old days of having a mediocre basketball program were preferable to the bustle and excitement inside the school and the spotlight on it. "They were getting overwhelmed," Downer said. "Somebody like Mary Murray was eager for the season to end."

For all that strain, Downer and the rest of the team couldn't wait for the season to start. The Aces, though still Kobe-centric, would have a slightly different look to them without Guy Stewart and Evan Monsky, both of whom had graduated. Emory Dabney would take over at point guard, joining Kobe, Jermaine Griffin, Dan Pangrazio, and Brendan

Pettit in the starting lineup, and two other new players gave Downer a deeper bench: forward Omar Hatcher, who had transferred from Archbishop Carroll, and freshman Kareem Barksdale. As he had done the year before, Downer loaded up the Aces' early-season schedule: a game against Donnie Carr and Roman Catholic at Drexel University; a rematch with St. Anthony, this time at the Fieldhouse at St. Joseph's; and three games at the Beach Ball Classic, a tournament in Myrtle Beach, South Carolina, that would feature several of the best players and teams in the nation, including Glen Oaks and Lester Earl, Eau Claire (South Carolina) and Jermaine O'Neal, and Shadow Mountain High School, from Arizona, and its point guard, Mike Bibby, the son of Joe Bryant's former teammate Henry Bibby.

Most important, for the team and for his own peace of mind, Downer brought on two more assistant coaches, assigning them unusual roles. He didn't have to find the first coach; the first coach found him. Jimmy Kieserman, who was six feet tall and twenty-six years old, who had grown up with Sam Rines Jr. and had started at point guard for both Rider University and the University of Miami, and who was now working in insurance and living in Narberth, happened to catch a feature about Kobe one night on a local TV news station. The grandson of legendary Temple head coach Harry Litwack, Kieserman asked himself something that a good coach, or a grandson of a great one, would ask: *How is this kid getting better in high school? Who is on staff to help him?* He called Downer and volunteered to be a quasi trainer for Kobe. Kieserman could dunk. Kieserman had played at the Maccabi Games in Israel and professionally in the Eastern Basketball League, had a killer crossover dribble, and had developed an athletic, aggressive game. "I felt like I was a man, he was a kid, and I could help him with his skill set, push him around," he said. Downer accepted.

Downer's second addition to his staff, Jeremy Treatman, was something of a formality, since the two men were already friends and since Treatman spent so much time with Downer, Kobe, and Joe. But Treatman wouldn't be so much a coach, Downer told him, as he would be a media-relations chief. Of all the responsibilities that accompanied having

Kobe on the team, the one that Downer genuinely hated was the incessant interview requests from newspaper and TV reporters. Stoic with strangers, careful with his words whenever he spoke publicly, Downer preferred to focus on coaching his team, and not only did Treatman have the professional contacts, experience, and know-how to handle the media onslaught, but he was jazzed about the chance to be an intimate to Kobe and to abandon any pretense of objectivity when it came to his relationships within the program. Why cover Lower Merion basketball when he could be part of Lower Merion basketball? It was, to Downer's credit, an innovative and modern way to build a high school basketball coaching staff. Mike Egan would remain the defensive specialist. Drew Downer would be the amateur sports psychologist. Kieserman would be Kobe's foil/tutor, and Treatman's presence allowed Downer to oversee and orchestrate the entire operation.

The journey would not be without its bumps in the season's early weeks. Egan's preseason notes—their heading: "4 Months to play, a lifetime to regret"—left little doubt that the tough-love methods that Downer and he employed during Kobe's junior season would carry over to his senior one: "Kobe—more forceful in paint, rebounds, altering, patrolling . . . Jermaine—finish, finish, finish, finish, finish, 2nd effort . . . DAN—court awareness, handle ball more, pump + go. Drew, think about agility work for him (heavy feet)." They would do their best to treat Kobe as if he were just another member of the team, even if he obviously wasn't. On the first day of practice, in fact, Kobe was aghast at the laziness of his teammates, particularly his newest ones. Dabney was late and—because he was, in his words, "just fucking around and not doing my work"—would be academically ineligible for three games. Hatcher was late, too, as was another backup, Cary "Butter" Walker. "They really had no clue," Kobe said later. "They tried out for the basketball team, but they did not know what to expect. They didn't know what we were about to go through emotion-wise, the hype, the media. They had no. Clue. They were at practice just dogging it." He pulled aside Griffin, his closest friend on the team.

"Jermaine," he told him, "we may have to do this all by ourselves. I might have to average forty, and you might have to average thirty."

Before a game had been played that season, Kobe's skills and white-hot need to win were beginning to separate him from his teammates, who struggled to live up to his expectations for them. Every practice, Downer had the team perform a rebounding drill: One player pursued the errant shot; the other tried to box him out. If the offensive player touched the ball, let alone grabbed the rebound, the defender had to stay on the floor. Kobe had never lost a scrimmage or competitive drill during his high school career. So when he and Pangrazio, set against each other, chased a loose ball toward a concrete wall, Kobe did what he felt had to be done. Just as Pangrazio put his hands on the basketball, Kobe shoved him in the small of his back. A metal plate hung at the bottom of the wall. As Pangrazio crashed into the concrete, his elbow struck one of the plate's screws, slicing a gash in his arm. Kobe plucked the ball from Pangrazio's blood-covered hands and carried it with him as he strode to center court, triumphant that he had remained unbeaten. Remarkably, Pangrazio bore no bitterness over the incident, even though he immediately went to the hospital to have three stitches laced into his arm. "As much as people might think Kobe went overboard," he said later, "we all loved his competitiveness. We knew we were part of something special. Kobe drove me to a level I never thought was possible to reach and asked all of us to do the same for him."

Generally, Robby Schwartz was a favorite target for torment. Those morning carpools earned him no quarter with Kobe. When the Aces scrimmaged full-court, Downer often had them play six-on-five, assigning Schwartz and another diminutive player, Leo Stacy, to guard and irritate Kobe. "I would always think to myself, 'One of these times, he's going to haul off and hit me,'" Schwartz recalled. "We were all over him. We'd try not to let him get the ball, and then once he got it, we'd double-team him and hack him and foul him. It got a little dicey sometimes. He'd smack our hand away. I got hit in the face with the ball after a dunk several times." Once, Schwartz at last exacted a measure of revenge, driving into Kobe on a fast break and spinning the ball off the backboard for a layup. Kobe flopped to the floor to try to draw a charge, and Schwartz caught the ball as it fell through the basket and threw it at him while he was still flat on his back. *Hell yeah. I just scored on the best player in the country.* Schwartz ran back on defense, pumping his fists as he approached half-court, when he saw his teammates pointing at him. "I turned around," he said, "and the ball was coming at my face." Kobe had hurled it at him, Nolan Ryan–style. Schwartz ducked. The ball whizzed past his head. Practice continued as if nothing had happened.

There was one moment involving Schwartz, though, that has long been stitched into the tapestry of the Kobe Bryant story, though its details have blurred over so much passing time and so many retellings that the anecdote might as well be folklore. From those who witnessed the incident, this seems the most accurate rendition of events: The Aces were having an intrasquad scrimmage, and Kobe and Schwartz were on the same team. With the score tied, with Kobe constantly drawing double- and triple-teams, Schwartz got the idea to use Kobe as a decoy. In the corner, Kobe clapped his hands and called for the ball—"Rob! Rob!"—but Schwartz faked a pass to him and drove to the basket instead. It was the first shot he took all game. "I missed the layup," Schwartz recalled. "I would tell you I got fouled, but we weren't really calling fouls."

The other team scored to win the scrimmage, Kobe's first loss of any kind to his teammates in four years. He slammed the ball down. He berated Schwartz: *That wasn't the smart play! What do you think you're doing?* "It started off like it was playful and kidding," Downer said. "Then we realized, 'He's not kidding.'" His anger escalated until Schwartz muttered, "Dude, relax."

To Schwartz, time then stopped. *Oh, shit, I shouldn't have said anything.* Kobe made some kind of motion toward him, and Schwartz didn't wait around to see what it was. He dashed through the double doors of the gym and ran to the top of the hallway. "I was terrified," he said. "I knew I had said something to someone who was significantly bigger than me. Fear took over, and I just fled. Walking back into the gym . . . talk about embarrassing."

Whether Kobe "chased" Schwartz down the hallway has become the subject of legend ever since. "He didn't chase him," Egan said. "The real story is better: He was just furious at the guy. It didn't matter that Robby was the last guy on the bench." Treatman insisted that Kobe never took his eyes off Schwartz for the remaining seventy-five minutes of practice, and as Treatman drove home that night, he couldn't shake what he had witnessed, the intensity of Kobe's reaction to what anyone else would regard as a meaningless loss in just another scrimmage. He stopped his car at a traffic light, and the significance of the scene occurred to him. *That's what makes him great. That's what makes him different from everybody else.*

"I think some of the kids were a little intimidated," Treatman said.

Maybe they had reason to be, and if Kobe's teammates couldn't handle his competitiveness, how would they handle Roman Catholic? Or St. Anthony? Or, come the district and state playoffs, Chester? Or, suppose the opposite problem developed, and the other players, because they trusted Kobe to bail them out, became overconfident? Downer saw potential pitfalls everywhere, including one born of the team's presumed improvement. The Aces' overall increase in talent had put Matt Matkov's roster spot in jeopardy, and Downer fretted over what Kobe's reaction would be if the coaches couldn't in good conscience keep Matkov on the team.

"What am I going to do with this guy?" Downer asked Egan. "He really can't play for us, but he's Kobe's best friend."

"Cut him," Egan said. "Kobe won't notice for two weeks."

As it turned out, Matkov left the team before Downer could cut him. Two weeks later, Kobe looked around practice and asked, "What happened to Matkov?"

TIME AFTER time over the previous two years, Joe Bryant had said to Speedy Morris, *If Kobe goes to college, he'll go to La Salle.* It was an easy thing for Joe to say to placate his boss and keep his job, but nothing had been finalized, and as far as Kobe and Joe were concerned, nothing would be. A breach had developed in Morris and Joe's relationship, and Morris wasn't fully aware of its depth.

Joe kept talking to Jeremy Treatman once a week, whispering into his office phone to him so that Morris wouldn't hear, updating Treatman on every conversation with Sonny Vaccaro. Struggling to balance being a parent and being a recruiter, Joe resented the tone of Morris's questions whenever he asked about Kobe. "He was asking me as a recruiter," Joe once said, "and I didn't appreciate that." When the *Philadelphia Daily News* published a story on October 5, 1995, titled, "La Salle, NBA top Kobe Bryant's list," Kobe had snickered with scorn at the headline. He had told Pam, "Mom, no way I'm going to La Salle, no way in hell," and he had told Joe, "Dad, it's not on you. I really don't like Coach Morris."

Morris didn't know any of this was happening—*suspected,* yes; *knew,* no—and because he didn't, he held out some hope that he could win Kobe over, get him to see the benefits of being a megastar for the Explorers. Joe and Kobe agreed to have dinner with him at a restaurant in Roxborough. With Kobe sitting at one end of the table and Morris at the other, Kobe said, "I'm coming." It was an oral commitment, but it wasn't binding beyond Kobe and Joe's word to uphold it.

The next morning, Joe entered Morris's office at La Salle, a sheet of paper in his hand.

"What's this?" Morris asked.

"These," Joe said, "are the schools he's looking at."

Morris took the sheet from Joe. There were fifteen schools on the list.

"All right, Joe," Morris said. *We're not getting him,* he thought, and he tore up the paper and threw it in the trash can.

THAT WAS just one sheet of paper, with just fifteen schools on it. Frank Hartwell had a basket in his office, filled to its lip every week with letters from every college and university in the country. And every week, Hartwell did with most of the contents of that basket what Morris did with Kobe's list: He dumped it into the trash. The larger envelopes and material, he would pass along to Gregg or Drew Downer, who would open them up in front of the team, making a lighthearted spectacle of each one: *Here's a FedEx package from . . . Kentucky! Kobe Bryant, come on down!*

Either way, Kobe had no interest in them, which surprised Hartwell, in that he presumed that the academic and social aspects of the college experience would hold some allure for Kobe, and they didn't. Kobe never took an official recruiting visit; he and Joe didn't want to waste their time or the schools'. "It seemed like he really knew what he wanted to do," Hartwell said, "and it seemed like he was getting encouragement and motivation from other sources."

He was, of course, and this was another contradiction that cut to the core of Kobe and his choices. In one regard, his teenaged basketball career was traditional, old school. He didn't transfer to a private-school powerhouse or to a tony prep school that recruited the country's best teenage players, drew them to a picturesque campus in California or Florida, and built itself an all-star team. He didn't rely on an unscrupulous AAU coach / athletic director falsifying records or grades at a wreck of a charter school so he could "qualify" academically to spend a year in one of college basketball's most prestigious programs. He did the simplest of things: He played for his local high school, where the people of his community, the classmates and parents he had known since he was in eighth grade, could follow him closely, could drive five minutes on a Friday night to one of his games, could have a higher stake in his success. One of his classmates and neighbors, Annie Schwartz (no relation to poor Robby), noticed that kids often approached Kobe for autographs, and he took the time to sign each one. "No one treats him any differently," said Annie, who grew up five houses away from the Bryants. "He's just a normal kid. For sure, he's not a Macaulay Culkin."

But in another regard, he was blazing a revolutionary trail, controlling his image and his outcomes, just as so many young athletes have done since, letting only so many people get an oblique glimpse of his mindset and thinking. One day in the library, for instance, Katrina Christmas asked Kobe about his plans after high school. Was he going to college, or was he going to play professional basketball, like all the rumors said? Christmas's desk was set across from a row of computers, and while he was sitting at one of the desks, Kobe doodled something on a piece of printer paper, then walked over, placed it on the top of her desk, and pushed it toward her. "This is your answer," he said. He had drawn himself in a basketball jersey, shooting a layup, and signed it on the bottom, a self-portrait that Christmas still has. "Wow," she said, "so you're going to the NBA?" He never said a word in response before leaving the library.

The media . . . it was easy to hide his true thoughts from them, just smile and deflect and mention one more time how much he had learned from his father about the process, how fun it was, how he was taking it all in. The chances that he would change his mind were slim, but he was happy to keep his options open—"Never say never, may go down there, have the best time of your life"—and to listen to him answer questions about his decision was to recognize, just from the tone and inflections of his voice, that he delighted in the speculation. It was a game to him, stringing people along, keeping them guessing. He liked Villa-nova, Michigan, and Arizona. Villanova? It would be cool to play close to home, with Tim Thomas. Michigan? Man, he loved Jalen Rose and the original Fab Five. Arizona? He had become friends with one of their recruits, Stephen Jackson. But none of those connections or reasons was strong or profound enough to get him to go to any of those schools, and with the exception of Duke and Krzyzewski, whom he talked to by phone here and there, even college basketball's blue bloods were stand-ing on tiptoes outside Kobe's window, hoping he'd see them. Kentucky? Rick Pitino couldn't get Kobe to visit Lexington, so he did what he thought was the next-best thing: He got Gregg Downer to visit Lexing-ton, flying him down there for a weekend. Downer, who had long ad-mired Pitino, watched the Wildcats practice and toured the campus and the town, but it didn't do Pitino much good in changing Kobe's mind. North Carolina? Kobe had received a recruiting letter from Dean Smith and had been so thrilled—Dean Smith!—that he had opened the enve-lope in English class while his teacher was droning on. But if he chose North Carolina, he would be choosing Michael Jordan's alma mater, and as much as he admired and emulated Jordan, how could he, Kobe Bry-ant, have his own identity there? Besides, Smith had cut to the chase: *We know you're turning pro, but if you change your mind, there's a scholarship here waiting for you.*

"Everybody's on the ground, wanting to know what school he's going to go to or hey, maybe he might go to the NBA," Kobe's friend Anthony Gilbert said, "and Kobe was on the bird's-eye view of that. Everything is a litmus test, and everything he's doing, he's assessing and testing. 'Yeah, naw, college ain't for me.' Dean Smith actually smelled it and was like, 'Naw, you're not coming here, dude.' UNC wanted him, and they got to a point where they were like, 'OK, we're not getting you, dude. You're clearly not going to college.' And that was *Dean Smith*."

Still, he told only so many people outright that he was planning to skip college—Matkov, Griffin, Treatman—trusting them to maintain his confidence, making Treatman's role as Kobe's unofficial PR rep all the more challenging. "I never discussed this with Gregg," Treatman said. "I didn't discuss it with any of the players because I was told not to. I absolutely knew that this was big-time, that this was going to be a huge story."

So why didn't Kobe just tell them all himself?

"I was trying to get the high school season down," Kobe said, "making sure everybody was on the same page, making sure everybody's working hard and practicing and, if not, you've got to get on them. That's what that was. During the season, I didn't want to come out and tell anybody because it would be a total distraction. I wanted to stay focused, the coaching staff, the teammates, so we can win this damn championship. . . .

"They always knew what I was going to do, even if I didn't tell them. To tell you the truth, I think they knew because they knew how competitive I was, and they knew I always wanted the ultimate challenge. I always need that. So I think they automatically knew that's what I was going to do. Know what I'm saying? I think it was understood."

Take Downer. Kobe listened to his counsel without explicitly revealing that he would turn pro right away, but Downer wasn't blind. He could tell which way Kobe was leaning, what his priorities were, and he expressed his concerns to him: *I know eventually you'll be a great player in the NBA. But right now, you have the world in the palm of your hand, and if you go to the NBA and don't produce, you're going to lose that. If you go to college, you won't have to worry.* Kobe didn't care. He wanted people to doubt him. "I didn't want to come in like Shaquille O'Neal, maybe like Chris Webber, who had all these expectations riding on them," he said. "Even if they're performing great, it's still not good enough, because it's never going to meet the expectations that people put on them. I just want to ease in, sneak up on people. Next thing people will be saying is, 'Oh, wow, he's doing great.' That's how I always want to be. I want to creep up on people, kind of like a shark."

KOBE WASN'T the only one creeping up on people, keeping secrets. All those hints and clues and overtures to him and his family from Sonny Vaccaro were the backbone of a scheme so smart and surreptitious that a British spy would have been envious. First, Vaccaro sold Adidas president Peter Moore on a theory: To sign a major player to a major endorsement deal, he had to be geographically closer to where most of them were, and most of them lived within a couple of hours of New York. So Adidas paid for Vaccaro and his wife, Pam, to move to and live in Manhattan for nine months; now he and his crony Gary Charles could go to work. They would drive down to the Philadelphia area, on the pretext that they were going to Villanova to watch Kerry Kittles play, and meet Joe for lunch or for a chat at the Pavilion after the game. Joe, in turn, would drive up to New York or New Jersey to meet with them. "If I had gone to the Bryants' house," Vaccaro said, "there would have been 'Sonny Vaccaro is on the move' or something. I didn't want to tip my hand." Vaccaro never went to a Lower Merion game himself. He didn't have to. Charles was his ears and eyes. "Around Christmastime," Vaccaro said, "I knew it was going to be Kobe. No one else knew. Nobody thought he was going pro, including everybody in Philadelphia. I knew." He had an agent, Arn Tellem, lined up and ready. All the arrangements could be formalized later. But Kobe would earn millions from his deal, and who knew? Maybe there would be a little something for Joe and the other people in Kobe's orbit, the Lower Merion Aces among them.

Sure enough, boxes of uniforms, warm-ups, and travel gear were delivered to the high school one day, all for the boys' basketball team, courtesy of Adidas.

HOURS BEFORE the brightest night of his basketball life, Donnie Carr fidgeted in a classroom desk at Roman Catholic High School, unable to concentrate, rivulets of sweat slickening his palms. All he could think about was his team's game that night against Lower Merion, against the friend and rival whom Carr had always held up as the standard by which to measure himself as a ballplayer. *I know Kobe's going to bring his game. I hope I bring mine. All these people are going to be there. I hope I don't slip up. I hope I don't play bad.*

The Aces had won their opener, beating Upper Darby by twelve, Kobe easing into the season with an eighteen-point effort. That game, against a Central League rival, might as well have been an exhibition compared to this matchup. This one, at the Physical Education Athletic Center at Drexel University, had an anticipatory hum to it, especially on La Salle University's campus. Joe Bryant had been recruiting Carr for the Explorers, and the prospect of the game's two stars, *Kobe and Donnie,* teaming up the following year was too thrilling for those affiliated with La Salle to put out of mind, even if it was, unbeknownst to anyone unfamiliar with Kobe's intentions, a pipe dream. Of the fifteen hundred spectators at the game—the Center held just more than twenty-five hundred—fifteen were teenagers and young men from Carr's neighborhood in South Philadelphia, all of whom were skeptical that he could hold his own against Kobe. "They didn't really know that Kobe and I would go at it all the time," he said. "They had heard all the hype about Kobe, and they were coming to see me get destroyed."

What they saw, instead, was a duel that would go down as a forever game—pro, college, high school, pickup—in Philadelphia basketball. Kobe, guarding Carr one-on-one, facing a triangle-and-two defense that Roman Catholic's coach, Dennis Sneddon, devised to limit Kobe and Dan Pangrazio, scored thirteen points in the first half. Carr had nineteen, a succession of dunks and jump-stop pull-ups, his friends in the stands now ragging and shouting at Kobe after each basket, Kobe yammering back, and as Carr sprinted off the court toward the locker room at halftime, roaring like a gladiator, Roman leading by three, he passed Joe Bryant, who was seated near a bleacher row of sportswriters and scouts.

"Yo, Donnie, take it easy," Joe said.

"Man," Donnie said, "if he's a pro, I'm a pro, too."

Carr kept up his energy throughout the second half, finishing with thirty-four points, enabling Roman to maintain a measure of distance between itself and the Aces, and he received more assistance from his teammates than Kobe did from his. Griffin had twelve points and twelve rebounds, but he was the only Aces player other than Kobe to score in double figures. Roman's triangle-and-two shut down Pangrazio; he finished with just seven points. Kobe finished with thirty, but it was a hard thirty. He took twenty-nine shots, missing five of his last six, chasing Carr around the court to the point of exhaustion. At the end of the 67–61 Roman victory, the friends embraced, and Kobe leaned close to whisper into Carr's ear.

"Great job, man," he said. "Congratulations. You guys deserved to win this game. Guess what, man? Why don't we just go to La Salle and do it together? Who could stop us two together?"

"Let's do it," Carr said, but he didn't quite believe that Kobe was being sincere. He thought that Joe might have planted those words in Kobe's mouth, to use as a recruiting tool. When Ted Silary, the *Philadelphia Daily News*'s longtime high school sports beat writer, pressed Joe and Kobe about Kobe's future, both were circumspect. Could Kobe and Carr wind up at La Salle together? "That would be pretty nasty," Joe said, "if it ever happened." Kobe told Silary that he would keep his intentions private until after the season. "But if I happen to wake up one morning after having a dream and I know what I want to do for sure," he said, "I'll go up to my dad and say, 'I'm ready to tell all.'"

So the following morning's *Daily News* didn't have the big reveal from Kobe. It had, instead, a piece from John Smallwood, the city's only Black sports columnist. Under the headline BRYANT ISN'T READY FOR THE NBA YET, Smallwood argued that, if Kobe really were capable of playing professionally in a year's time, "he should be that much better than Carr, a nice Division I prospect. . . . If Kobe Bryant enters the NBA now, he'll be a late first-round pick at best, and might never be heard from again."

Kobe dismissed the article as another example of prattle from "people who know nothing about the game of basketball. All they know is how to write paragraphs. I can take criticism. That just makes me work harder, makes me prove them wrong." He didn't care what Smallwood had written. "I wasn't upset," he said later. "I wasn't hurt or anything like that. I just said, 'I'll prove you wrong.' That's it. It comes in one ear, goes in my memory bank, goes in my motivation bank, goes out the other ear."

His mother did not react to the column with the same ostensible indifference. When he checked his messages in the newsroom the next day, Smallwood found a slew from Pam Bryant. She was enraged, not because Smallwood had suggested that Kobe shouldn't turn pro, but because he had included what he considered a throwaway descriptive clause: ". . . said Bryant, *who is Proposition 48-qualified, providing his grades don't slip drastically this school year.*" Kobe, Pam reminded Smallwood after he called her back, was an A/B student who spoke three languages and had scored 1080 on his SATs, and by merely mentioning Proposition 48, Smallwood had slapped a scarlet letter to her son's chest, perpetuating the stereotype that a Black kid couldn't go to college without basketball.

When people see Proposition 48, she told Smallwood, *all they see is a phrase that insinuates the person associated with it is dumb.*

A week later, Smallwood wrote a follow-up column, acknowledging that Pam Bryant had been right. He did not take back his prediction about Kobe and the NBA.

I made up my mind that if we were going to become a team that would win a state championship, I had to be the right kind of leader, and that meant respecting authority and working as hard as I could.

—KOBE BRYANT

14

THE CANCER
OF ME

N THE BLEACHERS OF THE Fieldhouse at St. Joseph's University, the country's best high school basketball coach and its best high school basketball player made time for each other, to talk about what one of them had yet to learn and how much he could still extract from himself. Sunken slightly, Bob Hurley's eyes remained a penetrating blue, and the respect he commanded—for his career at St. Anthony High School, as a former probation officer, as a Jersey City native whose pungent Jersey City accent lent authenticity to his accumulated experience and wisdom and his inclination to share both—was enough to draw and hold Kobe Bryant's attention like a tractor beam. This was no small thing. Hurley's team had just thumped Kobe's by fifteen points, yet in the minutes after that 62–47 loss, Kobe buried his frustration for a few minutes and sought out Hurley for some counsel.

Coach, Kobe asked him, *could we talk?*

Yes, Kobe needed some advice and reaffirmation, and yes, Hurley would provide some. Ordinarily, there would be no shame for a team in losing to Hurley and his Friars, but the circumstances of this loss were different. The game's original site was supposed to have been Lower Merion's gym, but anticipating a larger-than-usual crowd, Downer and Egan, a St. Joe's alumnus, had contacted Don DiJulia, the university's athletic director, and asked to relocate the game to the Fieldhouse. DiJulia not only said yes, but he didn't charge them any fee or rent. The day before the game, a snowstorm closed all of Jersey City's public schools, and expecting that St. Anthony would close, too, its two best basketball players, Anthony Perry and Rashon Burno, had not shown up for class. But St. Anthony had remained open, despite the weather, and Hurley benched Perry and Burno for their absences. The two still made the trip to City Avenue with the Friars and, when Kobe approached them before tip-off, explained to him why they weren't playing. This time, unlike in the summer with Donnie Carr, he knew better than to suggest that, if he had known he wasn't going against them, he wouldn't have bothered showing up.

Kobe had twenty-eight points, shooting ten-for-twenty-one from the field, and with four minutes, nine seconds left, he established a milestone in a high school career loaded with them, scoring his two thousandth point. That he had that many points in the game on so few shots, most of them jumpers from fifteen feet and beyond, was particularly impressive, given that the Friars hardly concerned themselves with his teammates, and for good reason. None of them scored more than seven points. "We were able to cheat off them and help against him," Hurley said. "He was brilliant. He got no help from the other players."

Nevertheless, there were aspects of Kobe's game—his situational awareness, his demeanor—that he could improve, bolts that he could tighten, and as they sat in the bleachers, Hurley pointed them out to him. Just before halftime, the Friars had trapped Kobe, stolen the ball from him, and scored a basket to stretch their lead to four. Kobe had walked to the locker room with his head down, his chin tight against his upper chest, telegraphing his disappointment in himself. Then, Hurley had thought Kobe passive during the first few minutes of the third quarter, when he could have tried to dominate the game and swing it in the Aces' favor.

"I talked to him about his reaction to that mistake and how important erasing that mistake would be with the way he played early in the second half," recalled Hurley, who coached at St. Anthony for thirty-nine years. "He totally understood, thanked me so much for it, and we parted ways.

He was just mature beyond his years. We played against unbelievable players over the years. He's the best player we ever played against."

The plaudits and praise that Kobe would earn from Hurley didn't help the Aces then and there, though. They were just 4–2. For the second time in eleven days, they had faced an opponent of the caliber they would have to beat come the district and state playoffs, and for the second time—first Roman Catholic, now St. Anthony—Kobe was the only Lower Merion player to meet the measure of the moment. It wasn't a matter of the team lacking talent around Kobe. There was something else, something intangible, that seemed to be holding the Aces back. Mike Egan left the Fieldhouse with his brother Tom, who said to him, "I can't believe you're not more upset."

"Tom," Egan said, "we need to lose a couple of games to shrink these kids' heads a bit."

"That's the No. 1 team in the country," Tom Egan said, still trying to look on the bright side. "You could have beaten them."

"Yeah, we could have."

HUGGING THE Atlantic's waters on the southern shore of Myrtle Beach, the Swamp Fox Motel beckoned to its guests during the final week of 1995 with its light blue placard along Ocean Boulevard, some spiky palm trees scattered around its parking lot, and a homey message on its marquee: MAINE LOBSTER $11, BEEF AND SHRIMP KABOBS, WELCOME BEACH BALL CLASSIC. The eight-team tournament had been a staple of the town since 1981, a wintertime event designed to increase the community's unity and visibility and to attract tourists to its beaches and surf-chill vibe, to its nightlife and its dozens of golf courses. Just the year before, the city had spent $23 million to expand the Myrtle Beach Convention Center to a capacity of between seventy-five hundred and eight thousand people, and the tournament's sponsors covered all the major costs for coaches and players—airfare, lodging, ground transportation, two meals a day—in exchange for providing a stage for the likes of Kobe, Jermaine O'Neal, Lester Earl, and Mike Bibby to show their stuff. It was, relative to what most high school basketball programs were used to, Lower Merion's included, a major event, with more spectators and scouts, with a college-like atmosphere, with news cameras and media time-outs.

Kobe and the coaches viewed the trip to Myrtle Beach and their three games there as a kind of midterm exam to gauge how good the Aces really were, whether they were really capable of winning a state championship. Through Philadelphia International Airport, on the way to their U.S. Airways flight to South Carolina, the Aces walked in single file, Downer at the front of the line, Egan at the end to make sure no one got separated from the group, and near the back sauntered Kobe, headphones on his ears, gym bag slung over his shoulder, passersby glancing at him. "He just had that specialness, that aura about him," Egan said. "Everyone just stared at Kobe." But the other players seemed to treat the trip like a spring break–style vacation. A few of them had never been on an airplane before.

Because Matt Matkov was no longer on the team, Kobe asked Downer if he could share a suite for the trip's five nights with Jeremy Treatman, which both flattered Treatman and put him on notice. "He wanted to feel completely independent," Treatman recalled, "and he knew he had a friend in me. I was the only one of the five coaches who would not say boo to him if he decided to venture out of his room." Their suite, all pastels and windows, had two rooms: a smaller one just inside the front door, with a television and a bed, and the main area, with a deck and a view of the ocean and a larger bed. Once they checked in and got their keys, Treatman dropped his bags in the bigger room. Then Kobe Bean Bryant came through the door. To mark his territory, he gestured for Treatman to move himself and his suitcases back into the smaller room.

"Why don't you put your stuff over here?" he said. "Then the Bean will come and hang out with you."

The Bean will hang out with you. Kobe had never talked like that to him before. *He's trying to charm me,* Treatman thought.

"Well," Treatman said, "I guess you're the reason we're here. If you want me to stay in this room, I'll stay in this room."

For the remainder of his week as Kobe's suitemate, Treatman, admittedly possessing a neurotic temperament, vacillated between serenity and alarm. There was one bathroom in the suite, and since Treatman tended to leave puddles of water on the floor after he showered, he spread out an extra bath mat, fearful that Kobe might slip and fall and that he, Jeremy Treatman, would be responsible for ruining the career of the next Michael Jordan before it even began. Kobe poured himself into the games and practices during the mornings and afternoons and filled the remaining daylight hours by napping, but at night he slipped out to socialize with O'Neal and Griffin, and Treatman fielded several phone calls to the room from giggling teenage girls asking to speak to Kobe. On one of the team's first nights in town, while Kobe was out, the phone rang. Treatman answered, but this time the female voice on the other end wasn't giggling.

"Is Kobe there?" Pam Bryant asked.

"No," Treatman said, "he's asleep."

She hung up, not wanting to wake up her baby. *Oh, God,* Treatman thought. *I just lied to Pam Bryant. I feel like such a jerk.*

Still, by protecting Kobe, even over such modest transgressions as hanging out with girls, Treatman earned his trust. So Kobe let him in on a secret.

"You know," he said to him, "Jermaine and I have been talking, and Jermaine's gonna go pro, too."

Treatman wasn't quite sure what he was hearing. Jermaine Griffin was an excellent high school basketball player, but a pro? And straight out of high school? Finally, Treatman interrupted.

"Kobe, I know he's your best friend and everything," he said, "and I'm not here to hurt anyone's feelings. But Jermaine Griffin? What are you talking about?"

"No!" Kobe replied. "Jermaine O'Neal!"

That made more sense. It also meant that Treatman had no more doubts about what Kobe's decision would be. And if even he did, Kobe's five days in Myrtle Beach would go a long way to eliminating them.

IN ITS first game of the tournament, Lower Merion faced Central Catholic High School, from Springfield, Ohio, a team with a decided height advantage over the Aces with its six-foot-six power forward, Jon Powell, and its seven-foot center, Jason Collier, himself a future NBA player. Collier blocked Kobe's first shot of the game, the crowd oohing, ahhing, and murmuring for seconds afterward. Downer immediately called a time-out, and in the huddle, Kobe made a demand of his teammates.

"Give me the ball. I'm gonna step on his fucking neck."

His teammates obliged him on the first offensive set after the time-out. Six inches shorter than Collier, Kobe nevertheless posted him up, spun toward the basket, and threw down a vicious dunk as Collier fouled him. On the bench, Drew Downer marveled at what he had seen. It wasn't just that Kobe had done what he said he would do. It was that he had done it on the very next play. Still, though Kobe's superiority to his peers and competitors was becoming more obvious to everyone, it was difficult for his teammates to appreciate how remarkable a player he was and might yet be. It was only after Brendan Pettit went to play Division III basketball at Wesleyan University, for instance, that he gained a broader frame of reference for Kobe. "You grow up watching videos of 'Air' Jordan, and you forget that he is a person, too," Pettit said. "Having Kobe as a classmate, a teammate, you know that he is a person. But it's funny, too. Moving on to college, continuing my playing career, you realize just how special Kobe was. No dunk, no play, no amount of points can impress you anymore." The tournament and Kobe's play in it changed Omar Hatcher's approach to basketball. "We got to see Kobe's game accelerate against the top teams in the country," he said. "He showed me that a good player's game has to travel. It can't be subject to place or atmosphere."

Kobe's game traveled, but the other Aces' didn't. Again, he was guarding the opponent's top scorer, this time the giant Collier, and again, he was the entirety of the offense. In the third quarter, the Aces trailed by five points. But to counteract their lack of size, Downer switched to a full-court press, and it neutralized Central, which went the game's final six minutes without a field goal. Lower Merion rallied to win, 65–60. Kobe scored forty-three points; made eighteen of his twenty-seven shots from the field, including three of his five three-point attempts; and pulled down sixteen rebounds. Dan Pangrazio had twelve points, and Dave Rosenberg was earning more playing time from Downer through sheer toughness and grit: His left shoulder would occasionally pop out of its socket whenever he collided with another player or dived to the floor for a loose ball, and he would just pop it back in so he could stay in the game. But the Aces, even with a 5–2 record and now in the Classic's semifinals, were less a harmonious ensemble than a breathtaking solo act with a discordant, sometimes indifferent, backup band. The next night would demonstrate just how out of tune they were.

KOBE'S PARENTS and sisters made it to Myrtle Beach in time for the Aces' semifinal game against Jenks (Oklahoma) High School. Joe was sitting in the stands next to Pam, wearing a La Salle baseball cap, when Wesley Gibson spotted him. Gibson had grown up just a few blocks from Joe in southwest Philadelphia, entered the National Guard and the Air Force, and split time between the city and South Carolina with his son, Jarid, who was thirteen, in sixth grade, and was with him in the arena.

"Hey, Joe, I remember you from back in the day," Wesley Gibson said. "What, are you down here scouting for somebody?"

"No," Joe said, "I've come to see my son play."

Wesley Gibson had never heard of Kobe Bryant, but Jarid had. Jarid read *SLAM* and all the scouting magazines and reports about the nation's top high school players, knew all about Kobe's terrific performance at the ABCD Camp. His and Wesley's shared love of basketball was maybe the strongest bond between a father and son who needed each other after Nathene Gibson, Wesley's wife and Jarid's mother, had died by suicide in 1988. Already, Jarid had been trailing Kobe like a puppy dog throughout the Beach Ball Classic, and now he had another reason, a hometown connection, to stay by his side for the rest of the tournament. Jarid got autographs from Kobe and "Mr. Joe," chatted with Kobe about their favorite cheesesteak spots in Philly and on the Main Line—"I'm a Jim's guy," Jarid recalled, "and he liked Larry's"—then settled in with Wesley to watch the game that would change everything for the Aces that season.

Jenks High School had more than twenty-four hundred students, twice the enrollment of Lower Merion, yet through the first eight minutes, it appeared the Trojans didn't belong in the same gym. The Aces led, 18–6, at the end of the first quarter, and even though Kobe collected four fouls and his teammates were once more lending him little support, they maintained a seven-point cushion entering the fourth. And they were ahead by nine when Kobe—in the sort of moment that so often defined his Lakers career, when he believed so deeply in his own magnificence that he crossed the boundary separating self-assurance from self-absorption—took on three Jenks defenders by himself, plowed over one of them, and was called for an offensive foul. He had played thirty minutes, scored thirty-one points, grabbed fourteen rebounds, and now he was out of the game.

"And we," Treatman recalled, "just completely unraveled."

No one more than the player who, because of his skills and his role on the team, complemented Kobe best. Kobe's core burned at a hotter temperature than anyone's, but no Aces player was wound tighter than Dan Pangrazio. His background as an elite youth soccer goalkeeper; the balance he provided the team with his outside-shooting ability; the pressure that he placed on himself and that his parents, Dorothy and Greg, placed on him: Those factors often drove him to excel, but this time, with the additional stress of Kobe's absence, they pushed him past his breaking point. He missed several foul shots down the stretch, finishing oh-for-six from the line. "And Dan never missed," said Dave Rosenberg, who bricked two late free throws himself after replacing Kobe in the lineup. The coup de grâce came with 0.4 seconds left in regulation when, with Lower Merion still leading 61–59, Jenks's Mike Bay went to the foul line for two shots. He made the first but missed the second . . . only for the Aces to commit a lane violation, giving Bay another chance. He sank his do-over to send the game to overtime, where the Aces crumbled completely. Rosenberg began the extra period by airballing a three-pointer. As Jenks continued steamrolling the Aces, outscoring them 17–2 in overtime and winning, 78–63, Kobe repeated two phrases over and over, his mumble loud enough for Treatman, seated next to him, to hear.

"No independence. No goddamned independence . . ."

In the locker room, Egan held out hope that the team still had time to pull itself together and reach its potential. "Guys," he said to the players, "you're just not as good as you think you are. Every one of you has to pick it up." Gregg Downer, too angry and distraught to say much more, asked, "Anybody have anything to say?" Kobe did: *You've got to go after people! You can't back down to no motherfuckers!* It was exactly what the Aces had done. Without Kobe, they had backed down.

"That was as mad," Egan recalled, "as I'd ever seen him."

The loss to Jenks, and Kobe's reaction to it, his fury unleashed on the other players, had brought to bear the Aces' biggest problem: Kobe's mere presence had created a Catch-22. He intimidated his teammates, and they were deferring to him to the point that they rendered themselves impotent to help him. Yet if he wasn't on the floor at all times, they had no chance to win at all. They were struggling to play with him, but they couldn't play without him. After the bus shuttled everyone back to the lobby of the Swamp Fox, Downer shouted out to all the players and coaches: "Room 107, ten minutes." As the team members gathered there, an uneasy tension simmered in the room. "I felt we were kind of entitled and arrogant," Downer recalled, "and I was pissed." The players feared a diatribe from their head coach. Kareem Barksdale, the team's only freshman, was so scared of what Downer might say that he trembled in his seat.

Then Downer stood up before them, holding a sheet of paper in his hands.

We have a problem on this team, he said. *When you have cancer, it starts attacking your body. Over time, it overwhelms the body. We have cancer. The Cancer of Me. And as long as we have it, we won't accomplish what we want to accomplish.*

He lifted the paper and, with a pen, started punching holes into it.

Everyone's got to step up. Stop worrying about whether your T-shirt fits. Stop worrying about where we're going to dinner. Stop worrying about who's buying the ice cream tonight. Let's get nasty. Let's get in the gym, because at 5–3, we're heading toward a .500 record. Some of you guys are expecting Kobe to do everything. We're too big for our britches. We aren't as good as our press clippings.

Kobe nodded in agreement. Downer turned to Emory Dabney.

If you don't start playing better, Downer told Dabney, *we're gonna send you down to JV.* The threat terrified Dabney. *I'm not fucking playing JV,* he thought.

Kobe kept nodding. Downer kept driving the pen through the paper. He turned to Brendan Pettit.

You don't get it. You're being a jerk. You need to be more serious. You need to be more focused. Your body language, your attitude, has got to change, and it's got to change fast.

Kobe kept nodding. Downer turned to Barksdale.

What are you contributing?

Kobe kept nodding. Downer pointed at Dave Rosenberg and allowed one compliment to one player.

If I ask Rosey to run through that brick wall, he'll say, "Fine, Coach. Where's the hospital?"

Kobe kept nodding as Downer went through all the players on the team save one, pointing out their shortcomings and the ways they had to improve. The coach held a thin, stringy net of pulp in his hands.

What do you have now? What do you have now, Kareem?

Barksdale, wide-eyed and scared, blurted out, "You got a sheet of paper with a big hole in it!"

Downer stifled a laugh. *Oh, no,* he thought, *there goes the speech.* But the room remained stone silent, the players locked on him.

You can't write on it anymore. You can't do anything with it. We're the same way. If everybody's not on the same page, we're broken. We're ripped apart.

He reached down and picked up his plane ticket back to Philadelphia.

If you want to go back, here you go. Anybody who wants to go back can leave right now.

Finally, he turned to Kobe, who stopped nodding.

You're Kobe Bryant. You're the best player in the country. But you've got to respect your teammates here. You can't be so aggressive. You can't take on every team by yourself. These guys are trying their best to play their roles on this team. You've got to make them feel comfortable. Everybody has to play their roles for this to work out.

He looked at the rest of the players while pointing at Kobe.

You have no idea what kind of pressure this guy is under. You've got to understand how hard he works. If you don't match his intensity, we don't have a chance. If we get back to hard work, if we put the team first, if we don't worry about the end result or who gets the credit, the outcomes will take care of themselves. Look around the room. We can be a great team. In case you don't know, gentlemen, we are trying to win a state championship this year. That's why we're here in South Carolina. That's why we're playing Bob Hurley and St. Anthony. That's why we're playing Roman Catholic. But things have to change in a hurry.

Downer finished. Treatman spoke up.

Twenty people made this trip. I'm the twentieth-most-important person here, and I'm going to tell you guys something. I feel like my responsibilities are pretty important. In March, I want to be part of history, and if you guys don't understand we could be a part of history, if you don't understand the opportunities that Coach Downer and Kobe Bryant are giving us, if you're not on board, you shouldn't be here.

The room was quiet for a while. Kobe broke the silence by clapping his hands rhythmically. His teammates joined him. Then everyone filed out.

To a man, the team members would remember Downer's speech as the season's cornerstone, its turning point. "It was one of those things where you clear the air so well that it helps the team relax," Drew Downer recalled. "All that tension just dissipates. You get it all out in the open, and it frees you up a little bit."

There was one player, though, who needed more time to process the pressure, to let go of the blame. When Drew, after talking with Gregg for a while, returned to his hotel room, his roommate for the week wasn't there, and Drew had no idea where Dan Pangrazio had gone. Eventually, after several minutes of searching the hotel and the night-fallen beach, their worry gradually escalating, Drew and the other coaches found him. He was sitting on the sand by himself, still wearing his Lower Merion jersey, the tide lapping in and out in its unceasing rhythm.

TOM PETTIT had gotten used to it. Kobe was the last player out of the locker room . . . again. Kobe was always the last player out of the locker room. The manager of the basketball team and Brendan's younger brother, Pettit had the humbling assignment after every game of staying at Kobe's side and carrying his duffel bag as Kobe walked to the team bus, signing autographs and shaking hands on the way. He was a sophomore, short and skinny with a thatch of blond hair, a pipe cleaner; the two made quite the contrasting pair, but for all the caddying Pettit did for Kobe, all the time they were alongside each other, they had never had a lengthy conversation, until now.

Come Lower Merion's third game at the Classic, against Lexington (Kentucky) High School, Kobe's right hand and forearm appeared mummified, wrapped in a thick bandage. He had sustained a thumb injury sometime during the first two games, but he had also complained about soreness in his right wrist that, as far as anyone could tell, was brought on by his own popularity, by his shaking so many hands and signing so many autographs. The demands on his time and for his signature did not bother him. "If you work hard to achieve something, if you set a goal—and my goal was to be a great basketball player and be famous—then you can expect that," he said late in his senior year. "You can't be on TV all the time and not expect people to know who you are and come up to you and ask you for autographs. So I accept it." By the tournament's end, he was using his left hand to scribble his name on basketballs, game programs, and slips of paper, but on Saturday, December 30, the Classic's last day, he was prepared to withstand some pain for the sake of the season and for a display of showmanship that was the Classic's centerpiece.

That afternoon, he scored forty-three points in a 76–70 win over Lexington, allowing the Aces to get their bearings back, earning the tournament's MVP award, giving him 117 points over the three games, the second most in the tournament's history to the 118 that Mike Bibby scored over *his* three games. Once more, Kobe had autographs to sign and interview questions to answer, and the bus driver shepherding the Aces back to the Swamp Fox couldn't wait any longer. He pulled away, leaving behind Kobe and Pettit. Fortunately, one of Lower Merion's host families, part of the contingent of Myrtle Beach residents who had volunteered to make the team's stay hospitable, offered to drive Kobe and

Pettit back to the hotel. The high schoolers climbed into the back of the family's SUV, and over the twelve-minute ride, Pettit engaged in the first and, really, the only conversation that he ever had with Kobe. How did he like being the team manager? What kind of music did he listen to? What TV shows and sports were his favorites?

That third question solicited Pettit's most detailed response. He told Kobe that, as much as he liked basketball, he followed hockey more closely.

"I love hockey," Kobe said. "I love Wayne Gretzky."

"You know hockey?" Pettit asked.

Yes, Kobe replied, especially Gretzky. "He's the best in his sport."

At the time, Pettit found Kobe's answer obvious and a little silly. This was the winter of 1995. Sure, Gretzky was still great then, but he was late in his career, about to turn thirty-five, and was no longer the National Hockey League's alpha and omega. There were other, younger players who had supplanted him, who were the newer, truer faces of the league, players whom even casual hockey fans already recognized. Pettit figured that Kobe had simply reached for the most familiar name associated with the sport, like someone describing himself as a classical-music fan because he liked Beethoven.

"I thought, 'Oh, yeah, you really know hockey, Kobe,'" Pettit recalled. "But now I think about it, and it was like, 'Wow, he was already in that I'm-going-to-be-the-best mindset.' That's where he was going with it. Of course he was talking about the greatest of all time.

"He was something special and different. It was a special time, even more special now."

CAPPING THE Beach Ball Classic was the event that every player and spectator enjoyed most: the dunk contest on Saturday night. Kobe was determined to compete in it, despite his teammates', coaches', and even family members' insistence that he shouldn't, that he risked injuring himself further. Sharia and Shaya knocked on the door of Kobe and Treatman's suite, pleading with their brother and practically in tears: *Please, don't do it.* "They were worried, and I don't think his parents wanted him to do it, either," Treatman said. "Kobe's like, 'I got this. I got this.'"

There was, Treatman and everyone else affiliated with the Aces had to admit, some curiosity over how Kobe would fare in the contest, curiosity that had nothing to do with whether he would exacerbate the pain in his arm. They had seen him deliver his standard dunks during games: powerful, incredible for a high school player, his creativity and athleticism constrained by the rules of basketball and the guise of sportsmanship. But what he could do with a running start, with stage props, with no limits? Wearing his white Lower Merion jersey, his arm still bandaged, before a packed Civic Center, Kobe lofted the ball toward the hoop on his first attempt, caught it after it bounced high off the court, and jammed it. The crowd was restrained in its reaction; each of the three judges gave him a nine out of ten. He pounded the ball against the floor in the left corner of the gym, deciding what to try next, then took off along the baseline, put the ball in his left hand, slipped it between his legs to his right hand as he lifted off, and dunked. That, the crowd and the judges appreciated: three tens and a burst of sustained sound.

In the finals were he and his friend Lester Earl, and as Kobe weighed the possibilities of his dunk, one voice, belonging to a young boy, could be heard, chanting, "Kobe! Kobe!" He took off from the foul line with the ball in his right hand, switched it to his left in midair, and hammered it down. Earl matched him with another perfect dunk, giving each of them one more chance in a tiebreaker round. To win, Earl recognized that he had to get imaginative, so he wheeled a basketball rack, with nine basketballs still on it, onto the court, positioning it on the right side of the floor, midway between the baseline and the foul line. From the right side, he dribbled twice, leaped to clear the rack with ease, and slammed the ball home with his left hand. It was a thrilling sight. Three tens again. Glen Oaks players poured onto the court to hug Earl. All Kobe could do was tie him now, and it would be a challenge.

He couldn't do it alone. He tugged the shirts of three teammates and dragged them toward the basket. He arranged them in a triangle five feet in front of the rim, then had each of them bend over at the waist and duck their heads. He walked back to half-court, dribbled the ball once between his legs when he got there, then turned back around to face his teammates and the basket.

Right-hand dribble . . . inside half-court . . .

Left-hand dribble . . . three-point arc . . .

Left-hand dribble . . . foul line . . .

He took off from inside the lane, just before he might crash into his teammates. Instead, he flew clear over them, not crashing into them, not touching them at all, cradling the basketball in his weakened right hand and slamming it through the hoop.

The crowd released a deafening noise, every person standing or hopping in place, clapping and shouting and cheering. Earl, standing near midcourt, lifted his hands in a what-can-you-do gesture. He and Kobe shook hands and hugged at half-court. The contest was ruled a tie, but everyone there knew who had won.

"It was like a rock star was born," Downer said. "That snowball was getting bigger and bigger."

Treatman and Drew Downer walked back to the Swamp Fox together, chatting about Kobe's performance, still not quite believing it. They had known him for four years, and neither of them had seen anything like what they had this night. Did these kids on the team appreciate what they were so privileged to witness? Did the coaches themselves, the adults with perspective, appreciate it? Did they get it, deep down? He was flying, throwing down circus dunks with a bad arm, with his family begging him not to risk himself, with the Convention Center crowd getting louder and more raucous by the second. If this was Kobe Bryant now, who might he be later?

The two of them stopped in front of the door to Treatman's suite.

"And he lives here," Treatman said.

They broke up laughing.

THROUGH MUCH of his first weeks as an undergraduate at the University of Maryland, Evan Monsky had listened to another freshman, a kid from Camden, New Jersey, who lived in the same dormitory that

Monsky did, tell him that Tim Thomas was "the greatest thing in the world." And yeah, Monsky had to admit that Thomas—headed for Villanova, where he'd stay one year before a thirteen-year NBA career—was a pretty incredible high school player. "But this was a kid who just talked shit," Monsky said later. "He had no idea. I told him, 'There's this guy from my hometown. Trust me. He's something else.'"

Kobe had come to Cole Fieldhouse in College Park, with Rip Hamilton and John Linehan and the Sam Rines All-Stars, for an AAU tournament early in Maryland's fall semester. Kobe had roomed with Linehan, and it had been a typical AAU experience for him in that he never left the hotel room except for the games themselves. "I'm trying to go out to the mall, hang out, play video games," Linehan recalled, "and it's eight, eight thirty, and it's lights out. I'm like, 'Kobe, what's going on?' He said, 'We got a game tomorrow.' Who does that at a young age like that? That's when I knew he was going to be special. He had a different approach to the game than I had or anyone else I had ever known." After one of the games at Cole, Monsky had a chance to say hello to and catch up with Kobe, and he asked him if he was considering going to Maryland. *No,* he said. *Don't like the rims here.*

Now it was early January, winter break at Maryland, Lower Merion's basketball team back from Myrtle Beach and settling into the routines and the lesser competition of its season, and Monsky was doing what a lot of college freshmen do during winter break: He had returned to his alma mater, to see old friends and bask a bit in having advanced to the next phase of his life. He was hanging out just before basketball practice began, talking to Kobe under one of the hoops, Treatman nearby and keeping his ears open, the rest of the team shooting around and warming up.

"Kobe, what's the deal?" Monsky said. "Where are you going to go to school? La Salle? I'm hearing Duke." That had been Monsky's assumption since his senior year: *Kobe will go to college, play for a year, and go to the pros. He'll be a decent sixth man, a journeyman, a nice player in the NBA, and what an amazing life that will be for him.*

"Ev," Kobe said, "I'm thinking about going to the league."

"No, seriously," Monsky replied. "Are you thinking La Salle or Duke?"

"No, really. Goin' to the league."

Downer blew his whistle to have the players meet him at half-court for the start of practice. Kobe trotted over, leaving Monsky alone to reconcile his expectations for his friend and Kobe's casual and surprising admission. *Guards don't go straight to the NBA. Kevin Garnett went, but he's not a guard. It just doesn't happen, and it certainly doesn't happen to kids with Kobe's excellent grades. And why would you want to do that? College is so fun!*

Meanwhile, Treatman had heard what Kobe said. He instinctively scanned the gym to see if any reporters were around, then sighed in relief when he remembered there weren't. He wasn't ready yet to assist Kobe in announcing his intentions, and having worked in the media for years, television in particular, he understood the accoutrements necessary—the scene, the buildup, the drama—to make the formal revelation unforgettable. More important, Kobe, despite what he had said to Monsky, understood them even better than Treatman did.

WEEKS AFTER the Beach Ball Classic, Jarid Gibson turned on his dad's Compaq computer. He wanted to write a letter to Kobe Bryant. Thirteen single-spaced pages later, he asked his father to look it over for him. *Here,* Wesley Gibson said to his son, *let's condense this for you.*

Months later, flames dancing and roaring in the family-room fireplace behind him, Kobe stretched out on the floor of the Bryants' home for a lengthy TV interview to be broadcast on ESPN. Fifteen minutes of the interview aired on the network. Kobe spoke of his childhood in Italy, the importance of his education, his desire to hear people say, *Kobe, you're a good person.* He had not yet announced whether he was going to college or the NBA. "It's something I'm really going to have to concentrate on before I make a decision," he said in the interview, as if he had not already made one.

Midway through, ESPN flashed on the screen the cover of the Beach Ball Classic program, an image of Kobe releasing a jump shot taking up most of the bottom two-thirds of the page.

"So," the interviewer said as the camera cut back to Kobe, "you met this young man where?"

"South Carolina," Kobe said. "Myrtle Beach."

"What's his name?"

"Jarid Gibson."

"A fan of yours?"

"Yes."

"You meet him at a tournament, and he writes you a letter afterward."

"A beautiful letter."

"What does it say?"

And Kobe looked down at the paper and began to read.

> *Dear Kobe,*
>
> *How's life treating you these days? I sincerely hope that this letter may find you in the best of health. I'm writing to thank you for your outstanding performance and character you displayed at the Beach Ball Classic. My name is Jarid Gibson, the little guy who continuously hung around you from Pennsylvania.*
>
> *Kobe, I just want you to know the tremendous impact you've had on my life in the short time I was in your presence, not only as a player but as a person. You are real, down to earth, and were accessible to your fans. But what I admire most is the 1000 you scored on your SATs, the special relationship you had with your dad. Neither fame nor money can buy you that. The game of life has dealt you the perfect hand. You are intelligent, have a loving family, and you are a very gifted basketball player. The pot of gold at the end of the rainbow of life awaits you. Grab it, but please remember these three things: One, always thank God and your family; two, the hard work it took you to succeed and what it is going to take to keep you there; three, never forget us little guys who saw you at the beginning of your rise to stardom.*
>
> *Just as you've touched me and given me the inspiration to be somebody, there will be thousands more in the future. Stay humbled. Stay focused. Stay real.*

Jarid Gibson eventually joined the Air Force, just like his father had, and from his encounter with Kobe in Myrtle Beach, he stayed in contact with him—more letters, five-minute phone calls to Jarid from Los Angeles once every couple of weeks, autographed balls and postcards and Lakers jerseys in the mail to South Carolina. "If I could be like anyone," Jarid said, "I would want to be like him." Their correspondence continued until the early months of 2001, after Kobe had won his first championship with the Lakers. "Once he became the Mamba," Wesley said, "we lost touch." He had become someone new, someone older, someone else, and he had decided not to carry that relationship with him into his future. It wouldn't be the only part of his past he'd leave behind.

Somebody says I can't do something, and I want to go out and do it on purpose and do it in an unbelievable way.

—*KOBE BRYANT*

15

RELAX,
I GOT THIS

THE CONTRAST WAS SO STARK, between the Kobe Bryant in the back of the bus and the Kobe Bryant in the front of the classroom. To road games, the team traveled amid a purr of low voices, a slight buzz of conversation and pregame strategy that blended with the white noise of the vehicle's hissing brakes and the rumble of its diesel engine. Kobe set that solemn mood as much as any player did: his headphones on, his face a clean canvas, the prospect of passing over a waterway no longer causing him tiny spasms of panic. There was a game to be won, and little else should occupy anyone's thoughts. But once they had arrived at their opponent's gym and kicked their opponent's ass, the Aces could let loose on the ride back to Wynnewood, let themselves be themselves. Closer to the driver, Jimmy Kieserman might be telling stories about what it was like to be a guard in the Big East or to attend a true fraternity party at Miami, but Kobe and Jermaine Griffin, the team's two dominant personalities, sat in the last row—"Kobe and Dan Pangrazio being the stars," Dave Rosenberg said, "Jermaine being the soul." Brendan Pettit and Robby Schwartz were the team's comics. Oral Williams's nickname was "Sarge." Dave Lasman had a cool, Hollywood demeanor. Kareem Barksdale would cap every victory by doing backflips on the court. Rosenberg and Phil Mellet were the academic standouts and the ever-hustling bench guys. Kobe, Griffin, and the other Black players—Emory Dabney, Omar Hatcher, Williams, Cary Walker, Barksdale—would engage each other in rap battles, and after the Fugees released *The Score* in mid-February 1996, Williams would tote his boom box, with its compact-disc player, onto the bus, and the album, with its reggae-rap grooves and swaggering lyrics, immediately became the entire team's soundtrack.

We used to be number ten
Now we permanent at one

It felt that way, like they would be on top forever and no one could take them down. Refocused after Downer had chewed them out in his suite at the Swamp Fox Motel, the Aces won their final fifteen regular-season games, emerging as one of the main attractions in Philadelphia basketball. "You started to hear rumblings across the county," recalled Jack McGlone, a sophomore guard for Ridley during that 1995–96 season. "You'd hear about other Central League teams playing Kobe and having a packed gym. You'd read newspaper articles and *SLAM* magazine about him." Before Ridley's first game against the Aces that season, at Lower Merion, McGlone was taken aback when one of the Green Raiders' assistant coaches told the team, *Remember, guys, when Kobe dunks and the crowd goes nuts, it's only two points.* "He was basically preparing us mentally to be ready for when Kobe dunks, not if he dunks," McGlone said. "It's not something you're used to worrying about from a high school kid." In his two games against Ridley, Kobe scored twenty-nine points in a sixteen-point win then twenty-seven points in a fifteen-point win, but more memorable for McGlone and his Ridley teammates—and, really, for every team that faced the Aces that season, and even for Kobe's teammates—was the sheer experience of playing with or against him. As heated as these suburban and neighborhood rivalries had been, they couldn't compare to the buildup and the thrill and the atmosphere that materialized whenever Kobe came to town: center stage, big game, crowd standing on every possession and going crazy when a player made a simple layup, the sight of children and even some adults lining up for autographs as Kobe stepped out of the locker room, a feeling never forgotten. "If you've ever played sports," McGlone said, "it's something you've always dreamed of doing, and I got to do it twice. That's better than some piece of paper with his name on it."

The fulfillment of those dreams would have to suffice for those players and teams, because Kobe and the Aces were a teenage basketball *kaiju*, destroying everything in their path. Of those fifteen straight victories, fourteen were by more than ten points, and seven were by at least twenty-eight. In a 95–64 romp over Marple Newtown, Kobe had forty-eight points with four minutes left in the fourth quarter when Gregg Downer called a time-out. "Look," he told Kobe, "just get one more basket." Fifty points, a nice plump number. Then Downer would have him sit out the rest of the game to be merciful . . . except Kobe proceeded to throw five perfect passes to set up five baskets from his teammates, just because he could, forcing Downer to call another time-out. "You have forty-eight points!" the coach yelled at his star. The next time the Aces had the ball, Kobe hit a layup and, at last, took a seat. "He could be so hardheaded," Downer said later.

Yes, he certainly could, and he was also filled with a carefree confidence about the Aces' prospects once the district and state playoffs began. Downer couldn't afford to be so cavalier about any game, any outcome. His professional future was thrown in doubt around Valentine's Day, when James Crawford, Episcopal Academy's headmaster, called him in for a meeting and told him that, because coaching Kobe and Lower Merion was occupying so much of Downer's time and keeping him from fulfilling his obligations to Episcopal, he would be fired at the end of the school year. *What are you talking about?* Downer responded. *I told you I've got to see this Kobe thing through. I told you that from day one.* (Crawford said later that he didn't recall the content of their conversation.) Never mind what would happen to Downer's reputation and future as a basketball coach if he didn't win a district and/or state championship in 1996. He gets handed four years of Kobe Bryant, and he can't get it done? To Kobe, though, that concept was inconceivable. *Relax, Coach,* he'd tell Downer.

I got this. And he would say the same thing to his teammates. *We're in high school. We're young. We've got the world ahead of us. Just have a good time. Play basketball. We're a great team.* "I'm trying to tell them, 'Emory, Omar, Butter, do you know how good we are? Smile! Have fun! Don't worry about it. I got this,'" he once said. "I'd joke around with them. They'll be nervous before a game or whatever. 'Relax. I got this.' They were real cool. They loosened up a bit. As practice went on and on, it started to get more competitive. Everything loosened up. 'Man, we can win this whole thing.'" And if anyone lapsed into the complacency that characterized the team's play before the trip to Myrtle Beach, he had an answer for that, too. Dabney was dealing with a hip injury, soreness flaring up like a Zippo spark whenever he ran, but Kobe showed him little sympathy, telling him that it was his responsibility to play through the pain, to go as hard as he could until he couldn't run anymore. So Dabney did. *Relax. I got this.*

TRUDGING THROUGH their first season in the Atlantic 10, the La Salle Explorers had lost seventeen of their twenty-two games ahead of a matchup against nationally ranked Villanova on February 12. Speedy Morris's contract had one year left on it, and the perception remained that only one person on the planet stood between him and unemployment: Kobe Bryant. Now, more than an hour before the Villanova game, in the bowels of the Spectrum, Morris encountered Bill Lyon, the longtime sports columnist for *The Philadelphia Inquirer.*

"How are you?" Lyon asked.

"Hangin'," Morris said.

"Literally?"

"Yep," Morris said, pulling back his shirt collar, "see the rope burns?"

Villanova beat La Salle that night, 90–50, the worst loss in the worst season of Morris's coaching career. Watching from the press box, Lyon concluded that the correct and courageous time to support a man is when the floodwaters are lapping at his feet. He wrote a 1,012-word column in which he argued that La Salle, amid the whispers and speculation that Morris might be fired, ought to be magnanimous and stand by him.

"Now the future of Speedy Morris, it is widely assumed, hinges on a decision by Kobe Bryant," Lyon wrote. "This is the senseless and agonizing part of the coaching profession. A seventeen-year-old man-child can control your destiny and that of your family."

The next morning, when the column appeared on the front page of *The Inquirer*'s sports section, Lyon's home phone rang. It was Morris's wife, Mimi. She was in tears.

"Thank you," she said.

THE KOBE in the front of the classroom wasn't quite as confident as the one on the court or among his teammates. He had approached Jeanne Mastriano about taking an elective that she taught in the spring called Speaking Arts, a one-semester course in which students learned, wrote, and delivered speeches and dramatic monologues, then critiqued each other. The purpose of the course, Mastriano said, was to teach students "to know your audience, know how to reach your audience, know what you want to achieve, and be flexible in your method." He signed up for the course, and not just because the training could come in handy for him later. He needed it immediately. Camera crews—from ESPN and from PRISM, a Philadelphia-based cable network—trailed him throughout the hallways for documentary-style reports on the daily life of America's most famous high school basketball prospect. When Mastriano's class attended a production of Ntozake Shange's *for colored girls who have considered suicide / when the rainbow is enuf,* she and the students settled into the theater only to notice, as the lights started to go down and the curtain started to come up, that everyone else in the audience was turning their heads away from the stage to catch a glimpse of Kobe. For the first time, Mastriano had an inkling of the fascination people had with her prized student. "What really hammered it home was when we left," she said later. "I couldn't get him on the bus. He had been swamped, mobbed."

He was accustomed to that kind of public attention. The requirements for Speaking Arts, though, put him in a more vulnerable position: standing before his peers in a hushed room, each of them judging and evaluating him, all in a setting where he was not necessarily the most gifted or practiced performer. During one of his assignments, a personal speech, he strode to a spot near the chalkboard, buried his hands under his oversized white fleece and in the pockets of his sleek navy athletic pants, and spoke about himself for four and a half minutes, pausing every few seconds to search for the next set of just-right words, never lapsing into "ummm"s or "ahhh"s, his nervousness manifesting itself as he shifted his weight from one foot to the other and swayed back and forth, his tongue darting out of each side of his mouth.

"My name is Kobe Bryant. I'm seventeen years old. And I've been lucky enough. To live not only in different parts of the United States. But Europe as well."

He felt isolated when he first arrived at Lower Merion, he told the class, playing basketball to fill his days and pass the time.

"I think that was the best thing that could have ever happened to me. Because during those lonely hours in the rec room. I discovered the hunger, the motivation, and the desire. To be the best possible basketball player that I could be. And here I am today. . . . I have a big decision coming up. And that's whether to go to college. Or straight to the NBA."

What bothered him most about the decision were the strangers who, while he was walking down the street or in the mall, stopped to tell him what he ought to do. But he understood that such unsolicited advice and input were unavoidable.

"I've admired a lot of people: Magic Johnson, Michael Jordan, Emmitt Smith. And entertainers such as Michael Jackson and Janet Jackson. But the two people I admire the most. Are my mother and my father."

He sat at his desk after finishing, turned to one of the cameras, and, half joking, half serious, wiped his brow and said, "Whew." The students weighed in. They didn't mind his swaying. They thought he was passionate. They pointed out his tics. He laughed in the way that a person laughs to avoid an awkward silence. A minute into the speech, Kobe had described his father's decision to retire from the NBA and begin his playing career in Italy: "After his eighth year, he decided it would be best for him to move on . . . and take his talent elsewhere." No one in the room reacted to or seemed to think anything of that turn of phrase.

★ ★ ★

WITH THE postseason approaching and Lower Merion sure to be one of
the favorites not only to win the District One championship but Pennsylvania's Class AAAA state championship, Gregg Downer sought to make
certain that his players were well motivated. Downer never had to worry
about Kobe taking anything lightly or not appreciating the gravity of a
game or situation. But some of the other kids . . . he wasn't sure. The
school hadn't won a state championship since 1943. . . . He got an idea.

Villanova had agreed to open up the Pavilion, which would again be
the site of the district-title game, to the Aces for a practice. The day before
that workout, Downer gave Jeremy Treatman an assignment: Treatman
was to record himself calling play-by-play for a simulated championship
game featuring Lower Merion and a team from the western side of Pennsylvania. Downer wanted to give the players a taste of what playing in—
and winning—a state championship would be like. "I don't think the
kids realize what we're about to do here," he said to Treatman.

That night, Treatman did as he was told. He took out a microcassette recorder, the same one he had used to conduct interviews when he
was writing stories for *The Inquirer.* He picked an opponent that would
resonate with the players: Williamsport, which had reached the state-
championship game the year before. And he began. *Hello, everybody, and
welcome to Hersheypark Arena. . . .*

The fictitious game, conjured completely from Treatman's imagination, lasted an hour. Every Aces player got in the game. Kobe hit a jumper
at the end to win it.

At Villanova the next day, Downer gathered the players at midcourt,
had them sit down, and had Treatman play the entire tape. Most of the
players were smiling, laughing, cheering. Treatman looked down at Kobe
and saw him silent and transfixed. "I think it had more of an effect on
the other guys," Treatman said later, "because they weren't dreaming it
the way Kobe was dreaming it."

When the recording ended, Downer let the boys' cheering subside until there was perfect silence in the Pavilion.

"Now," he said, "let's get to the game."

The tape wasn't Downer's only motivational ploy. He arranged to have the numbers 27 and 53 affixed to the backs of the Aces' warm-up shirts. The meaning behind the numbers was obvious: The team had lost to Chester in the previous year's district-title game by twenty-seven points, and it had been fifty-three years since Lower Merion had won a state championship. "We just wanted to send everybody a message," Kobe said, "send Chester a message, to say, 'Hey, we're here. Last year was last year. This year is a new year. So you guys had better be prepared and bring it all. If not, we're going to spank you.' That was a message that we're not intimidated and we're not going to let you intimidate us." But the Clippers, the No. 1 seed in the district, were only one threat to Lower Merion's championship aspirations. Coatesville entered as the No. 2 seed, with just one loss. The Aces were No. 3.

Knowing how much that lopsided loss to Chester still ate at Kobe, Treatman seized an opportunity, during a pre-practice shootaround, to needle him about it. Pennsylvania's district and state tournaments were separate entities; a team qualified for the latter by reaching the quarterfinals of the former. It was possible, then, for Lower Merion to win the district championship, beating Chester and/or Coatesville along the way, then lose to one of them in the state bracket—a scenario that would surely torment Kobe, given his friendships and rivalries with Chester's John Linehan and Coatesville's Rip Hamilton. So Treatman wanted to get a sense of how Kobe was approaching the prospect of facing such formidable opponents during the playoffs, maybe facing them more than once.

"Linehan and those guys are pretty good," Treatman said.

"I ain't afraid of those n—s," Kobe said.

The remark caused Treatman to recoil. Maybe he had been naive all this time, but he had never heard Kobe use that word before. He didn't quite know how to respond.

"What about Coatesville?" he said.

"I ain't afraid of those n—s, either."

What was there to fear? The Aces won each of their first two district-playoff games by twenty-seven points, Kobe scoring fifty again and hitting seven three-pointers in the second victory, over Academy Park, drawing the interest of *New York Times* sports columnist Ira Berkow, who headed down to suburban Philadelphia to see the phenom for himself. In the quarterfinals, against Norristown, which had a lineup full of players with the length and quickness to harass him, Kobe saved his only bad game of his senior season for Berkow, missing nineteen of his twenty-four shots from the field—the worst shooting performance, Downer said later, that he'd ever seen from him—and fouling out with one minute, ten seconds left in regulation. Kobe's poor game irritated him for days thereafter, mostly because he felt it had given Norristown's players the mistaken impression that they had stopped him, instead of Kobe stopping himself. "I didn't want them to think, 'Yeah, we shut down Kobe Bryant,'" he said. "When the state tournament started, I wanted them to win and keep winning so we could play them again and I could go for fifty, sixty, something like that, and show them, 'You didn't do it. I did it.'"

The Norristown game was perhaps the best worst-case scenario for the Aces: Kobe had been terrible, yet they had survived anyway. Dan Pangrazio, his Myrtle Beach nightmare long behind him, drilled four three-pointers in the fourth quarter, and the Aces held on, 60–55. If there were ever a game that they might lose, that one appeared to be it, and they didn't. They would face Coatesville four nights later, with Chester taking on Plymouth Whitemarsh in the other semifinal, and before he had showered and changed out of his uniform, Kobe realized fully that Lower Merion would play again in the Palestra, and he began to cry. "The road seemed real cloudy at the beginning of the year," he said. "I didn't know what to expect." After collecting himself and leaving the locker room, he gave Berkow a quick quote—"And we go on"—as Berkow strode alongside him, scribbling notes and later describing him as a "young man, even on a lackluster shooting night, properly confident of his talent and full of the pleasures of life," watching as Kobe hugged Joe, slung his bag over his shoulder, and jogged to join his teammates for the raucous bus ride back to Wynnewood.

"He had so much confidence," Treatman said later. "I personally thought his confidence was out of control. I learned so much from him because

I don't live my own life like that. He was the most confident person I've ever met, in any field, and I believe that to this day."

FORGET THE court. Forget the classroom. If you wanted to see Kobe Bryant, teenager, at his most apprehensive, you put him in a room with a girl he thought pretty. Among his female friends, he could vacillate between pally playfulness and near courtliness, aware that his celebrity and good looks made him a catch but declining to exploit those attributes in the way a stereotypical high school jock might. As the senior prom approached, he asked Katrina Christmas for advice on potential dates, suggesting names of his female classmates to solicit Christmas's opinion on them. *Do you think she's OK? Do you think I should ask her?* Jocelyn Ebron, his pseudo-girlfriend, might have seemed the logical choice. Except . . .

"Then I introduced him to Kristen Clement," Treatman said.

Kristen Clement, it does not go too far to say, was the Kobe Bryant of Philadelphia-area girls' basketball: a guard/forward at Cardinal O'Hara High School in Delaware County, just eight miles from Lower Merion, who would score more than two thousand points in her career, lead O'Hara to three Philadelphia Catholic League championships, and play for coach Pat Summit at the University of Tennessee. Her nickname was "Ace," and she had been linked romantically to Eric Lindros, the star player for the Philadelphia Flyers—a morsel of local gossip that, if it didn't quite lift her to Kobe's tier of fame, made her more visible and recognizable than the average high school athlete. Treatman had covered her for *The Inquirer High School Sports Show,* and he mentioned her to Kobe: *beautiful girl at O'Hara, incredible player.*

"Jeremy," Kobe said one day, "we're going to see Ace play. When does she play next?"

"Actually," Treatman said, "my birthday: February 11."

So Treatman spent the afternoon of his thirtieth birthday in the bleachers of O'Hara's gym, sitting next to Kobe. "At the end of the game," Treatman recalled, "Kristen turns around and does a double take. 'Oh, hi.' I saw them exchange numbers, and I totally thought it was just a friendship thing. Next thing I know, everywhere we were, he was on a pay phone talking to Kristen Clement. She came to all our games from that point on. They were arm in arm from the bus."

The couple's fledgling romance presented them with challenges intrinsic to those who live their lives in the public eye. One night, after the Aces had played a road game that Clement had attended, Kobe sidled up to Robby Schwartz as the two of them deboarded the team bus. Kobe was supposed to meet Clement that night at a restaurant in Ardmore, and she was bringing a friend.

"Wanna come?" Kobe asked him.

"Of course!" Schwartz said.

It didn't take long, once they arrived at the restaurant, for Schwartz to understand why Kobe had invited him to be his wingman on his double date. "I just remember looking around," Schwartz recalled, "and everyone was staring at our booth. I don't think I said more than ten words the whole night. It was definitely a 'Come with us so we're not alone' thing." He didn't blame Kobe for wanting company. How else could he experience some sanity in his social life? "Basketball was ninety-nine percent of his life, but he was as normal as the best player in the country could be," Schwartz said. "People acted differently around him. If you were introduced to someone, if you met me—'Hey, there's a guy who plays Lower Merion basketball over there'—you'd come up to me and say hi and be normal. But people never acted normal. They would just say dumb shit, and they forgot how to act around him. Like, just come say hi! He's a normal dude!"

A normal dude who, come the spring, would have a normal experience at his normal senior prom, one would think.

ON FEBRUARY 27, two weeks and a day after Bill Lyon's column defending Speedy Morris appeared in *The Inquirer,* La Salle University held a press conference to announce that its administration had extended Morris's contract for two years, through 1999. "Without that article, I don't get that extension," Morris recalled. "I'm sure of that."

There was no mention at the press conference of Kobe Bryant, who would be playing in the District One semifinals, against Coatesville at the Palestra, that night.

I definitely one day want to sit down with him and talk with him, and hopefully he can give me some advice . . . so I can break all his records.

—KOBE BRYANT, ON MICHAEL JORDAN, 1996

16
THE
TUNNEL

HERE WAS HIS CHANCE, MAYBE Rip Hamilton's final chance, to prove himself better than Kobe Bryant, and how could he know then, as a senior stepping on the Palestra floor for another District One semifinal game, what was ahead for him and the friend and adversary he had come to love and respect and, in the healthiest sense of the word, fear? The gym was shaking and shuddering, spectators spilling out into the aisles. Gene Shue—once the Sixers' head coach, now their director of player personnel—was among them, seated close to the court for Lower Merion–Coatesville, so many people, nine thousand or more, in such tight quarters that Kobe, after the game, would assert that every player on both teams "was in shock." Hamilton, presumably, was among those who needed a few minutes to acclimate himself to the kind of setting that would become commonplace for him as his basketball career continued. Just two weeks earlier, he had verbally committed to play at the University of Connecticut for Jim Calhoun, who was in the Palestra stands, too, for the game, to see how his recruit handled as pressured a moment as high school basketball could present, to see whether Hamilton could step out of the shade that Kobe would cast over him for most of their careers. Yes, Hamilton, over his three seasons at UConn and his fourteen years in the NBA, would surpass Kobe in certain ways. An NCAA national championship—Kobe never gave himself a shot at one, but Hamilton, by choosing UConn, would. And he would win one, in 1999. An NBA title—OK, Kobe would win five, but none of them came at Hamilton's expense. And when they did go head-to-head in the 2004 Finals, when Hamilton and the Detroit Pistons beat the Lakers in five games, he was as good as or better than Kobe: shot a higher percentage from the field, shot a higher percentage from three-point range, averaged more rebounds and assists, at last extracted some satisfaction from his rivalry with him.

And now he had him. He *had* him. Lower Merion had held a ten-point lead after the third quarter, the Aces scoring most of their points either by throwing alley-oop passes to Kobe or by handing him the ball, spreading out to the four corners of the half-court, and letting him go one-on-one against whatever Coatesville player or players happened to be guarding him. "It was a personal-duel type thing" with Hamilton, Kobe said later. "A lot of people were saying he could compete with me, give me some work. When people say that, I just kind of laugh and smile and think in the back of my mind, 'Man, I can kill this guy.'" But the Red Raiders wiped away that deficit in the first three minutes of the fourth, and when Hamilton's teammate John Henderson dropped in a layup, Coatesville led by six with less than three minutes to go. The first meeting . . . Kobe had made that twenty-five-foot three-point shot and that six-foot buzzer-beater, and Hamilton couldn't beat him. The second meeting . . . Kobe had fouled out, and Hamilton still couldn't beat him. This was it. This had to be it.

This was not it. Emory Dabney flushed a three-pointer, then made a steal and layup to cut the lead to one. Kobe found open space in the Coatesville defense—how he could he, of all people and players, find open space?—and, with 1:43 left, slammed the ball home to put the Aces on top again. Jermaine Griffin scored four points in the final minute. "There's nothing like the Palestra," Kobe said after the 70–65 victory, after scoring twenty-nine points and limiting Hamilton to just sixteen, after the Aces had set up a district-championship rematch with Chester. "This was a once-in-a-lifetime opportunity."

No one had to tell Hamilton. After his first game against Kobe, he had realized that he had never played against someone at his position who had outscored him and beaten him in the same game. Now Kobe had done it again, for the third time.

"How come every time I play you," Hamilton asked him after the game, "I always seem to lose?"

Kobe laughed. "I have no clue," he said. It would be eight years until the 2004 NBA Finals, until Rip Hamilton could acquire some feeling of equilibrium between himself and Kobe Bryant, eight years too late for the Coatesville Red Raiders.

LOWER MERION–COATESVILLE was the first game in the semifinal doubleheader. Chester had no trouble with Plymouth Whitemarsh in the second, 65–45.

Chester coach Fred Pickett: "We're happy Kobe gets all the accolades he does. We're happy he's an all-American. But we're going to shut him down. Period."

Chester forward Greg Hollman: "He's a great player, but he still has to slip his shorts on one leg at a time, like the rest of us."

Chester guard Brahin Pharr: "We're going to go after him. We're going to take it right to him."

THE ACES had two school days and one practice bridging their victory over Coatesville and their rematch with Chester, forty-eight more hours for the hype and demands around Kobe and the team to increase. Athletic director Tom McGovern happened to have his daily lunch duty, his hour of keeping an eye on student behavior in the cafeteria, coincide with Kobe's lunch period, and it became common for a different commotion to occupy his attention. The cafeteria was at ground level, and lined up elbow-to-elbow outside its tall, paneled windows, congregating on the school's baseball field just twenty-five feet away, were reporters, television camerapeople, and photographers. McGovern had stopped letting media members into the building, but they knew Kobe had to eat. So they'd stay there, filming, clicking, watching, as if Kobe were an animal and they were glimpsing him in his natural habitat. "There was a jock table," McGovern said. "Sometimes he'd go there, but not always. He'd also sit with whatever kids knew him from class. The poise he had for that age was stunning. He wouldn't pay any attention to the cameras as they were rolling."

Practice was his respite. Even as a high school player, long before *falling in love with the journey* and *staying in the moment* became mantras of the Mamba Mentality, he savored the necessary routine of preparation. At the Aces' team workout the night before the Chester game, Marcella Shorty, the program's athletic trainer, helped him balance three bags of ice on his body as he sat in her office: one bag on each knee, one on his right hand. He was not injured in any way; these were merely the preemptive measures he had always taken to keep his body fine-tuned. As if to reaffirm he was ready for Chester, he waited an hour into practice before, during a lull, snatching the ball, driving to the basket with a couple of crisp dribbles, and rattling the gym walls with a dunk. Everyone in the place, including Gregg Downer and the coaches, let out an "OHHHH!" Later, after a drill, he cleared his throat to speak to his teammates, his voice having deepened, as he had aged, into a rich baritone. His aim was to usher them into the tunnel with him, into the condition that psychologists call *flow,* that place where there are no wayward thoughts or ambient sounds, just a state of concentration so immersive that everything else in their lives would seem unimportant and unnecessary, a diversion or distraction, and would fall away, dead leaves from a rose cane.

"Just don't practice this and forget it," he said. "When you go home tonight, think about it. Think about what you're going to do tomorrow night in the game. See yourself doing it."

He needed the tunnel. He needed the tunnel because there, he could call John Linehan every day for a week—even before Lower Merion had beaten Coatesville—to trade smack talk with him. He needed the tunnel because it would protect him, keep him calm and cocky and focused and certain that he could carry his team to a district championship or a state championship or both. He needed the tunnel because the reporters and cameras weren't going away. The tension wasn't going to dissipate. The state tournament, if the Aces reached the title game, would last another three weeks. Kobe still had his decision to announce—anyone who knew him well knew the decision was already made—sometime thereafter. The phone calls would continue to flood into the athletic office: for questions, for demands on people's time, for tickets. Not everyone relished the limelight and its effects as Kobe did. Treatman, more than once, overheard school administrators muttering to themselves, *When will this end?* The wrestling team was having a strong season, and McGovern had to listen to the team's coaches complain that the success of Kobe and the basketball program was hogging all the attention. The wrestling team used the gym before the basketball team, and often, McGovern had to help Downer drag away wrestling mats that had been left on the court—an archipelago of passive-aggressive resentment—so Kobe and the players could practice. One day, a call came into the athletic office from Pam Bryant, who left a message to make sure that she and Joe and the rest of the Bryants would have tickets for a playoff game. But they hadn't yet paid for the tickets, and the deadline was approaching, and Drew Downer happened to be in the office when Mary Murray started dialing the phone to tell Pam that it was too late, too bad, no tickets for you to see Kobe play in the biggest games of his high school career. "Drew was everybody's big brother," Kobe said. "Everybody looked up to him. He got everybody pumped up. Coach Downer was the motivator, the guy who's going to punish you when you mess up, but Drew was the big-brother type who would smack you on the behind when you weren't do-ing well, cheer you up when his brother just punished you." And he would stand up for you and your family when an athletic secretary was being unreasonable. Drew pressed his finger down on the phone's receiver. "This is Pam Bryant," he told Murray. "You're not going to do that." Chubby Cox, Kobe's uncle, came to pay for and pick up the tickets.

SET ON the east side of Villanova University, the John E. DuPont Pavilion seemed on this late-winter Friday night the site of a national political rally or a Springsteen concert, not a high school basketball game. Its surround-ing parking lots were choked with cars. Yellow crime-scene tape cordoned off a quarter-mile stretch of sidewalk from the arena's entrance gate to Lancaster Avenue, the main artery through campus. Those who already had purchased their tickets to the Pennsylvania District One Class AAAA championship game and awaited access to the Pavilion had to stand in a line that, in its stagnancy, rivaled any backup on the Schuylkill Expressway. Those who hadn't planned ahead could only conduct a furtive search for a scalper or two and shell out anywhere from $30 to $60 for a seat. Or more. When Lynne Freeland and her husband, Michael, arrived at the Pavilion, their tickets already in hand, he dropped her off so she could hold their place in line, then went to park their car. As he walked back to join her, a stranger offered him $100 for his ticket. He turned down the offer.

Inside, the arena was a stew of bodies and colors and noise: students and parents, basketball fans and scouts and media, the Aces in maroon, the Clippers in white trimmed with orange and black, cheerleaders chanting, step team kicking and stomping, taunts and—it does not go too far to say this— threats traded in the bleachers. Chester fans shouted at Lower Merion fans and players that they were "garbage," that they were "afraid to come down to the 'hood" and "scared to play the street-ball boys"; a student reporter for *The Merionite* took care to log each of the insults. It is fair to presume, of course, that the Lower Merion contingent responded in kind, but the contentious atmosphere couldn't be reduced to a clash between a Black city school and a white suburban school. It was as much about class and culture as it was about skin color, and Kobe was at the center of that conflict, threatening to steal Chester's birthright, a piece of the town's very identity.

"The parents were trying to fight us in the stands," Kobe's friend Dayna Tolbert said. "A lot of people outside of the Main Line were jealous that a Black kid from the Main Line was making it. That's not how the story is supposed to go. It's supposed to be that a Black kid from the inner city is supposed to make it to the NBA. 'Kobe doesn't deserve it because he was already born to an NBA player.' It was that way everywhere. That's why we were very protective over him. There were a lot of jealous people and jealous parents, and it didn't rear its head in our community. But the second we stepped out of it—woo, it was not good. It was not good."

That conflict, that pressure . . . it wouldn't bother Kobe. No one had to worry about that. The worry was that even Kobe's best, even the Aces' best, might not be good enough against the Clippers. Gregg Downer had seen it himself, had coached Chester kids at the Keystone Games in

Harrisburg, had sat down in a Central Pennsylvania Denny's at 3:30 in the morning with another coach, the two of them ready to dig into a couple of Grand Slam breakfasts, when into the restaurant bopped a group of Chester players. *Hey, Coach.* And they scarfed down their eggs and pancakes, too, just like Downer, and what could he say? He wasn't going to be mealymouthed and tell them, *Hey, guys, curfew was at eleven.* No way, because he knew what would happen, and did happen, the next afternoon: that on three hours of sleep, after a brunch of Cheetos and grape soda, those same Chester kids would run forever without tiring, would ball out for him, as if they'd just had the most restful eight hours of shut-eye in their lives. And that was just a summer-league tournament, meaningless compared to a district championship. Chester was 25–1, and John Linehan was a senior, heading to Providence College the following fall, and even if the Aces managed to get the ball across half-court against him, the Clippers would have one or both of their six-foot-eight post players, center Tyran Watkins and forward Garrett McCormick, waiting for them near the rim.

Kobe began the game at point guard; having him handle the ball was the easiest, most efficient way for the Aces to break Chester's full-court press. But it was proving too difficult to get the ball back in his hands once he gave it up, and the Aces weren't scoring enough to counteract the Clippers' size advantage. Watkins finished a fast break by jamming the ball with two hands. McCormick displayed a deft shooting touch by hitting a ten-footer as the second quarter was winding down. Chester led at halftime, 29–22. The Aces had trailed by the same deficit, seven points, at the midpoint of their 1995 game against the Clippers. A year had gone by. Had they really made no progress at all against the kings of the district?

"Even though we had Kobe, I really always thought we were the underdogs," Dave Rosenberg recalled. "I don't know if that's the right feeling to have, but certainly against Chester, for the most part, I felt that way. Lower Merion was not the perpetual powerhouse. We had never beaten Chester. They had such a legacy."

Somehow, Downer needed to demystify Chester in his players' minds, to show them that the Clippers weren't some irresistible machine. He had to make this game, the most important of these kids' lives, feel like any other game, and there was one characteristic common to just about every Lower Merion game: Kobe scored easily, whenever he had to or wanted to, in any manner he chose. So Downer made a tactical adjustment: He took Kobe off the ball, counting on the team's point guards, Dabney and backup Dave Lasman, to beat the Chester press. Dan Pangrazio would remain on the wing, but Kobe and Jermaine Griffin—two of the team's tallest and most mobile players—would roam the baseline on offense and defense, which allowed Downer to replace Brendan Pettit, who had gotten into foul trouble, with the scrappy and tenacious Rosenberg. Now, with their new lineup, the Aces could at least approximate Chester's speed and pace, and Kobe and Griffin could pull Watkins and McCormick away from the basket.

The changes changed the game. Kobe dived to the floor for a steal, sparking a 14–1 run in which he and Griffin combined for twelve points. With three minutes, twenty-one seconds left in the third quarter, Pangrazio lofted an alley-oop pass to Kobe for a thunderous dunk, and Kobe capped the quarter by swishing a deep three-pointer for an eight-point lead. In the game's final 2:40, he made ten free throws; after a foul call on Hollman, he waved at him and said, "Bye, bye." If any player had earned the right to rub it in, Kobe had, with his thirty-four points, eleven rebounds, nine blocked shots, and six assists. When Pangrazio chucked the basketball toward the rafters as the clock expired on the 60–53 victory, the Aces danced at center court before lining up to have their gold medals placed around their necks.

The Clippers' players were reserved in their reaction to the game's outcome—"We will keep our head high," Linehan said—compared to the adults in the program. Coach Fred Pickett, noting the Aces' jubilation, believing that the aftermath of a close loss was no time to show doubt in his team, decided to ramp up the bravado in anticipation of the teams' meeting again in the state tournament, as both presumed they would. "We saw them," Pickett said. "They celebrated, all right. They celebrated *their* state championship tonight." Randy Legette, Chester's athletic director, told Jack McCaffery, the sports columnist for the *Delaware County Daily Times,* "Hey, we would rather win a state championship than a district championship. Put that in the paper."

McCaffery did. The next morning, Kobe read it.

THROUGHOUT HIS recruiting process, Donnie Carr had assumed that Kobe would go to college. Duke, probably, because Kobe loved Coach K. The rest of the ACC—Maryland, Florida State, Clemson—had shown interest in Carr. Bobby Knight had offered him a scholarship to Indiana. But his decision was coming down to two local schools: La Salle and St. Joseph's. He called Kobe one night to chat.

"I'm really thinking about La Salle," Carr told him.

"That would be a great spot for you," Kobe said, "because you can go there and showcase your skills."

There was a subtle distance to Kobe's answer that Carr came to understand later, when Joe Bryant invited Carr and his older brother, Darren, to La Salle for a meeting.

Listen, man, Joe told Carr, *my son's not going to college. Kobe is going to have the chance to be the first guard to make the jump. They're saying he's going to be a lottery pick. Listen, Don, in my heart, I still believe that this is the right school for you. You're going to play forty minutes a game. They're going to put the ball in your hands. You have the chance to do some unbelievable things here.*

On March 8, 1996, Carr scored nineteen points at the Palestra, leading Roman Catholic to a 57–47 victory over Archbishop Carroll in the Philadelphia Catholic League championship game. On March 11, he called Kobe again. He was going to La Salle, he told him, and he was announcing his decision the next day. Neither of them said much after that, as if Carr were waiting for Kobe to fill the expectant silence . . . and Kobe never did. "We talked about other things," Kobe said later.

Donnie Carr did do some unbelievable things at La Salle. He ranked sixth in the country in scoring as a freshman, averaging nearly twenty-four points a game. Then, he made what he later acknowledged to be a mistake: Instead of entering the NBA draft, he returned for his sophomore year. He was a local kid playing at a local school for, in Speedy Morris, a local legend, so he took what had been the traditional route to success, the route that Kobe had barely bothered to consider. "You as a player are a penny stock," Carr said. "They draft on potential. Once it reaches a certain plateau, it can only go down." He stayed at La Salle for four years, finishing with more than two thousand points, but a case of meningitis his senior year hampered him, and he never matched the production of his freshman season again. In the 2000 NBA draft, no team selected him. He went overseas to play in France and Turkey, and his luck worsened: bone-spur surgery, a torn right meniscus, a torn left meniscus, a torn patella tendon. By his twenty-fifth birthday, Donnie Carr—who at one time had thought of himself on par with or better than Kobe Bryant . . . and was justified in thinking so—had lost any realistic hope of a playing career in professional basketball.

He ricocheted from job to job, getting hired and fired as an environmental services supervisor, ballooning to three hundred pounds, falling into depression, before a friend offered him a volunteer high school coaching position. He worked his way up, and La Salle hired him in 2017. He's still on staff there, an assistant to another of Kobe's childhood friends: Ashley Howard. The passage of time has helped to heal him, has acted as a salve for the wound on his spirit. The past and its unfulfilled possibility, the constant juxtaposition with Kobe, don't sting as much anymore.

"It took me years to get over it," he said. "The funny thing about it is, when people used to come up to me and say, 'Oh, man, Don, you and Kobe used to go at it,' they would think that it helped me, helped my morale, and it would crush me. It brought me back to that place. I was right there with him, and he goes on to be the best player in the world, and I fell short of my ultimate dream."

IT WAS, Kobe said later, the "ugliest alley-oop of the century," Dan Pangrazio near the top of the key and heaving the ball toward the general vicinity of the rim, Kobe starting in the right corner, dashing toward the lane, going up, up, up, seeing the ball and thinking at first that he would catch it with his left hand and lay it in the basket, then bringing his left hand down, closer to the rim, and closing his eyes . . .

"And then," he said, "everybody started going crazy."

He was fashioning at least one of these each game now, at least one moment that, even if he had done nothing else of note that night, validated his reputation and the murmurs trailing him through the first three rounds of the state tournament. This one was at Coatesville, of all places, in the second quarter of the Aces' first-round game against Cedar Cliff, and it brought them within two points after they'd been down by nine, and it's tempting to say that Kobe was making all of this up as he went along, but no. That wasn't him. He relegated his improvisational skills to those tiny slivers of time on the court that he could elevate a play from terrific to breathtaking, sprinkling in just enough razzmatazz to let everyone in the gym know that they had seen him make a play that a high schooler ought to be incapable of making. Just after that dunk, he brought the ball down court, sized up the defender in front of him. *I want to dunk again, but I might as well try to make this guy look a little foolish.* Juke right, spin left, complete the 360-degree revolution, face the basket again, give 'em the finger roll with the left hand, tie game. The levity stopped there, midway through that 74–62 win, because to Kobe all of this was dead-serious business. On the sixty-mile bus ride to Liberty High School in Bethlehem for the team's second-round game against Scranton, he considered the mindset that Scranton's players might be in. He had read up on the Knights. They were 15–10, a young team that in the first round had upset defending state finalist Williamsport, a result so surprising that Scranton's coaches hadn't bothered to scout Lower Merion because they hadn't believed their team was capable of beating Williamsport. Scranton's players, Kobe reasoned, would be excited that they had won such a big game, perhaps a little too satisfied with themselves. "Coming in and facing a team like us," he said later, "that can be intimidating." When the bus arrived, the rest of the Aces entered the gym first. Kobe followed them, flanked by two security guards. Liberty had been the site of the state-playoff loss to Hazleton the previous year, and every sensory experience—the sight of the school building, the musty odor of the gym—jarred his memory and reminded him of that night. He smirked at the Scranton players.

"When I walked in," he said, "this guy from around their way gave me a nice little article. It had their star player talking about dreaming about the day he could guard me and come out and play against me. He said it was a dream come true. 'I really look up to him. I know I can't stop him.' Little things like that. I said, 'Oh, my God. I got you.' I said, 'Like a shark: When he smells blood, he's going to go after it. He's going to attack it.' I knew that he was intimidated, that he looked up to me like that. I just went after him."

On Scranton's first four possessions, Kobe blocked one shot, altered two others, and stole the ball once. He dunked five times and had twenty-five points and twelve rebounds. Lower Merion scored the game's first twenty-two points and won 79–39. The Knights weren't intimidated as much as they were deferential, honored just to be on the same court as Kobe. "Obviously," John Lyons, their coach, said, "that is the greatest high school team and the greatest high school player I've ever seen." Afterward, every Scranton player asked for, and received, Kobe's autograph, a request that both flattered and puzzled him. *My God,* he thought, *didn't we just blow y'all out? You're supposed to be upset.* "But they smiled, and I'm signing," he said later. "It was cool. I enjoyed it."

One more win—71–54 over Stroudsburg, Kobe with thirty-six—had the feel of a formality, the real thrill coming afterward in the locker room, when Downer and the coaching staff got word that Chester had won its quarterfinal game, too. The teams would indeed play again, on a Wednesday night at the Palestra, a berth in the state-championship game at stake. His teammates whooping and hollering at the news, Kobe remained quiet, first in a corner of the room then on the bus ride home. The newspaper articles following the first Chester game, the quotes from the Clippers, had drained his excitement about the district championship, had framed it as an empty achievement. What did that victory matter, what did it mean, if he lost this time around? *Beating Chester. Beating Chester. Have to do it. Gotta do it.* It was all that filled his mind as the bus rolled on through the night.

MONDAY, MARCH 18, marked the Aces' first practice before facing Chester, and though Kobe had a pressing appointment that night—one that, for anyone else his age, surely could have been distracting—he felt himself the only player fully engaged in the workout. A state championship could be planned, could be prepared for, could be won, he believed, if he and his teammates did everything as it ought to be done, if no one deviated, if everyone locked in on the *now.* They had done that most of the season, but they weren't doing it at this practice, not to his standard. "We were going through the motions," he said, "not concentrating, not running through screens hard." He and Downer were aggravated over the lack of effort, so during one drill, "I tried to pump the team up," Kobe said, taking the ball near midcourt and, while little Leo Stacy got in position to guard him, mulling the fastest route he could take to the basket for a ferocious dunk.

Kobe moseyed forward with a slow, deliberate dribble, pulled back, and tried to zoom past Stacy with a crossover. Stacy reached in to try to bat the ball out of Kobe's hands, and the top of his head slammed into Kobe's nose and knocked him to the floor.

Downer cringed immediately. He had long feared that Kobe might get hurt during a practice. But for months his players had prided themselves on their hustle, had shown off their floor burns to each other like war wounds. How could he tell them to take it easy now? Dazed, his eyes watering, Kobe thought, *Oh, well. I bumped my nose. I'll get up, start playing some more.* He tried to stand up. Blood gushed from his face.

Shorty rushed out to the court with an ice pack wrapped in a towel. With his right hand, Kobe pressed the towel to his nose, which was, quite obviously, broken. The entire team watched him in horror, wondering whether he would be healthy enough to play in forty-eight hours. He took a step toward the trainer's room, then stopped.

"Ball," he said.

Someone threw him a soft bounce pass. He caught the ball with his left hand, five feet beyond the three-point arc. He turned to Treatman, who was standing next to him.

"Jeremy, I'll bet you five dollars I can make this three-point shot with my left hand," Kobe said. "I bet you I can make this shot."

Treatman took the bet. One-handed, off-handed, Kobe lofted the ball toward the basket.

Swish.

He kept walking to the trainer's room.

"The rest of us are just standing there," Robby Schwartz said, "like, 'What the hell is even going on here?'"

Kobe told Shorty that he wanted to go back out to practice some more. His jump shot hadn't been falling before Stacy's head smacked into him.

It annoyed him that he couldn't work on his game, that Leo Stacy—Leo Stacy!—"Five foot nothing, weighs a hundred and nothing pounds," Kobe said—had been the one to break his nose. But Shorty and the coaches were adamant; they wouldn't let him back on the court. Besides, he had somewhere else to be.

IT WAS a night for Kobe to hang out with old friends, to pal around with his summertime pickup-game buddies, Jerry Stackhouse and Vernon Maxwell, in the home locker room of the Spectrum, a couple of hours before the Sixers' game against the Chicago Bulls. John Lucas had invited Kobe to the game, all the better to maintain and strengthen their relationship as the NBA draft, still three months off, approached. Now Lucas interrupted the conversation with Stackhouse and Maxwell with an offer that Kobe couldn't refuse.

Let's go meet Michael.

Lucas led Kobe to the visitors' locker room. A horde of reporters encircled Jordan. Kobe slid up as close as he could and leaned against a nearby wall.

"Kobe," Jordan said, "what's up?"

Kobe looked around. *Is there another Kobe here? I know he's not talking to me.* Jordan extended his hand. "Hey," he said, "nice meeting you, young man."

Kobe didn't know that Jordan knew anything about him. Did he remember their brief interaction when Kobe was an eighth grader? Had Lucas mentioned something to him? Had Jordan heard or read about him? Kobe reached out his hand and shook Jordan's. *His hand is so . . . strong . . .* Kobe was not nervous. This person standing in front of him, this person whom the world adored, was a human being, just like everybody else. Just a basketball player, like Kobe.

Unlike in their previous meeting, Jordan this time talked to Kobe at some length. *Enjoy the game,* he told him. *With the pressure and hype that's going on, you can become easily distracted, and the game won't be enjoyable. Don't let people do that to you. Stay yourself. Have fun on the court, and everything will be fine.* The last piece of advice Jordan gave him: *Man, if it was up to me, you'd go to North Carolina. Go to Carolina.* He said it three or four times, having no idea, of course, that Kobe already had made up his mind about the NBA, that he already had said to Jeanne Mastriano, "The window's closing. I'm not going to have a chance to play against Michael if I don't go now."

The sands of power and popularity in an institution, in a culture, can begin to shift without anyone noticing. The Bulls, on their way to a seventy-two-win season and the fourth of their six championships with Jordan, beat the Sixers, 98–94. Kobe's introduction to him merited nothing more than a throwaway line in a *Philadelphia Inquirer* feature a couple of days later: "There was also an audience with Michael Jordan on Monday . . ." To fashion a stronger link between the two of them then, between the most famous and admired athlete in the world and a seventeen-year-old aspirant, would have been absurd. And yet, remember: Just two years separated Jordan's last NBA championship from Kobe's first. The transition from one to the other was more direct than anyone could have imagined in 1996, and by 2020, Jordan had felt enough of a need to reaffirm his standing in the sport, to reacquaint everyone with his magnitude, that he partnered with the NBA for the ten-part ESPN documentary *The Last Dance*. "What you get from me is from him," Kobe says during the series. "I don't get five championships here without him." There is a subtle but telling detail in the interview: At the instant that Kobe utters those words, he moves his right hand as if he is pushing away either the interviewer or the question, as if he is saying, *Slow down. Don't forget. Michael came first.* The reminder is necessary, not because Kobe had surpassed Jordan as a player, but because he had surpassed him as a story. He had traveled the redemptive narrative arc: ruining his good name and nearly his marriage and leaving a stranger scarred in that hotel room in Eagle, Colorado; destroying relationships with who knows how many coaches and players and peers before reconstituting them; somehow scrubbing away much of that grime to emerge as someone perceived to have matured, to have found the elusive balance between peace and ambition; persuading people that the arrogance and atrocious choices and actions of his past weren't so relevant anymore; forging a new identity as an emotional and psychological touchstone, the possessor of a mentality that all should admire and emulate and adopt. It was a greater trick than anything Michael Jordan ever pulled off.

I can remember getting in an argument with one of the teachers in school, a substitute teacher. This is when I was a junior. He's talking all this trash. We had just lost to Chester, and he said, "Y'all never will win a state championship. Do you honestly think you can win a state championship?" I'm like, "Yes." He's like, "You can believe that all you want. You will never win a state championship. There are too many great players out there, too many great teams out there. You'll never, ever win." I looked at him: "Man, you're wrong. Watch."

—KOBE BRYANT

17

THE FINAL
GAME

FOR THE THREE DAYS BEFORE the state semifinals, Kobe could have spent his time basking in the gratifying news of perhaps his greatest individual honor to date: He had won the Naismith Award as the best high school basketball player in the nation. But his thoughts were a swirl of anxiety and excitement, of possible outcomes elating and intolerable. So he fed his mind with familiar nourishment. As if he were again in Italy, learning basketball at his father's feet, he watched and rewatched game tapes of Magic Johnson. All of the tapes had one thing in common. Each of them was of one of the four Game Sevens that Johnson had played in his career. (Jordan would play just two in his.) This time, he wasn't focusing on Magic's no-look passes and slope-shouldered dribble as he led a fast break, his precognition of where all his teammates would be on the court and when they would be there. This time, Kobe focused on something else: How did he handle the pressure? Did he let the game come to him? Did he go out and take it? How did he lead his team to victory? Then Kobe focused on himself: What if his shots didn't fall? What if his teammates' shots didn't fall? How would they withstand the crowd noise in the Palestra? How would they react if and when Chester took the lead? How would they handle the adversity? "I was very nervous," he said later. "At the same time, I was excited because I knew it was the chance of a lifetime. I knew that we could beat them. There wasn't any doubt that we could beat them. We just had to play our game."

Gregg Downer wasn't so certain. During a Tuesday practice, one day after Kobe's collision with Leo Stacy, one day before the Chester game, Kobe had worn a protective face mask, and Downer had stationed Lynne Freeland outside the gym doors, having her stand sentry to make sure no media or students or onlookers caught a glimpse of Kobe's resemblance to the Phantom of the Opera. He planned to wear the mask during the game, as well. Should he? Would it make him a target? Chester's coaches and players knew nothing about the injury. No one outside the team did, and revealing the broken nose would make Kobe vulnerable to a not-so-accidental elbow. He didn't like the mask anyway. It limited his peripheral vision. But he might put himself at greater risk of injury if he didn't wear it at all.

Kobe answered those questions minutes before tip-off. "Guys, let's go to war," he said. "I'm not wearing this thing." He ripped the mask off and threw it against a wall.

NOW KOBE had no mask. He also had no legs. He could feel it in the pregame layup line. They were gone, limp. He tried stretching them out. He tried relaxing, hoping that keeping them loose would restore their bounce and spring. Nope. His defiant hurling of his mask against the locker-room wall had been dramatic in the moment, but whatever emotional inspiration and adrenal boost he and the Aces received from it had faded like a sugar rush. He missed ten of his fourteen shots in the first half, the Clippers making him labor just to get open. Every jump shot he took was short. After the game, he would deliver, to *The Philadelphia Inquirer,* a quote so colorful and nostalgic that he had to be thinking of his father when he said it: "I was making too many moves. There was too much jelly on my jam." He was dog tired, and though Pangrazio sank two three-pointers and had nine points, John Linehan was too often preventing Lower Merion from running its offense. Linehan had five steals in the first quarter alone. Chester led by two at halftime. The lead felt larger.

Now Kobe had a choice to make and a conundrum to solve. If he continued to remain on the perimeter, he would reduce the risk that a stray elbow or forearm would strike him in his broken nose and knock him out of the game. But if he continued shooting as he had been, every jumper grazing or clanking off the front of the rim, the Aces would have no chance to come back. "At halftime, I just regrouped," he said later. "I worked too hard to get in shape in the off-season. I'm not losing this because I'm tired. I just pushed myself. I said, 'I may be tired, but I've got to attack the rim.'"

It took him until the end of the third quarter to assert his will on the game, driving to the hoop and dunking to give the Aces a 41–39 lead. He had made just four of his ten shots in the period, but an invaluable piece of information had revealed itself: The referees were calling a particularly tight game—at least, they were against Chester—and the more frequently Kobe drove to the basket, the more likely it was that he could pile up easy points at the foul line. Settling for jump shots wasn't an option for him anymore, and his relentlessness in going to the basket sucked Chester's defensive attention and alignment toward him, opening shots for his teammates. He scored twelve points in the fourth quarter, and when Emory Dabney drilled a three-pointer with 1:19 left in regulation, Lower Merion led 61–56.

Then the meltdown began. Linehan hit a free throw. Off the ensuing inbounds play, Kobe threw a soft pass to Pangrazio, who fouled Linehan as they jostled for the ball. Linehan made both free throws. Now the lead was down to two. Dabney caught the inbounds pass and, as if he couldn't get rid of the ball fast enough, threw a pass for Pangrazio into the maw of the Chester press. Another steal. As a Clippers player missed a jump shot, Pangrazio, on the other side of the court, took two steps backward, anticipating that the Aces would get the rebound. The ball caromed out of bounds off Kobe's hands, and on his second step, Pangrazio set his left foot down atop the sneaker of a Chester player. His ankle turned. He dropped in a heap. One spectator yelled out, "Is it broke?" It was not. But it was badly sprained.

In the tussle under the basket, someone had elbowed Kobe in the nose, which started it bleeding again. As he squeezed his nose to stanch the flow of blood, he turned around to find Pangrazio lying on the floor, writhing in pain, grabbing his leg. *Oh, my God,* Kobe thought. *I lost my damn shooter.* Four coaches rushed out to tend to Pangrazio, leaving Treatman alone as Kobe and the three other Lower Merion players who had been in the game wandered, zombie-like, back to the bench. The training staff carted Pangrazio away on a stretcher.

Treatman had no encouraging speech to give, and even if he had, it might not have made a difference. On the ensuing possession, Chester guard Tahir Lowrie nailed a pull-up jumper with 27.5 seconds left to tie the game. Panic was swelling within the Aces now, within one player in particular. Dabney caught the inbounds pass along the left sideline and froze, again throwing the ball blindly into the middle of the floor. Chester's Garrett McCormick intercepted the pass and missed a short bank shot, but the ball again went out of bounds off Kobe. The Clippers would have the ball with a chance to win. They called a time-out.

Dabney was starting to lose it, hot tears forming in his eyes, the cheers and groans of nine thousand people inside the Palestra bearing down on him. Kobe could imagine what he was thinking: *God, the season's right here, and I'm throwing the ball away.* But before Kobe or anyone else on the team could console Dabney, Drew Downer sprinted over and, above the din, shouted at the sophomore guard.

"NOT NOW! WE'RE NOT GOING DOWN LIKE THIS. DON'T YOU FUCKING GIVE UP ON ME! DON'T LET UP NOW. ONE MORE PLAY! DO NOT LET UP!"

Had Kobe or any other coach . . . *encouraged* . . . him like that, Dabney might never have recovered. But Drew could reach Dabney, could motivate him and level with him in a way no one else on the team could. When Dabney had missed those three games early in the season, it was Drew who had snapped him out of his academic doldrums. "He had to pull me aside and say, 'Emory, what the fuck? Some kids have problems and struggle, but you're not having those problems. You're just bullshitting,'" Dabney recalled. "And I had to say to myself, 'You know what? He's right.'"

Out of the time-out, Chester swung the ball twice near the top of the key until it ended up in Linehan's hands on the right side of the court, forty-five feet from the basket. In the Clippers' huddle, Fred Pickett had called a set play that required Linehan to give up the ball. But Kobe had peeled back to the center of the lane to protect the rim and provide rebounding support, and Linehan saw that the defender guarding him one-on-one was Dabney. He decided not to run the play. Sensing that he had a fragile opponent before him, he wanted to win the game by himself.

He dribbled to his right, then crossed over to his left. Dabney stayed on Linehan's right hip like a walkie-talkie clipped to a cop's belt. Just as he reached the foul line, Linehan rose to shoot. Dabney, two inches taller, jumped with him, reached up with his left hand, and blocked the shot. The ball bounded across the half-court stripe as the regulation clock ran out.

Kobe sprinted back to the bench with his right fist high in the air. *There's no way we're losing this game. No way in hell.* With two minutes left in overtime, he split a double-team, burrowed into the lane, and dropped in a leaner to put Lower Merion ahead, 67–65. He made two free throws to extend the lead to four. Less than twenty seconds remained when, with the Aces up seven, Linehan missed a three-pointer and Dabney rebounded the ball and passed it to Kobe, who tucked it under his right arm, a few feet near the baseline, the length of the court before him. He could wait for a Chester player to foul him to stop the clock. If the Clippers were ready to surrender, he could run out the rest of the game by lofting a pass to a teammate or dribbling the ball around the backcourt himself. He did neither of those things.

All those previous games, all those times when Kobe had gone side to side and behind his back and around again, when he had treated opposing players as if they were traffic cones, when Gregg Downer had cautioned him against embarrassing his opponents just because he could:

Those moments of flash and unnecessary ostentatiousness would reveal their purpose and utility now. Three dribbles put him at half-court. Linehan reached in for one last desperate steal. Kobe pushed past him. Two Chester post players stepped up to meet Kobe above the three-point arc, to try to block his path to the basket. Before they could establish position, he shake-dribbled and darted between them, batting the ball in front of him. It was, to Gregg Downer, the consummate Kobe play, everything on display, the lateral movement, the agility, the desire. *There's the rim. I'm going there. You're not stopping me.*

Kobe caught up to the ball just inside the foul line and didn't take another dribble, and when he leaped, the baggy white T-shirt he wore under his tank top billowed like a skydiver's flight suit. A Chester player bumped him from behind, a tweet from a referee's whistle following to signal a foul, as Kobe slammed the ball home with his right hand. He threw his arms into the air, and his teammates streamed toward him, then dispersed, and he remained alone, pumping his fists, cupping his right hand and putting it to his ear to exhort the crowd, screaming just to scream. He looked up at the scoreboard. *This game is over.* He swished his foul shot.

OF HIS thirty-nine points in the Aces' 77–69 victory, Kobe had scored twenty in the fourth quarter and overtime. He had shot just twelve of twenty-nine from the field, but he had made four of his final five field-goal attempts and had missed just two of his seventeen foul shots. When the game ended, when he realized that he and the Aces would play in the state-championship game, "I had a big smile on my face," he said. "It was such a great feeling. All the reporters who had written all the stuff about Chester, I could laugh in their face." In three days, on Saturday at 8:00 P.M., televised throughout the state on the Pennsylvania Cable Network, Kobe Bryant would play his final high school basketball game, for the last high school championship he had left to win.

JIMMY KIESERMAN kept a basketball in his car, just in case an opportunity arose for him to get Kobe's autograph. One day after practice, Kobe asked him for a ride home, and the coach told him to hop in.

"Would you mind signing this for my nephew?" Kieserman said.

Sure, Kobe said. "Do you want my high school number or my NBA number?"

He signed the ball "KOBE BRYANT #27." He said 27 was his favorite number.

JOE BRYANT and Sonny Vaccaro remained in touch throughout March 1996, mostly through their intermediary, Vaccaro's friend Gary Charles. Adidas was in. Adidas wanted Kobe, and if, as part of a deal, Adidas were to pay his father as well, Vaccaro and Charles could do that. But Joe didn't mind exploring other options or keeping the doors to them propped open. Becoming the head coach at La Salle was no longer a possibility. Speedy Morris, after his contract extension, was entrenched there now, and once La Salle's season ended, Joe's relationship with the coaching staff pretty much did, too. Sharia and Shaya started picking up their father's paychecks.

So Joe talked to other agents, other potential sponsors, and he made it clear to Kobe: If Kobe wanted to go in another direction, if he wanted to sign with Nike or Fila, they would look into it. Believing that Kobe and his family ought to remain as much in control of his future as possible, Joe and Pam had formed what they called "Team Bryant": they themselves, Sam Rines Sr. and Jr., and Ron Luber—friends whom they trusted to put Kobe and his best interests first. But Kobe had his own ideas. Fila already had signed Grant Hill and Jerry Stackhouse, and Kobe thought Vaccaro was "the greatest guy. . . . He was there when Michael Jordan first started with Nike. He was there with him. He was there for his mistakes, his positive things. He knows what I have to do to go in the right direction. Nike's on top. I don't want to go with somebody who's on top. This is my time to bring Adidas to the top." Joe handled the legwork. Joe collected the contacts. Joe could lend his son advice, maybe even nudge him toward a choice, but only so far. Kobe, at all times, was the one wielding the power. All that was left was to negotiate and settle on a price.

★　★　★

IN 1996, Pennsylvania's eight state-championship basketball games—four classifications based on enrollment, boys and girls—were held in the same town, in the same edifice, where the greatest offensive performance in the sport's history had taken place. Hershey was distinguished not merely by the candy factory founded by its namesake, Milton Hershey, and the pleasing smell that, issuing from the factory's two sandy brown spires, enveloped the town and started visitors craving chocolate. On March 2, 1962, just more than thirty-four years earlier, Wilt Chamberlain had scored one hundred points for the Philadelphia Warriors, in a victory over the New York Knicks, at Hershey Sports Arena. It was a record that Kobe would come closer to matching than any NBA player before or since, torching the Toronto Raptors for eighty-one points in January 2006, and as he prepared to play in Hershey for the first and only time, he carried enough confidence to believe that he could score 101 points, and would, if he had to. At a school-wide pep rally, he stood before the student body and said, "There's no way in hell we're losing this game. We're going to bring it back. I guarantee it." That week, he had perhaps his best practice of his career. "I just lit the place up," he said. "I didn't miss a shot. I was on fire. Nobody was nervous. Nobody. Well, Coach Downer probably was."

Yes. Yes, he was, as were the members of his coaching staff. Pangrazio's left ankle was encased in a boot. Omar Hatcher would replace him in the starting five, and while Hatcher would lend the lineup more speed, a good defensive presence, and the unusual wrinkle of being left-handed, the absence of Pangrazio and his shooting ability promised to be particularly debilitating against the Aces' opponent. Erie Cathedral Prep was 24–6 and was as close to a basketball dynasty as Western Pennsylvania—a region renowned for its love affair with high school football—could produce. The Ramblers had won the Class AAAA championship in 1993, had advanced to the state-title game in 1994, and had reached the state quarterfinals in 1995. Their coach, Marcel Arribi, had them run a patient, patterned offense that would lull opponents into a collective stupor before a wide-open jump shot or a backdoor layup revealed itself. They would control the ball, and within their man-to-man defensive system, they would have a plan for Kobe, whether to deny him the ball or badger him once he caught it. By Arribi's design, Kobe would have the ball only so much, would get only so many chances to score. The Aces' full-court pressure was unlikely to rattle Erie Cathedral Prep, and they would struggle to pull the Ramblers into a fast-paced, up-and-down game. He and his teammates would have to be sharp, precise in their play, to win.

At lunch, Kobe, picking up on Downer's anxiety, tried to calm him. "Coach, don't worry about it," he said. "I got this. I'm going to win this game for you. After everything you pulled us through, there's no way we've come this far, all the way to the championship game, to lose." But the precision that the Aces would need against Erie Cathedral did not apply to their journey west from Wynnewood to Hershey late that afternoon, a ride that was supposed to include a stop along the Pennsylvania Turnpike for a team dinner, for a chance to relax and relieve the players' mental and emotional pressure before the game. During the bus ride, Downer reached into his grab bag of motivational tactics: He had the team watch the movie *Hoosiers,* the fictional underdog tale of Indiana's Hickory High School Huskers, who win the 1951 state basketball championship with a hard-driving coach, one star player, and a capable supporting cast. Kobe had never seen *Hoosiers* before. "It was similar to our story, really," he said later. But as the bus took an off-ramp to the restaurant, just a few minutes away from Hersheypark Arena, a strange sequence of events shattered the veneer of relaxed confidence that Downer had hoped to create.

Drew Downer had awakened that morning with the flu or some iteration of it. So instead of boarding the bus with the rest of the team, he and Treatman drove themselves, trailing the bus on the turnpike. Dehydrated and light-headed, Drew began moaning as he reclined in the passenger seat. "What do you want me to do?" Treatman said. "Do you want me to stop at a hospital?" Drew passed out without answering. When he arrived at the restaurant, Treatman dashed in to tell Gregg that his brother was sick, at which point Gregg turned to the other patrons and asked in a half shout, "Is there a doctor here?" There was not, but Hershey Medical Center was a short drive from both the restaurant and the arena.

Treatman said that he would take Drew to the emergency room, then try to rendezvous with the team before or during the game. Kobe, sitting at the table, goofing around with Jermaine Griffin, was oblivious to the commotion until he got back on the bus and, after a while, wondered why it was still idling in the parking lot. *Drew is sick? What do you mean Drew is sick? How the hell did he get sick?*

At the hospital, nurses outfitted Drew with an IV to feed him fluids, and once friends of the Downer family arrived to mind Drew, Treatman hopped back in his car and sped over to the arena. Kobe and the other players had written "DD" on their sneakers, in honor of their flu-stricken coach, but they might have done well to add "GD" to their inscriptions. Treatman noticed, once the players were warming up on the court after Downer's pregame speech, that Gregg himself was not on the court. He went back into the locker room and found Downer still there, sitting in one of the bathroom stalls, his face wan.

"Jeremy," he said, "I can't come out. We're not going to win this game."

"I'll tell you one thing," Treatman replied. "If you stay in here, we're not going to win."

Throughout the first quarter, it appeared that, whether Downer was on the sideline or not, Lower Merion had saved its worst game of the season for its most important game of the season—and that Kobe had, too. Double- and triple-teaming Kobe and daring the other Aces to score, Erie Cathedral got out to a 7–0 lead, a run that didn't end until Hatcher hit a pair of free throws more than three and a half minutes into the game. Off a Hatcher steal, Kobe had an open three-pointer from the top of the key. It clanked off the front of the rim, and as he trotted back down court, he yelled at and motioned toward the Lower Merion bench that the basketball was slippery, an unforeseen problem that threatened the Aces' ability to function on offense. "We handle the ball, go between our legs, come out the back, crossovers, pulling up on a dime," he said later. "And those guys, all they do is pound the ball, pound the ball, pass." The quarter ended with Kobe missing another top-of-the-key three. With the Ramblers ahead 13–5. With Kobe scoreless. With the Erie Prep fans in the sold-out, seven-thousand-seat arena chanting,

"OVERRATED!" With one spectator shouting at Kobe that he had "put too much jelly on his jam," a sign that someone had been reading *The Philadelphia Inquirer*.

Frustrated, Kobe kept up his complaints about the basketball's slick surface to the referees, demanding that they switch out the ball for a tackier one. The refs offered to wipe the ball with a towel but refused to do anything more. *Man, you're gonna cheat?* Kobe thought. *All right. Fine.* During the break between quarters, he picked up a small aerosol can of adhesive spray that trainer Marcella Shorty carried with her. Shorty used the spray on an athlete's ankle before taping it up; the sticky substance allowed the tape to stay on the skin longer. Kobe covered each of his hands with it.

On the opening possession of the second quarter, Kobe posted up on the right block. Hatcher lobbed him the ball, and it stuck to Kobe's hands without his having to close them. He shot without hesitating, rattling in a fifteen-foot fadeaway from the right baseline. Later, Kobe dribbled the ball thirty-five feet from the hoop, scanning the court, and three Erie defenders moved, amoeba-like, with him. He found Griffin for a driving layup, the only Lower Merion basket of the quarter that Kobe himself didn't score. The Aces trailed at halftime, 21–15, a familiar position for them but an uneasy one nonetheless. It was one thing to trail Chester, Coatesville, or another high-scoring team by six; the nature of those opponents and pace of those games would afford ample opportunity for a comeback. It was another to trail a plodding, deliberate team like the Ramblers. If the Aces weren't careful, if they didn't make up the deficit in the third quarter, the game could get short fast.

In an uneasy locker room, Kobe couldn't conceive of Erie Cathedral continuing to withstand the Aces' full-court, man-to-man defense. *They're gonna crack. There's no way they can stand our pressure the entire game.* Team manager Tom Pettit, picking up on Kobe's idea, spritzed every player's hands with Shorty's pre-tape spray. Downer, balancing his agitation with his understanding that the Aces could still seize control of the game with a strong start to the second half, dispatched Treatman to the bleachers to find Pangrazio's mother, Dorothy, to see if she would let him play. "He's in a boot," she told Treatman. "He's not playing." While Treatman made his plea, Downer reentered the locker room and, before addressing the team, removed something from his duffel bag: a pair of Adidas sneakers, white with three blue stripes. He slipped off his dress shoes and put the sneakers on. The players were puzzled until he started to speak.

I want good traction for the postgame celebration. When we win this game, I'm going to run around the court and jump around like a madman, and I need to wear my Adidas for that.

"That sent a message," Kobe said later. "We're in the championship game. How come we're playing like this? If we're going to do it, we've got to do it now."

The Aces received another positive jolt when, just before the second half began, Drew Downer—looking like he had been in a fight, his hair disheveled, his shirt untucked, having persuaded the nurses that they had squeezed enough fluid into him that he could leave the hospital—staggered back into Hersheypark Arena and wobbled his way to the bench. Gregg yanked him into the huddle to cheers from the players. "I said something—I don't remember what—and almost passed out again," Drew recalled.

He would have been disappointed if he had. He would have missed Griffin turning two Erie Cathedral turnovers into baskets. And Dabney hitting a three-pointer, then leading a fast break and feeding Kobe for a dunk. And Brendan Pettit corralling a loose ball and scoring inside. The 11–0 burst put Lower Merion up by five. After all those weeks, all those games of counting on Kobe to carry them, his teammates were bearing their share of the burden and more. The Aces led, 37–31, after three quarters. They were eight minutes away.

IT IS a marvelous feature of human nature: The way we remember things, the way we see and shape them in our mind's eye, is often the way we wish we had seen and shaped them in the moment. It's a kind of retroactive foresight. *I knew I would marry her the instant I touched her hand. . . . Those lottery numbers felt lucky as soon as I saw them. . . .*

"I knew," Kobe once said, thinking back on that state-championship game, "that once we got up by four points, we were not going to turn back. That was all she wrote right there."

Except it wasn't. Lower Merion didn't score through the first four and a half minutes of the fourth quarter, and Erie Cathedral slowly, deliberately, as was its method, retook the lead, 41–39, running a smart set play to get a layup. After the Ramblers' go-ahead basket, Dabney set up the Aces' offense. Kobe ran from one corner to the other, an Erie Prep player tracking him, and when he cut toward the foul line, a second player, point guard Julian Blanks, slid over to double him. Kobe caught Dabney's pass. Blanks reached in. Foul. A one-and-one, with 3:11 left. Make both, and the game would be tied. Make one, and the pressure would remain. Miss the first . . . and the dream, in all likelihood, would disappear.

Kobe exhaled deeply and took his first shot. Had a film director choreographed the basketball's flight and route for dramatic effect, the audience would have thought it over-the-top. The ball hit the front of the rim, catapulted softly backward, bounced four more times, little hops, on the back of the rim . . . and fell through the hoop.

Kobe exhaled again and took his second shot. He swished it: 41–41.

Hatcher, who had learned from Kobe in Myrtle Beach that a good player's game has to travel, has to be excellent even in the most challenging of situations and environments, hauled in a defensive rebound, was fouled, and knocked down both free throws with 2:43 left. The Aces led by two. The teams traded baskets, Lower Merion now up 45–43, and with 1:22 to go, the Ramblers' Keith Neis—their leading scorer in the game, with twelve points—back-rimmed a baseline jumper. After contesting the shot, Kobe, amid a thicket of bodies, clutched the rebound. Two Erie Prep players hounded and harassed him as he remained rooted under the basket. There was nowhere for him to go. He jumped and threw the ball toward Dabney on the right sideline . . .

. . . but Blanks darted across Dabney's face, deflected the pass, hurled himself into the row of reporters to save the ball from going out of bounds, and flung it to a teammate. The Ramblers had possession with a chance to tie the game. Because of a turnover. By Kobe Bryant. So much for knowing, a few minutes earlier, that the game was won. So much for *all she wrote.*

The Ramblers worked the ball around the perimeter, waiting, probing the defense for a good shot, for the right shot. Thirty seconds remained on the clock when Blanks penetrated the three-point line and let go a one-handed runner from twelve feet. It struck the rim firmly and caromed to the right. Kobe, the lone Lower Merion player in the paint, encircled by Blanks and three other Ramblers, tipped the ball to the corner, controlled it, and, before Erie Cathedral could trap him there, took off up court, dribbling with his left hand along the sideline, moving past Blanks, cutting to his right, away from another Ramblers player, until he reached midcourt.

What now? Against Chester, in a game in which victory was already assured, Kobe had not given up the ball, had not shared the glory. Now there were twenty-two seconds left, and his team was up by two, and it had been nearly eight months since he had bent ever so slightly to Sam Rines Jr.'s wishes in Las Vegas and given the ball up to a teammate at the end of a game, and it had been nearly three months since Gregg Downer had turned to him in that motel room and said, *You have to respect your teammates* and *You can't take on every team by yourself,* and so what would Kobe do now?

He never looked up. Without any visible indication that he knew Hatcher was ahead of him, he fired a pass forward, to the left of the lane. Hatcher took one dribble and—being left-handed made this so much easier for him—laid the ball off the backboard and through the hoop. "Kobe could have dribbled through that double-team," Hatcher recalled. "He trusted his friend to make a layup to win a championship. The same thing we struggled with early on was our strength at the end." Lower Merion led by four. The clock kept running. Neis, pushing back up the floor for a quick shot, was called for traveling. He let the ball fall from his hands, and it bounced once to Kobe, who cradled it under his arm as he jumped up and landed on both feet at once, as if he were stomping something.

A time-out . . . an inbounds pass to Kobe . . . a foul. He missed the first free throw, made the second . . . an airballed Erie shot . . . a horn sounding . . . the scoreboard showing LOWER MERION 48, ERIE CATHE-DRAL PREP 43 . . . the scoreboard showing Kobe with seventeen points, his second-lowest total of the season, and Kobe, for once, not caring in the least . . . a dozen high school basketball players at center court hugging each other . . . Gregg Downer making good on his promise to run like mad around the court . . . Kobe hugging him . . . Treatman and Egan and Drew Downer and Jimmy Kieserman celebrating . . . Pam Bryant and the rest of Kobe's family in the stands . . . Kobe turning around, trying to climb over the security ropes and wires surrounding the court to get to his mother and sisters and grandparents and . . .

"The next thing I know," he said, "my dad was down there."

The length of their embrace is what stayed with Mike Egan, nearly twenty-five years later. It's what made Kobe's eventual falling out with his family so heartbreaking for Egan and Downer and Treatman and everyone who knew them then. "Man," Joe said to Kobe, "I'm proud of you." And father and son remained wrapped in each other's arms for ten seconds . . . twenty . . . Egan would swear it was a full minute, as if they would never let go.

WENDELL HOLLAND—BASKETBALL star of the late 1960s, judge, business executive, public servant, father, grandfather, the man who could credibly claim to have been Kobe's closest precursor at Lower Merion— had watched the game on TV at his home in Bryn Mawr. It wasn't until 2010, when he introduced Kobe at the ceremony dedicating the school's gymnasium to him, that Holland had the opportunity to tell him just how much pride he felt in Kobe's accomplishments.

"We got, as a result of Kobe, what I always wanted: a state champi-onship," Holland recalled. "You have no idea, no idea, how much that means to me. I am such a Lower Merion curmudgeon. I'm very proud of what other cultures and cities have achieved, but I'm very, very, very proud of my school. Put all those little stories together, silly as they might sound, about Vernon Young and Chester. Put all of them together. I'm proud of that, and at alumni association and Hall of Fame functions, the basketball alums are so multicultural. Downer won games with this rainbow of players. Isn't that the way it's supposed to be?

"You have no idea how many people come up to me now and talk about Lower Merion basketball. You have no idea how this No. 33 beamed with pride and pain when Kobe died, because of what he and Downer did together. It killed me because he was the dream realized. He was the dream realized for all of us."

THE TEAM arrived back in Wynnewood late that night, and already arrangements had been made. Lynne Freeland had contacted the fire department. There would be a championship parade Sunday, through Ardmore, students and faculty and residents lining the streets. And Kobe and Jermaine Griffin would stand atop one of the fire trucks, both of them holding on to a handlebar to keep them steady, a dalmatian leashed up there with them. And Kobe would look down at the crowd and see that substitute teacher, the one who had told him he would never win a state championship. And he would see that teacher standing on a corner and cheering.

"This is all I ever wanted," Kobe said later. "When I first came to high school, I knew I was a pretty good player, and I was going to work hard to accomplish all those individual goals. But, after going four and twenty, I said, 'Man, I hate losing. There's no way in hell I want to go through this again.' The next year, we improved. The year after that, we improved. Throughout the whole time, I remember thinking, 'I want to be known as the best—not only as the best player, but as the best player on the best team.' That meant so much to me. I just wanted to prove to everybody that I could carry us to a state championship."

But that would be Sunday afternoon. First, he and his teammates had a party to go to, at a cheerleader's house. A few players, Robby Schwartz and Brendan Pettit among them, were there all night, trudging home at 7:00 A.M. Kobe Bryant, having scored 2,883 points over the previous four years—the most in southeastern Pennsylvania high school history—having achieved everything he wanted out of his career at Lower Merion, with the chance to enjoy one of the last normal nights of his adolescence, stayed at the party an hour before driving himself home.

I've never wanted to offend anybody. I never was like that and never will be. I try to be as sincere as possible.

—*KOBE BRYANT*

18

THE SPEED AT WHICH
THINGS CHANGE

TOM KONCHALSKI, THE MOST RESPECTED grassroots basketball scout in America, was as devout a Roman Catholic as a man could be without having become a priest. Six foot six, lanky in his build, measured and gentle in his demeanor, he believed in the sanctity of Sunday Mass, and he believed in the sanctity of sports' capacity to shape a boy's or girl's character, and he believed in them with equal fidelity. God sent sports to young children, he once said, as preparation for the later years of their lives; the competition would stir different parts of their souls, and sometimes those stirrings would be painful, but they would always be instructive. Konchalski's role in that mission, as he saw it, was to locate and evaluate young athletes who were worthy of that blessing. For nearly two decades, he had been writing for, and eventually taken over publication of, a scouting newsletter, *High School Basketball Illustrated,* mailing out his reports to his subscribers. Hundreds of college coaches around the country regarded those mimeographed pages as essential to their recruiting, which was why Konchalski annually attended the McDonald's

All-American Game, the nation's most prestigious high school all-star game. It was why he attended the 1996 game, held at the Civic Arena in Pittsburgh, and the annual pregame banquet, held the night before. And it was why, at the banquet, he was seated at a table with Kobe Bryant and his family.

Konchalski had scouted Kobe ever since the Bryants had returned from Italy, remembering that his first visit to a Boston Market restaurant—he spent so much time on the road that he had not eaten a meal at home in five years—had come on December 1, 1994, during a trip to suburban Philadelphia to see Kobe. "He had an iron will," said Konchalski, who died of cancer, at seventy-four, in February 2021. "He just worked so uncommonly hard. When you look at the Jordans and Kobes, what made them was their will." He disliked the McDonald's game itself, too many players trying to do too much, trying to show off. (Kobe would be no different, scoring thirteen points in nineteen minutes but not playing especially well.) But the banquet was always worthwhile. John Wooden, the legendary UCLA coach, was the guest speaker each year, delivering his remarks without notes, quoting Emerson, Thoreau, Shakespeare, and all the players wore tuxedos to the event. "They'd all complain about that," Konchalski said, "but who looks better in tuxedos than the twenty-four best athletes in America? And Kobe looked regal. What a handsome young man he was."

As the banquet neared its end, cake forks jangling against plates, coffee burbling as the waitstaff poured it into cups, the lights in the room dimmed, and on a projection screen appeared the face of Michael Jordan, giving a pre-taped video message to the players. *It was a great honor to be a McDonald's All-American,* Jordan told them. *It gave me the confidence to keep working. Make sure you get your education.* Then he finished: *I hope all of you get to the NBA. But if you do get there, I'll be waiting.* And he winked.

After the dinner, Konchalski lingered for a while, posing for photos with Kobe, Joe, Pam, Sharia, and Shaya. Kobe's parents and sisters had walked away before he turned to Konchalski, who had no idea at the time that Kobe had planned on skipping college.

"I can't wait to play against the greatest players in the world," Kobe told him. "And I'll be ready."

And he winked.

SATURDAY, APRIL 6, 1996

ANOTHER CITY, ANOTHER AWARD, ANOTHER banquet. He was in Atlanta, at the Georgia World Congress Center, to receive the Naismith Award. Over there was Marcus Camby, the national college player of the year, from the University of Massachusetts. Over there was John Calipari, the national college coach of the year, also from UMass, two months away from signing a five-year, $15 million contract to become the head coach and executive vice president of basketball operations of the New Jersey Nets.

Asked by a reporter whether he would emulate Kevin Garnett and go right from high school to the NBA, Kobe shrugged. "I haven't figured it out," he said. As a perk of winning the Naismith, he could take a group of family members or friends out to dinner, courtesy of the Atlanta Tipoff Club, which sponsored the award. Once he was back home, he made a reservation at a steakhouse in Manayunk for him and his Lower Merion coaches and teammates.

MONDAY, APRIL 8 TO WEDNESDAY, APRIL 24, 1996

KOBE'S OFFICIAL ANNOUNCEMENT WAS APPROACHING, and it was becoming clearer what his decision would be, so Mike Krzyzewski called Gregg Downer to see if there was still time to persuade Kobe that coming to Duke was his best course of action.

"If you've got a seventy-yard bomb," Downer told him, "you've got to throw it right now."

Krzyzewski started listing the reasons that Kobe should choose Duke. *I'm going to turn him into the next Grant Hill . . . I have a lot of experience as a gemologist, shining diamonds . . .* For five to ten minutes, he gave what was, for Downer, an inspirational pep talk, and if, when he was playing for Penncrest High School, Downer had been good enough to play for the Blue Devils, if he had been a Bobby Hurley or Johnny Dawkins, he would have tossed his bags in his car and driven down to Durham in a heartbeat. But Downer wasn't the talk's true target, and the target's mind was already made up.

Later, Kobe called Krzyzewski himself to tell him of his decision. Krzyzewski wished him luck, told him that if he ever needed advice, he shouldn't hesitate to call him. "I know that you're going to be fine," he told Kobe. "You have a great attitude toward the game, and you love to play." At the 2008 Summer Olympics, in Beijing, and the 2012 Games, in London, Krzyzewski would finally get the chance to coach Kobe, crediting him with establishing the standards of work ethic and selflessness that would contribute to the U.S. men's basketball team's two gold medals. It might seem a discordant description, to call Kobe "selfless." But before the '08 Games, at USA Basketball's headquarters, in Colorado Springs, Kobe knocked on Krzyzewski's office door and told him that he wanted to guard the opposing team's best player during every scrimmage and every game, growing so consumed with this self-imposed responsibility, with helping his country win gold, that Krzyzewski once joked that he was the only coach who ever had to remind Kobe to shoot.

KEITH MORRIS was twenty-six, a rookie financial adviser at Prudential Securities, and his father's biggest fan and closest confidant. So it didn't surprise him completely when his assistant answered the office phone one day in late April and told him that Joe Bryant was on the line. Of course, neither Keith nor Speedy Morris had seen Joe on La Salle's campus in weeks. No one had.

"Hello."

"Keith, I've got a problem," Joe said. "Kobe wants to go to the NBA."

"What's the problem with that?" Keith asked.

"I don't know how to tell your father," Joe said.

"You be a man," Keith said, "and tell him." But Keith didn't bother waiting to find out if Joe would follow through. He hung up, then called his father himself.

"I was happy to hear he was going to the NBA and not to Duke," Speedy Morris said years later. "I was heavy in prayer for a while: 'Please God, I hope we get him.' And God answers all our prayers. Sometimes He says, 'No.'"

FRIDAY, APRIL 26, 1996

OH, MY GOD, HOW AM I here? Of course Kobe had that question swirling in his head and his gut and who knows where else as he took in the scene around him on a Friday night at Madison Square Garden, at the 1996 Essence Awards. Halle Berry, Tyra Banks, Naomi Campbell, Toni Braxton—all of them were there, as anyone would have expected them to be, but how was it that Kobe and Sharia were there, too, and how was it that this night would lead to the answer to the most pressing and mysterious piece of gossip at Lower Merion: Who was Kobe taking to the prom?

A winter fashion show at La Salle. That's how it began. Shaya was participating in the show, held in a ballroom in the student union building. There, she overheard a couple of guys talking about Kobe, and when she told them that he was her brother, one of them, Mike Harris, a marketing manager and promoter, said to her, *Well, tell him Boyz II Men want to meet him.* Harris could make such a meeting happen; he counted the R & B trio, all of whose members were Philadelphia-born, among his clients. Weeks later, Kobe met Harris himself at a Villanova basketball game. The two exchanged phone numbers and developed a friendship, Kobe confessing that he had a crush on Brandy, whose sitcom, *Moesha,* had just debuted on UPN. Harris soon called Kobe and invited him to the Essence Awards—a gesture that Kobe, still low on guile when it came to matters away from basketball, might have thought purely generous but that had an additional aim for Harris. Here was a chance for him to branch out into basketball, to take on Kobe as a client. If only there were a way for Kobe to make a splash on the national social scene . . .

After the award show—Sharia, as agog as Kobe was at the models and dancers and singers and celebrities, had accompanied him to the

Garden—Kobe hopped in a limousine with Harris and two members of Boyz II Men, Mike McCary and Wanya Morris, for a ride to the Four Seasons. Harris and Morris told Kobe to come down to Morris's suite. When he and Kobe walked in, Harris began to giggle. *What the hell is going on here?* Kobe thought. Then he turned to his left. There, sitting on the hotel room bed, was Brandy.

Kobe's mouth fell open. He laughed, too, out of nervousness. *Oh, my God, you guys did not just do this to me.* "How are you doing?" Brandy asked him, and Kobe could barely speak, his little "Hi" drowned out by the guffaws from Harris and the group members. He left the room, barely able to remember what he had said, certain only that he had embarrassed himself.

Back in his room, Harris asked Kobe, "Do you want to take Brandy to your prom? Do you want to do that?" Of course Kobe did. That was the easy part. And earlier, Harris already had knocked down a possible impediment to his bid for publicity. Wanya Morris was twenty-two, and Brandy was seventeen, and for a year they had been involved in a relationship that was something more than a friendship, something less than an open romance; Brandy and her handlers, too, worried about protecting her wholesome image to allow her to reveal the secret publicly. According to *Showboat,* one of author Roland Lazenby's two biographies of Kobe, Harris had persuaded Morris to go along with his scheme, to let Kobe and Brandy ride the wave of awww-aren't-they-cute exposure that the pair would generate from one night together. So Harris called Brandy that night and said, "Brandy, Brandy, Brandy, my man Kobe wants to ask you to his prom. It would mean the world to him if you would go with him."

Brandy said yes. She just first had to clear it with her mother, Sonja Norwood, who was also her manager. Like that, Kobe had a celebrity prom date, and he didn't even have to ask her himself.

LATER THAT weekend, Kobe, at Boyz II Men's request, played in a charity/celebrity basketball game at Community College of Philadelphia. Brandy accompanied Morris to the game, and after Kobe enlivened the crowd with a tomahawk dunk the first time he touched the ball, he made small talk with her at halftime, finding her sweet, the kind of girl he could hang out with and talk to as if she were one of his female friends at school. Pam Bryant and Sonja Norwood spoke later, confirming details, making sure everyone was on the same page about the prom, and Kobe and Brandy began chatting regularly by phone.

"I admired her for what she was doing," Kobe said later. "I knew at the time I wanted to go to the NBA, and I was going to be the young guy in front of the cameras and lights. She was young. She started at fourteen, and she was in front of the cameras and the lights. She handled everything very well, and I admired that, and I respected that, aside from the fact I loved her songs."

He was no longer spending time with Jocelyn Ebron. He was still friends with Kristen Clement, he told Treatman, though they had not spoken in a long time. As people learned of his date's identity, his friends reacted with good-natured disbelief. When Treatman heard that Kobe was going with Brandy, he thought at first it was one of Clement's teammates at Cardinal O'Hara: Brandi Batch. During a study hall one day at school, Susan Freeland asked him who he was taking to the prom.

"Brandy," Kobe said.

"Brandy who?"

"*Brandy,* Suze."

"Where did you meet her?"

"One of the guys from Boyz II Men."

"Shut up!"

Freeland couldn't get over it. *Brandy, Suze. Boyz II Men.* He had said it like it was the most normal thing in the world.

MONDAY, APRIL 29, 1996

THE IDEA OF KOBE'S HOLDING a press conference to say that he was making himself eligible for the NBA draft was not his. Joe asked him if he wanted one.

"Come on," Kobe said. "It doesn't matter to me."

But he sensed that it mattered to Joe and Pam. As much as a formal announcement would lend validity and credibility to Kobe's decision, his parents seemed fixated on what he might say and how he might say it. For what would such an event be if not an insight into—or, for some, an instant referendum on—how they had raised their prodigy of a son? For a week, after Joe first made his suggestion, he and Pam pestered Kobe, making certain he would handle himself with the proper proportions of maturity, composure, and humor. "I was kind of teasing them: 'Hey, you're more nervous than I am,'" he said later. "It really wasn't that big of a deal to me." He did not care where or when the press conference would be held; he left it up to Joe to decide, so Joe picked a Monday afternoon. Treatman took care of most of the arrangements, working with Tom McGovern to prepare the gym for the crowd of reporters and students who would attend and to alert media outlets about the event. He didn't tell them, even when they asked, what Kobe had decided. Did he have to? Would Kobe hold a press conference, at this point, if he were going to Duke or La Salle?

Classmates approached him all morning, pressing him for a morsel of information. *Kobe, I have a lacrosse game this afternoon. Why don't you just tell me now?* With them, Kobe was as coy about the NBA as he was about the prom, telling them that he didn't know yet, that he would make up his mind at the spur of the moment. In his metal-jewelry class, the other students crowded around him, forgetting momentarily about the bracelets they were supposed to be crafting, and his teacher tried to listen in on Kobe's conversations and vague answers. His friend Deirdre Bobb asked him, "What are you going to do?"

"I don't know," Kobe said. "What do you think?"

"Honestly, Kobe," Bobb said, "from a friend to a friend, you should go to school. Your gift will never leave you. What you have is a gift from God, and whatever school you go to, you'll be the best player on that team. The NBA will always be there."

Lynne Freeland tracked him down in another class and called him out of it. Gregg Downer would be there for the press conference, and he already knew anyway, without Kobe having to say it, what the announcement would be. But Freeland asked: Did Kobe want to call Drew Downer and tell him personally? "Lead the way," Kobe said. Freeland took him to the guidance office, gave him Drew's phone number, and told the counselors and secretaries that Kobe needed some privacy. As she closed the door behind her, she heard him say, *I'm gonna go play with the big boys.*

"What I wanted him to know," Drew said later, "and I would say this to him every time I saw him for years afterward, when he was an adult, was 'We care about you. We care about you as a person,' especially when he became the villain of the NBA. I stopped going to Sixers games down in South Philly because I was afraid I'd get in a fight with somebody. I don't want to overstate what I did. I tried to be his protector. I tried to be an adult. Some weird-looking guy would show up and say, 'Sign this stack of magazines.' I'd be like, 'Who are you?' I built some trust in that I never really asked him for anything. I never expected anything from him."

One period remained in the school day when he drove home to get ready, skipping English class. Pam helped him pick his outfit. Kobe chose a white shirt, a brown silk tie, and a beige silk suit that Ron Luber and his family had given to him as a gift, Luber said, "to wish him luck in his next career." (When Luber had purchased the suit, which had cost more than five hundred dollars, the salesman had told him, "Did you know that his wingspan measured seven foot two?") To complete the ensemble, Kobe set a pair of designer sunglasses, black ovals, atop his forehead. "That was my idea," he said later. "I've always loved glasses. I figured, 'Why not start something new?'"

The Bryants drove back to the school, arriving not long after the final bell of the day rang at 2:25, parking in the back. Television camera lights burned in Kobe's eyes as soon as he entered the gym, a warm and muggy spring day, seventy-four degrees outside, made warmer and muggier inside by the crush. Joe clutched a clunky cellular phone in one hand and wiped his brow dry with the other. Kobe asked Matt Matkov to update him on the English class he had missed. His grandmother, seeing the hubbub over him, said, "Well, I've got to make my baby an apple pie now," and Kobe's ears perked up. "Oh, yeah, Grandma," he said, "you've got to make me a couple of those." He'd had no idea what to expect when he walked into the building, and now the gym was full, everyone there to hear what he would say, to hear what Kobe Bryant thought was best for Kobe Bryant, everyone there for him . . . and it was . . . *fun*. It was so much damn fun.

The moment of revelation is a marvel to rewatch. The gym's rich brown bleachers providing a neutral background to frame him in any camera shot, Kobe was completely self-assured as he stood at a lectern, a bundle of microphones at his chest. His family, coaches, teammates, classmates were seated and standing among the media, a large crowd waiting for him to speak.

"I, Kobe Bryant . . ."

Pause. Head-wiggle, as if he were shaking a defender.

". . . have decided to take my talent . . . to uhhh . . ."

Another pause. This time, he feigned indecision or forgetfulness or a combination of both. He put his left hand to his chin as if he were mulling something over, playing to the cameras, playing to the moment.

Then he broke into a gigantic smile.

"No, I have decided to skip college and take my talent to the NBA."

It took nineteen seconds. There was a roar.

IN 1996, for a sizable segment of the population, the notion of a high school athlete holding a press conference to make a declaration about his future was regarded not as an appropriate, newsworthy event, not as an indication of how much interest there was in such an announcement, but as a display of such naked arrogance that it could barely be abided. Deirdre Bobb had come to the gym after she had finished with classes for the day. Her heart broke a little when she heard Kobe say he would not go to college. *All right, Kobe,* she thought. *You're smelling yourself. But if that's what you want to do, I'll encourage you and pray for you.* Neil Cooper, a rabbi for a synagogue in the township, gave a sermon in which he criticized Kobe, arguing that his decision would send the wrong message to young people, that it would undermine the value and importance of higher education. Bill Lyon, in *The Philadelphia Inquirer,* wrote, "All of this is warm and wonderful. But he is also seventeen years old, and the father in me has only one possible reservation: I hope that he has not ransomed away his youth." Kobe instantaneously became a debate topic on sports-talk radio, a microwavable meal of outrage delivered piping hot during morning and afternoon drive time.

"A lot of people probably thought that press conference was ridiculous," Gregg Downer said. "There were people who didn't know sports that well who didn't fully understand it. There were people in that building who didn't know what was happening. I knew what was happening. This is not just another tall athletic basketball player. This is something different."

TUESDAY, MAY 21, 1996

AT 10:00 A.M. IN A showroom in Manhattan's SoHo neighborhood, Kobe was everywhere. Kobe was dunking in four different places on one wall, all four dunks captured in six-foot-high photos, all four photos having the effect of enormous exclamation points. A highlight video played and replayed Kobe dunking, dunking, dunking, with a jump shot or two to break up the monotony. Adidas had unveiled a new logo: three stripes of increasing length from left to right, symbolizing progression, improvement, the future. One reporter went around the room and tallied up the total: fifty-six logos. Logos on walls. Logos on basketballs. Logos on chairs and microphones. And those were just the ones he counted. There were more logos on press credentials and staffers' shirts and even the smallest flat surfaces. The company had no reason to be subtle. This was a coronation for its newest client. This was the king-making of Kobe Bryant.

"He's one of a new generation of athletes who will help transform sports in the next decade or two," Steve Wynne, the president of Adidas America, said.

The day after his I'm-off-to-the-NBA press conference, Kobe and his teammates had gone to Harrisburg to meet Pennsylvania governor Ed Rendell, and they had traveled as most high school state basketball champions travel: They rode a leaky school bus on a rainy day. It was the sort of episode that Kobe had been used to, that once might have grounded him, and that he wouldn't have to experience again. At Lower Merion, he had been a player. Now he was a *player,* a spokesman for a sneaker company, a rocket ship breaking through the ozone, and it was crazy to think how close this deal, and the lengthy courtship with Sonny Vaccaro, had come to falling apart.

At Joe and Pam's request, Ron Luber had solicited legal opinions from a New York firm that had a branding operation and that could, in theory, handle Kobe's shoe contract. The Bryants, Luber recalled, had a choice to make: They could stick with Vaccaro and Adidas, or they could go on their own. The choice practically made itself. At a meeting in Atlantic City, the members of Team Bryant proposed that they pick Kobe's agent. In response, Vaccaro laid out his list of ultimata: The sneaker deal would be with Adidas, and Arn Tellem would be Kobe's NBA agent, and the William Morris Agency would represent Kobe in any and all endorsements and interests unrelated to basketball—acting, music, whatever caught Kobe's fancy. Then Vaccaro got up and walked out. "Why would he stay?" Sam Rines Jr. said. "There was nothing anyone could say, because he was the one in charge." With Vaccaro aware that he had leverage, with the Bryants not wanting their best and longest-standing endorsement offer to slip away, both parties had arranged a second meeting, at Il Vagabondo, an Italian restaurant on the Upper East Side of Manhattan. It had culminated in Joe's and Pam's consenting to hire Tellem in what Rick Bradley, Kobe's William Morris representative, called "a major contract by Adidas." Kobe and the company reached a multiyear agreement worth $10 million, including a guaranteed $1 million for him in the first year. (At one point, Kobe had asked Vaccaro, "If I had gone to Duke, would I have been able to sign my own shoe contract?" When Vaccaro told him no, that NCAA regulations would have prohibited it, Kobe replied, "Well, I certainly made the right decision, didn't I?") A national television campaign for his new line of shoes—the slogan: "Feet You Wear"—would start in August and highlight him exclusively later that fall. In a partnership of that scale, Joe could get his own signing bonus, just for delivering Kobe. In a partnership of that scale, it was nothing for Adidas to throw in another $150,000 for Joe. Which it did.

So there were Joe and Pam and Sharia and Shaya, in the showroom's front row, supporting their son and brother as always. There was Joe, telling the reporters on hand that the Bryants would move wherever Kobe happened to end up, as if he were a beautiful hot-air balloon and the family would pile into the basket below him. And there was Kobe, asked about the perils of playing professional basketball as a teenager, saying, "This is the ultimate challenge. You get a chance to learn from the best. If they're killing you, if they're beating you up, they're teaching you at the same time. Only positives can come from it." All that remained was the question of which NBA team, in a month's time, would draft him.

"We'd prefer the Lakers or the Knicks, Philadelphia, Chicago, a major-market center," Bradley said. "But we obviously have no control over that."

Obviously. Right.

SATURDAY, MAY 25, 1996

THE PROM COULD WAIT. THERE was basketball on TV. Not just basketball. Chicago Bulls basketball. Not just Chicago Bulls basketball. Michael Jordan basketball. Kobe and Jermaine Griffin lounged around all afternoon, watching Jordan labor through a lousy shooting performance (five of fourteen from the field, seventeen points), watching the Bulls coast past the Orlando Magic anyway, 86–67, to win a first-round playoff series in a three-game sweep. The game had tipped off at 2:30 P.M. eastern time, and only when it was over did Kobe and Griffin start getting ready. What, were they going to have the prom without Kobe and Brandy?

The game was Kobe's moment of downtime in a busy weekend. Team Bryant, Sam Rines Sr. in particular, had taken care of everything, hooking Kobe and Brandy up with tickets to a Barry White concert and a fireworks show in Atlantic City on Friday night, then planning another late-night trip down there Saturday (with Brandy's mom along to chaperone). The

prom was being held, of all places, at one of Kobe's favorite and most familiar pickup-basketball spots: the Bellevue Hotel in Center City. On Broad
Street, outside the hotel's entrance, a phalanx of Philadelphia police officers and fifteen television news cameras awaited the arrival of the celebrity
"couple," and they would be waiting awhile. Kobe dropped off Griffin at
the home of his date—Tarvia Lucas, John's daughter—then drove into the
city to pick up Brandy at the Marriott where she was staying, he in a black
tuxedo and a banded-collar shirt, she in champagne Moschino, her hair to
her shoulders in flowing braids. "Man, she glowed," Kobe said later. They
drove back to pick up Griffin, Lucas, and Matt Matkov—complicating
matters was that Matkov's date had bailed on him at the last minute, so he,
as usual, would be Kobe's plus-one—before a white limousine shuttled the
five of them to the Bellevue, Brandy's entourage of bodyguards and stylists
following.

Impatient as they scanned the streets for Kobe and Brandy's car, the
TV reporters at the Bellevue stopped other seniors to get their reactions
to the fuss at their formal. "It's not Kobe's prom; it's Lower Merion's
prom," one female student said. Another echoed her: "We're not the class
of Kobe. We're the class of 1996." To Susan Freeland, such resentment
was misplaced. Of course the prom wasn't *all* about Kobe, but "that
magic and momentum we had as a class was because of him," she said,
and none of those security guards and police officers and reporters were
there because of anyone else.

"He took Brandy to the prom for his image," Matkov, ever the loyal
Kobe defender, once said, "because he needed to go with someone who
approached his status. Finally, it was like there was a girl who didn't like
him just because he was Kobe Bryant. That wasn't her motive, because
she was just as big as he was. It was the same for her. He was a guy who
didn't like her just because she was Brandy. He didn't *need* her. So they
had that in common. It doesn't mean they were made for each other. . . .
It meant he knew he couldn't go to the prom with just another dumb
high school girl."

Finally, three hours after the prom had begun, the white limo pulled
up outside the Bellevue. The cameramen rushed in. The cops and secu-

rity created a halo of space around Kobe and Brandy. Someone asked her if she would sing at the prom.

"I'm just here to have a good time," she said.

The two seventeen-year-olds ascended a marble staircase to the hotel's second floor, and the reaction of the prom's other attendees angered Kobe. "You had all the classmates bad-mouthing the whole thing," he said later. "We get in there, and they're like, 'Oh, can we have a picture with y'all? Can we talk to y'all?' I was like, 'Get up out of my face, man.' They were mouthing. Jealous, I guess. I didn't care about them. They're not my friends anyway. My friends are the people who are close to me and have been close to me, the basketball team. Fake friends: that's what they are." Sonja Norwood shared Kobe's contempt. "Everybody's asking her for autographs, asking her for pictures," she said. "It's like she's working." The irony of the evening was apparently lost on them: that they were complaining about the attention that two young stars received at the prom . . . when the entire ersatz courtship had been arranged to cultivate attention for two young stars.

Besides, Norwood was wrong. Not everybody was dazzled. Kobe's friend Audrey Price requested a photo with the couple, but not an autograph. "It wasn't because he was a superstar," Price recalled. "It was just more, I took photos with all my friends. It was just a memory. It was to seal that memory. I told Brandy that her dress looked pretty, and she told me she was nervous. I don't think it subtracted in any way from the evening. Everyone still went about their business. It was still very much a normal prom."

After her second night in Atlantic City with Kobe, Brandy flew home to Los Angeles. One Philadelphia news station reported that the prom had been her first date. It was a storybook detail, one that Wanya Morris would have been surprised to learn.

JUNE 1996

KOBE BRYANT SPENT HIS LAST day as an official Lower Merion student and his first night as an official Lower Merion alumnus at Lower Merion.

Following their commencement ceremony, the seniors gathered within the school building's walls, where they would be locked inside for an all-night party—dancing, swimming, obstacle courses, socializing—a measure taken to encourage them to remain together and avoid underage drinking, drunken driving, or any other reckless behavior. One senior toted a video camera around, conducting faux interviews with the graduates, and when the camera turned to Kobe, he came up with a four-line rap song, apparently off the top of his head.

> *My beeper is beeping*
> *So let me quick pause*
> *As I grab the microphone*
> *For all y'all*

Half the gymnasium had been partitioned off into a dance club with a DJ. There, Kobe lowered himself to the floor, curled himself up like a turtle, and spun himself on his back, breakdancing to Kool & the Gang's "Jungle Boogie." He took off his T-shirt, his torso resembling old-fashioned bottles of Coca-Cola stacked on their sides, and, still holding the microphone, grooved and lip-synced to LL Cool J's "Doin' It."

> *No doubt, I'm the playa that you're talkin' about . . .*
> *Right, I'm in the zone*
> *One of a kind when it's time to do mine*

In another section of the gym, he did what came most naturally to him, playing a game of half-court three-on-three, his T-shirt still gone, two dozen students along the sideline watching, some with their mouths agape.

"That was the first time I saw what was under Kobe Bryant's shirt, and for the majority of the girls in my high school, that was the first time we saw his hard, cut body," Price recalled. "There was a different side of Kobe that night that was hilarious. That wasn't him. He was prim and proper. He was never the type of guy, even with abs and everything, who would walk around without his shirt. All of a sudden, to see him let loose like that was out of the ordinary and hilarious. It just added to the fun of the night.

"He was coming out of his shell, and it was the last time I saw him."

NEXT TO his senior headshot in the 1996 edition of *Enchiridion,* the school's yearbook, Kobe wrote, "Thanx Mom, Dad for giving me the opportunity to go to school here in the U.S. For being there in good and bad times Sharia Shaya Ti Amo Moltissimo Matt you my main man always be. . . . Thanx 4a great 4 years Love you all."

He was voted the male student "Most Likely to Succeed" in the class of '96. In a candid yearbook photo, he wore a black leather jacket and wrapped his right arm around the female winner, Antje Herlyn, who became an anesthesiologist. Because he was such an overwhelming choice for that honor, his classmates did not select him as their best male athlete. That distinction went to Sean Furber, a standout on the soccer, wrestling, and lacrosse teams. After all, Kobe had played only one sport.

The main thing is getting in shape. From what I hear, it's a very long season, a lot of basketball to be played, a lot of bumping and grinding. I have to prepare myself physically so I get in shape and my legs won't get tired. A lot of rookies nowadays tend to hit a wall in the middle of the season. A lot of the great players of the past—Magic, Michael—I don't think they've ever hit that wall. I don't want to hit that wall. If I work as hard as I possibly can this summer, and I still hit the wall, then I'm going to have to work even harder.

—KOBE BRYANT, SUMMER OF 1996

19

NOW I'M
A LAKER

THE TWO MEN WHO, MORE than anyone else, conspired to orchestrate
Kobe Bryant's relocation from Wynnewood to the West Coast had
their friendship blossom out of the strangest of places: a "Mommy
and Me" class. Arn Tellem and Jerry West had been contemporaries and
colleagues in the NBA, West as the Lakers' general manager, Tellem as
a powerful player agent. But it wasn't until their wives gave birth to sons
in the late 1980s—Karen West to Jonnie West, Nancy Tellem to Matty
Tellem—and bonded as their toddlers played with finger paint and building blocks that West and Tellem themselves turned into more than just
competitors on opposite sides of a negotiating table. Their families va-
cationed together at the Greenbrier, the luxury resort in West Virginia,
near West's childhood home. Jonnie and Matty became best friends. The
trust that Tellem and West had in each other would prove the key factor
in the lengthy and risky gambit that they pulled off to have Kobe land in
Los Angeles, to initiate the regeneration of the Lakers' dynasty.

Kobe entered the 1996 draft as a mystery. He had hired Joe Carbone
to be his full-time personal trainer, having told Carbone in March that
he would enter the draft, and Joe Bryant asked his friend Tony DiLeo—a
fellow La Salle alumnus, a former professional player in Europe, and the

Sixers' director of scouting—to tutor Kobe for his pre-draft workouts. For an hour or so each day in the Fieldhouse at St. Joseph's, DiLeo had Kobe carry out a drill that required him to shoot three hundred shots: shots off the dribble, shots on the move, shots from behind the three-point arc. If Kobe missed three straight from any spot, he'd have to begin the drill again. "That's when I saw this inner drive he had, this drive to be great," DiLeo recalled. "He would miss and get frustrated and want to do it again. He was relentless."

But what did teams around the league really think of Kobe and his potential? Tellem wasn't sure. Rob Babcock, the Minnesota Timberwolves' player-personnel director, compared Kobe unfavorably to Kevin Garnett: "Kevin's ability as a six-eleven player was so overwhelming, it came through immediately. He's a very special player. You watch Kobe Bryant, and you don't see that. His game doesn't say, 'I'm a very special talent.'" John Outlaw, the Denver Nuggets' director of college scouting, had said flatly, "I don't think he's ready." The Sixers, having gone 18–64 in 1995–96 and won the draft lottery, held the No. 1 overall pick, but most of the other early-first-round picks belonged to small-market franchises, and neither Kobe nor Adidas would maximize one's investment in the other if Kobe ended up in Vancouver, Indianapolis, or Cleveland. "The Lakers were the team I wanted to play for," Kobe said, but the Lakers were twenty-fourth in the draft order. If they wanted Kobe as much as he wanted them, they'd have to find a way to acquire a higher pick.

So Tellem devised a way to use the uncertainty around Kobe to their advantage. "We had to recognize," he recalled, "that we might have a unique opportunity." Joe Bryant insisted to Tellem that Kobe was among the best players in the draft. To get a better sense of where Kobe might fall in the pecking order of prospects, Tellem arranged workouts with teams near the top of the first round . . . but not all of them. By having Kobe refuse to work out for certain teams, by denying them the opportunity to assess him in person, Tellem could influence the process, cooling those teams on the idea of drafting Kobe. The strategy probably wouldn't work in the modern NBA, when general managers are more likely to draft the best available player, regardless of his agent's behind-the-scenes machinations. But this wasn't the modern NBA. This was 1996. Offense was taken at the idea that Tellem, at his young client's behest, could so manipulate the process. *Who did this kid think he was?*

Kobe worked out for just a few teams. Then Tellem called in a favor with his friend, setting up a private session for Kobe with West.

"I wanted to get Jerry's opinion," Tellem said. "I asked him: 'I want to do this confidentially. I need to know what you think.'"

What followed were two workouts—at the Inglewood YMCA, "on a side street somewhere," Kobe recalled—that convinced West that Kobe would be the NBA's next Greatest Player. In the first, Kobe so dominated recently retired Lakers guard Michael Cooper—forty years old at the time, still in good shape, one of the league's best perimeter defenders during his career—that West stopped the workout after fifteen minutes. "I thought that Kobe was possibly better than the players we had on the team at the time," he wrote in his autobiography, *West by West*. "Never in my life have I seen a workout like that. When I said enough, I meant it." What struck Cooper was how physically strong Kobe was, especially in the low post, an indication of how much Kobe's training with Carbone had helped. In the second, in front of West and Lakers coach Del Harris—Joe's coach with the Houston Rockets—Kobe manhandled Dontae' Jones, a six-foot-eight small forward who, as a senior, had led Mississippi State to the Final Four just in March. *I'm beating up on a regional MVP in the NCAA tournament,* he thought. *If I had gone to college, I would have busted out. I would have killed.*

Back at his hotel, Kobe called Tellem.

"How'd you do?" Tellem asked, his anxiousness apparent to Kobe. "How'd you do?"

"I did great. It went well."

"All right. Really? Really? I love you, man. I love you."

"Hey, Arn, take a chill pill."

The Lakers had won just one postseason series in the five years since they had advanced to the 1991 NBA Finals, where they had lost to Michael Jordan and the Bulls in five games. West told Tellem, "I'm about to shake up this team this summer. I'd like to have Kobe and build around him and this other player I'm targeting." The "other player" was Shaquille O'Neal, who was entering free agency after four years with the Orlando Magic. So West eventually put together the makings of a deal with the Charlotte Hornets, who had the No. 13 pick: If none of the first twelve teams had selected Kobe, the Hornets would draft him, then trade him to the Lakers for center Vlade Divac. It was on Tellem, Sonny Vaccaro, and the Bryants to make sure that Kobe was still available when lucky No. 13 rolled around.

KOBE WAS ambivalent about the remote possibility of the Sixers' taking him with the draft's first pick. The prestige that would come with being "the best player in the draft" was appealing. But then . . . his benefactor, John Lucas, was no longer there. The Sixers had fired Lucas in May, hiring a new general manager, Brad Greenberg, and a new head coach, Johnny Davis. And if Kobe were the first player selected, there would be no team against whom he could hold a grudge. The No. 1 pick isn't passed over. The No. 1 pick isn't explicitly underestimated by any of the league's other teams, because none of them had the opportunity to draft him. The No. 1 pick can't prove anyone wrong. "I want people to say, 'Awww, you messed up because you did not take him,'" he said not long after the draft. "That's what I want."

For their part, the Sixers—though they, like the rest of the league, regarded Georgetown guard Allen Iverson as the draft's top player—did consider taking Kobe. Both DiLeo and Gene Shue, now a scout for the team, lobbied Greenberg to open his mind to the possibility, even suggesting that the Sixers trade Jerry Stackhouse to acquire another first-round pick, which would allow them to draft Iverson and Kobe. "I knew how much they believed in him," Greenberg recalled, "and I do think, if Gene or Tony had the chance to make the call on the pick, they very well could have selected Kobe." (After going 22–60 during the 1996–97 season, the Sixers fired Greenberg and Davis, and DiLeo, as the acting director of basketball operations, one day called Mitch Kupchak, the Lakers' assistant general manager, and asked if he and West would be open to trading Kobe. He was not on the phone with Kupchak long. "They knew what they had," DiLeo said. "They didn't really laugh at me, but basically, they did.") Mike Egan even called the Sixers' offices the day before the draft, telling the receptionist that he was one of Kobe Bryant's coaches and needed to speak to Greenberg. Egan was stunned when, later that afternoon, Greenberg called him back. Greenberg said later that he had no recollection of speaking with Egan, but Egan described in detail their conversation.

Egan: *I know what a good player looks like. He's the best player in the draft. And I would never forgive myself as a Sixers fan if I didn't tell you that.*

Greenberg: *What do you like about him?*

Egan: *He's the whole package. He's so talented, so aggressive, so mature, works so hard with all that skill.*

Greenberg: *He didn't look too mature with those sunglasses on his head.*

Egan: *That's probably the worst thing you could find to say about him.*

But to Greenberg and many others, Iverson was "the fastest and quickest and perhaps even the toughest player in the draft." The call was Greenberg's, and the call was easy: The Sixers would take Iverson. Tellem had done the necessary reconnaissance to feel safe that there were just two other teams that might pick Kobe before the Hornets went on the clock at No. 13. His nightmare scenario was that the Milwaukee Bucks, coached by Joe's former teammate Mike Dunleavy, would take Kobe at No. 4, exiling him to southeastern Wisconsin. But Milwaukee would instead go with Stephon Marbury, who had left Georgia Tech after his freshman season, making him a surer bet in the eyes of NBA scouts than Kobe. The Bucks would then trade Marbury to Minnesota for the player whom the Timberwolves would select with the No. 5 pick: University of Connecticut guard Ray Allen.

"Brad Greenberg and Mike Dunleavy both said that if they had the balls, they would have taken him," Tellem recalled.

That left the Nets, at No. 8. That left John Calipari and the team's new general manager, John Nash.

THE WASHINGTON Bullets had not had a winning season during Nash's six years as their general manager, and in the spring of 1996, he left the franchise in the kind of forced resignation that is common throughout professional sports and is often papered over with euphemistic phrasing. *The Bullets parted ways with Nash.* The Nets hired him soon after to work alongside and guide Calipari, who had never worked in the NBA before, and Nash's familiarity with Kobe and his friendship with Joe Bryant gave the Nets an edge in the Kobe sweepstakes. He worked out for them three times, each more impressive than the previous one. Willis Reed, the Nets' vice president of basketball operations and formerly the center on the Knicks' great teams of the early 1970s, was a strapping six foot ten, with hands that opened like golf umbrellas. He wrapped one of his mitts around Kobe's biceps, jiggled it, and said, "You ain't so little." (Carbone took pride in that compliment.) Kobe played one-on-one against former UCLA forward Ed O'Bannon, the Nets' 1995 first-round pick, a contest that Calipari paused so he could test Kobe's shooting range. After Kobe knocked down a succession of three-pointers, Calipari challenged him to shoot from closer to half-court.

"Let's see if you can make something from back here," he said.

Kobe took five shots and made all of them.

"What the hell?" Calipari said. "Where did this come from? We thought you couldn't shoot."

Kobe shook his head. *Fine. Let people think I can't shoot. Better for me.*

Better for the Nets, too. Jerry West already had called Nash and offered him Divac in exchange for the No. 8 pick. Nash had turned him down. The Nets, he told West, weren't ready to win immediately. They wanted to build through the draft. "We zeroed in on Kobe," Nash recalled. "We knew he was going to be our guy."

ON TUESDAY, June 25, the night before the NBA draft, held that year at the Continental Airlines Arena in East Rutherford, New Jersey, the Nets' home arena, Calipari and Nash—both living out of a local hotel because the team had hired them so recently—hosted Joe and Pam Bryant for dinner. They told the Bryants that the Nets would draft Kobe.

Well, Joe said, *I think he'll start as a rookie, and he'll be an All-Star in his second season.*

"After they left," Nash said, "we both thought, 'Typical father, high aspirations.' It would be amazing if he could do that, but we weren't anticipating that."

THE NEXT day, not long after noon, the draft still more than seven hours away, Kobe lay in bed in the hotel where all the prospective draftees were staying. Tellem and Joe reviewed everything with him one last time.

"We can for sure have the Nets," Tellem told him. "Do you still want to go for the Lakers? There is a risk that some team, even though I feel like I've controlled it, could say they're still going to take you. The Nets might not take you, and you could end up in a place you don't like as much as New Jersey."

Kobe reached up, grabbed some of Tellem's shirt, and pulled him toward him.

"That's why I hired you," he said. "You'll get it done."

MEANWHILE, CALIPARI and Nash were having lunch with Joe Taub, the point man among the seven members of the Nets' ownership group, to brief him on their plans for the draft. The idea of selecting Kobe, or any high school player, disappointed Taub, who preferred that the team pick Syracuse forward John Wallace. More, Taub suggested to Nash that the Nets would be wasting time and money on Kobe. The team had mustered just two winning seasons in eleven years and existed in the shadow of the New York region's other, traditionally superior NBA franchise, so Taub assumed that Kobe would leave at his first opportunity anyway. "The Nets had a terrible second-class mentality because of the Knicks," Nash recalled. "They thought they were never going to overtake the Knicks."

Calipari and Nash had just returned to the office, around 2:00 P.M., when Kobe called Calipari and Tellem called Nash. Both delivered the same message: Kobe appreciated the Nets' interest in him, but he didn't want to play for them. In fact, if they did draft him, he would sooner return to Europe and sign with a team there than consign himself to the swamps of Jersey.

Nash, Tellem figured, would draft Kobe if given the chance, but Calipari was a soft target, a young coach eager to please his bosses, mindful of the culture he hoped to create for his new team, and inclined to avoid having to manage a relationship with a player who already had said he didn't want to play for the Nets. Nash worked the phones and learned of the deal between the Lakers and the Hornets, but Tellem received a helping hand from a surprising source: his primary rival, agent David Falk. Falk represented Kerry Kittles and had been pushing the Nets to take him at No. 8. "We liked Kerry Kittles a lot," Nash said, "but he would have been our second choice. So Falk called Calipari and assured him that if we didn't take Kittles, we would never get one of his free agents."

Nash regarded Falk's threat as an agent's idle ploy, but to Calipari, the pressure *not* to take Kobe was double-barreled now. As the two men walked through the arena's catacombs toward the Nets' locker room, where the team's front-office members were having dinner at six, they passed Tellem, Falk, and Vaccaro, huddled together. One of the trio asked, "What are you going to do?"

"You'll know when we make the pick," Nash shot back.

Except Nash himself didn't know. Continuing to the locker room, Nash tried to convince Calipari to call all these bluffs, stick to their original plan, and draft Kobe. *John, don't worry,* Nash told him. *You've got a five-year contract. Even if we swing and miss on this pick, it's a freebie. You're not going to get fired over this draft.* He still didn't know what Calipari's decision would be until after the dinner had begun, when Calipari stood up and told the personnel on hand: If Kerry Kittles was on the board at No. 8, the Nets would take Kerry Kittles. If he wasn't, they would take Kobe Bryant.

"The wind," Nash recalled, "went out of my sails."

WOULD KOBE really have spurned the Nets to play in Europe? "I'm not going to answer that," Tellem said in 2020. "That will always be unanswered." Such a move wouldn't have been unprecedented. Just seven years earlier, Duke's Danny Ferry, the No. 2 overall pick in the 1989 draft, had signed with an Italian team rather than report to the sad-sack Los Angeles Clippers. But Ferry hadn't had the marketing and endorsement dollars at stake that Kobe did.

"Kobe's not going to turn down being the eighth pick in the draft to go to Europe," Vaccaro said. "Use common sense. What the hell are you afraid of if taking him is what you thought was best? Why are you getting paid? He's going to Italy instead of going eighth in the N-B-fucking-A? Are you crazy? I didn't need him in fucking Italy. This is what happens to history based on lies. It perpetuates itself. The bigger you are as a company, as an individual, as a mythological talent, the bigger the lie is. What the fuck? Kerry Kittles was a good player. He was a good pro. But don't use Kobe as the foil because you 'thought he was going somewhere.' What you did was make a professional opinion."

DRAPED FROM high rods, thick, dark curtains along the arena floor created a green room, where the players, clad in boxy, too-big suits, sat with their families and agents at tables near a buffet. No one ate. Too many nerves. Sitting with Kobe were Joe and Pam, Sharia and Shaya, Chubby and John Cox, Sonny and Pam Vaccaro, and Tellem. Gregg Downer and Mike Egan were in the stands, looking down at NBA commissioner David Stern each time he revealed a pick. Kobe could hear Stern through the curtains, but he could see him only on a nearby television. Joe and Pam squirmed. Each squeezed one of Kobe's hands.

Iverson to the Sixers . . .

Marcus Camby to the Toronto Raptors . . .

Shareef Abdur-Rahim to the Vancouver Grizzlies . . .

If I'm the fourth pick, or if I go to New Jersey or Sacramento or wherever, it does not matter. I'm the truth.

Antoine Walker to the Boston Celtics at No. 6 . . .

Lorenzen Wright to the Clippers at No. 7 . . .

If Coach Calipari takes me, I'm going to be a great player.

Kerry Kittles to the Nets . . .

L.A., here I come . . .

Todd Fuller to the Golden State Warriors at No. 11 . . .

Vitaly Potapenko to the Cleveland Cavaliers at No. 12 . . .

Kobe, don't trip. Do not trip.

When they heard Stern announce that the Hornets had selected Kobe, Downer and Egan were pleased. Charlotte was a short flight or a manageable drive away; they could road-trip to some of Kobe's games. It took Joe twenty minutes to break away from the post-pick interviews and afterglow to find them.

"Kobe," he told them, "is going to be a Laker."

AND THEN, it appeared he wouldn't be. Divac said that, rather than go to the Hornets, he would retire. Bob Bass, Charlotte's general manager, called West to say that he was backing out of the trade. "Bob, we have a deal, goddamn it," West told him. "Vlade is not going to retire. Trust me." Tellem called Bass and unleashed a fusillade of fury that Elissa Fisher Grabow, Tellem's assistant, would remember for years thereafter: screaming, stomping his feet, his neck veins popping, his mouth throwing spittle, "so much physical chaos," Grabow said, to compel Bass to complete the trade. Which, when Divac's wife persuaded him not to retire, the teams did, on July 1.

The fallout for Kobe and Tellem was swift and fierce. One was a seventeen-year-old prima donna dictating terms to the entire NBA; the other, the enabler behind a summer-long scheme to force his client to a favorable destination. Jerry Reynolds, the player-personnel director for the Sacramento Kings, said that "it's depressing that any player and his representation, who have their choice of entering or electing not to enter the draft, turn around and don't follow the rules of the draft." Timothy Dwyer of *The Philadelphia Inquirer* wrote that Kobe "didn't help himself or his image. He turned off a lot of sneaker-buying fans with his adolescent power play." The stress of acquiring Kobe and signing O'Neal in mid-July threw West into so deep a state of exhaustion and depression that he spent several days in the hospital. Kobe, though, had gotten what he wanted, and he felt neither guilty about the means to his end nor fatigued from the process.

"Now I'm a Laker," he said later that summer. "I was kind of surprised and shocked at first. Now, it's just like, I want to win a championship. I'm not stepping in there saying, 'I want to have a nice rookie season, and if we get a championship, fine. If we get to the Western Conference finals, fine.' It's not like that. I want to get a championship. I want to get there *now*. It's going to be like that every, every year. If I win a championship next year, the next year I'm going to come back saying, 'Look, man, I want to get a championship again. Shaq, come on, man. Let's go. Let's get another one. Michael got four. Let's get five then. Let's get five.' That's how it's going to be from this point on."

INDEPENDENCE DAY, a nighttime concert featuring Patti LaBelle and the Philadelphia Orchestra, a fireworks show on the Benjamin Franklin Parkway, outside the Philadelphia Museum of Art, the temperature never breaking seventy-five degrees, a zephyr cleansing the evening, leaving it refreshing and cool after a recent rain. Eight days since the NBA draft, three days since the trade became official. Kobe, hanging out with his cousin Sharif Butler, wore a baseball cap tugged low on his head so no one would recognize him.

Someone recognized him.

He hated it. It was so stupid, all of it so stupid, what people said to him, how they acted around him, how emboldened they felt. He had been at a party in West Philadelphia just that weekend, ten-dollar cover. He was at the door, and a girl he didn't know approached him and asked him to lend her ten dollars so she could get into the party. Lend? *Don't worry,* she said. *I'll pay you back. I'll mail the cash to the Lakers. I know you got money.* Could you believe this shit? Was he the national bank or something? *Sorry,* he told her. *All I got is plastic. If they take Visa or Mastercard, I got you. If not, what you want to do? Break the plastic in half?* It was her attitude that infuriated him, her entire social posture, like he was supposed to give her the money, like she was entitled to ask him for it, even though he had no idea who the hell she was.

"I don't trust nobody," he said later.

Trust? Forget it. Trust was gone. Trust was dead. Look at the parkway on the Fourth. A person should have the intelligence to be discreet, to approach him and whisper . . . *Kobe Bryant? Aren't you Kobe Bryant?* That was smart. That was considerate. But no, here were hundreds of people around him, and one guy had to turn and look at him and half yell, *Kobe Bryant?!* And now his cover was blown, and there were so many people, and they were asking and begging for and insisting upon his autograph . . . *Sign this for me . . . Come on, Kobe . . . Saw you beat Chester, man* . . . and you didn't know who or what could jump at you at any time. No security. No patting down. Nothing like that. Guy could get jealous, start saying something. Guy could have a gun . . .

"Man," he told Butler, "I feel uncomfortable. This is the last time I go out without a bodyguard."

They stayed ten more minutes, a half hour in all, watched the fireworks, and left. People had recognized him before. People had known his face. But in just this short time, he had noticed: They were reacting to him differently, expecting something from him, making demands of him, total strangers with their hands out. And he had not reacted to them before like he was now, as if all of them were hazards in waiting, as if any of them might be wielding something terrible in those hands. This was his life now.

ON JULY 27, 1996, Kobe and his friends Kevin Sanchez and Anthony Bannister, the three of them still bonded by their love of rap, met Charlie Mack, a bodyguard and promoter for the actor/rapper Will Smith, at the Jewish Community Center in Wynnewood. Kobe, Sanchez, and Bannister had formed a group called CHEIZAW, a cumbersome acronym for a cumbersome name: Canon *Homo sapiens* Eclectic Iconic Zaibatsu Abstract Words. Mack had gotten to know Kobe and Joe Bryant through the Bryants' connections to the music industry, and he had agreed to listen to some of the group's songs. For three to four hours, with Sanchez and Bannister taking a fifteen-minute break to run to McDonald's for some food, CHEIZAW rhymed for Mack. Kobe left around 6:00 P.M. The audition led to a recording contract for CHEIZAW a couple of months later, but Kobe's career in rap lasted less than four years. Sony dropped him in 2000.

During that afternoon, a man, his face masked with a Stroehmann bread bag, held up a 7-Eleven on City Avenue. A witness picked a photo of Sanchez, who had a juvenile police record, out of an array of eight headshots. Sanchez was six feet and 185 pounds. The witness described the suspect as being five foot eight and 120 pounds. Yet after a two-day trial in September 1998, Sanchez was convicted of armed robbery, eventually serving more than five years in prison before his release in 2007. "It isn't Kobe's fault I went to jail," he once said. He had assumed there was no way he'd lose at trial, so he had not insisted that Kobe act as an alibi witness on his behalf. So Kobe had never testified, and his friend had absolved him of his absence. This was his life now, too.

WEEKS PASSED in that summer of 1996. Kobe was in Los Angeles, a gym at UCLA, stretching on the court before getting some pickup run in. Through the door strode someone he hadn't met yet.

Man, that's Magic.

Magic Johnson was thirty-seven and had just played thirty-two games during the 1995–96 season, the final thirty-two games of his Lakers career. He wasn't a has-been. He wasn't even Michael Cooper, six years removed from his most recent game in the league.

"Hey, how you doin', young fella?"

"I'm doing good," Kobe said.

Kobe noticed right away how he was dressed: shorts, a tank top, sneakers.

I get to go up against Magic. Cool.

They were on the same team for the first couple of games, freelancing, playing off each other. Then they split up. Kobe's team won three games. Magic, not pleased, came back the next day and won three himself, banter flying between them like corn in a popper.

"I can remember one time," Kobe said later, "we had a pick-and-roll, and we forced him to switch out, so I had the wing. So I'm isolated with Magic. I'm looking, and I'm not really paying that much attention. I'm like, 'Hold up. I got Magic on me. I'm gonna take him to the hoop.' So, bam, I go to the hoop, and I go up for a layup on one side, and he tries to foul me. Another guy comes up and steps up from the baseline, so I hang and go to the other side and scoop it, lay it off the glass, get an and-one. He's like, 'Yeah, man, OK, OK, OK, nice move.'"

No crowd. No cheers. No state championship on the line. Just Magic, just the man with the world's most famous smile, with a question implicit and unsaid, the question that matters most on every basketball court: What have you got? No envy. No resentment. No bitching that Kobe was shooting too much or holding back a lesser player. Just Magic, confirming that he belonged. *Yeah, man. Nice move.* This was his life now, too.

It's always been my dream and goal to play professional basketball. I've always loved the game. I love the smell of the leather, the hardwood, the concrete of the playground, the swish of the net. I just really love the game. I don't know where that came from. It's always been there.

—KOBE BRYANT

20

OPEN
GYM

N HER TOWN HOUSE IN Marina del Rey, across the street from Jerry's Famous Deli, Elissa Fisher Grabow contemplated what she would say to Kobe Bryant when he called her, because as he shot one air ball . . . two air balls . . . three . . . *four?* . . . at the Delta Center in Salt Lake City, she knew that, eventually, he would call her.

As Arn Tellem's assistant, Grabow served a vital purpose in Kobe's rookie season with the Lakers: She was the normal person in his life who had nothing to do with basketball, who was there to help him make the transition from high school to the NBA. She didn't follow the sport, didn't watch a game unless one of Tellem's clients was playing, but this one was on her television: Game Five of the Western Conference semifinals, the Utah Jazz up three games to one on the Lakers, Kobe taking the potential game-winning shot at the end of regulation and hitting . . . nothing, taking three more shots in overtime that hit . . . nothing, his legs wet pasta after playing eighty games in the NBA, the Lakers having their season end with a 98–93 loss.

One might have called Grabow a fixer, but that term didn't quite capture all that she did for Kobe. He called her "E," always "E"; a former preschool teacher, just eleven years older than he was, Grabow felt that she was of Kobe's generation, or at least close enough to it that she could communicate with him better than Tellem often could. She didn't need anything from him. She was there only to help him, and she assumed that he would need her help now. Surely he would be distraught. *Holy shit, how am I going to pick up his spirits?*

Finally, the call. Kobe hadn't bothered to wait until the Lakers' team plane had touched down in Los Angeles. It was still in the air when he rang her up.

"Have Palisades' gym open for me," he told her. "I want to go shoot."

Palisades High School was located less than three miles from Kobe's house. Kobe's brief order couldn't have been clearer to Grabow. She was to wake up whomever she had to wake up, call whomever she had to call, do whatever she had to do to get him access to the school's basketball gym that night. He was not angry. There was no quaver in his voice, no indication that his performance had brought him any shame. It was well after 10:00 P.M., West Coast time, on a Monday night in May. There would be school the next morning.

"Make sure it's open," Kobe said.

MAYBE HE had that awful night coming. Maybe the embarrassment of those air balls was karmic justice for a conversation that he had with Tellem the summer before his rookie year, for eleven months of juggling all the conflicting qualities that would make him an incredible basketball player and, at the time, made it fair to wonder if he was setting himself up for an Icarus moment. Kobe and Tellem would argue about all kinds of topics—sports, politics, music, history—and one day, Tellem asked him what he thought about the prospect of facing John Stockton, the Jazz's point guard.

"Well," Kobe said, "I grew up playing against all these Catholic League guys. I played against a ton of guys like that."

Tellem was aghast. He understood immediately what kind of guys Kobe meant: guys who scratch and claw and play defense that's always aggressive and often a little dirty, guys who are short and scrappy and white. "This is fucking John Stockton," he reminded Kobe. You know, John Stockton, member of the U.S. "Dream Team" at the 1992 Summer Olympics, in Barcelona. John Stockton, who had led the NBA in assists in each of the previous *nine* seasons, who would go on to play in ten All-Star Games and set the league's career records for assists and steals, who would be inducted into the Naismith Memorial Hall of Fame. John Stockton, whom Kobe was now shrinking into a cultural stereotype.

"No problem," Kobe said. "I know who John Stockton is."

An ESPN reporter had asked him, *Any games circled on your calendar?* And Kobe had said, *Of course not,* which was . . . how to put this . . . not true. "You know damn well I'm looking forward to Charlotte," he had said later. "The 76ers, November 26, I'm waiting for that. I've got a bounty on Stackhouse." He was still fighting his father's wars, just as he had learned to do in Italy, just as Anthony Gilbert had seen and heard from him on those playground courts. "I'd hear it from Joe: He was ahead of his time. He never got his fair shake," Tellem said. "A son absorbs and picks up these things from childhood, and this was a very close family. Kobe took this all in, and it helped shape who he was." Grabow always thought Kobe's cockiness a facade, a mechanism that an ambitious adolescent relied on to get him where he wanted to go. To her, what else could it be? After finalizing his Adidas deal and the three-year, $3.65 million contract he signed with the Lakers, after purchasing a house high on a hill in Pacific Palisades, Kobe had welcomed Grabow there with Joe, Pam, and Shaya, all of whom had moved in with him, and with Sonny and Pam Vaccaro, who lived a few houses away. Kobe's home was spectacular: an all-white exterior; an ocean panorama; white marble floors inside; a winding staircase; couches with gigantic, inviting pillows; ever-present aromas of vanilla sugar, of cookies warming in the oven, of Pam's homemade fried chicken and macaroni-and-cheese that her baby loved so much; a mother and a family sheltering him, taking care of him, feeding his soul.

"It's real simple to me," Kobe said before his first season with the Lakers. "I grew up in Italy. I didn't have anybody to rely on but my sisters, my mother, and my father. From that, we built such a strong relationship, such a great friendship, and when we came back here, we put it into play. When I would see my classmates not getting along with their brothers and sisters and arguing and saying 'I hate her' or 'I don't like him' or whatever, me, I just can't wait to get home to see my mother, to see my father, to enjoy the family atmosphere that I have, because I know it's not going to be there forever.

"That's why it's real important for my mother and father to come out there and live with me, so I can enjoy the company. Then, when it's time for the bird to leave the nest, then that's the time. But I'm going to enjoy it now while I have them, because you never know what can happen."

GREGG DOWNER and Jeremy Treatman flew out to Los Angeles for a visit, one that coincided with the start of the Lakers' regular season, and they arrived to Sharia and Shaya sitting on Kobe's bed and eating popcorn during a family movie night on a Friday, to Kobe's airplane hangar–size closet loaded with Lakers jerseys and Adidas gear and designer clothes—Tommy Hilfiger, Perry Ellis, Guess, Polo—that companies had sent to him. It was so weird, Kobe told Treatman. He figured that he would have the money to buy whatever shirts and sneakers he wanted, but it turned out that rich people didn't have to buy things, because everybody wanted them to endorse their clothes and products. So the companies raised their prices on poor people but gave him the stuff for free. *That tripped me up.*

"There was an innocence about what was going on," Downer said. "He was naive, but there was a tenderness."

He took them on a tour of the house, and the area around his bed was empty but for two items: a VHS tape of Lower Merion's season-in-review, a highlight montage that Treatman had produced and set to the song "One Shining Moment," the soundtrack of CBS's coverage of the NCAA men's basketball tournament, and his state-championship medal, which was dangling from one of the bedposts.

"Where is everything else?" Treatman asked.

"I don't need anything else!" Kobe said. "This is all I need until I start accomplishing things in the NBA."

It was perfect, maybe too perfect, as if Kobe might have left out those mementos on purpose, just for Downer and Treatman. No, they said. Kobe wouldn't do that. Kobe just loved Lower Merion.

THE COCKINESS wasn't a facade, as Grabow believed then. Innocence and arrogance could swirl inside Kobe at the same time, manifest themselves in different settings, in different ways. Three weeks before training camp, he had broken his wrist during a pickup game in Venice Beach. "It wasn't going to stop me from doing my thing," he said. No, but Del Harris did. Kobe's wrist healed in time for him to return to play in a couple of preseason games, but in one, after making a flashy move and missing a pull-up jump shot, Kobe had come to the sideline only to have Harris admonish him: That sort of thing might have worked in high school, but it wouldn't work in the NBA. *Awww, shit,* Kobe thought. *Gonna be a long motherfucking season.* And from his perspective, it would be. That Harris had coached Joe in Houston years earlier earned Kobe no special privileges with him, and Kobe gave him no grace in return.

What was Harris doing, benching Kobe for two games in late November, having him play less than ten minutes at the United Center in December, in his first game against Michael and the Bulls, then having him play just three minutes more in the teams' February rematch? Sure, the Lakers would win fifty-six games. Sure, Shaquille O'Neal would take Kobe under his wing, so much so that Kobe would invite him over for home-cooked meals, that Kobe would say, "Shaq's like my older brother. We've been tight since day one." Sure, Kobe would score thirty-one points in the NBA Rookie Game. But he would dwell on what he didn't do, or what Harris wouldn't allow him to do. No matter that Kobe would play seventy-one games in the regular season, averaging 15.5 minutes and 7.6 points a game, a hell of a workload for an eighteen-year-old rookie. No matter that Harris didn't clamp down on Kobe's offensive tendencies at all, that Kobe would average 13.8 shots per thirty-six minutes, the second-highest rate on the entire team, ahead of starting guards Eddie Jones and Nick Van Exel, behind only O'Neal. No matter that Kobe played twenty-one minutes in his first game in Philadelphia, a victory over the

Sixers, scoring twelve points while his Lower Merion coaches and friends cheered him on. No matter that Harris would trust him enough to play him more than twenty-eight minutes in Game Five against the Jazz, that with the game tied late in the fourth quarter he would gather the Lakers in the huddle and call a play *for* Kobe. Let the kid bring the ball up. Let him go one-on-one against Bryon Russell, Utah's best defender. Let the NBA's youngest player determine the postseason fate of one of its most decorated franchises. All Kobe saw were shackles. All Kobe saw was Allen Iverson playing forty minutes and scoring twenty-three to twenty-four points a night for the Sixers, Kerry Kittles playing thirty-six minutes and scoring sixteen to seventeen points a night for John Calipari and the Nets, and a coach in Los Angeles who was holding him back and burying him on the bench out of spite.

"You're against the whole thing I'm doing, coming into the league in the first place," he said after the season, explaining his reaction to Harris's coaching. "He's just looking for every little thing to shoot me down the whole season. It's kind of funny because people either don't want to see what's going on or don't know what's going on. But I think it's impossible not to see what's going on. Shaq had told me a couple of times: 'Go in there and do your thing. Play your game. Let the game come to you, but go out there and do your thing. If he pulls you out, he pulls you out. He's gonna pull you out anyway.' He's always looking for a time to sit me down and try to get me frustrated. I don't even care, though. Fuck him."

He was isolated—how could he not be?—hungry for independence but unaccustomed to it. His teammates were men. He was not quite one. More and more as the season went along, he wouldn't drive back to Pacific Palisades immediately after games but would call Grabow instead. *I want to come over.* He didn't want to go home, but he didn't have anywhere else to go. She was twenty-nine, like another big sister. She would bake him brownies, and sometimes they would, for hours, watch episodes of *Mr. Bean,* the British sitcom, on HBO. "He was *obsessed* with *Mr. Bean,*" Grabow said. But sometimes, she would be hosting a dinner party, or her roommate would have friends over, and he would stop by then, too. He would sit on Grabow's couch in a room separate from everyone else, the

TV on, not even secure enough to introduce himself, everything awkward, until those partygoers' reactions would shift from *He's a Laker!* to *Why is this guy coming over again?*

"It wasn't like he entered my friend world," Grabow said later. "Kobe did not have great social skills; he wasn't comfortable just talking to strangers. But he trusted me, and he trusted very few people. So, it was 'OK, the babysitting continues.'

"He loved being taken care of. But I saw a shift, which is normal, of 'I don't want to be with my parents anymore. I don't want to have that anymore. I want to be a grown-up.' He was so desperate to prove everyone wrong because everyone was like, 'He's a bust.' It felt like it was tunnel vision: 'I'm going to do this.'"

Except now that tunnel vision had led to that excruciating stretch against the Jazz, a fourteen-footer and three three-pointers in five minutes, all of them wide open, none of them close . . . what was the proper parallel? Maybe a singer forgetting the words to the national anthem, or the *Hindenburg* disintegrating, a choke or collapse or catastrophe so naked and public that, if you were watching it, you would feel compelled to reach out and offer the poor kid some help . . . and this kid would say, *No, I don't need you. I'm fine. Fuck you. I can do this myself. Make sure the gym's open.*

GRABOW HUNG up the phone. Kobe had a problem. She would fix it. She called Palisades High's administrators and coaches. They would go to the school in the middle of the night, unlock the doors, give Kobe all the time there he needed. Once he got there, he would stay all night, see the sun rise, then have Joe Carbone put him through another three days of workouts, drills, lifts, until his legs and his jumper came back to him, until he would allow his off-season to begin. First, the Lakers' plane had to touch down safely. It did, at 2:00 A.M.

From the airport, he drove straight to Palisades High, never stopping home. He hadn't and couldn't read the newspapers yet, of course. He couldn't read the upcoming story in *The New York Times,* which would describe his four air balls as "a scene straight out of Ripley's." Or the columnist in San Bernardino, who would be baffled: "How come the ball is in his hands for the final shot with the score tied in regulation? . . . In the final game of the season, the Lakers treated Kobe as if he were Michael Jordan." In the locker room, he might have overheard Van Exel tell the *Los Angeles Times,* "He's going to be a great player in this league, but maybe the season caught up with him a little on those threes. He came up a little short." But it would be another few days before Rockets forward Matt Bullard said, "By the time I was eighteen, I had not shot four air balls in my life. I think it reinforces . . . about young kids coming up not being able to make shots. They don't work on their shot. They work on the open-court game and on breaking guys down off the dribble and dunking." He would ingest it all, tell everyone that none of that criticism bothered him when in fact every slight, every doubt, every reservation about his future infiltrated his being like a germ and burned in his brain like a fever. Chester. Utah. The draft. Del Harris. He would read everything. He always had.

He pulled into the parking lot. A state-championship medal on his bedpost. Purple and gold in his closet. Nothing had changed. Everything was changing. He was eighteen years old and alone in a high school gymnasium, with sneakers on his feet and a basketball in his hands. The world thought him a failure. That was fine. That was *ideal.* Most people didn't see him in the way that he saw himself. They couldn't see what he had done, and was still prepared to do, to turn his dreams and compulsions into something lasting, into the existential mortar and stone of an unforgettable life. They didn't know his story, not fully, not yet. A baby named after a restaurant. A kid who had united a community. A teenager whose youth was just now beginning to recede into the distance and darkness of his memory. They would learn. He would make sure they would learn. He had time. He had so much time.

The first shot left his fingertips.

AFTERWORD
HIS STORY,
AND HIS VOICE

JEREMY TREATMAN WAS SITTING IN Section 121 of the Wachovia Center in South Philadelphia, the pyrotechnics of an average NBA game's player introductions reverberating around him. It was a late-winter Friday night, March 2007, and Treatman had come to the arena (now called the Wells Fargo Center) to watch Kobe and the Lakers play the Sixers. On the morning of the game, Treatman had seen and spoken to Kobe during Kobe's annual visit to Lower Merion. The two had talked about the dynamic between Kobe and Philadelphia's basketball fans, about the fans' reluctance to embrace him—this man, twenty-eight years old at the time, whose comportment suggested that he considered himself above them and not one of them. Kobe had taken such pleasure in the Lakers' five-game victory over the Sixers in the 2001 NBA Finals—he had said during the series that he wanted to "cut the hearts out" of the Sixers and their followers—that many Philadelphians harbored a grudge against him. His personality could come off as artificial. He appeared to lack authenticity, and there is no greater sin among such a parochial populace. Nevertheless, Treatman remained loyal to him, optimistic that people eventually would come to regard him more favorably.

"I genuinely think he loves Philadelphia," Treatman said, "appreciates Philadelphia, appreciates his background."

More than twenty thousand people were there, a rare full house. The Sixers long ago had faded into irrelevance, and the Lakers themselves were in the midst of a 42–40 season and eventually would lose in the playoffs' first round to the Phoenix Suns. Three years had passed since they had last reached the Finals, five years since they had won the third of their three consecutive championships with Shaquille O'Neal and Kobe as their nuclei, and much of the blame for the franchise's fall to mediocrity had been laid at Kobe's feet. Dropped in September 2004, the sexual-assault charges against him—the implications of them—had intensified any contempt of him: If people had found him vain and off-putting, now he was villainous, too. He had engaged in a power struggle with O'Neal to determine who ultimately would be the centerpiece of the Lakers. The cutting and cold-blooded Kobe, not the jovial Shaq, had won that battle. O'Neal was traded to Miami after the 2004 season; the Lakers had struggled since; and Phil Jackson had been quick to point to Kobe as the primary problem, the cause of the dynasty's disintegration. Yet Treatman held firm to his belief that redemption awaited his old friend.

"When he finishes his career here," Treatman said, "they'll really cheer him. I'll bet he'll end up here with his last contract. I have a feeling."

There had been no apparent hint that Kobe had considered ending his playing career in Philadelphia, but Treatman's suggestion carried some weight, given their history and relationship. After the game, a 108–92 Lakers loss, I asked Kobe in the visiting locker room about the possibility of his joining the Sixers someday, and he cleared his throat before he responded, weighing his answer.

"It would be nice to play here," he said. "In high school, that's all I thought about."

The answer was pure Kobe. Was he trying to say exactly the right thing to exactly the right audience, whether his words were true or not? His image and its rehabilitation were obviously on his mind, and his comments seemed part of a concerted effort to cleanse his legacy. That sellout crowd had responded negatively to his every move throughout his

twenty-seven-shot, thirty-point performance. They had booed his introduction, had celebrated each of his fifteen missed shots, had jeered him
when he was charged with each of his four personal fouls, had groaned
with grudging respect whenever he hit a jumper or contorted himself,
Plastic Man–like, around several defenders for an acrobatic layup. Earlier
in the day, the tone had been so different at Lower Merion, where the
students saw only a superstar willing to spend time with them.

"A lot of people don't know I come back and go to my old stomping grounds," he said. "A lot of people think I've just forgotten about
it. That's not the case, and the more people understand that, the better
glimpse they'll get of me."

There it was, another cryptic answer that led to a question: Who is the
real Kobe Bryant? By the time Kobe talked to the media, Jeremy Treatman had left the Wachovia Center. Kobe would win two more NBA
championships with the Lakers, in 2009 and 2010, and the notion that
he would leave them for any team, let alone for the Sixers, would forevermore seem ridiculous. But Treatman walked out of the building that
night believing that Kobe needed to return to the Philadelphia area,
where he had first entered the public consciousness, for proper closure
to his playing career. Los Angeles would come to be regarded as Kobe's
home, but it wasn't his birthplace, and only those who had guided and
befriended him during those early years of his life could appreciate how
much those years had shaped him. Everything that anyone needed to
know about Kobe, Treatman felt, was rooted in his time at Lower Merion High School. It was there that his personality and persona had been
molded and first made manifest.

TREATMAN AND I have known each other since 1996. We met not
long after Kobe had finished high school and made off for the NBA,
just after one journey had ended, just before another began. In 2009,
Treatman—having tried to co-author a Kobe memoir in the late
1990s, having conducted his interviews with him back then—had approached me about collaborating on a book. It would focus on Kobe's
senior year. He couldn't find the tapes of those interviews, but he did

have transcripts of several of them, and he had remained in close contact with Gregg Downer, Robby Schwartz, and many other members of the Aces' 1995–96 state-championship team. Would Kobe help us? Not much, but maybe we could catch him for a couple of minutes at his old high school or in the locker room after a game. It would be enough. We could do this.

No, we couldn't. Not then. I was offered a new job in New York that I couldn't turn down. I had to relocate. We scuttled the project.

Kobe's death and the near-universal posthumous reverence for him, though, gave his life a new, more intense resonance. Writing about him as a columnist, I could go and had gone only so deep. There was so much more there, yet it seemed certain anecdotes about him had been repeated incessantly over time, as if those at-the-ready memories alone explained him. More, because of the scope and controversies of his life since, the story of his leading Lower Merion to that state title had receded into a throwaway line in his biography, despite its inherent drama: A high school basketball team, once just another high school basketball team, climbed to a championship that, without this single figure, it would not have won. It was a story worth telling with as much honesty and accuracy as possible, by examining the context of Kobe's rise and its forgotten and oft-unseen effects on those around him, and I found that there were people—Downer, John Cox, Kobe's friends, coaches, teammates, competitors—who were eager to help me tell it. I am grateful to all of them—Treatman, in particular. We spoke at length, and he gave me access to his interview transcripts, which were invaluable for their insights into Kobe's thinking.

Then he called me on December 22, 2020, three nights before Christmas. He was about to move from his Manayunk town house, which he had owned for years, to Boca Raton. He had been cleaning out his garage and loading up his car for the trip.

"I found the tapes," he said.

I'm still surprised I didn't drop the phone.

Early the next morning, I drove forty-five minutes from my home to his. Both of us masked against COVID-19, he reached into a cardboard box on a shelf and removed a plastic zip bag of microcassettes, twenty in all, and a recorder/player. Some of the cassettes had "KOBE" written on them. One said "JOE." Not all of them were interviews with Kobe, but enough of them were. In them, there were glimpses of the man and athlete he became, especially in one segment, in which he spoke of how he would approach his career in professional basketball.

"You have to realize that, on a nightly basis, a guy can come out and kill you," he said. "You have to prepare yourself, and I know I'm gonna prepare myself. If a guy comes out and kills me, I'm not just gonna sit back and let him. I'm going to do everything I can to stop him, and if he does light me up, I'm going to have to look at the videotape to see what he did that beat me. Next time I play him, I'm going to know every move—when he touches his nose, when he touches his ear. I'll know everything."

To listen to those tapes, to hear Kobe at eighteen and nineteen years old, was to be whipsawed by a chilling sensation, as if a spirit had crept into the room, and a warm, wistful sadness. Though I reached out to Vanessa, Joe, and Pam Bryant and asked them to speak with me for this book (I asked Sharia and Shaya, as well, through their parents), they declined. It would be obscene for me to do anything other than understand and accept their reticence. My hope is that they will have the opportunity to hear those tapes someday, and that Kobe's voice will bring them something beyond their pain and grief, something closer to joy.

ACKNOWLEDGMENTS

IN WHAT WAS, FOR SO many reasons, for so many people, the worst of years, I was fortunate to have many reasons to be thankful for many people. COVID-19 created obvious obstacles to researching and writing about Kobe Bryant, but the generosity of strangers and acquaintances and friends allowed me to overcome most of them, I think. I hope.

Once a week during the spring and summer of 2020, Gregg Downer and I would sit down for a lengthy, socially distanced interview at his home. It didn't take long for those conversations—and his daughter's presence at them—to become a leavening agent for life in a pandemic. I owe Gregg, Colleen, and Brynn Downer a debt. As I do, of course, to Jeremy Treatman.

Mike Egan did more than share Kobe stories that only he knew. I could barely contain my glee—any reporter knows this feeling—when he handed me a box full of notes, documents, and newspaper clippings from his two years coaching Kobe and said, "Keep it as long as you need it." He also has impeccable tastes in sportswriting and beer.

Dayna Tolbert and Doug Young were committed to helping me understand the history and reality of Lower Merion before, during, and after Kobe's time there. They are at the top of a long list of people who went above and beyond in answering my questions about topics ranging from the Bryants to Philadelphia basketball to life on the Main Line.

That list includes, but is not limited to, Amy Buckman, Joe Carbone, Donnie Carr, John Cox, Drew Downer, Lynne Freeland, Susan Freeland Barber, Anthony Gilbert, Elissa Fisher Grabow, Frank Hartwell, Wendell Holland, Ashley and Mo Howard, Phil Martelli, Evan Monsky, Keith and Speedy Morris, John Nash, Sam Rines Sr. and Jr., Robby Schwartz, Sultan Shabazz, Guy Stewart, and Julius Thompson.

I would have loved to have taken a high school English course taught by Jeanne Mastriano.

Sean Hughes and Sarah Stout opened the doors of Lower Merion High School and Bala Cynwyd Middle School to me, so that I could walk where Kobe had walked and see what he had seen.

Ted Goldsborough and Jerry Francis of the Lower Merion Historical Society allowed me to travel back in time, into the community's past, into Kobe's.

Al Tielemans was generous and accommodating in providing me several of his first-class photographs of Kobe.

Regina Ventresca Creedon and Meghan Mueller Creedon graciously took the time to translate and transcribe an entire book, one that had been written in Italian, so that my research into the Bryant family's years in Europe would be richer and more accurate.

The support that my direct editors at *The Philadelphia Inquirer*—Michael Huang, Pat McLoone, Gary Potosky, Shemar Woods—lent me as I wrote this book was as strong and unflagging as their support for my work there.

Several of my colleagues offered their insights and assistance as I tried to find the right words to tell Kobe's story: Kevin Armstrong, Dan Barbarisi, Zach Berman, Jerry Brewer, Scott Cacciola, Dom Cosentino, Ray Didinger, Bob Ford, Dan Gelston, Mike Jensen, Abbott Kahler, Tyler Kepner, Rob Knox, Ian O'Connor, Keith Pompey, Mike Sager, Ben Shpigel, Mike Vaccaro, Seth Wickersham, Adrian Wojnarowski. Their contributions were essential, as is their friendship.

Susan Canavan has been everything I could have asked for in a literary agent since the moment I asked her if she would be interested in representing me. She has championed this book from its inception. I cannot thank her enough.

During the first conversation in our working relationship, Pete Wolverton promised that he would give this manuscript a rigorous edit and that the book would be better for it. He was right on all counts. He was the perfect editor for this project.

Mike and Lauren Triana gave me a piece of advice so valuable that, without it, this book likely would not exist.

The encouragement I received from all my friends and family members made the work of writing this book seem easier, the journey's end seem nearer. Thank you for blessing me with your good humor and grace.

I am lucky to have an immediate family full of love, loyalty, and laughter: Jessica, Martin, Regan, and Patrick Cunningham; Bob and Pam Zilahy; Chuck and Ann Sielski. My wife, Kate, and my sons, Evan and Gabe, make me proud every day. They have my heart, and always will.

—*MIKE SIELSKI*
MARCH 2021

NOTES AND SOURCES

BETWEEN THE INTERVIEWS WITH KOBE Bryant that he already had transcribed and the microcassette tapes that he hadn't, Jeremy Treatman provided me with more than thirty thousand words' worth of insight into Kobe's thinking and experiences during his Lower Merion career and his first season with the Lakers. Treatman also conducted an interview with Joe Bryant that I uncovered among the tapes. In citing those sources, I have designated the material I used from them as "Kobe Bryant Transcripts" and "Kobe Bryant Tapes," depending on whether Treatman transcribed Kobe's words or I did. All of the quotes from Kobe that bridge the chapters came from those transcripts and interviews.

In the months after Kobe's death, I wrote several columns for *The Philadelphia Inquirer* about him, including a co-authored piece with Gregg Downer. I obtained written permission from *The Inquirer* to replicate or republish excerpts from those columns or reuse their raw material here.

I interviewed—in person, by phone, by email—more than one hundred people for this book and reached out to many more who declined to speak with me. Some of the interviews I conducted were merely for the sake of background, context, and fact-checking. All of them were invaluable.

The digitization of newspaper and document archives allowed me to bunker in my home office during the pandemic and still be productive in my research. I relied particularly on Ancestry.com, Newspapers.com, the *Philadelphia Daily News, The Philadelphia Inquirer,* and *The Philadelphia Tribune.* The remarkable people at Basketball-Reference.com created a page with the game log of Kobe's entire high school career, which was a handy and essential reference point. The Lower Merion Historical Society had the 1996 *Enchiridion* and several files bulging with newspaper articles about Kobe. Its back copies of *The Merionite* were a gold mine. Mike Egan had plenty of terrific stuff that I would have struggled to find otherwise. During a day at Temple University's Charles Library, I carefully thumbed through its archive of articles from *The Philadelphia Bulletin,* which helped in collecting details about Joe Bryant and his basketball career. The clippings were so delicate that I took care to make sure they wouldn't disintegrate at my clumsy touch.

Any direct quotations here came from transcripts of interviews that I conducted, interviews that Treatman conducted with Kobe, published accounts, or those who said or heard the quote. Where there were differing recollections of what someone said (the exact wording of Downer's "Cancer of Me" speech, for instance), I have put those words common to all the recollections in italics. Where there were differing recollections of an event or anecdote, I have tried to account for those differences by presenting the varying perspectives. Where I used the attribution "he thought" or "she thought" and/or italicized sentences or phrases to reflect what someone thought, I have done so because that person told me what he or she was thinking in that particular moment or because my reporting and research revealed it with total clarity. That standard held even with Kobe: Often in the transcripts and tapes, he made his thoughts so obvious that no one could doubt them. On YouTube and Facebook, I watched Lower Merion games from 1992 through 1996, Kobe highlights, Kobe interviews, and Kobe's take-my-talent press conference, senior prom, and post-commencement party.

Where possible, I relied on firsthand witnessing and observations to report and reconstruct scenes. I attended the press conference that Gregg

Downer and Doug Young held two days after Kobe's death. On Labor Day 2020, while I asked her questions and she provided detailed answers, Kate Bayer gave me a tour of 1224 Remington Road. Early one morning in the fall, before the sun came up, I drove from that house to Lower Merion High School, taking one of the routes that Kobe would have at the hour he would have taken it.

PREFACE: THE SIGNS OF THINGS TO COME

Interviews: Gregg Downer, Bob McIlvaine, Helen McIlvaine, Jeff McIlvaine, Ben Relles, Jeremy Treatman.

vii **On the day after Kobe Bryant died:** Mike Sielski, "How Kobe Bryant's Death Brought Bobby McIlvaine—an Athlete, a Scholar, the Friend I Should Have Known Better—Back to Life," *Philadelphia Inquirer,* April 9, 2020.

viii **"Remember this name":** Jeremy Treatman, "Injuries and Departures Will Take Toll on Aces," *Philadelphia Inquirer,* Dec. 7, 1992.

x **"It taught me how to be tough":** Sielski, "Bryant Finally Feels the Love in Hometown," *Philadelphia Inquirer,* Dec. 2, 2015.

1: AFTER THE FIRE

Interviews: Amy Buckman, Gregg Downer, Elissa Fisher Grabow, Sean Hughes, Phil Mellet, Jeremy Treatman, Doug Young.

3 **It had been forty-eight hours:** Marie Moler, Performance Study and Specialist Report, National Transportation Safety Board, Jan. 26, 2020. Dave Philipps, Tim Arango, and Louis Keene, "Flying into Patchy Fog, Kobe Bryant's Pilot Had a Decision to Make," *New York Times,* Jan. 27, 2020.

4 **A sixty-four-year-old Lakers fan:** Jere Longman and Sarah Mervosh, "Kobe Bryant, Philly Guy," *New York Times,* Jan. 28, 2020.

6 **The gym:** John P. Martin, "School Gym to Be Named after Kobe Bryant," *Philadelphia Inquirer,* Oct. 20, 2010.

13 **But Kobe's relationship with his parents:** The Associated Press, "Kobe Bryant: Mom Can't Have My Stuff," May 9, 2013.

14 **One month later:** Gregg Downer and Sielski, "'My Beloved Kobe,'" *Philadelphia Inquirer,* March 20, 2020.

17 **He began to scribble down thoughts:** Ibid.

2: A SAFE HAVEN

Interviews: Christ Dhimitri, Sonny Hill, Mo Howard, Vontez Simpson, Julius Thompson, Littel Vaughn.

19 **Lankenau was located:** *The First 300,* 214.

19 **The day after Kobe was born:** "Peoplenotes," *Philadelphia Inquirer,* Aug. 24, 1978. "Sports of All Sorts," *Philadelphia Daily News,* Aug. 24, 1978.

20 **When he told *Sports Illustrated*:** Ian Thomsen, "Show Time!," *Sports Illustrated,* April 27, 1998.

21 **But the block itself:** U.S. Census records.

21 **At one point:** *The Great Migration: A City Transformed,* Historical Overview, https://greatmigrationphl.org/node/24.

21 **He had made that same journey:** Donald Hunt, "Bryant Family Keeps Close Ties," *Philadelphia Tribune,* May 16, 2000.

22 **Philadelphia throughout the 1960s:** Menika Dirkson, "Safe Streets, Inc.: The 'Hustle' to End Black Gang Violence in Philadelphia, 1969–1976," Arlen Specter Center for Public Service Research Fellowship, 2019.

22 **Once, he and several friends:** Alan Richman, "Bryant Has Bigger Worries Than Game," *Philadelphia Bulletin,* Dec. 26, 1973.

22 **After his family:** John Rhodes, "Joe Bryant, the Best Freshman Forward," *Philadelphia Tribune,* April 17, 1976.

24 **His playground model:** Ibid.

24 **Joe averaged 27.4 points:** Julius Thompson, "Bryant Picks La Salle: 'Only Forty Cents Away," *Philadelphia Bulletin,* May 25, 1972.

24 **"I eat about four pounds":** Ibid.

25 **Jack Farrell told a reporter:** Bob Savatt, "Bryant Bomb Bartram's Big Basket," *Philadelphia Bulletin,* Feb. 16, 1972.

3: GOD AND THE DEVIL IN THEM

Interviews: Aleta Arthurs, John Cox, Gregg Downer, Steve Mix, Vontez Simpson, Julius Thompson, Sonny Vaccaro, Littel Vaughn, Paul Westhead, Pat Williams.

27 **Founded in 1893:** Lou Baldwin, "Through Ups and Downs of 125 Years, St. Ignatius Parish's Faith Endures," CatholicPhilly.com, July 6, 2018.

27 **One of its earliest congregants:** Rev. M. R. Jordan, S.J., "St. Ignatius Parish: 50 Years of Progress," *Philadelphia Tribune,* July 7, 1973. "Three Catholics Admitted to Knights of Columbus," *Philadelphia Tribune,* Feb. 21, 1956.

27 **Both sides:** Howard Jones, "Under the Hoop," *Philadelphia Tribune,* Feb. 18, 1950.

27 **He enlisted in the Army:** "Cox-Williams Ceremony at St. Ignatius Church," *Philadelphia Tribune,* Aug. 18, 1953.

27 **The couple:** City of Philadelphia records, https://www.phila.gov/2018–02–15 -black-history-month-8-things-to-know-about-the-fire-department/.

27 **He finished his career:** "COX, JOHN, A.," *Philadelphia Inquirer,* Oct. 1, 2001.

28 **Within Pam:** Nita Lelyveld, "Bryant: A Wonder of Nurture," *Philadelphia Inquirer,* March 31, 1996.

28 **A panel of Wanamaker's employees:** "O.H.S. Girls Chosen for Wanamaker Teen Board," *Philadelphia Tribune,* Feb. 1, 1969.

28 **Her grandparents:** Lelyveld, "Bryant: A Wonder of Nurture."

29 **As he winnowed:** Thompson, "Bryant Picks La Salle."

29 **"I might get homesick":** Ibid.

30 **In his first game for La Salle:** Allen Lewis, "La Salle Rips Lehigh, 87–37," *Philadelphia Inquirer,* Dec. 2, 1973.

31 **"It was kind of a Miss Piggy and Froggy thing":** Lelyveld, "Bryant: A Wonder of Nurture."

31 **Joe had had a girlfriend:** Lazenby, *Showboat,* 14.

31 **One writer:** Chris Ballard, "Where Does Greatness Come From?," *Sports Illustrated,* May 14, 2012.

32 **As a sophomore:** https://www.sports-reference.com/cbb/players/joe-bryant-1.html.

32 **Initially:** Jim Barniak, "Proper Offer Could Lure JB," *Philadelphia Bulletin,* March 27, 1975.

32 **Of course, it was Joe's decision to make:** Frank Brady, "Bryant Hardship Case? Coach Isn't Rushing Him," *Philadelphia Bulletin,* Feb. 13, 1975.

33 **After the game:** Frank Bilovsky, "Bryant Paces Explorer Win," *Philadelphia Bulletin,* March 2, 1974.

33 **The NCAA had banned the dunk:** Frank Fitzpatrick, "When College Basketball Outlawed the Dunk," *Philadelphia Inquirer,* March 23, 2014.

34 **Everyone, including Joe:** Bill Livingston, "Taylor Clicks for 32 as Explorers Rally," *Philadelphia Inquirer,* March 9, 1975.

34 **And he could make even that game:** Livingston, "Syracuse Defeats Explorers in OT," *Philadelphia Inquirer,* March 16, 1975.

35 **One by one:** Brady, "Bryant Hardship Case?"

35 **Pam still had her doubts:** Ibid.

36 **"I know where I'm at":** Ibid.

37 **"We haven't gotten a contract":** Williams and Lyon, *We Owed You One!,* 33.

37 **Williams once wrote:** Ibid., 34.

37 **"It's unbelievable":** Herm Rogul, "JB (Sr.) Glad It's Over," *Philadelphia Bulletin,* Sept. 11, 1975.

37 **"Just talking jive":** Mark Heisler, "76ers Top Kings as Bryant Excels," *Philadelphia Bulletin,* Dec. 7, 1975.

37 **He had the summer ahead of him:** Montgomery County, PA, property records.

38 **At 11:37 P.M.:** John B. Rhodes, "Drug, Auto Charges against 76ers' Joe Bryant Are Dismissed," *Philadelphia Tribune,* June 12, 1976. Bill Livingston, "76er Is Arrested on Cocaine Charge," *Philadelphia Inquirer,* May 8, 1976.

38 **One of the officers:** Ibid.

38 **"I grabbed him":** Ibid.

38 **When they searched the Datsun:** Livingston, "76er Is Arrested."

39 **At Joe's trial:** Phil Jasner, "Bryant: I Hope It Makes Me a Better Man," *Philadelphia Daily News,* June 11, 1976.

39 **He wiped Joe's slate clean:** "76ers Bryant in Clear," United Press International, June 11, 1976.

39 **Joe returned:** Jasner, "Bryant."

40 **One night in September 1979:** Brady, "Bryant: A Legend in His Own Mind," *Philadelphia Bulletin,* Oct. 8, 1979.

40 **He welcomed:** Ibid.

4: CHILD OF THE WORLD

Interviews: Donnie Carr, Tamika Catchings, John Cox, Leon Douglas, Ashley Howard, Mo Howard, Mike Sager.

43 **Look at the child, three years old:** Herm Rogul, "Bryant's Son—Dunking at Three?" *Philadelphia Tribune,* June 18, 1982.

43 **Because, throughout his adolescence:** Mike Sager, *Tourist Information* podcast, May 22, 2020.

44 **The Sixers, Joe said:** Leroy Samuels, "Joe Bryant: He's Sizzling Hot," *Philadelphia Bulletin,* Aug. 17, 1980.

45 *My daddy's team won last night:* "Bryant Due for Surgery," *Philadelphia Bulletin,* March 30, 1981.

45 **"The younger guys":** Elmer Smith, "Jellybean for Ombudsman?," *Philadelphia Daily News,* Oct. 29, 1982.

45 **He was also considering:** "Joe Bryant Eyes Big 5 Job," *Philadelphia Bulletin,* no date listed.

46 **Look at the child, four years old:** Lee Jenkins, "Reflections on a Cold-Blooded Career," *Sports Illustrated,* Oct. 21, 2013.

46 **In Kansas City:** Norm Frauenheim, "NBA Players' Strike? Dr. J Would Rather Play," *Arizona Republic,* March 20, 1983.

46 **Pam joked:** Lazenby, *Showboat,* 78.

47 **Sonny Hill gave him an idea:** Barocci, 18.

47 **Joe's brother-in-law:** Mark Palmquist, "This is NOT a Story about L.A. Lakers Star Kobe Bryant," *SF Weekly,* Feb. 27, 2002.

47 **He drove his Mercedes:** Herm Rogul, "Joe Bryant 'The Show' in Football in Italy," *Philadelphia Tribune,* April 5, 1985.

49 **Immersed in Italian:** Ibid.

49 **"People treat others as equals there":** Lelyveld, "Bryant: A Wonder of Nurture."

50 **Now he shot baskets:** Robert McGill Thomas Jr. and Peter Alfano, "At Home in Italy," *New York Times,* March 18, 1985.

50 **"He would watch those games":** Thomsen, "Show Time!"

50 **He started rolling up:** Kobe Bryant, "Dear Basketball," *The Players Tribune,* Nov. 29, 2015.

50 **He was waiting:** Barocci, 33.

51 **He was recruited:** Ibid., 37.

51 **"The travel helped them see":** Helene Elliott, "Kobe Bryant Humbly Begins His Jump from Preps to Pros," *Los Angeles Times,* Oct. 15, 1996.

51 **Sometimes, when Pam was out on her morning jog:** Barocci, 63.

52 **She would expose them:** Ibid., 43.

52 **She would keep Catholicism:** Corriere TV, https://video.corrierefiorentino .corriere.it/pistoia-l-infanzia-kobe-bryant-ricordi-un-amica/3456842a-40f4–11ea -ac4b-cc121ffa8ffd.

52 **During Kobe's early years:** Pearlman, 116.

52 **"We had a vision":** Barocci, 48.

53 **A few years later:** Lazenby, *Showboat,* 89.

53 **After plopping down on the floor:** Ibid., 93.

54 **At home:** Barocci, 88.

54 **It was that Kobe:** Kobe Bryant Transcripts, Kobe Bryant Tapes.

55 **His coach in the league:** Barocci, 59.

55 **But once the scrimmages:** Ibid., 60.

55 **He carried himself:** Margherita Stancati, "Before Mamba, a Panther: Italy Mourns Bryant, Who Learned Basketball There," *Wall Street Journal,* Jan. 27, 2020.

56 **Joe brought Kobe with him:** Barocci, p. 66.

56 **There is one photo:** Emiliano Carchia, https://twitter.com/Carchia/status /1221563958714339336.

56 **In the summer:** Ted Silary, "When He Was One of Us," *Philadelphia Daily News,* Sept. 12, 2000.

57 **It occupied so much of it:** Palmquist, "This Is Not a Story."

58 **In twenty-five games:** Pearlman, 18.

58 **"It was a turning point for me":** Sielski, "Bryant Finally Feels the Love."

59 **When Magic Johnson was diagnosed:** Thomsen, "The Evolution of Kobe Bryant," *Sports Illustrated,* June 4, 2008.

59 **He was always quick:** John Smallwood, "Bryants Want What's Best for Kobe," *Philadelphia Daily News,* April 30, 1996. Rogul, "Joe Bryant 'The Show' in Football in Italy."

5: ANGELS AT SUNRISE

Interviews: Kate Bayer, Gregg Downer, Wendell Holland, Sean Hughes, Evan Monsky, Arn Tellem, Dayna Tolbert.

63 **Rimmed with a gold frame:** https://www.blackartdepot.com/products /guardian-angel-by-shahidah.

65 **"More than any other person or entity":** *The First 300,* 72.

66 **To this day:** Shelly Hagan and Wei Lu, "This Is America's Richest Zip Code," Bloomberg, April 10, 2018.

66 **"Life in the golden era":** David Schmidt, The Lower Merion Historical Society, http://www.lowermerionhistory.org/texts/schmidtd/mansions.html.

67 **The train depots alone:** *The First 300,* 240.

69 **Just 9 percent of students:** Kristen E. Holmes, "Marking a 1963 Equality Moment," *Philadelphia Inquirer,* Sept. 12, 2013. Linda Stein, "1963: The Moment of Integration for the Lower Merion School District Remembered," MainLineMediaNews.com, June 7, 2013.

70 **Under pressure:** Stein, "1963."

71 **Lower Merion won:** https://AcesHoops.com/history.

72 **By 2004:** Debra J. Dickerson, "What If Bill Cosby Is Right?" *Philadelphia Magazine,* September 2004.

6: BATS AND MICE AND THE RIDE OF A LIFETIME

Interviews: Donnie Carr, Drew Downer, Gregg Downer, John Dzik, Mike Dzik, Lynne Freeland, Susan Freeland Barber, Ashley Howard, Tom McGovern, Keith Morris, Speedy Morris, Dave Rosenberg, Allen Rubin, Sultan Shabazz, George Smith, Matt Snider, Guy Stewart, Jay Wright, Doug Young.

80 **When Mike Manning retired:** https://AcesHoops.com/history.

81 **In the school's locker room:** Marcia C. Smith, "Chapter One," *Orange County Register,* June 10, 2001.

83 **"They'd say":** Kobe Bryant Tapes.

83 **"Everybody started laughing":** Ibid.

84 **Lock up his valuables:** Elliott, "Kobe Bryant Humbly Begins."

85 **And he did:** Kobe Bryant Transcripts.

86 **He got his nickname:** M. G. Missanelli, "Making It: The Morris Story," *Philadelphia Inquirer,* March 1, 1989.

87 **He was, one writer put it:** Bill Lyon, "It's La Salle's Turn to Be Loyal to Morris," *Philadelphia Inquirer,* Feb. 13, 1996.

7: LOSING

Interviews: Corella Berry Moten, Sterling Carroll, Katrina Christmas, Gregg Downer, Frank Hartwell, Tim Legler, Jack Maher, Tom McGovern, Evan Monsky, Speedy Morris, Audrey Price Gornish, Sam Rines Jr., Sam Rines Sr., Allen Rubin, Matt Snider, Guy Stewart, Dayna Tolbert, Jeremy Treatman, Sonny Vaccaro, Doug Young.

95 **The older students:** Dan Ackerman, "Administration to Prevent Freshman Day Massacre," *Merionite,* Dec. 9, 1994.

95 **In 2007:** John N. Mitchell, "Memo: Lower Merion District Hindered Blacks," *Philadelphia Tribune,* Sept. 6, 2011.

96 **A federal appeals court:** Mark Walsh, "Appeals Court Rejects Suit Alleging Race Bias in Special Education Placements," *Education Week,* Sept. 15, 2004.

96 **Only twenty-seven:** Dickerson, "What If Bill Cosby Is Right?"

96 **"She is weak on fundamentals":** Chuck Newman, "Ex-Sixer's Daughters Go Their Own Way at L. Merion," *Philadelphia Inquirer,* Dec. 14, 1992.

98 **From grades six through twelve:** Pete Schnatz, "'Jelly Bean' Devoting Time to Coaching Career," *Philadelphia Inquirer,* Jan. 20, 1993.

98 **"My objective":** Jeremy Treatman, "Akiba Picks Bryant as Basketball Coach," *Philadelphia Inquirer,* Oct. 27, 1992.

99 **Fittingly:** Jessie Torrisi, "Bryant Brings NBA Experience and a Big Smile to LM," *Merionite,* Dec. 19, 1992.

105 **"There was a lot of jealousy":** Bill Doherty, "Dixon Happy He Stayed with Aces," *Philadelphia Inquirer,* Dec. 20, 1993.

8: SWAGGER

Interviews: Gregg Downer, Mike Egan, Jeanne Mastriano, Evan Monsky, Audrey Price Gornish, Matt Snider, Guy Stewart, Jeremy Treatman, Doug Young.

115 **"Whenever I step on the court":** Kobe Bryant Transcripts.

116 **One of their games:** David T. Shaw, "L. Merion about to Begin Work on Turn-around Season," *Philadelphia Inquirer,* Dec. 9, 1993.

117 **Once, Mastriano:** Mark Medina, "How Kobe Bryant's Forgotten Homework Assignment Sparked His Post-NBA Career," *USA Today,* Jan. 23, 2020.

117 **"She was so good":** Ibid.

118 **The "call to adventure":** Campbell, 48.

118 **Kobe's was titled:** Karen Abbott, "Paging Kobe Bryant, 1998," Medium.com, Jan. 28, 2020.

119 **He'd had the tough childhood:** Nancy V. Greene, "Just a Slam-Dunk from Queens to Lower Merion," *Main Line Times,* May 2, 1996. Chris Morkides, "For Griffin, New Chance to Test Himself," *Philadelphia Inquirer,* March 14, 1995.

120 **"Jermaine was the savior":** Kobe Bryant Tapes.

122 **Yet *The Inquirer*'s coverage:** Doherty, "Dixon Happy."

124 **Williamsport:** Eric Hunt, "Bryant Shut Down in His 1993 Trip to the Magic Dome," *Williamsport Sun-Gazette,* Jan. 28, 2020.

125 **It was Kobe about whom:** Frank Bertucci, "L. Merion Sophomore Hits Pennsbury Hard in First Round," *Philadelphia Inquirer,* Feb. 28, 1994.

125 **And it was Kobe:** Bertucci, "Colonials Make the Most of Free-Throw Chances, Beat Aces," *Philadelphia Inquirer,* Feb. 28, 1994.

9: *SE DIO VUOLE*

Interviews: Donnie Carr, Gregg Downer, Anthony Gilbert, Keith Morris, Speedy Morris, Sam Rines Jr., Sam Rines Sr., Dave Rosenberg, Allen Rubin, Guy Stewart, Jeremy Treatman, Sonny Vaccaro.

127 **Vaccaro had his own remarkable story:** Nocera and Strauss, 35.

128 **He had seen Jordan:** Wetzel and Yaeger, 10–11.

130 **"The way I think about it":** Mike Biglin, "Vacation Eluding Basketball Stand-out at Lower Merion," *Philadelphia Inquirer,* Aug. 2, 1994.

130 **The irony of the discovery:** Tom Cobourn, "Like His Dad, Bryant Can Fill It Up," *Wilmington News-Journal,* April 9, 1995.

132–3 **A future celebrity and star:** https://www.youtube.com/watch?v =sZVDqmrl9sM, https://www.youtube.com/watch?v=wDSAmdgFswQ.

134 **In the Narberth League:** Biglin, "Vacation Eluding."

136 **There were 157 players:** Lenn Robbins, "July Madness Hits College Recruiting," *Record,* July 8, 1994.

10: OK, LET'S PLAY

Interviews: Deirdre Bobb, Sterling Carroll, Katrina Christmas, John Cox, Gregg Downer, Mike Egan, Susan Freeland Barber, Anthony Gilbert, Dan Gross, Rick Hicks, Bob Hurley, Ross Kershey, Rob Knox, Jack Maher, Evan Monsky, Keith Morris, Speedy Morris, Brendan Pettit, Dave Rosenberg, Jim "Scoogie" Smith, Guy Stewart, Dayna Tolbert, Jeremy Treatman.

141 **Already an elite soccer goalkeeper:** Dave Ruden, "Boy Shoots to the Top in Basketball," *New York Times,* April 9, 1989.

144 **There was a girl:** Allison Samuels, "Kobe Off the Court," *Newsweek,* Oct. 12, 2003.

147 **"I look around at those other teams":** Stacy Moscotti, "Bryant Burns Up Basketball Court with Professional Fire," *Merionite,* Dec. 9, 1994.

148 **The game featured:** Samuel Davis, "Kobe Bryant Developing Ahead of Jelly-bean's Pace," *Philadelphia Tribune,* Jan. 3, 1995.

148 **It was Shaya:** Ibid.

149 **Early on:** Doherty, "L. Merion's Bryant Burns Malvern," *Philadelphia Inquirer,* Dec. 30, 1994.

151 **"That's why":** Davis, "Kobe Bryant."

151 *If you hold Kobe to fifteen points:* Tom McGrath, "The NBA Kid," *Fan,* January 1996.

151 **"Dan told me":** Rob Knox, "Aces Top Ridley in Central Battle," *Philadelphia Inquirer,* Jan. 9, 1995.

152 **"Someday":** Morkides, "Aces Storm to Win over Strath Haven," *Philadelphia Inquirer,* Jan. 13, 1995.

154 **Kobe gathered in the rebound:** Steve Wartenberg, "Bryant's Shot in Last 2 Seconds Aces the Raiders," *Philadelphia Inquirer,* Jan. 16, 1995.

154 **Back at home:** *All the Smoke* podcast, https://www.youtube.com/watch?v =mVyd47lOaSo.

159 **In February 1995:** Abrell Camron, "February's Voice," *Merionite,* Feb. 10, 1995.

160 **"We felt":** Morkides, "Lower Merion Drops Ridley to Clinch Central," *Philadelphia Inquirer,* Feb. 7, 1995.

11: THE PIT

Interviews: Dana Barros, Gregg Downer, Mike Egan, Jim Fenerty, Bob Ford, Rob Knox, John Linehan, Evan Monsky, Brendan Pettit, Sam Rines Jr., Guy Stewart, Jeremy Treatman.

164 **"I've finally seen":** Bob Ford, "How Kobe Almost Landed with the Philadelphia 76ers Early On," *Philadelphia Inquirer,* Nov. 30, 2015.

165 **The night before the game:** Sally Pollak, "Gratz Was There Again, but Where Was FLC?" *Philadelphia Inquirer,* March 2, 1995.

166 **"I knew that Lower Merion was the right spot for me":** Kobe Bryant Tapes.

166 **As he stepped from the late-winter chill:** Jason McGahan, "Kobe's Friends, Teammates, Coaches, and Rivals Reflect on the Rise of a Legend," *L.A. Magazine,* Feb. 28, 2020.

167 **Afterward:** Morkides, "Lower Merion Tops Coatesville, Gains Final," *Philadelphia Inquirer,* March 2, 1995.

168 **From a thriving city:** U.S. Census records.

168 **It was the poorest city:** Mele, 4.

168 **Its housing projects:** Ibid., 121.

171 **"They just wore us down":** Morkides, "Watkins Gets It Right as Chester Takes Title," *Philadelphia Inquirer,* March 6, 1995.

171 **The game:** Morkides, "Aces Ousted in OT," *Philadelphia Inquirer,* March 16, 1995.

172 **The Aces didn't score a point:** https://www.youtube.com/watch?v=1C3YgxoLbvM.

12: MYTH AND REALITY

Interviews: Joe Carbone, Donnie Carr, John Cox, Emory Dabney, Drew Downer, Gregg Downer, Bob Ford, Paul Hewitt, Mo Howard, Bob Hurley, Bobby Johnson, John Kunzier, Ron Luber, Phil Martelli, Keith Morris, Speedy Morris, John Nash, Sam Rines Jr., Sam Rines Sr., Arn Tellem, Jeremy Treatman, Sonny Vaccaro, Michael Weil.

176 **For the one year:** *La Salle University Academic Bulletin,* 1995–96.

177 **That the university:** Kobe Bryant Transcripts.

177 **Teaming up:** Ibid.

178 **From his contacts:** Ibid.

178 **Speedy Morris . . . was Speedy Morris:** Kobe Bryant Tapes.

180 *College basketball wouldn't be ready:* Ibid.

182 **Stackhouse wasn't:** *The Woj Pod,* April 8, 2020.

183 **John Lucas thought:** Ford, "How Kobe Almost Landed."

183 **Willie Burton:** Shaun Powell, "Ready or Not, Here He Comes," *Newsday,* Dec. 17, 1995.

184 **After the Sixers practiced:** Ford, "How Kobe Almost Landed."

185 **Kobe played a game of P-I-G:** Melanie Amato, "You Can't Touch This," *Merionite,* Dec. 4, 1995.

185 **Kobe picked up Emory Dabney:** https://twitter.com/Ian_OConnor/status/1221984129543286785.

187 **"Could you imagine":** *The Woj Pod.*

189 **In October 1994:** Feinstein, 366–70.

190 **Amaker thought Kobe:** Statement by Tommy Amaker from Harvard University, July 9, 2020.

190 **Kobe, however, was talking to Krzyzewski:** Kobe Bryant Transcripts.

191–2 **"You wouldn't believe":** Michael Amsel, "Bryant Drawing Attention as an Elite Hoop Prospect," *Central Jersey Home News,* July 12, 1995.

192 **"I'm trying to steer talk away":** Ibid.

198 **"If John says something":** David Aldridge, "Bullets Ready to Name Nash General Manager," *Washington Post,* June 18, 1990.

200 **And when Kobe capped:** "Philly File," *Philadelphia Daily News,* Aug. 7, 1995.

201 *There's no way I'm going to La Salle:* Kobe Bryant Transcripts.

13: SECRETS AND SHARKS

Interviews: Donnie Carr, Katrina Christmas, Drew Downer, Gregg Downer, Mike Egan, Lynne Freeland, Susan Freeland Barber, Anthony Gilbert, Frank Hartwell, Jimmy Kieserman, Tom McGovern, Keith Morris, Speedy Morris, Brendan Pettit, Lauren Rodrick Nevin, Robby Schwartz, Jeremy Treatman, Sonny Vaccaro.

206 **Construction:** Scott Tillman, "Parking Situation Worsens, Becoming Costly and Unfair," *Merionite,* Oct. 5, 1995.

208 **When a vagrant:** Abbott, "Paging Kobe."

208 **Matkov got into a fight:** Ibid.

208 **One night:** Ibid.

209 **During an English class analysis:** Ibid.

210 **A rumor circulated:** Amato, "You Can't Touch This."

211 **In March 1995:** David Rosenberg, "Sexual Harassment Policy Unveiled," *Merionite,* Oct. 5, 1995.

214 **"They really had no clue":** Kobe Bryant Tapes.

215 **"Jermaine":** Ibid.

215 **Every practice:** Bryant, *The Mamba Mentality,* 155.

215 **So when he and Pangrazio:** Ian O'Connor, "Kobe Drove Merion First," *Asbury Park Press,* June 10, 2001.

215 **Remarkably:** Josh Egerman, "Lower Merion HS Teammate Learned of Kobe Bryant's Competitiveness the Hard Way," *New York Post,* Jan. 29, 2020.

215 **"As much as people might think":** O'Connor, "Kobe Drove Merion First."

218 **"He was asking me as a recruiter":** Kobe Bryant Tapes.

218 **When the *Philadelphia Daily News*:** Ibid.

219 **Kobe never took an official recruiting visit:** Kobe Bryant Tapes.

219 **One of his classmates and neighbors:** Elliott, "Kobe Bryant Humbly Begins."

220 **The chances that he would change his mind:** Kobe Bryant Tapes.

220 **Kobe had received:** Peter Vecsey, "Kobe Shunned, Bypassed by Several Teams Heading into '96 Draft," *New York Post*, Feb. 12, 2012.

221 **"I was trying to get the high school season down":** Kobe Bryant Tapes.

222 **"I didn't want to come in like Shaquille O'Neal":** Ibid.

223 **Of the fifteen hundred spectators:** Ted Silary, "Bryant's Not the Only Star," *Philadelphia Daily News*, Dec. 12, 1995.

224 **Could Kobe and Carr:** Silary, "What If Both Bryant, Carr Played for La Salle?" *Philadelphia Daily News*, Dec. 12, 1995.

224 **Under the headline:** John Smallwood, "Bryant Isn't Ready for the NBA Yet," *Philadelphia Daily News*, Dec. 12, 1995.

225 **Kobe dismissed the article:** Kobe Bryant Tapes.

225 **His mother did not react:** Smallwood, "Prop 48's Stigma Worth Considering," *Philadelphia Daily News*, Dec. 19, 1995.

14: THE CANCER OF ME

Interviews: Emory Dabney, Drew Downer, Gregg Downer, Mike Egan, Jarid Gibson, Wesley Gibson, Omar Hatcher, Bob Hurley, Jimmy Kieserman, Evan Monsky, Brendan Pettit, Tom Pettit, Dave Rosenberg, Jeremy Treatman.

229 **Hugging the Atlantic's waters:** Photograph from Dave Rosenberg.

229 **Just the year before:** Associated Press, "Convention Center Expansion Pays Off," *Charlotte Observer*, Oct. 12, 1995.

232 **Kobe scored forty-three points:** "Boys Basketball," *Philadelphia Inquirer*, Dec. 29, 1995.

233 **Jenks (Oklahoma) High School:** https://www.schooldigger.com/go/OK /schools/1572000739/school.aspx?t=tbStudents#aDetail.

234 **He had played thirty minutes:** "Boys Basketball," *Philadelphia Inquirer*, Dec. 30, 1995. Official box score from the Beach Ball Classic.

234 **He missed:** Ibid.

238 **Come Lower Merion's third game:** https://www.youtube.com/watch?v =KPw7MCAXHBk.

238 **The demands on his time:** Kobe Bryant Tapes.

240 **Wearing his white Lower Merion jersey:** Ibid.

243 **Months later:** https://www.youtube.com/watch?v=5zr6Xm5IjPM.

244 ***Dear Kobe:*** Ibid.

15: RELAX, I GOT THIS

Interviews: Katrina Christmas, James Crawford, Drew Downer, Gregg Downer, Mike Egan, Omar Hatcher, Jimmy Kieserman, Jeanne Mastriano, Jack McGlone, Phil

Mellet, Keith Morris, Speedy Morris, Brendan Pettit, Tom Pettit, Dave Rosenberg, Robby Schwartz, Jeremy Treatman.

250 **"I'm trying to tell them":** Kobe Bryant Tapes.

250 **Now, more than an hour before:** Lyon, "It's La Salle's Turn."

251 **"Now the future":** Ibid.

252 **During one of his assignments:** https://www.youtube.com/watch?v=XWTIY21JKf0

254 **"We just wanted to send everybody a message":** Kobe Bryant Tapes.

255 **Kobe's poor game:** Ibid.

255 **They would face Coatesville:** Ibid.

255 **"And we go on":** Ira Berkow, "Basketball: A High School Star Ponders His Future," *New York Times,* Feb. 27, 1996.

257 **On February 27:** Joe Juliano, "Morris' New Deal Answers One Question," *Philadelphia Inquirer,* Feb. 28, 1996.

16: THE TUNNEL

Interviews: Donnie Carr, Emory Dabney, Drew Downer, Gregg Downer, Mike Egan, Lynne Freeland, Omar Hatcher, John Linehan, Tom McGovern, Brendan Pettit, Dave Rosenberg, Robby Schwartz, Dayna Tolbert, Terry Toohey, Jeremy Treatman.

259 **The gym was shaking and shuddering:** Morkides, "Bryant Lifts L. Merion to District Final," *Philadelphia Inquirer,* Feb. 28, 1996.

260 **"It was a personal-duel type thing":** Kobe Bryant Tapes.

260 **"There's nothing like the Palestra":** Morkides, "Bryant Lifts L. Merion to District Final."

261 **"How come every time I play you":** Kobe Bryant Tapes.

261 **It would be eight years:** James Herbert, "Q&A: Rip Hamilton on Kobe Bryant, His High School Friend and Rival," CBSSports.com, April 8, 2016.

261 **Chester coach Fred Pickett:** Morkides, "P-W Can't Catch Top-Seed Chester, Falling by 65–45," *Philadelphia Inquirer,* Feb. 28, 1996.

261 **Chester forward Greg Hollman:** Terry Toohey, "Kobe Hype Doesn't Bug Chester? Pickett Doesn't Think So," *Delaware County Daily Times,* March 1, 1996.

261 **Chester guard Brahin Pharr:** Ibid.

262 **At the Aces' team workout:** Timothy Dwyer, "For Kobe Bryant, No Letting Up," *Philadelphia Inquirer,* March 1, 1996.

262 **His aim was to usher them:** Csikszentmihalyi.

262 **"Just don't practice this and forget it":** Ibid.

263 **"Drew was everybody's big brother":** Kobe Bryant Tapes.

263 **Yellow crime-scene tape:** Neil Wimmer and Mike DiPasquale, "Chester: Only Hurdle on Road to States," *Merionite,* April 8, 1996.

264 **Chester fans shouted:** Ibid.

266 **Downer made a tactical adjustment:** Ibid.

266 **In the game's final 2:40:** Jack McCaffery, "Chester Will Tend to Affairs of State," *Delaware County Daily Times,* March 2, 1996.

266 **The Clippers' players:** Ibid.

266 **"We saw them":** Ibid.

267 **On March 8:** Sam Carchidi, "Roman Reigns Again Over Catholic League," *Philadelphia Inquirer,* March 9, 1996.

267 **"We talked":** Kobe Bryant Tapes.

268 **It was, Kobe said later:** Ibid.

268 **"And then":** Ibid.

269 **This one was at Coatesville:** L. D. Kerstetter, "Colts Show Plenty of Heart in Loss to Bryant's Aces," *Carlisle Sentinel,* March 10, 1996.

269 *I want to dunk again*: Kobe Bryant Tapes.

269 **On the sixty-mile bus ride:** Ibid.

269 **"Coming in":** Ibid.

269 **Kobe followed them:** Marty Myers, "Scranton Star Recalls Lessons from 1996 Matchup Against Kobe Bryant," Accessnepa.com, Jan. 27, 2020.

269 **"When I walked in":** Kobe Bryant Tapes.

270 **On Scranton's first four possessions:** Myers, "Bryant Just Too Much for Knights," *Times-Tribune,* March 14, 1996.

270 *My God*: Kobe Bryant Tapes.

270 *Beating Chester*: Ibid.

270–1 **"We were going through the motions":** Ibid.

271 **Dazed:** Ibid.

271 **"Jeremy, I'll bet you five dollars":** Ibid.

272 **It annoyed him:** Ibid.

272 **It was a night for Kobe to hang out with old friends:** Ibid.

17: THE FINAL GAME

Interviews: Emory Dabney, Drew Downer, Gregg Downer, Mike Egan, Bill Flanagan, Lynne Freeland, Susan Freeland Barber, Wendell Holland, Jimmy Kieserman, John Linehan, Ron Luber, Brendan Pettit, Tom Pettit, Sam Rines Jr., Sam Rines Sr., Jeremy Treatman, Sonny Vaccaro.

275 **"I was very nervous":** Kobe Bryant Tapes.

276 **He also had no legs:** Ibid.

276 **After the game:** Morkides, "L. Merion Needs OT to Oust Chester," *Philadelphia Inquirer,* March 21, 1996.

277 **"At halftime, I just regrouped":** Kobe Bryant Tapes.

277 **Then the meltdown began:** https://www.youtube.com/watch?v=HbE9yYPnI-4.

278 ***Oh, my God***: Kobe Bryant Tapes.

278 **Kobe could imagine**: Ibid.

279 ***There's no way we're losing this game***: Ibid.

280 **Kobe caught up to the ball**: https://www.youtube.com/watch?v=HbE9yYPnI-4.

280 **"I had a big smile on my face"**: Kobe Bryant Tapes.

281 **Fila already had signed Grant Hill**: Ibid.

282 **At a school-wide pep rally**: Ibid.

283 **At lunch**: Ibid.

283 **Kobe had never seen *Hoosiers* before**: Ibid.

284 ***Drew is sick?***: Ibid.

284 **Throughout the first quarter**: https://www.youtube.com/watch?v=npyUwyq3J9Y.

284 **"We handle the ball"**: Kobe Bryant Tapes.

285 **With one spectator shouting**: Morkides, "Kobe Bryant an Easy Choice for Boys' Player of the Year," *Philadelphia Inquirer*, March 29, 1996.

285 **Frustrated**: Kobe Bryant Tapes.

285 ***They're gonna crack***: Ibid.

286 **"That sent a message"**: Ibid.

287 **"I knew"**: Ibid.

287 **Kobe exhaled deeply**: https://www.youtube.com/watch?v=npyUwyq3J9Y.

289 **"The next thing I know"**: Kobe Bryant Tapes.

290 **And Kobe and Jermaine Griffin**: Eric Mencher, "A Victory Parade for State Champions," *Philadelphia Inquirer*, March 25, 1996.

290 **"This is all I ever wanted"**: Kobe Bryant Tapes.

18: THE SPEED AT WHICH THINGS CHANGE

Interviews: Deirdre Bobb, Drew Downer, Gregg Downer, Mike Egan, Susan Freeland Barber, Omar Hatcher, Tom Konchalski, Ron Luber, Tom McGovern, Keith Morris, Speedy Morris, Audrey Price Gornish, Sam Rines Jr., Sam Rines Sr., Robby Schwartz, Jeremy Treatman, Sonny Vaccaro.

293 **Six foot six**: William Doino Jr., "Tom Konchalski's Quiet Witness," *First Things*, April 15, 2013.

294 **Konchalski had scouted Kobe**: Corey Kilgannon, "Basketball Prospector," *New York Times*, Feb. 1, 2013.

295 **Another city, another award, another banquet**: Wendy Parker, "Award Puts Cap on Roundtree's Career," *Atlanta Journal-Constitution*, April 7, 1996.

295 **"I haven't figured it out"**: Ibid.

296 **Later, Kobe called Krzyzewski**: Kobe Bryant Transcripts.

296 **At the 2008 Summer Olympics**: *The Old Man and the Three* podcast, Oct. 15, 2020. Jonathan Abrams, "How Kobe Bryant Led the Rebirth of USA Basketball,"

Bleacher Report, Sept. 11, 2018. Jace Evans, "Former USA Basketball Coach Mike Krzyzewski Remembers Olympic 'Leader' Kobe Bryant," *USA Today,* Jan. 29, 2020.

297 ***Oh, my God, how am I here?*:** Kobe Bryant Transcripts.

297 **Here was a chance:** Lazenby, *Showboat,* 208.

298 ***What the hell is going on here?*:** Kobe Bryant Transcripts and Tapes.

298 **Kobe's mouth fell open:** Ibid.

298 **Wanya Morris was twenty-two:** VH1, "Brandy: Behind the Music," https://vimeo.com/452766467.

298 **So Harris called Brandy:** Kobe Bryant Transcripts.

299 **"I admired her":** Kobe Bryant Tapes.

299 **The idea:** Ibid.

300 **"I was kind of teasing them":** Ibid.

300 ***Kobe, I have a lacrosse game*:** Ibid.

301 **Kobe chose:** https://www.youtube.com/watch?v=8WH2L0oTxng.

301 **"That was my idea":** Kobe Bryant Tapes.

301 **The Bryants drove back to the school:** Michael Bamberger, "School's Out," *Sports Illustrated,* May 6, 1996.

302 **"I, Kobe Bryant":** https://www.youtube.com/watch?v=8WH2L0oTxng.

302 **Neil Cooper:** Neil Cooper, "Kobe Bryant Was a Neighbor and a Light to Lower Merion," *Philadelphia Inquirer,* Jan. 27, 2020.

302 **Bill Lyon:** Lyon, "Will It Be Big Money Now and Regrets Later?" *Philadelphia Inquirer,* April 30, 1996.

303 **At 10:00 A.M.:** Rich Hofmann, "Feet First: Selling of Kobe Bryant Begins as He Signs with Adidas, William Morris Agency," May 22, 1996.

303 **"He's one of a new generation":** Ibid.

304 **It had culminated:** Ibid.

304 **Kobe and the company:** Dustin Dow, "Vaccaro Built the Empire," *Cincinnati Enquirer,* July 2, 2006.

305 **So there were Joe and Pam:** Hofmann, "Feet First."

305 **And there was Kobe:** Ibid.

305 **"We'd prefer":** Ibid.

305 **The prom could wait:** Kobe Bryant Tapes.

306 **On Broad Street:** Jennifer Weiner, "NBA Hopeful, Pop Star Put Cameras in Overdrive at L. Merion Prom," *Philadelphia Inquirer,* May 26, 1996. https://www.facebook.com/100011548841224/videos/934991770229109/?fref=gs&dti=110990665587523&hc_location=group.

306 **"Man, she glowed":** Kobe Bryant Tapes.

306 **"It's not Kobe's prom":** https://www.facebook.com/100011548841224/videos/934991770229109/?fref=gs&dti=110990665587523&hc_location=group.

306 **"He took Brandy to the prom for his image":** Abbott, "Paging Kobe."

307 **"I'm just here to have a good time":** https://www.facebook
.com/100011548841224/videos/934991770229109/?fref=gs&dti
=110990665587523&hc_location=group.

307 **"You had all the classmates":** Kobe Bryant Tapes.

307 **Sonja Norwood shared:** Weiner, "NBA Hopeful."

307 **One Philadelphia news station:** https://www.facebook.com/100011548841224
/videos/934991770229109/?fref=gs&dti=110990665587523&hc_location=group.

307 **Kobe Bryant spent his last day:** Ibid.

19: NOW I'M A LAKER

Interviews: Joe Carbone, Tony DiLeo, Gregg Downer, Mike Egan, Elissa Fisher
  Grabow, Brad Greenberg, John Nash, Arn Tellem, Jeremy Treatman, Sonny
  Vaccaro.

312 **Rob Babcock:** Raad Cawthon, "Scouts Wonder If Bryant's Ready," *Philadelphia
  Inquirer,* April 30, 1996.

312 **John Outlaw:** Ibid.

312 **"The Lakers":** Kobe Bryant Transcripts.

313 *I'm beating up*: Ibid.

313 **"How'd you do?":** Kobe Bryant Tapes.

314 **"I want people to say":** Ibid.

316 **"Let's see":** Kobe Bryant Transcripts.

319 *If I'm the fourth pick*: Ibid.

319 *If Coach Calipari takes me*: Ibid.

320 **"Bob, we have a deal":** West and Coleman, 170–171.

320 **Jerry Reynolds:** Stephen A. Smith, "Kobe Criticized after Arranging Trade to
  Lakers," Knight-Ridder News Service, July 2, 1996.

320 **Timothy Dwyer:** Dwyer, "OK, Kid, Let's See If You Can Cut It in that Big
  Playpen," *Philadelphia Inquirer,* July 3, 1996.

320 **The stress:** West and Coleman, 169.

320 **"Now I'm a Laker":** Kobe Bryant Tapes.

321 **Independence Day:** "Sweet Sounds of Liberty Concert and Fireworks," *Philadelphia Inquirer,* July 4, 1996.

321 **Kobe, hanging out:** Kobe Bryant Tapes.

322 **On July 27, 1996:** Thomas Golianopoulos, "The Secret History of Kobe Bryant's
  Rap Career," Grantland.com, April 12, 2013. Nicole Weisensee, "Convict's Full-
  Court Press for Justice," *Philadelphia Daily News,* Sept. 7, 1999.

323 **Weeks passed:** Kobe Bryant Tapes.

323 **"I can remember one time":** Ibid.

20: OPEN GYM

Interviews: Joe Carbone, Gregg Downer, Elissa Fisher Grabow, Arn Tellem, Jeremy Treatman.

325 **She didn't follow the sport:** https://www.youtube.com/watch?v=bi6fftt43xo.

327 **"You know damn well":** Kobe Bryant Tapes.

327 **After finalizing:** Earl Bloom, "Bryant Is Wealthy Teenager," *Orange County Register,* July 25, 1996.

327 **"It's real simple to me":** Kobe Bryant Tapes.

328 **He figured:** Ibid.

329 **"It wasn't going to stop me":** Ibid.

329 **Sure, Shaquille O'Neal:** Ibid.

330 **"You're against the whole thing I'm doing":** Ibid.

331 **He couldn't read:** Tom Friend, "Lakers' O'Neal Is Willing to Accept Some of the Blame," *New York Times,* May 14, 1997.

331–2 **Or the columnist:** Paul Oberjuerge, "Kobe Not Ready for Prime Time," *San Bernardino County Sun,* May 13, 1997.

332 **In the locker room:** Tim Kawakami, "Van Exel, Who Thought He Should Have Taken Last Shot in Regulation, Says He Can't Co-Exist with Harris," *Los Angeles Times,* May 13, 1997.

332 **But it would be:** *Daily Herald,* May 15, 1997.

AFTERWORD: HIS STORY, AND HIS VOICE

333 **Jeremy Treatman was sitting:** Sielski, "Kobe Bryant Once Said He Might Join the Sixers to End His Career. What If He Had?," *Philadelphia Inquirer,* Jan. 31, 2020.

SELECTED BIBLIOGRAPHY

Abrams, Jonathan. *Boys Among Men: How the Prep-to-Pro Generation Redefined the NBA and Sparked a Basketball Revolution.* New York: Crown Archetype, 2016.

Barocci, Andrea. *An Italian Named Kobe: Our Friend Bryant, the Untold Story.* Rome: Absolutely Free, 2015.

Bryant, Kobe. *The Mamba Mentality: How I Play.* New York: MCD Books, 2018.

Campbell, Joseph. *The Hero with a Thousand Faces.* 3rd ed. Novato, CA: New World Library, 1949, 2008.

Croatto, Pete. *From Hang Time to Prime Time: Business, Entertainment, and the Birth of the Modern-Day NBA.* New York: Atria Books, 2020.

Csikszentmihalyi, Mihali. *Flow: The Psychology of Optimal Experience.* New York: Harper-Collins, 1990.

Deveney, Sean, ed. *Remembering Kobe Bryant: Players, Coaches, and Broadcasters Recall the Greatest Basketball Player of His Generation.* New York: Sports Publishing, 2016, 2020

Lazenby, Roland. *Mad Game: The NBA Education of Kobe Bryant.* Chicago: Masters Press, 2000.

———. *Showboat: The Life of Kobe Bryant.* New York: Little, Brown, 2016.

The Lower Merion Historical Society. *Lower Merion and Narberth.* Charleston, SC: Arcadia Publishing, 2010.

———. *The First 300: The Amazing and Rich History of Lower Merion.* Collingsdale, PA: Diane Publishing, 2000.

Lyons, Robert S. *Palestra Pandemonium: A History of the Big Five.* Philadelphia: Temple University Press, 2002.

Mele, Christopher. *Race and the Politics of Deception: The Making of an American City.* New York: New York University Press, 2017.

Meyers, Mary Ann. *Art, Education, & African-American Culture: Albert Barnes and the Science of Philanthropy.* New Brunswick, NJ: Transaction Publishers, 2004.

Miller, Alice. *The Drama of the Gifted Child: The Search for the True Self.* New York: Basic Books, 1997.

Nocera, Joe, and Ben Strauss. *Indentured: The Inside Story of the Rebellion Against the NCAA.* New York: Penguin, 2016.

Pearlman, Jeff. *Three-Ring Circus: Kobe, Shaq, Phil, and the Crazy Years of the Lakers Dynasty.* Boston/New York: Houghton Mifflin Harcourt, 2020.

Purcell, Kevin. *Philly War Zone: Growing Up in a Racial Battleground.* Xlibris, 2012.

Sernett, Milton C. *Bound for the Promised Land: African American Religion and the Great Migration.* Durham, NC: Duke University Press, 1997.

The Staff of the Philadelphia Daily News. *Philly Hoops: The Magic of Philadelphia Basketball.* Philadelphia: Camino Books, 2003.

Weigley, Russell F., ed. *Philadelphia: A 300-Year History.* New York: W. W. Norton, 1982.

West, Jerry, and Jonathan Coleman. *West by West: My Charmed, Tormented Life.* New York: Back Bay Books, 2011.

Wetzel, Dan, and Don Yaeger. *Sole Influence: Basketball, Corporate Greed, and the Corruption of America's Youth.* New York: Warner Books, 2000.

Wilkerson, Isabel. *The Warmth of Other Suns: The Epic Story of America's Great Migration.* New York: Vintage Books, 2010.

Williams, Pat, and Bill Lyon. *We Owed You One! The Uphill Struggle of the Philadelphia 76ers.* Wilmington, DE: TriMark Publishing, 1983.

INDEX